Other books in The Princeton Review Series

Cracking the SAT and PSAT
Cracking the ACT
Cracking the LSAT
Cracking the GRE
Cracking the GMAT
Cracking the MCAT
Cracking the Biology Achievement
Cracking the Chemistry Achievement
Cracking the English Achievements
Cracking the French Achievement
Cracking the History Achievements
Cracking the Math Achievements
Cracking the Physics Achievement
Cracking the Spanish Achievement
How to Survive Without Your Parents' Money
Grammar Smart
Math Smart
Study Smart
The Student Access Guide to College Admissions
The Student Access Guide to Paying for College
The Student Access Guide to the Best 286 Colleges
The Student Access Guide to the Best Law Schools
The Student Access Guide to the Best Medical Schools
Word Smart: Building a Better Vocabulary
Word Smart II: How to Build a More Educated Vocabulary

Also available on cassette from Living Language

Word Smart
Grammar Smart

THE **PRINCETON** REVIEW

STUDENT ACCESS
GUIDE TO

THE

BEST

BUSINESS

SCHOOLS

1994 Edition

THE **PRINCETON** REVIEW

STUDENT ACCESS
GUIDE TO

THE

BEST

BUSINESS

SCHOOLS

By Nedda Gilbert

1994 Edition

Library of Congress Cataloging-in-Publication Data
Gilbert, Nedda.
    Student access guide to the best business schools/by Nedda Gilbert.
        p.   cm.
    At head of title: The Princeton Review.
    ISBN 0-679-74628-5
    Includes indexes
    1. Business schools—United States—Evaluation.   2. College, Choice of—United
States—Handbooks, manuals, etc.   3. Master of business administration degree—
United States—Handbooks, manuals, etc.
I. Princeton Review (Firm).   II. Title.   III. Title: Best business schools.
HF1131.G5 1993   650'.071'173—dc20   93-6057

Manufactured in the United States of America on paper using partially recycled fibers

9 8 7 6 5 4 3 2

First Edition

FOREWORD

In the late '80s, The Princeton Review began working with Fortune 500 companies to provide their employees with on-site preparation classes for the GMAT. In the course of our work, it became clear that most of these prospective business school students were lacking critical information about the business school admissions process on which they were about to embark. Over and over, students asked:

- "How many times should I take the GMAT?"
- "If I take it twice, which score will they count?"
- "How high does my score need to be?"
- "What points do I need to make in my essays?"
- "What if all I've done is work? I don't have any extracurriculars to write about?"
- "Should I interview?"
- "How much do my grades count?"
- "Who should write my recommendation—an immediate boss who knows me well or a senior V.P. who's a power alum of the school?"
- "When's the best time to send in the application—early or close to the deadline?"

These students were confused with good reason. Unlike high-school students—who can turn to guidance counselors and professional advisors for help navigating the undergraduate admissions process—prospective MBAs have almost nowhere to turn for advice on selecting and applying to the right business school. Even the information that is available—mainly guidebooks and magazine rankings—is obscure and contradictory. What, then, is a B-school applicant to do?

Read This Book

We surveyed 10,000 current students, hundreds of admissions officers, and dozens of recruiters and business school grads to bring you the real scoop on B-school.

Want to know what really happens to the applications you toiled, sweated, and bled over? This book gives you an exclusive inside look at the deliberations of a top admissions committee, and shows you what they're looking for in an applicant. Ever wonder who actually reads your essays? We not only tell you, we show you what they liked about fifteen essays submitted to twelve top schools. This book tells you what admissions officers are looking for, what your life as a business school student will be like, what to talk about in your interviews, when to apply, and more. But, most importantly, this book gives you important facts, unique insights, and up-to-the-minute information on the nation's top 70 B-schools, so you can make an educated decision about where you should apply.

Why These 70 Schools?

For several years now, two leading magazines have been trying to tell you which school is number one, which is number eight, which is number thirty-seven. These rankings make headline news and sell millions of magazines. Business schools take these lists very seriously. But these rankings are too precise, to the point of being arbitrary, and, if you think about it, they really don't reveal much about the schools in question. One magazine says a school is number five. Another says the school is number eleven. With that knowledge, you can deduce one thing: these magazines are obviously using different criteria. But aside from the numbers "five" and "eleven," do you know anything useful about the school? Not much.

We are not completely debunking the idea that there are better and worse schools. After all, this book is called *Student Access Guide to the Best Business Schools*. There are about 900 graduate business programs offered in the United States. Of these, roughly 250 are accredited by the American Assembly of Collegiate Business Schools. Of these, we determined that about 70 are, on the basis of reputation, curriculum, quality of professors, and student opinion, the top schools in the country. Those schools are included in this book—with three exceptions. Rice University is not accredited by the AACBS but is included in this book because of its excellent programs and the national reputation it enjoys and deserves as an exceptional business school. The University of Florida and State University of New York-Albany graduate business programs are both among the finest in the country. We were unable to poll students at these schools because of difficulty obtaining permission to come on campus. We regret that we could not include them in this edition of *Student Access Guide to the Best Business Schools*, and hope to bring you full profiles of these schools in next year's edition.

After arriving at our list, we decided that any rank-ordering of the schools would be pointless: every school in this book is top-notch. We've chosen to list schools in our book alphabetically. We believe our profiles highlight each program's major strengths and weaknesses as well as capture its personality. The profiles take into account the reputation, prestige, and status of a school. The question is, which school is best for you? We hope this book helps you make the right choice.

Good luck!

ACKNOWLEDGMENTS

This book absolutely would not have been possible without the help of my husband, Paul. His insights and support were invaluable—this book is as much his as it is mine.

The following people were also instrumental in the completion of this book: my father, Dr. Irving Buchen, for his razor's-edge editorial suggestions; Julian Ham, who designed this book; Rob Zopf, for his tireless phone interviews with business school administrators; Andrew Dunn, Joe Keith, Bruce McAmis, Mark Stein, and Thane Thomsen, who gathered all manner of facts and figures and processed the endless flood of surveys; Cynthia Brantley and Lee Elliott, for putting all the pieces together; Alicia Ernst and John Katzman, for giving me the chance to write this book; and to the folks at Villard, who helped this project reach fruition. Special thanks goes to Andy Goldfarb and to all those section-A mates, HBNS-92, who lent a hand and provided valuable feedback.

Thanks are also due to the business school folks who went way out of their way to provide essential information:

Will Makris, Director of Admissions—Babson University

David Irons—University of California, Berkeley

John Gould, Outgoing Dean, and Allan Friedman, Director of Communications—University of Chicago

Meyer Feldberg, Dean, and Ethan Hanabury, Director of Admissions—Columbia Business School

Skip Horne, Director of Admissions, and Elaine Ruggieri, Director of Public Relations—University of Virginia

Pat Wetherall, Assistant Director of Communications—Dartmouth University

Cathy Cassio and her staff at the News and Publications Office—Stanford University

CONTENTS

ALL ABOUT B-SCHOOL

HOW TO GET IN

THE SCHOOLS

INTRODUCTION

The B-school Hustle

According to current data, there are fewer MBA-wannabes these days. The number of folks taking the Graduate Management Admission Test (GMAT) has fallen by almost twenty percent since its peak in 1990-1991. At many B-schools, applications have likewise dropped, from ten to twenty percent. The drivers of this decline include: the recession, a renewed interest in professions such as teaching, public service, and medicine, and the general impression that an MBA may not lead to the huge payoffs it used to.

B-school admissions officers can no longer count on a bottomless cup of applications, much less their fair "yield" of those from the best and the brightest. If it was a seller's market in the '80s, it's more of a buyer's market in the '90s. All things being equal, you have a better chance of getting into the school of your choice today than you did a few years ago.

From administrators to admissions officers, B-schools have started to hustle for students. Here's what you can expect from some of them: 800 numbers, computer disk applications, and Saturday interviews—all part of making the admissions process a user-friendly experience. MTV-esque videos, and personal phone calls from Deans, Faculty, and current students—intended to convince you their school is best. The programs have also stepped up recruiting efforts in foreign countries to tap into new sources of applicants. Although the hustle-factor will vary from school to school (and year to year), these days, B-schools need you as much as you need them. Maybe even more.

Getting In

Nevertheless, admission to the top programs is still extremely competitive. Thousands and thousands of prospective MBA candidates spend loads of time and money making sure they select, and are in turn, admitted to the "best" school. Their time and money goes toward working in jobs they think will impress a B-school, studying and preparing for the GMAT, writing essays, interviewing, visiting prospective schools, and buying guides like —but not as good as—this one.

This book is your best bet. It takes you into the heretofore secret deliberations of the admissions committees at the top schools. You get a firsthand look at who decides your fate. More important, you learn what criteria are used to evaluate applicants. As we found out, it isn't always what you expect. You also get straight talk from admissions officers—what dooms an application and how to ace the interview.

In addition to getting inside information on the application process, you learn when the best time is to apply, how to answer the most commonly asked essay questions and the key points to make in your essays. There's also loads of information on what you can do before applying to increase your odds of gaining admission.

We've also given you the facts—from the most up-to-date information on major curricula changes and placement rates to demographics of the student body—for the seventy best B-schools in the country. And we've included enough information about them—which we gathered from admissions officers, administrators, and students—to let you make a smart decision about going there.

Why These 70 Schools?

For several years now, two leading magazines have been telling you who's hot and who's not. They've smooshed together objective and subjective data into a quantified format to create the perception of precise numerical rankings. But the rankings are as imprecise as they are abitrary. One magazine says a school is number five. Another says it's number eight. The weighting of different criteria leads to dramatically different interpretations of a program. While the rankings make news, and sell a lot of magazines, in real-life prospective students are as much, if not more interested in those characteristics that distinguish one school from another. What makes a program tops?

To find the answers, we took a more holistic approach and gathered input from a variety of sources. First on our list was student opinion. Mass-interview style, we surveyed over 10,000 currently matriculated B-school students. We surveyed hundreds of admissions officers and administrators. In addition, we also looked at more traditional measures including: a school's acceptance rate, average GPA, average GMAT scores, placement rate, curriculum, learning environment, and caliber of student body. As we progressed, we learned that many lesser-known schools belonged in this book because of their regional reputation, star faculty, "bang for the buck," or unique course offerings. Finally, we sought to focus on those schools that are accredited by the American Assembly of Collegiate Business Schools (of the approximately 900 business programs in the nation, roughly 250 are so accredited). All of the schools included in this book are accredited by the AACBS with the exception of Rice University. Rice University is included in our book because of its special programs and the national reputation it enjoys and deserves as a top business school. In a few cases, schools which might have met our criteria for inclusion had to be omitted because they wouldn't allow us to poll their students.

A final note: As you might have expected, we've chosen to list schools in our book alphabetically, rather than rank them. We believe our profiles highlight each program's major strengths and weaknesses, as well as capture their distinct personalities. The profiles take into account the reputation, prestige, and status of a school without ranking it.

A warning about the GMAT: The Princeton Review has learned that, as of October 1994, the GMAT will be administered in a new format. A one-hour analytical writing test will be added. It will consist of two essays on two different topics. It will be scored holistically. The readers scoring the writing tests will be primarily business school professors who require written essays as part of their business school course work.

In order to be able to continue to administer the GMAT in one morning without a lunch break, ETS and the GMAC have decided to cut approximately five minutes from each of the existing six 30 minute sections, including the experimental section. The GMAT will be four hours in length. However, many details have not been worked out and it is likely that the Reading Comprehension section will not change in length.

The six multiple choice sections will continue to be scored on a scaled 200–800 measure: 0–60. No change here. The essay will most likely be scored on a scale of 1–6 which will be derived by averaging the two scores provided by the readers. Again, these details have not yet to be worked out and this scoring process is not conclusive.

Don't panic. These changes will not affect the GMATs that are to be administered on October 16th, 1993, January 15th, 1994, March 19th, 1994, and June 18th, 1994. If you are considering taking the GMAT during or after October 1994, you have plenty of time to prepare for the changes in the test. And as soon as we know more, you'll know more. Good luck!

THE **PRINCETON** REVIEW

STUDENT ACCESS
GUIDE TO

THE

BEST

BUSINESS

SCHOOLS

1994 Edition

CHAPTER ONE

Picking the Right Business School for You:

How to Use This Book

Making the Decision to Go

The first step for you may be B-school. Indeed, armed with an MBA you may journey far. But the success of your trip and the direction you take will depend on knowing exactly why you're going to B-school and exactly what you'll be getting out of it.

The most critical questions you need to ask yourself are: Do you really want a career in business? What do you want the MBA to do for you? Are you looking to gain credibility, accelerate your development, or move into a new job or industry?

Knowing what you want doesn't just affect your decision to go. It also affects your candidacy; admissions committees favor applicants who have clear goals and objectives. Moreover, once at school, students who know what they want make the most of their two years. If you're uncertain about your goals, opportunities for career development—such as networking, mentoring, student clubs, and recruiter events—are squandered.

You also need to find a school that fits your individual needs. Consider the personal and financial costs. This may be the single biggest investment of your life. How much salary will you forego by leaving the workforce? What will the tuition be? How will you pay for it? If you have a family, spouse, or significant other, how will getting your MBA affect them?

If you do have a spouse, you may choose programs that involve partners in campus life. If status is the be-all and end-all, you may simply choose the most prestigious school you can get into.

The MBA presents many opportunities, but no guarantees. As with any opportunity, you must make the most of it. Whether you go to a first-tier school, or to a part-time program close to home, you'll acquire the skills that can jump start your career. But your success will have more to do with you than with the piece of paper your MBA is printed on.

Why the Rankings Aren't a Useful Guide to School Selection

All too many applicants rely on the magazine rankings to decide where to apply. Caught up with winners, losers, and whoever falls in between, their thinking is simply: Can I get into the top five? Top ten? Top fifteen?

But it's a mistake to rely on the rankings. Mark Twain once said, "There are lies, damn lies, and statistics." Today, he'd probably add B-school rankings. Why? Because statistics rarely show the whole picture. When deciding on the validity of a study, it's wise to consider *how* the study was conducted and *what* exactly it was trying to measure.

First, the rankings have made must-read news for several years. Not surprisingly, some of the survey respondents—current B-school students and recent grads—now know there's a game to play. The game is this: give your own school the highest marks possible. The goal: that coveted number-one spot. Rumor has it that some schools even remind their students of how their responses will affect the stature of their program. This kind of self-interest is known as respondent bias, and the B-school rankings suffer from it in a big way.

The rankings feature easy-to-measure differences such as selectivity, placement success, and proficiency in the basic disciplines. But these rankings don't allow for any intangibles—such as the progressiveness of a program, the school's learning environment, and the happiness of the students.

To create standards by which comparisons *can* be made, the rankings force an evaluative framework on the programs. But this is like trying to evaluate a collection of paintings—impressionist, modern, classical, and cubist—with the same criteria. Relying on narrow criteria to evaluate subjective components fails to capture the true strengths and weaknesses of each piece.

The statistically measurable differences that the magazines base their ratings on are often so marginal as to be insignificant. In other words, it's too close to call the race. Perhaps, in some years two schools should be tied for the number one spot. What would the tie-breaker look like? A rally cry of "We're number one" with the loudest school winning?

A designation as the number-one, number-five, or number-ten school is almost meaningless when you consider that it changes from year to year—and from magazine to magazine. (At least Olympic medalists enjoy a four-year victory lap.)

Judging for Yourself

Depending on what you're looking for, the rankings may tell you something about the B-schools. But it's wise to use them as approximations rather than the declarations of fact they're made out to be.

The rankings don't factor in *your* values or all of the criteria *you* need to consider. Is it selectivity? The highest rate of placement? The best starting salary? Surprise! The number-one school is not number one in all these areas. No school is.

The best way to pick a program is to do your homework and find a match. For example, if you have limited experience with numbers, then a program with a heavy quantitative focus may round out your résumé. If you want to stay in your home area, then a local school that's highly regarded by the top regional companies may be best for you. If you know that you want to go into a field typified by cutthroat competition, or a field in which status is all-important . . . well, obviously, keep your eyes on those rankings.

You also need to consider your personal style and comfort zone. Suppose you get into a "top-ranked" school, but the workload is destroying your life or the mentality is predatory. It won't matter how prestigious the program is if you don't make it through. Do you want an intimate and supportive environment or are you happy to blend in with the masses? Different schools will meet these needs. Lecture versus case study, specialization versus broad-based general management curriculum, and heavy finance versus a heavy marketing are other kinds of trade-offs.

One last thing to consider is social atmosphere. What is the spirit of the student body? Do students like each other? Are they indifferent? Perhaps a bit hostile? If you go through graduate school in an atmosphere of camaraderie, you'll never forget those two years. But if you go through school in an atmosphere of enmity . . . OK, you'll still remember those two years. It's up to you to decide *how* you want to remember them.

Remember when you applied to college? You talked to friends, alumni, and teachers. You visited the campus and sat in on classes (or should have). It's not all that different with B-school. Here are some of the things you should check out:

ACADEMICS

- Academic reputation
- International reputation
- Primary Teaching Methodology
- Renown and availability of professors
- General or specialized curriculum
- Range of school specialities
- Opportunities for global/foreign study
- Emphasis on teamwork
- Fieldwork/student consulting available
- Student Support—extra study sessions, accessible faculty, tutoring
- Academic Support—libraries, computer facilities and expertise
- Grading/Probation Policy

- Workload/Hours per week in class
- Class and section size
- Pressure and Competition

CAREER

- Summer and Full-Time Job Placement (number of companies recruiting on and off campus)
- Placement Rate
- Average Starting Salaries
- Salaries at five-year mark
- Career Support—assistance with career planning, résumé preparation, interview skills
- Networking with visiting executives

QUALITY OF LIFE

- Location
- Campus
- Orientation
- Range of student clubs/activities
- Diversity of student body
- Housing
- Social life
- Spouse/Partner group
- Recreational facilities

EXPENSE

- Tuition
- Books, computer
- Cost of living
- Financial Aid

How to Use This Book

Each of the business schools listed in this book has its own two-page spread. Each spread has eight components: two "sidebars" (the narrow columns on the outside of each page that contain charts and statistics) and four "boxes" (the big boxes in the middle that contain text). Look at the sample page below:

Here's what's in each section:

The Sidebars

The sidebars contain various statistics which were gathered either from the questionnaires we sent to the schools, from our own surveys, or from College Counsel, an independent educational consulting group.

■ *Type of School*
Whether the school is public or private.

■ *No. Men, No. Women, No. Minorities, No. International Students*
The demographic breakdown of last year's entering class.

■ *Equality Meter*
Based on the opinions of the students we surveyed at the schools, these graphs reveal whether women and minorities feel they are afforded equal treatment as compared to the white, male majority. Their responses are compared to the national average (also based on our student survey).

■ **Admissions Statistics**

Gives the average GMAT score, average undergraduate GPA, average age at entry into business school, number of applicants, number of students accepted, and number of students enrolled for last year's entering class.

■ **Deadlines and Notification**

Gives the application deadline and acceptance notification dates.

■ **Focus of Curriculum**

Those academic areas the school is particularly noted for.

■ **Academic Specialties**

This will either read "general" or "specialized." A business school with a general curriculum gives students very broad coverage of all functional areas. A specialized curriculum allows students to major or specialize in one or two areas.

■ **Joint Degrees**

Lists any special graduate degrees offered by the school.

■ **Special Programs**

Lists any exchange, internship, or job programs.

■ **Financial Facts**

In-state tuition, out-of-state tuition, and costs of on-campus housing.

■ **Student's Overview Book**

At each school, the students we surveyed were asked to rate their overall happiness and their satisfaction with their school's program. The results are shown on a scale of 50 to 100, and are compared with the national average (also gathered from our student surveys).

■ **Faculty Rating**

Our survey asked students how they would rate their professors as teachers. The results are shown on this scale. The national average is also shown.

■ *Hits and Misses*

Summarizes the results of our survey. The lists show what students felt unusually strong about, both positively and negatively, at their schools. Following are the categories:

- Gym—if this appears under the "hits" list, the students at the school love the gym facilities; if it appears under the "misses" list, the students are dissatisfied with the facilities.

- Helping other students—if this appears under the "hits" list, the students feel that students are willing to help each other; if it appears under the "misses" list, the students feel that their classmates aren't willing to help each other.

- Accounting dept.—students rated their improvement in the area of accounting. If this listing appears under the "hits" list, the students were happy with the quality of accounting instruction; if it appears under the "misses" list, they were not satisfied.

- Finance dept.—same as above, only for finance skills.

- Marketing Skills—same, only for marketing skills.

- Quantitative Skills—same as above, *mutatis mutandis*.

- Placement—a rating of the efficiency of the school's job placement office.

- Ethnic and Racial Diversity—students were asked whether their school is ethnically and racially diverse. If it is, this rating appears in the "hits" list; if not, it appears under "misses."

- Classmates are smart/classmates are stupid—reveals students' opinions about the intelligence of their classmates.

- Recruiting—rates students' satisfaction with their school's recruiting efforts.

- Social Life—if students have active social lives, this rating appears in the "hits" list; if not, it appears in the "misses" list.

- Diverse Work Experience—this rating appears in the "hits" list if students said their classmates had come from diverse work backgrounds; if it appears in the "misses" list students came mostly from the same type of company.

- Off-campus Housing—students' rating of the quality of off-campus housing.

- On-campus Housing—students' rating of the quality of on-campus housing.

- Library—a rating of the usefulness of the library.

- Location—this is a rating of whether or not students like the town their school is in.

- Cozy student community—students were asked whether they liked to hang out with their classmates. If they did, "Cozy student community" appears in the "hits" list; if not "Don't like classmates" appears in the "misses" list.

- School clubs—a rating of the breadth and number of extracurricular clubs and organizations on campus.

- Staying in touch—students were asked whether their classmates were the kind of people they'd want to stay in contact with after business school. If this rating appears in the "hits" list, they did want to stay in touch with their classmates; if it appears in the "misses" list, they felt they wouldn't stay in touch.

■ *Applicants Also Look at*
Lists other schools applicants also consider.

■ *For More Information, Contact:*
The address and phone number of the school's admissions office can be found here.

The Boxes

Academics

This section describes the academic atmosphere of each school, what the professors are like, where the curriculum is headed, and what students think about the education they are receiving.

Placement and Recruiting

One of the most important issues to MBAs is the quality and efficacy of their school's recruiting and placement offices. This box explains the programs each school offers.

Student Life/Campus

From dating to off-campus housing, this box describes the social atmosphere and quality of life at each campus.

Admissions

This box tells you what aspects of your applications are most important to the school's admissions officers. We used the admissions officer's responses to our questionnaire, as well as telephone interviews with many admissions officers, to write these boxes.

A Glossary of Insider Lingo

You've probably already noticed this, but business school students, graduates, and professors—like most close-knit, somewhat solipsistic groups—seem to speak their own weird language. With that in mind, here's one last set of tools that will help you on your way through this book and into the business world: a list of MBA jargon (with English translations):

Air Time: a precious opportunity—speaking or making comments in class.

Air Hogs: students who monopolize classroom discussion and love to hear themselves speak.

Analysis Paralysis: not being able to make a decision because you've gotten lost in the thicket of your own analysis.

Back of the Envelope: an abbreviated analysis of the numbers.

Barriers to Entry: conditions that prevent entry into a particular market.

Beta of a stock: the inherent volatility of a stock.

Bottleneck: the point in a plant or process that determines or blocks the pace.

Burn Rate: amount of cash a company consumes each day.

Case Cracker: a comment in class that gets to the essence of the case.

Case Study Method: popular teaching method that uses real-life business cases for analysis.

Chip Shots: unenlightening comments made during class discussion for the sole purpose of getting credit.

Cold Call: unexpected, often dreaded request by the professor to open a case.

Core Courses: courses in the basic disciplines of business, usually mandatory.

Corner Office: office location that all MBAs aspire to and the exclusive province of partners, managing directors and senior executives.

Cost Benefit Analysis: calculating whether something is worth doing on the basis of the real dollar cost versus real dollar benefit. This is often used as a shortcut in analyzing the numbers.

Cycle Time: how fast you can turn something around.

Deliverable: what your end product is.

Finheads: finance heads who also tend to be sharks.

Four-P's: elements of a marketing strategy—Price, Promotion, Place, Product.

Fume Date: date the company runs out of cash reserves.

Functional Areas: the basic disciplines of business.

Globalization: trend of the '80s and '90s; expanding the definition of your market to include the challenges of operating in a multi-country, multi-consumer market.

Hard Courses: anything with numbers.

HP12-C: the calculator of choice for number crunching.

I-Bankers: investment banking analysts coming out of the two-year training programs and into B-school.

Incentivize: a bastardized version of the word incentive, used as a verb.

MBA Weenies: students who believe that once they get their MBAs they'll be masters of the universe.

Net net: End result.

OOC: out of cash.

Opportunity Costs: the cost of pursuing an opportunity, i.e., for B-school, tuition and loss of income for two years.

Poets: students with little quantitative skills or experience (numerically challenged).

Power Naps: quick, intense in-class recharge for the continually sleep deprived.

Power Tool: someone who does all the work and sits in the front row of the class with his hand up.

Pre-enrollment Courses: commonly known as MBA summer camp—quantitative courses, generally offered in the summer before the first year to get the numerically challenged up to speed.

Pro forma: financial presentation of hypothetical events; for example, how much new debt would a company require if it grows 10 percent a year?

Quant Jock: a numerical athlete who is happiest crunching numbers.

Quick and Dirty: an abbreviated analysis, often involving numbers.

Run the Numbers: analyze quantitatively.

Sharks: aggressive students who smell blood and move in for the kill.

Shark Comment: comment meant to gore a fellow student in class discussion.

Soft Courses: touchy-feely courses such as human resources and organizational behavior.

Soft Skills: conflict resolution, teamwork, negotiation, oral and written communication.

Slice and Dice: running all kinds of quantitative analysis on a set of numbers.

The Five Forces: Michael Porter's model for analyzing the strategic attractiveness of an industry.

Three-C's: the primary forces—Customer, Competition, Company.

Total Quality Management: the Edward Demming method of management that caught on with the Japanese and is now "hot" in American business—managing the quality of products, service, work, process, people and objectives.

Valuation: adds up projected future cash flows into current dollars.

Value-Based Decision Making: value and ethics as part of the practice of business.

CHAPTER TWO

Suspenders and Power Breakfasts:

What Does an MBA Offer?

Nuts-and-Bolts Business Skills

Graduate business schools teach the applied science of business. The best business schools, the ones in this book, combine the latest academic theories with pragmatic concepts, hands-on experience, and real-world solutions.

To equip students with the broad expertise they need to be managers, most business schools start new MBAs off with a set of foundation or "core" courses in what are known as the "functional areas": finance, accounting, management, marketing, operations, and economics. These courses introduce you to the basic vocabulary and concepts of formal business culture. They also develop your practical skills—skills you'll be able to use immediately in your new career.

Your learning occurs on three levels: You become familiar with *concepts*. For example, in finance you learn that a company's cost of equity is greater than its cost of debt. You acquire *tools* such as ratio analysis, valuations, and pro formas. Finally, you experience *action-based learning* by applying your skills and knowledge to case studies, role-plays, and business simulations. Over the course of this three-tiered study, you will explore the complete business cycle of many different kinds of organizations.

B-schools also teach the analytical skills used to make complicated business decisions. You learn how to define the critical issues, apply analytical techniques, develop the criteria for decisions, and make decisions after evaluating their impact on other variables.

After two years, you're ready to market a box of cereal. Or prepare a valuation of the cereal company's worth. You'll speak the language of business. You'll know the tools of the trade. Your expertise will extend to many areas and industries. In short, you will have acquired the skills that open doors.

The Fast Track and Big Bucks

Applicants often have big bucks in mind when they decide to go to business school, believing that earning an MBA is equivalent to winning the lottery. At some schools, this is (sort of) the case. The top talent at elite schools are commonly offered salaries from $50,000 to $90,000. In fact, thirty percent of all Harvard B-school graduates accept positions in the six figure range. But this is hardly a common experience.

Many factors have an effect on a student's first-job-out-of-school salary. First, there's a correlation between school reputation and average starting salary. The better the school (or the better the current perception of the school), the better the compensation. Second, compensation varies by industry. For example, consulting and investment banking are at the high end of the salary spectrum these days. Some companies in these industries even offer students "sign-on bonuses" and reimbursement of their second-year tuition. By contrast, advertising firms and small businesses offer smaller compensation packages and fewer perks.

Third, previous work experience and salary will boost or deflate your perceived value. A clear track record of success before school is likely to secure a bigger package after graduation.

Another common reason for pursuing an MBA is to get on the proverbial "fast track." Many students do find that the degree allows them to leapfrog several notches up the ladder. But the guaranteed fast track is something of an illusion.

B-school students these days are older than they used to be: the average age is twenty-seven, as opposed to twenty-two twenty years ago. This indicates that students typically spend more time working after college before entering a graduate degree program. Their age, maturity, and previous work experience allow these graduates to move into substantive, responsible positions right after completing their programs. In contrast, twenty years ago a recent MBAs first job out of school was in a management development track, but at a fairly low level in the organization.

All that said, the MBA can lead to accelerated career development. But like your salary, much of this depends on the industry you enter and the program you graduate from.

Access to Hundreds of Recruiters, Entry to New Fields

Applicants tend to place great emphasis on "incoming" and "outgoing" statistics. First they ask, "Will I get in?" Then they ask, "Will I get a job?"

The latter is not as easy to answer at it used to be. In an economic downturn, the immediate financial reward of the MBA is reduced. So is the access to jobs. Mainstream MBA recruiters typically spend less on the recruiting process, cut back on their hiring, become more selective in their choices, and expect more of their new employees.

MBAs are affected in several ways. First, the cost benefits of hiring newly-minted MBAs aren't always favorable. They command large salaries, yet offer little real-world experience in return. They also have a high rate of turnover in their first job out of school. During tough economic times, many companies opt for cheaper BAs (or a mix of BAs and MBAs) and train them in-house.

Second, in a recession, companies focus more on short-term profits; they just want to survive to the next quarter. They want employees who can instantly do the job exactly the way it needs to be done. Although MBAs do make immediate contributions,

RECRUITER SPELLS IT OUT

David Tanzer,
Booz - Allen & Hamilton

"It may be kind of self-limiting, but we hire MBAs from the Business Schools that use the case method. Students trained in this methodology get exposure to a wide variety of business situations. They learn to quickly figure out what's truly important and focus on that. This is an important part of the consulting process.

"As a recruiter, when you read a résumé, you look for some continuity: that what you're hiring an MBA for is some logical progression of what they've done before. The MBA will allow you to switch careers, but it's still a good idea to build on prior experiences.

"In general, the MBA is a screening device. Somebody who got into a good business school has something going for him or her. You find in an MBA the level of maturity you're looking for and the interpersonal skills of some one who has had several years of work experience."

they can't always operate at this level of expertise. Under these conditions, graduates of B-schools with specialized curricula, such as finance, may offer more bang per hire.

Third, many companies are hiring less than half the number of MBAs they did before the downturn. Some have backed out of campus recruiting completely. This has made securing an interview, much less an offer, more difficult. Even at the elite programs, getting a job is no longer the mating dance it used to be. While many still get wined and dined, fewer receive offers. Where once students could choose from four to six offers, now they pick from one or two—luckier ones from three. In some cases, students don't receive a single, solitary offer until after graduation.

Last, during tough times, recruiters are interested in yielding the greatest number of hires for the least expense—meaning they don't have the budget to fly all over the country hiring MBAs. Rather than interviewing at dozens of smaller schools, some companies minimize their "cost per hire" by going to only those with the largest number of students. The best *and* biggest schools thus have great appeal.

A related career concern is that the MBA has become commonplace. Once it was a credential that pushed recent grads to the front of the line; now it's what's needed merely to qualify. In fact, in some industries the MBA is the only ticket to entry. Many applicants now considering B-school witnessed the mega-deal days and abundance of the '80s. During this time, expanding companies had a great need for MBAs. Everyone thought of the degree as a golden ticket because for a short period (one which may go down in history as reckless and fraudulent), it bought instant success. These days expectations for the MBA have simply returned to more realistic levels. The change in perception is partly a reconciliation of the difference between a degree whose value was once artificially elevated and an MBA that is now poised for more traditional accomplishments.

MBA CORPORATE RECRUITING—MIXED MESSAGES?		
Corporation	MBA Hires for 1992	Projected MBA Hires 1993
Morgan Stanley	40	40
Microsoft	25	25
Merck	55	25
First Boston	34	35
United Airlines	30	0
Leo Burnett	5	10
Kidder-Peabody	15	no estimate for '93
Banker's Trust	58	no estimate for '93

Despite a cyclical slowdown in placement and a spate of recent MBA-bashing, you shouldn't be deterred from seeking the degree. More than a million MBAs are out there prospering and harboring grand ambitions. There's certainly room for more.

The history of the American economy is one of cycles and growth, and an attendant surge in jobs will likely occur eventually. Until that happens, both schools and students are taking a creative and aggressive approach to the job search. For example, one spirited group of students organized a phone-athon to alumni for leads on internships and jobs.

Most important, the MBA is a long-term investment. It's meant to see you through a lifetime of economic cycles, as well as boost your success over an entire career.

Finally, although companies no longer want to pay lots of money to fresh-faced know-it-all MBAs, they *do* want the new breed of graduates—teamwork-oriented MBAs with ethics and the skills to manage the grittier, more complex world of business.

Getting a Job

For most would-be MBAs, B-school represents a fresh beginning—either in their current profession or in an entirely different industry. Whatever promise the degree holds for you, it's wise to question what the return on your investment will be.

As with average starting salary, several factors affect job placement. School reputation and ties to industries and employers are important. At the top programs, the lists of recruiters read like

RECRUITER SPILLS THE BEANS

Liz Tunkiar,
Senior V.P. - Director of Personnel,
Ogilvy and Mather

"We've gone back and forth on whether we should hire MBAs. We've finally come to the conclusion that from an account point of view, they fit well into our organization.

"Many of our clients have MBAs—Kraft, General Foods, Unilever—so it makes sense that we hire MBAs to work on those businesses. They tend to have instant credibility with the client.

"MBAs have an advantage over BAs in that they bring a certain maturity to the account work. They also bring marketing knowledge and problem-solving and analytical skills.

"MBAs cost us more. We pay them higher salaries. In return we expect them to understand the business much more quickly than non-MBAs. We also expect them to move quickly up the learning curve and make immediate contributions.

"Obviously, this puts them on a faster track."

a "Who's Who" of American companies. These schools not only attract the greatest volume of recruiters, but consistently get the attention of those considered blue-chip.

Not to be overlooked are lesser-known, regional schools that often have the strongest relationships with local employers and industries. Some B-schools (many of them state universities), are regarded by both academicians and employers as number one in their respective regions. In other words, as far as the local business community is concerned, these programs offer as much prestige and pull as a nationally ranked program.

Student clubs also play a big part in getting a job because they extend the recruiting efforts at many schools. They host a variety of events that allow you to meet leading business people, so that you can learn about their industries and their specific companies. Most important, these clubs are very effective at bringing in recruiters and other interested parties that do not recruit through traditional mainstream channels. For example, the high-tech, international, and entertainment student clubs provide career opportunities not available through the front door.

Another important factor is the industry you enter. Newly rediscovered fields such as marketing and manufacturing are red-hot. Consulting and investment banking are popular because salaries have stayed high. Brand management positions in packaged-goods companies are always appealing; you get to manage a product as though you were a mini-CEO. Companies off the beaten track, such as start-up ventures, offer unique opportunities but many more unknowns.

Your background and experiences also affect your success in securing a position. Important factors are academic specialization (or course of study), academic standing, prior work experience, and intangibles such as your personal fit with the company. These days, what you did before B-school is particularly important; it helps establish credibility and gives you an edge in competing for a position in a specific field. For those using B-school to switch careers to a new industry, it's helpful if something on your resume ties your interest to the new profession. It's smart to secure a summer job in the new area.

Finally, persistence and initiative are critical factors in the job search. Since the beginning of this decade, many fast tracks have been narrowed. Increasingly, even at the best schools, finding a job requires off-campus recruiting efforts and ferreting out the hidden jobs.

Friends Who Are Going Places, Alumni Who Are Already There

Most students say that the best part about B-school is meeting classmates with whom they share common goals and interests. Many students claim that the "single greatest resource is each other." Not surprisingly, with so many bright and ambitious people cocooned in one place, B-school can be the time of your life. It presents numerous professional and social opportunities. It can be where you find future customers, business partners, and mentors. It can also be where you establish lifelong friendships. And after graduation, these classmates form an enduring network of contacts and professional assistance.

Alumni are also an important part of the B-school experience. While professors teach business theory and practice, alumni provide insight into the real business world. When you're ready to interview, they can provide advice on how to get hired by the companies recruiting at your school. In some cases, they help secure the interview and shepherd you through the hiring process.

B-schools love to boast about the influence of their alumni network. To be sure, some are very powerful. But this varies from institution to institution. At the very least, alumni will help you get your foot in the door. A resume sent to an alum at a given company, instead of "Dear Sir or Madam" in the personnel department, has a much better chance of being noticed and acted on.

After you graduate, the network continues to grow. Regional alumni clubs and alumni publications keep you plugged into the network with class notes on who's doing what, where, and with whom.

Throughout your career, an active alumni relations department can give you continued support. Post-MBA executive education series, fund-raising events, and continued job placement efforts are all resources you can draw on for years to come.

CHAPTER THREE

What B-School Is Really Like

The Changing Face of Business

In the last decade, B-schools have been taken to task. A recent article in *The Chronicle for Higher Education* observed, "Hardly a month passes without a new article in the business press lamenting the narrow, overly quantitative focus of graduate business curricula, the irrelevant research done by business schools' faculty members, and the inability of graduates to grapple successfully with the nation's economic problems. Reporters gleefully interview unemployed graduates of business schools and pump corporate executives for unflattering comments about their employees with Masters Degrees in Business Administration."

Things have certainly changed. In the 1980s, for example, Wall Street was the place to be. Investment bankers surfed on a monster wave of mergers and acquisitions. Students studied finance with an eye toward mega-deals. Today, with a soft Wall Street job market, high finance falling into discredit, and an economy besieged by invigorated foreign competitors, the focus is on building and delivering better products and services. Jobs may be easier to find in the Rust Belt than on Wall Street.

B-schools are responding to these challenges by carving out a new image for themselves. Many programs have sprouted social consciences. The '90s MBA student hardly resembles the Gordon Gekko stereotype (remember that evil arbitrager from the movie *Wall Street*?) of the '80s. Gone is the tolerance for avaricious, self-important MBAs. B-schools are recruiting students with broader, more humanitarian outlooks—students interested in contributing as much as in profit-taking. And, importantly, schools are trying to break down the rich-white-male stronghold on the business world by actively recruiting women and minorities.

Schools are also training students differently, both in content and in style. There's a move toward the medical-school model of education—learning by doing. Business "residencies," product "laboratories," and fieldwork augment classroom instruction with real-world experiences. Greater emphasis is being placed on public service and citizenship. Professional ethics classes are now mandatory in many schools. Outward-Bound style orientation and leadership programs are in vogue. Interpersonal communication skills, such as negotiation, conflict resolution, and team playing, have moved to the forefront. In short, the "bottom line" is no longer the bottom line.

Much has been made in recent years of the rise of a global economy. To make sure MBAs have the skills necessary to be effective in this economy, leading business programs have developed courses on global business operations and international economics. To teach sensitive leadership in an increasingly multicultural workforce, they've enhanced offerings on cultural diversity and human resources.

One other change is worth noting. The reason that the average age of the business school student has steadily increased to the current high of twenty-seven is that B-schools have sought older students to satisfy the new demands of the marketplace. Recruiters want graduates with more than a degree; they want the skills that come with maturity, and the maturity that comes with several years of work experience.

An Academic Perspective

The objective of all MBA programs is to prepare students for a professional career in business. One business school puts it this way:

Graduates should be

1. Able to think and reason independently, creatively, and analytically

2. Skilled in the use of quantitative techniques

3. Literate in the use of software applications as management tools

4. Knowledgeable about the world's management issues and problems

5. Willing to work in and successfully cope with conditions of uncertainty, risk, and change

6. Astute decision makers

7. Ethically and socially responsible

Sound like a tall order? Possibly. But this level of expectation is what business school is all about.

All MBA programs feature a core curriculum that focuses students on the major disciplines of business: finance, management, accounting, marketing, manufacturing, decision sciences, economics, and organizational behavior. Unless your school allows you to place out of them, these courses are mandatory. Core courses provide broad functional knowledge in one discipline. For example, a core marketing course covers pricing, segmentation, communications, product line planning, and implementation. Electives provide a narrow focus that deepens the area of study. For example, a marketing elective might be entirely devoted to pricing.

Students sometimes question the need for such a comprehensive core program. But the functional areas of a real business are not parallel lines. All departments of a business affect each other every day. For example, an MBA in a manufacturing job might be asked by a financial controller why the company's product has become unprofitable to produce. Without an understanding of how product costs are accounted for, this MBA wouldn't know how to respond to a critical and legitimate request.

At most schools, the first term or year is devoted to a rigid core curriculum. Some schools allow first-years to take core courses side by side with electives. Still others have come up with an entirely new way of covering the basics, integrating the core courses into one cross-functional learning experience, which may also include sessions on '90s topics such as globalization, ethnics, and managing diversity. Half-year to year-long courses are team-taught by professors who see you through all the disciplines.

Teaching Methodology

Business schools employ two basic teaching methods: case-study and lecture. Usually, they employ some combination of the two. The most popular is the case-study approach. Students are presented with either real or hypothetical business scenarios and are asked to analyze them. This method provides concrete situations (rather than abstractions) that require mastery of a wide range of skills. Students often find case studies exciting because they can engage in spirited discussions about possible solutions to given business problems and because they get an opportunity to apply newly acquired business knowledge.

The other teaching method used by B-schools is lecture, in which—you guessed it—the professor speaks to the class and the class listens. The efficacy of the lecture method depends entirely on the professor. If the professor is compelling, you'll probably get a lot out of the class. If the professor is boring, you probably won't listen. Which isn't necessarily a big deal, since many professors make their class notes available on computer disc or in the library.

The Classroom Experience

Professors teaching case methodology often begin class with a "cold call." A randomly selected student opens the class with an analysis of the case and makes recommendations for solutions. The cold call forces you to be prepared and think on your feet.

No doubt, a cold call can be intimidating. But unlike law school, B-school professors don't use the Socratic method to torture you, testing your thinking with a pounding cross-examination. They're training managers, not trial lawyers. At worst, particularly if you're unprepared, a professor will abruptly dismiss your contributions.

Alternatively, professors ask for a volunteer to open a case, particularly someone who has had real industry experience with the issues. After the opening, the discussion is broadened to include the whole class. Everyone tries to get in a good comment, particularly if class participation counts heavily toward the grade. "Chip shots"—unenlightening, just-say-anything-to-get-credit comments—are common. So are "air hogs," students who go on and on because they like nothing more than to hear themselves pontificate.

Depending on the school, sometimes class discussions degenerate into wars of ego rather than ideas. But for the most part, debates are kept constructive and civilized. Students are competitive, but not offensively so, and learn to make their points succinctly and persuasively.

Your First Year

The first six months of B-school can be daunting. You're unfamiliar with the subjects. There's a tremendous amount of work to do. And when you least have the skills to do so, there's pressure to stay with the pack. All of this produces anxiety and a tendency to overprepare. Eventually, students learn shortcuts and settle into a routine, but until then, much of the first year is just plain tough. The programs usually pack more learning into the first term than they do into each of the remaining terms. For the schools to teach the core curriculum (which accounts for as much as 70 percent of learning) in a limited time, an intensive pace is considered necessary. Much of the second year will be spent on gaining proficiency in your area of expertise and searching for a job.

The good news is that the schools recognize how tough the first year can be. During the early part of the program, they anchor students socially by placing them in small sections. You take many or all of your classes with your section-mates. Sectioning encourages the formation of personal and working relationships and can help make a large program feel like a school within a school.

Because so much has to be accomplished in so little time, getting an MBA is like living in fast-forward. This is especially true of the job search. No sooner are you in the program when

A RECENT GRAD LOOKS BACK

"I went to work for IBM straight out of undergraduate school. Within a year or two, I decided to get my MBA—part-time. I never considered going full-time. Not having any money? I couldn't deal with that. Unfortunately, after one year in the program I quit because I didn't have clear goals for myself. Several years later I returned. This time I was ready.

"Depending on your background, some of the core courses are not exactly pleasant or stimulating. If you don't have a business background, you'll benefit from them tremendously. They provide a good foundation. I had some waived because I had taken them as an undergrad. The courses I really enjoyed were advanced electives like strategic management.

"Most of my professors left successful careers in business to teach. They brought their practical experience into the classroom. You know the expression, 'Those who can do—do. Those who can't—teach.' This isn't so at business school."

continued on the next page

recruiters for summer jobs show up, which tends to divert students from their studies. First-years aggressively pursue summer positions, which are linked with the promise of a permanent job offer if the summer goes well. At some schools the recruiting period begins as early as October. At others, in January or February.

In Your Second Year

Relax, the second year is easier. By now, students know what's important and what's not. Second-years work more efficiently than first-years. Academic anxiety is no longer a factor. Having mastered the broad-based core curriculum, students now enjoy taking electives and developing an area of specialization.

Anxiety in the second year has to do more with the arduous task of finding a job. For some lucky students, a summer position has yielded a full-time offer. But even those students often go through the whole recruiting grind anyway, because they don't want to cut off any opportunities prematurely.

Most MBAs leave school with a full-time offer. Sometimes it's their only offer. Sometimes it's not their dream job. Which may be why most grads change jobs after just two years.

One University of Chicago Business School student summed up the whole two-year academic/recruiting process like this: "The first-year students collapse in the winter quarter because of on-campus recruiting. The second-years collapse academically in the first quarter of their second year because it's so competitive to get a good job. And when a second-year does get a job, he or she forgets about class entirely. That's why pass/fail was invented."

Life Outside of Class

Business school is more than academics and a big-bucks job. A spirited student community provides ample opportunities for social interaction, extracurricular activity, and career development.

Much of campus life revolves around student-run clubs. There are groups for just about every career interest and social need—from "MBAs for a Greener America" to the "Small Business Club." There's even a spouse group for significant others on most campuses. The clubs are a great way to meet classmates with similar interests and get in on the social scene. They might have a reputation for throwing the best black-tie balls, pizza and keg events, and professional mixers. During orientation week, these clubs aggressively market themselves to first-years.

Various socially responsible projects are also popular on campus. An emphasis on volunteer work is part of the overall trend toward good citizenship. Perhaps to counter the greed of the '80s, "giving back" is the B-school style of the moment. There is usually a wide range of options—from tutoring in an inner-city school to working in a soup kitchen to renovating public buildings.

Still another way to get involved is to work on a school committee. Here you might serve on a task force designed to improve student quality of life. Or you might work in the admissions office and interview prospective students.

For those with more creative urges there are always the old standbys: extracurriculars such as the school paper, yearbook, or school play. At some schools, the latter takes the form of the B-school follies and is a highlight of the year. Like the student clubs, these are a great way to get to know your fellow students.

Finally, you can play on intramural sports teams or attend the numerous informal get-togethers, dinner parties, and group trips. There are also plenty of regularly scheduled pub nights, just in case you thought your beer-guzzling days were over.

Most former MBA students say that going to B-school was the best decision they ever made. That's primarily because of non-academic experiences. Make the most of your classes, but take the time to get involved and enjoy yourself.

"Females at my school were well-represented. But in terms of minority ethnic groups—black and hispanic, and that applies to myself—these were under-represented. I could count on my two hands how many minorities were in that program. This is not an indictment of the school, it's just that as a minority, you have to be comfortable with the numbers.

"There's a lot of press out there that says the MBA is not the golden ticket it's cracked up to be. But it does make you more competitive. I remember interviewing for a job in one of the other IBM offices. I had just started the MBA program again, and this manager said, 'It's really good you're doing that. All the other people who work for me have MBAs. Every one of them.' So I can see the degree helping with my short- and long-term career goals.

"The MBA gave me credibility. It helped me understand my customers' needs better. Business school changes HOW you think about a problem. And I've made better business decisions because of that."

Female MBA, Graduate School of Business, Claremont College, 1991 Manager, IBM

A DAY IN THE LIFE OF A STUDENT

Male MBA, First Year
Kenan-Flagler Business School,
The University of North Carolina at Chapel Hill

7:00 am: Review notes for my first class.

7:30 am: Eat some high-energy flake cereal; read the *The Wall Street Journal*—professors like to discuss news items that relate to the class topics.

8:00 am: Read review for quantitative methods exam; do practice problems; re-read case on control systems for organizational behavior class.

9:00 am: Arrive at school. Go to "reading room" to hang out with everyone. Check student mailbox for invitations to recruiter events.

9:30 am: Integrative Management Class: Guest speaker from case-study discusses how the company approached problems.

10:45 am: Hang out.

11:00 am: Organizational Behavior Class: Get in a couple of good comments; debate the effectiveness of a management decision with another student in class.

12:15 pm: Grab some lunch and sit with friends. Talk about the lousy cafeteria food and who's dating whom.

1:00 pm: Go back to reading room to review for 2:00 class.

2:00 pm: Microeconomics Class: Listen to lecture on monopolistic competition.

3:15 pm: Arrive at home, change into work-out clothes. Go running, lift weights—relax.

6:00 pm: Eat dinner; watch the news. Read the next day's case.

7:30 pm: Head back to campus for study group.

7:45 pm: Discuss cases, help each other with homework problems on interpreting regression statistics; discuss how to account for capital leases versus operating leases.

10:00 pm: Back at home. Review more cases, read next class assignment in textbook, work on problem set.

Midnight: Sports on ESPN till I fall asleep. Boardroom dreams.

Female MBA, Second Year
The Fuqua School of Business, Duke University

6:45 am: Get dressed, listen to CNN and pick up *The Wall Street Journal* on way to school.

8:00 am: Arrive at school. Bargaining and Negotiations class. Perform role-play on conflict resolution.

10:15 am: Hang out—grab a bagel.

10:30 am: Intermediate Accounting Class—Discussion on cash flow statements—nothing exciting.

12:45 pm: Arrive at admissions office to review resume of applicant to B-school.

1:00 pm: Conduct interview of applicant.

1:45 pm: Write evaluation of candidate. Hand in to admissions secretary.

2:00 pm: Attend quality advisory board meeting—discuss creation of corporate survey.

3:30 pm: Competitive Strategy class. Lecture on barriers to entry.

5:45 pm: Attend recruiter event. Tell the recruiter how interested I am in the industry (I know nothing about it).

7:45 pm: Over to the health club for aerobics.

8:45 pm: Drive home, eat dinner, and finally read *The Wall Street Journal*—of course, it's not news by now.

9:30 pm: Study class notes, prepare next day's case.

11:45 pm: Quality phone time with my boyfriend.

12:30 pm: Boardroom dreams.

CHAPTER FOUR

Preparing to Be a Successful Applicant

Get Good Grades

If you're still in school, work on getting good grades. A high GPA says you've not only got brains, but discipline. It shows the admissions committee you have what you need to make it through the program. If you're applying directly from college, or have limited job experience, your grades will matter even more. The admissions committee has little else on which to evaluate you.

It's especially important that you do well in courses such as economics, statistics, and calculus. Success in these courses is more meaningful than your success in classes like "Monday Night at the Movies" film appreciation. Of course, English is also important; B-schools want students who communicate well.

Strengthen Math Skills

Number-crunching is an inescapable part of B-school. Take an accounting or statistics course for credit at a local college or B-school. If you have a liberal arts background, did poorly in math, or got a low GMAT math score, this is especially important. Get a decent grade and this will go a long way toward convincing the admissions committee you can manage the quantitative challenges of the program.

Work For a Few Years—But Not *Too* Many

Business schools favor applicants who have worked full time for several years. There are three primary reasons for this: 1) With experience comes maturity. 2) You're more likely to know what you want out of the program. 3) Your experience enables you to bring real-work perspectives to the classroom. Since business school is designed for you to learn from your classmates, each student's contribution is important.

How many years of work experience should you have? Two to five seems to be the preferred amount, although there is no magic number. The rationale is that at two years you've worked enough to be able to make a solid contribution. Beyond four or five, you may be too advanced in your career to appreciate the program fully. You may also have reached a salary level too pricey for most recruiters.

If your grades are weak, consider working at least three years before applying. The more professional success you have, the greater the likelihood the admissions committee will overlook your GPA.

Let Your Job Work For You

Many companies encourage employees to go to B-school. Some of these companies have close ties to favored B-school and produce well-qualified applicants. If their employees are going to the kinds of schools you want to get into, these may be smart places to work.

Other companies, such as investment banks, feature training programs at the end of which trainees go to B-school or leave the company. These programs hire undergraduates right out of school. They're known for producing solid, highly skilled applicants. Moreover, they're full of well-connected alumni who may write influential letters of recommendation.

Happily, the opposite tactic—working in an industry that generates few applicants—can be equally effective. Admissions officers look for students from underrepresented professions. Applicants from biotechnology, health care, not-for-profit, and even the Peace Corps, are viewed favorably.

One way to set yourself apart is to have had two entirely different professional experiences before business school. For example, if you worked in finance, your next job might be in a different field, like marketing. Supplementing quantitative work with qualitative experiences demonstrates versatility.

Finally, what you do on your job is important. Seek out opportunities to distinguish yourself. Even if your responsibilities are limited, exceed the expectations of the position. B-schools are looking for leaders.

March from the Military

A surprising number of business school students hail from the military (although the armed forces probably had commanders in mind, not CEOs, when they designed their regimen).

Military officers know how to be managers because they've held command positions. And they know how to lead a team under the most difficult of circumstances.

Because most have traveled all over the world, they also know how to work with people from different cultures. As a result, they're ideally suited to learn alongside students with diverse backgrounds and perspectives. B-schools with a global focus are particularly attracted to such experience.

The decision to enlist in the military is a very personal one. However, if you've thought of joining those few good men and women, this may be as effective a means of preparing for business school as more traditional avenues.

Check Out Those Essay Questions *Now*

You're worried you don't have interesting stories to tell. Or you just don't know what to write. What do you do?

Ideally, several months before your application is due, you should read the essay questions and begin to think about your answers. Could you describe an ethical dilemma at work? Are you involved in anything outside the office (or classroom)? If not, now is the time to do something about it. While this may seem contrived, it's preferable to sitting down to write the application and finding you have to scrape for or, worse, manufacture situations.

Use the essay questions as a framework for your personal and professional activities. Look back over your business calendar and see if you can find some meaty experiences for the essays in your work life. Keep your eyes open for a situation that involves questionable ethics. And if all you do is work, work, work, get involved in activities that round out your background. In other words, get a life.

Get involved in community-based activities. Some possibilities are being a big brother/big sister, tutoring in a literacy program, or even initiating a recycling project. Demonstrating a concern for others looks good to admissions committees, and hey, it's good for your soul, too.

It's also important to seek out leadership experiences. B-schools are looking for individuals who can manage groups. Volunteer to chair a professional committee or get elected to an office in a club.

It's a wide-open world; you can pick from any number of activities. The bottom line is this: the extracurriculars you select can show that you are mature, multifaceted, and appealing.

We don't mean to sound cynical. Obviously, the best applications do nothing more than describe your true, heartfelt interests and show off your sparkling personality. We're not suggesting you try to guess which activity will win the hearts of admissions directors and then mold yourself accordingly. Instead, think of projects and activities you care about, that maybe you haven't gotten around to acting on, and act on them now!

Pick Your Recommendors Carefully

By the time you apply to business school, you shouldn't have to scramble for recommendations. Like the material for your essays, sources for recommendations should be considered long before the application is due.

How do you get great recommendations? Obviously, good work is a prerequisite. Whom you ask is equally important. Bosses who know you well will recommend you on both a personal and professional level. They can provide specific examples of your accomplishments, skills, and character. Additionally, they can convey a high level of interest in your candidacy.

There's also the issue of trust. Business school recommendations are made in confidence; you probably won't see what's been written about you. Choose someone you can trust to deliver the kind of recommendation that will push you over the top. A casual acquaintance may fail you by writing an adequate, yet mostly hum-drum letter.

Cultivate relationships that yield glowing recommendations. Former and current professors, employers, clients, and managers are all good choices. An equally impressive recommendation can come from someone who has observed you in a worthwhile extracurricular activity.

Left to their own devices, a recommendor may create a portrait that leaves out your best features. You need to prep them on what they write. Remind them of those projects or activities in which you achieved some success. You might also discuss the total picture of yourself you're trying to create. The recommendation should reinforce what you're saying about yourself in your essays.

About "Big-Shot" recommendations: don't bother. Getting some golf pro who's a friend of your dad's to write you a recommendation will do you no good if he doesn't know you very well, even if he is President of the Universe. Don't try to fudge your application—let people who really know you and your work tell the honest, believable, and impressive truth.

Prepare for
the Graduate Management Admission Test (GMAT)

Most B-schools require you to take the GMAT. The GMAT is a three-and-a-half-hour standardized multiple-choice exam with math and verbal sections. It's the kind of test you hate to take and schools love to demand of you.

Why is the GMAT required? The B-schools believe it measures your verbal and quantitative skills and predicts success in the MBA program. Some think this is a bunch of hooey, most notably the Harvard Business School, which does not require the exam. But for most other schools, the GMAT is weighed heavily in the admissions decision. If nothing else, it gives the school a frame of reference with which to compare you against other applicants.

Most people feel they have no control over the GMAT. They dread it as the potential bomb in their application. But you have more control than you think. You can take a test-preparation course which reviews the math and verbal material, teaches you test-taking strategies, and builds your confidence. Test-prep courses can be highly effective. But if the course you select won't guarantee you a score improvement of at least 85 points, don't take it. You haven't found the best test-preparation course out there.

How many times should you take the GMAT? More than once, if you didn't ace it on the first try. But watch out: multiple scores that fall in the same range make you look unprepared. Don't take the test more than once if you don't expect a decent increase, and don't even think of taking it the first time without serious preparation. Two tries is best. Three, if there were unusual circumstances or you really need another shot at it. If you take it more than three times, the admissions committee will think you have an unhealthy obsession with filling in dots. A final note: if you submit more than one score, most schools will take the highest. Otherwise, they'll take the average.

If you don't have math courses on your college transcript or numbers-oriented work experience, it's especially important to get a solid score on the quantitative section. There's a lot of math between you and the MBA.

CHAPTER FIVE

Admissions

HOW THE ADMISSIONS CRITERIA ARE WEIGHTED
What They Count

Admissions requirements vary from institution to institution. Most rely on the following criteria (not necessarily in order): GMAT score, college GPA, work experience, essays, letters of recommendation, interviews and extracurriculars, of which the first four are the most heavily weighted. The more competitive the school, the less room there is for weakness in any one of these areas.

Most applicants suspect that the GMAT score or GPA pushes their application into one of three piles: "yes," "no," or "maybe." But that's not the way it is. Unless one or more of your numbers is so low it forces a rejection, the piles are "looks good," "looks bad," "hmmm, interesting," and all variations of "maybe." In B-school admissions, the whole is greater than the sum of the parts. Each of the numbers has an effect, but doesn't provide the total picture.

What's fair about the system is that you can compensate for problem areas. Even if you have a low GMAT score, evidence of a high GPA, quantitative work experience, or the completion of an accounting or statistics course will provide a strong counter-balance.

As we've said, no one single thing counts more than everything else. Your scores, work experience, and essays should give the admissions committee a clear idea of your capabilities, interests, and accomplishments. Any particular weakness can be overcome by a particular strength in another area—so make sure you emphasize whatever strengths you have, and don't take them for granted.

The GMAT and GPA

The GMAT score and GPA are used in two ways. First, they're used as "success indicators" for the academic work. In other words, if admitted, will you have the brain power and discipline to make it through the program? Second, they're used to compare applicants against the larger pool. In particular, the top schools like applicant pools with high scores. They think that having an incoming class with high score and grade profiles is an indicator of their program's prestige and selectivity.

Some schools look more closely at junior and senior year grades than the overall GPA. Most consider the academic reputation of your college and the difficulty of your curriculum. A transcript loaded with courses like "Environmental Appreciation" and "The Child in You" isn't valued as highly as one with a more substantive agenda.

Work Experience

Of all the criteria, your work history is perhaps the most crucial to acceptance. It provides tangible evidence of your performance in the business world thus far and hints at your potential. This helps B-schools determine if you're going to turn out to be the kind of graduate they'll be proud to have as an alum. Your work experience also reveals whether you've progressed enough (or too far) to benefit from a B-school education. Last, your experience sheds light on the industry perspective you'll bring to the program.

Five elements are considered. First, the stature of your company: Does it have a high reputation? Does it produce well-qualified applicants?

Secondly, diversity of work experience. Have you started your own business, invented a new software program, or worked in an industry that is under-represented at the prospective school?

Third, your advancement: Did you progress steadily to ever-more responsible positions, or did you just tread water? Do your salary increases prove that you are a strong performer? Did you put in your time at each job, or just jump from company to company?

Fourth, your professional and interpersonal skills: Did you get along well with others? Work as part of a team? Do your recommendors see you as future manager material?

Fifth (and this is critical), your leadership potential: Did you excel in your positions, go beyond the job descriptions, save the day, lead a team?

The Essays

Admissions committees consider the essays the clincher, the swing vote in the "admit/deny" issue. Essays offer the most substance about who you really are. The GMAT and GPA reveal little about you, only that you won't crash and burn. Your work history provides a record of performance and justifies your stated desire to study business. But the essays tie all the pieces of the application together and create a summary of your experiences, skills, background, and beliefs.

The essays do more than give answers to questions. They create thumbnail psychological profiles. Depending on how you answer a question or what you present, you reveal yourself in any number of ways—creative, witty, open-minded, articulate, mature—to name a few. Likewise, your essay can reveal a negative side, such as arrogance, sloppiness, or an inability to think and write clearly. In essence, the essays don't just complete the picture. They are the inside picture.

The Recommendations

Admissions committees expect recommendations to support and reinforce the rest of the application. They act as a sort of reality check. When the information from your recommendor doesn't match up with the information you've provided, it looks bad.

Great recommendations are rarely enough to save a weak application from doom. But they might push a borderline case over to the "admit" pile.

Mediocre recommendations are potentially harmful: an application that is strong in all other areas now has an inconsistency that's hard to ignore.

Bad recommendations—meaning that negative information is provided—cast doubt on the picture you've created. In some cases they invalidate your claims. This can mean the end for your application. Again, be careful whom you ask for recommendations.

The Interview

Like the recommendations, the interview is used to reinforce the total picture. But it is also used to fill in the blanks, particularly in borderline cases.

A great interview can tip the scale in the "admit" direction. How do you know if it was great? You were calm and focused. You expressed yourself and your ideas clearly. Your interviewer invited you to go rock climbing with him next weekend. (O.K., let's just say you developed a solid personal rapport with the interviewer.)

A mediocre interview may not have much impact, unless your application is hanging on by a thread. In such a case, the person you're talking to (harsh as it may seem) is probably looking for a reason *not* to admit you, rather than a reason to let you in. If you feel your application may be in that hazy, marginal area, try to be inspired in your interview.

Did you greet your interviewer by saying, "Gee, are all admissions officers as pretty as you?" Did you show up wearing a Karl Marx tee-shirt? Did you bring your mother with you? If so, it's probably safe to say you had a poor interview. A poor interview can doom even a straight-A, high-GMAT, strong-work-history candidate. Use good taste, refrain from belching, avoid insulting the interviewer's tie, and you'll probably be O.K.

Not all B-schools attach equal value to the interview. For some, it's an essential screening tool. For others, it's used to evaluate borderline cases. Still others strongly encourage, but do not require, the interview. Some schools make it simply informative. If you can't schedule an on-campus interview, the admissions office may find an alum to meet with you in your hometown.

If an interview is offered, take it. In person, you may be an entirely more compelling candidate. You can further address weaknesses or bring dull essays to life. Most important, you can display the kinds of qualities—enthusiasm, sense of humor, maturity—that often fill in the blanks and sway a decision.

In general, B-school interviews are not formulaic. The focus can range from specific questions about your job responsibilities to broad discussions of life. Approach the interview as a conversation to be enjoyed, not as a question-and-answer ordeal to get through. You may talk more about your hobbies or recent cross-country trip. This doesn't mean that it won't feel like a job interview. It just means you're being sized up as a person and future professional in *all* your dimensions. Try to be your witty, charming, natural self.

Interviews are conducted by students, faculty, admissions personnel and alumni. Don't dismiss students as the lightweights; they follow a tight script and report back to the committee. However, because they're inexperienced beyond the script, their interviews are most likely to be duds. You may have to work harder to get your points across.

Prepare for the interview in several ways: Expect to discuss *many* things about yourself. Be ready to go into greater depth than you did in your essays (but don't assume the interviewer has read them). Put together two or three points about yourself that you want the interviewer to remember you by. Go in with examples, or even a portfolio of your work, to showcase your achievements. Practice speaking about your accomplishments without a lot of "I did this, I did that's." Finally, be prepared to give a strong and convincing answer to the interviewer's inevitable question, "Why here?"

How to Blow the Interview

1. Wear casual clothes.

This is an automatic ding. Wearing anything but professional attire suggests you don't know, or want to play by, the rules of the game.

2. Bring your mom or dad. Or talk about them.

Business schools value maturity. If Mom or Dad brings you to the interview, or your answer to the question "Why an MBA," begins with "Dad always told me . . .", the interviewer is going to wonder how ready you are for the adult world of business school.

3. Talk about high school.

Again, they'll question your maturity. Stories about high school, and even college, suggest you haven't moved on to more mature, new experiences.

Exceptions: Explaining a unique situation or a low GPA.

4. Show up late.

This is another automatic ding at some schools. Short of a real catastrophe, you won't be excused.

5. Say something off the wall or inappropriate.

No doubt, the conversation can get casual and you may start to let your guard down. But certain things are still off-limits: profanity, ethnic jokes, allusions to sex, your romantic life, and anything else that might signal the interviewer that the cheese fell off your cracker.

6. Forget to write a thank-you note to your interviewer.

Sending a thank-you note means you know how to operate in the business world, and it goes a long way toward convincing the interviewer you belong there.

MAKING THE ROUNDS: WHEN TO APPLY

You worked like a dog on your application—is there anything else you can do to increase your odds of getting accepted? Perhaps. The filing period ranges anywhere from six to eight months. Therefore, the *timing* of your application can make a difference. Although there are no guarantees, the earlier you apply, the better your chances. Here's why:

First, there's plenty of space available early on. As the application deadline nears, spaces fill up. The majority of applicants don't apply until the later months because of procrastination or unavoidable delays. As the deadline draws close, the greatest number of applicants compete for the fewest number of spaces.

Second, in the beginning, admissions officers have little clue about how selective they can be. They haven't reviewed enough applications to determine the competitiveness of the pool. An early application may be judged more on its own merit than how it stacks up against others. This is in your favor if the pool turns out to be unusually competitive. Above all, admissions officers like to lock their classes in early; they can't be certain they'll get their normal supply of applicants. Admissions decisions may be more generous at this time.

Third, by getting your application in early you're showing a strong interest. The admissions committee is likely to view you as someone keen on going to their school.

To be sure, some admissions officers report that the first batch of applications tend to be from candidates with strong qualifications, confident of acceptance. In this case, you might not be the very first one on line; but closer to the front is still better than lost in the heap of last-minute hopefuls.

Of course, if applications are down that year at all B-schools, or—thanks to the latest drop in its ranking—at the one to which you are applying, then filing later means you can benefit from admissions officers desperately filling spaces. But this is risky business, especially since the rankings don't come out until the spring.

Conversely, if the school to which you are applying was recently ranked number one or two, applying early may make only a marginal difference. Swings in the rankings from year to year send school applications soaring and sagging. From beginning to end, a newly minted number-one or -two school will be flooded with applications.

Rounds and Rolling Admissions

Applications are processed in one of two ways—rounds admissions or rolling admissions. With rounds, the filing period is divided into three to four timed cycles. Applications are batched into the round in which they are received and reviewed competitively with others in that grouping. A typical round might go from February 15th to March 15th.

With rolling admissions, applications are reviewed on an ongoing basis as they are received. The response time for a rolling admissions decision is usually quicker than a decision with rounds. And with rolling admissions, when all the spaces are full, admissions stop.

QUOTAS, RECRUITMENT, AND DIVERSITY

Business schools don't have to operate under quotas—governmental or otherwise. However, they probably try harder than most corporations to recruit diverse groups of people. Just as the modern business world has become global and multi-cultural, so too have the B-schools. They must not only preach diversity in the classroom, but make it a reality in their campus population, and if possible, faculty.

Schools that have a diverse student body tend to be proud of it. They tout their success in profiles that demographically slice and dice the previous year's class by sex, race, and geographic and international residency. Prospective students can review this data and decide whether the school will provide them with the experience they desire: a cosmopolitan, international group of classmates.

But such diversity doesn't come naturally from the demographics of the applicant pool. Admissions committees have to work hard at it. While they don't have quotas per se, they do target groups for admission. Most notably, these are women and minorities. In some cases, enrollment is encouraged with generous financial aid packages and scholarships.

But those targeted for admission are not limited to women and minorities. The committees seek demographic balance in many areas. Have they admitted enough foreign students, marketing strategists, and liberal arts majors? Are different parts of the country represented?

Only toward the end of the admissions filing period do shortages in different categories emerge. Although you can't predict, women and minorities are almost always on the short list.

WHO ARE THOSE ADMISSIONS OFFICERS?
One School's Committee Revealed

Just who are those nameless, faceless people who pore over thousands of applications and determine the future of budding CEOs like you?

Most applicants picture a committee of white male MBAs in blue suits and power ties. But that's not the whole picture. Although many admissions officers do hold MBAs, they represent a wider slice of the demographic spectrum than do the business school classes they admit. There are more women. And more studied liberal arts and worked in fields such as human resources and teaching. In short, they're a diverse group.

But as diverse as they are in background, they share a certain perspective: they believe that *qualities*, such as drive and discipline, rather than *skills*, such as financial analysis, are the true and enduring engines of success. In other words, at least as much value is placed on who you are as on your accomplishments.

Why does knowing this help you? Because in writing your application you need to consider your audience. Admissions officers aren't necessarily the people you thought they were. Moreover, they don't necessarily share your love of business. Their role in the business world is different from yours: They sustain the profession by launching inductees, while you actually practice business. Many officers, even some with MBAs, have limited business experience.

Remember, they're not only admissions officers, they're daughters, sons, mothers, fathers, and grandparents too—in other words, regular people. Would you write the same kind of essay for them that you would for your boss? The essays for B-school should be a combination of the two: strong on substance and heavy on personality.

Here's who reads your application at the Columbia B-school:

THE DIRECTOR OF ADMISSIONS

Gender: Male
Race/Ethnicity: White
Age: Mid-30s
Marital/Family: Single
College Major: Accounting/Economics
Graduate Degree: MBA
First Job out of Graduate School: Brand Manager

> "In the '80s, applications were just flowing in.
> But now, admissions is a real marketing chal-
> lenge. I enjoy it; I'm out meeting students,
> helping them identify their goals, and talking
> about how our school might be right for them.
> Because I went through this program, I have an
> understanding of what it takes to be successful in
> this environment. I can gauge how realistic the
> applicant's expectations of B-school are."

ADMISSIONS OFFICER

Gender: Female
Race/Ethnicity: African-American
Age: Mid-30s
Marital/Family: Married/Mother
College Major: French/Political Science
Graduate Degree: M.A. in French, M.S. in Law and Diplomacy
First Job Out of Graduate School: French instructor;
 Developing public policy for higher education.

> "My previous work in undergraduate admissions
> gives me a unique point of view in reviewing
> MBA applications: I expect an applicant to be
> able to fully articulate why getting the degree is
> important. If the reasoning isn't clear, it's a
> problem. I also look for applicants who can bring
> something special to the student community—
> really add to the program and yet take advantage
> of all that we have to offer."

ADMISSIONS OFFICER

Gender: Female
Race/Ethnicity: White
Age: Late 40s
Marital/Family: Married, Grandmother
College Major: English Literature
Graduate Degree: One year in law school—dropped out to be "ski bum";
    M.S. in Reading; Candidate for Ph.D. in philosophy
First Job Out of Graduate School: Teacher in an inner-city high school

> "Based on my experiences as a teacher, I can see
> how some applicants will succeed even with a
> weak academic history. I err on the side of
> 'wait—don't reject this student just because the
> GMAT or academic cum isn't high on the
> charts.' Other things will refocus me on their
> application: a unique job experience, compli-
> ments that people made about the applicant that
> are very telling, or something that alludes to
> depth or potential."

ADMISSIONS OFFICER

Gender: Female
Race/Ethnicity: Indian
Age: Late 20s
Marital/Family: Married
College Major: Art History/Asian Studies
Graduate Degree: MBA
First Job out of Graduate School: Strategic Planning and Financial Manager

> "As a recent graduate, I try to bring several
> perspectives to the admissions process: that of an
> applicant, a matriculant, and a young profes-
> sional. Because of my international background, I
> understand the importance of diversity. I look for
> applicants who show this in both their profes-
> sional and personal experiences."

ADMISSIONS OFFICER

Gender: Female
Race/Ethnicity: White
Age: Early 30s
Marital/Family: Married
College Major: English
Graduate Degree: M.A. in Writing
First Job Out of Graduate School: English teacher for grades 9–12

"Admission to B-school is not the experiment of science nor game of roulette that people often think it is. When I review an applicant's profile, I don't fill in columns and rows with data. Making a decision is a very difficult, thought-filled, and time-intensive process. I'm always aware that I'm working with the summary of a person's intellect, talent, culture, and aspirations. On Commencement Day, it's a fact that after the students, the admissions officers are the second happiest group in the school. On that day, everyone knows the decision and the relationship was successful!"

ADMISSIONS CONSULTANT

Gender: Female
Race/Ethnicity: White
Age: Mid-30s
Marital/Family: Married
College Major: Stage and Theater
First Job Out of School: Actress
Career Prior to Admissions: Stage Director/Administrative Consultant

"I look for clear goals that are realistic and born of experience. When applicants can't articulate why they want the MBA, it's a concern. They don't have to have all the answers, but they should have a sound reason for wanting to be here. I'm also looking for people who have a sense of personal responsibility in the world. It's not a bad thing when a candidate says 'the MBA will help me strengthen the family business.' But I'd like to see somewhere else in the application that their universe is greater than themselves."

WHOM DO YOU THINK READS YOUR ESSAYS?

Now that you know who those admissions officers are, here's the next surprise. Many top business schools farm out the essays to paid readers. Why would the schools use readers instead of trained admissions officers to evaluate the essays? The answer is volume. As the number of applications to top business schools has soared, it has become cost-effective to hire part-timers to do the most time-intensive work. Admissions officers are then free to make the higher-level admissions decisions.

Most applicants wouldn't be pleased to know that the essay they worked on for two weeks isn't being read by an admissions officer. But admissions committees couldn't be more pleased. Now instead of an enormous pile of unread essays—some terrific, some not—they have a pile that's been evaluated. Moreover, they point out, the essays are now read in greater depth than before.

But what you need to know is this: How do readers affect the admissions decision?

At most schools readers make general recommendations, then pass it on to other members of the committee for other opinions. They don't have the authority to make a final judgment. They're trained to evaluate essays in the same way admissions officers do—writing style, content, message, etc. More than one staff member usually reads them, often a combination of reader and admissions officer, so a reader's opinion is not the only one. Also, readers don't examine or have input into the evaluation of the applicant's total candidacy.

INSIDE BABSON'S ADMISSIONS DEPARTMENT:
What Really Happens to Your Application

Are specific weights or scores assigned to each component of the application?

Do admissions committees get together and read them at one big table—or do they take them home and cover them with coffee stains?

How many people read your essays? How do they decide if it's good or terrible? If there is a system for standardizing the reading of the essays? Are they graded? Are there disagreements? How are they resolved?

Who are the surprise admits? Who are the surprise rejects? Why are some students put on the wait list? What can be done to pull them off?

These are just a few of the questions surrounding an admissions process that often operates with the concealment strategies of the CIA. But all is not lost. The Babson Graduate School of Business agreed to open its files for our review. And while this is only one school's admissions process, there are certainly some interesting conclusions to be drawn. Here's a flow chart of their process:

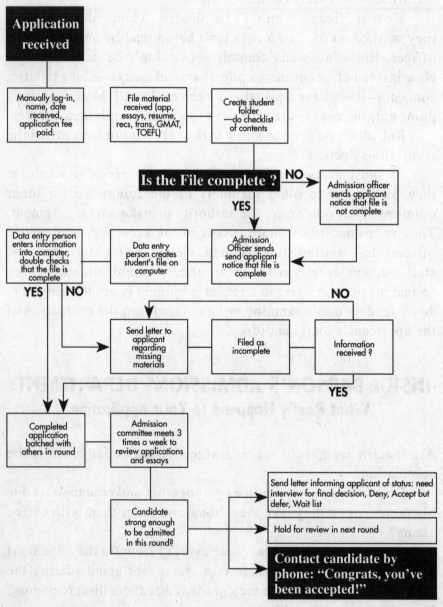

NOW WE CAN TAKE A CLOSER LOOK:
The Babson Admissions Challenge

The Babson admissions committee define their challenge in four ways:

First, will they be presented with the right types of applicants for their program? Second, will they yield enough applications that year to give the committee room for choice? Third, will the applicants they admit make it through the program; and will they be competitive in the marketplace because of the MBA when it's time to get a job? Fourth, will they be the kind of graduates the institution will be proud to have among its alumni?

Sorting Out Candidates

Even before reading the applications, Babson expects applicants will fall into three general categories: those who have exactly what the institution is looking for, those who fall below standard admissions requirements, and the intriguing group—those who possess qualities that capture the attention of the committee, yet are short of securing initial and clear acceptance.

Timing Can Make a Difference

Babson batches applications based on when they are received. Early applicants have the advantage; they're reviewed earlier when more spots are available.

No Homework Allowed

At some schools, admissions officers "sign" applications out to be read at home. But at Babson, applications are read on-premises in regularly scheduled "group reads" attended by admissions staff. The aim is to ensure that all applications receive the committee's comprehensive and equal attention and that, as a result, decisions are consistent. The sessions take place in a long rectangular conference room. There are no windows or phones. A DO NOT DISTURB sign hangs on the door. In short, there are no distractions.

At least three admissions officers read each application, essays and all.

An officer spends approximately 30–45 minutes on each. Essays are judged on how well they answer the question, style, writing ability, overall content and message, and maturity; also, if the applicant appears to be trying too hard to impress or has obtained help from a ghost writer. They try not to form opinions on the views expressed in the essay. Because the committee shares the same standards of evaluation, these assessments are qualitative. Essays are not subjected to an internal grading system or checklist of criteria.

Decisions, Decisions, Decisions

Occasionally there is disagreement about a particular essay. But since the admissions decision is based on the entire package, agreement on one essay is not as important as the agreement on the overall candidacy of the applicant. When the committee doesn't agree on this, a lengthy discussion about the applicant takes place. If a consensus isn't reached, one of two steps is taken. Either the application is placed into a pile of "re-reviews" to be read again against each other at a later date (up to two weeks); or, depending on the problem area, the applicant is asked to have an additional interview with a dean or faculty member, do some extra coursework, or retake the GMAT. Applicants in the latter category may be put on conditional admit or wait lists. If they satisfy the additional requirements and a place is available, they're in.

After the "group read" and review session, the three admissions officers are joined by the remaining admissions staff for a presentation of the applicant's candidacy.

CASE STUDIES

Here are the dossiers of four hopeful applicants to Babson, and the admissions committee's evaluation:

Applicant I is an undergraduate finance major from the University of Connecticut. She has a B grade point average and scored in the high 500s on the GMAT. Her work experience is substantive: five years, including two spent in the Peace Corps. The essays are descriptive and full of enthusiasm for her Peace Corps experience. The admissions committee learned she was up against major odds trying to secure loans from various funding sources for native African business people.

The committee used the interview with this applicant to obtain further insight into why she chose to go into the Peace Corps rather than pursue her original career. A small but important point the applicant had overlooked—what had motivated her decision? In the interview, the admissions officer found her poised, well prepared, and able to articulate why she wanted the MBA. Her clarification of her job experience helped the committee better understand why she made the career decision she made.

Decision: *Admit*

> **Applicant II** is a pharmaceutical salesman for a major international firm. His GMAT score is borderline, his GPA from a small liberal arts school in Maine is a low B. In reviewing his file, however, the committee found that he played a star position on his college's varsity hockey team and held a leadership position in student government. This helped explain and balance his marginal grades.

This applicant requested an interview early in the admissions process (this showed initiative even though interviews are required). He communicated clear expectations of the degree and what he wanted to accomplish. His essays also reflected a concise and persuasive presentation of his ideas. The letters of recommendation strongly supported his candidacy. His successes at work (many of them involving quantitative skill) also gave weight to his future business potential.

Decision: *Admit*

> **Applicant III** is an art major from the Art Institute in Chicago. In addition to her current position as a marketing assistant at a special events planning company, she has been recognized as one of the most creative students in the school and won the opportunity to present her work in the gallery at the museum. The committee felt a gallery show in such a prominent institute is a great accomplishment, particularly for a recent undergraduate.

This applicant took a "risky" approach to the essays, disclosing very personal information about emotional challenges she faced as a young adult. The essays were forthright, strong, and well structured. Most compelling was that her art exhibit was a pictorial essay of young women experiencing the same emotional challenges. The committee saw this as evidence that she had moved beyond the limitations of her emotional issues.

The greatest concern for this applicant was whether she would be able to manage the quantitative demands of the program. She has performed poorly on the math section of the GMAT. Her undergraduate coursework and limited work history provide no evidence of quantitative experience. For her benefit and the benefit of her classmates, she needs to bolster her skills before she can begin.

Decision: *Denied. Needs to retake the GMAT, quantitative courses, and reapply.*

> **Applicant IV** is a Venezuelan banker, one of many applying to the school because of its program's ties to Latin America.

This applicant was visiting Boston on a business trip and thought she would use the opportunity to come in for an interview before she applied. She was outstanding interpersonally. Her application later revealed an undergraduate GPA of a B+, eight years of work experience, and a mid-400 GMAT score. She has progressed in her job from being an economist with a bank to a senior loan officer—a nice progression. But her low GMATs blocked a clear "accept." Moreover, the committee needed to balance the number of students so there was not a predominant presence in any class from any one country.

Decision: *Hold her application for review in the next round and within the Latin American pool of candidates; ask her to retake the GMAT.*

CHAPTER SIX

The Right Stuff:

Filing a Winning Application

No one ever said it was going to be easy. Depending on where you're applying, and how prolific a writer you are, a B-school application will take anywhere from 50 to 100 hours to complete. Sound excessive? Go ahead and try it. You'll probably scrap and rewrite an essay many times over. It takes time for thoughts to gestate. Indeed, it might feel like a fine wine ages faster than it takes you to write an essay.

This chapter should speed the process along. It deciphers some of the most commonly asked essay questions. It also provides you a list of mistakes applicants most often make.

COMMON ESSAY QUESTIONS:
What They're Really Asking

Each school has its own set of essay questions. Although posed differently, all search for the same insights. Here's a list of commonly asked questions and what's behind them.

1. Theme: Career Goals and the MBA

"Describe your specific career aspirations. How will your goals be furthered by an MBA degree, and our MBA program in particular?"

"How do you feel the X school MBA degree can help you attain your specific career and personal goals for the five years after you graduate?"

"Discuss your career progression to date. What factors have influenced your decision to seek a general management education? Based on what you know about yourself at this time, how do you envision your career progressing after receiving the MBA degree? Please state your professional goals, and describe your plan to achieve them."

Translation:

"What do I want to be when I grow up, and how will the MBA get me there?"

This may be the most important essay question. It lays out the reasons why you should be given one of the cherished spots in the program. Even if your post-MBA future is tough to envision, this question must be answered.

A good way to frame this essay is to discuss how the MBA makes sense in light of your background, skills, and achievements to date. Why do you need this degree? Why now? One common reason is being stymied in your work by a lack of skills that can be gained in their program. Or you may want to use the MBA as a bridge to the next step. For example, an actress wants an MBA to prepare for a career in theater management. The more specific, the better.

It may be easier to provide specifics by breaking your plans into short- and long-term objectives.

Don't be afraid to present modest goals. If you're in accounting and want to stay there, say so. Deepening your expertise and broadening your perspective are solid reasons for pursuing the degree. On the other hand, feel free to indicate you'll use the MBA to change careers; 70 percent of all students at B-school are there to do just that.

If you aspire to lofty goals, like becoming a CEO or starting your own company, be especially careful that you detail a sensible, pragmatic plan. You need to show you're realistic. No one zooms to the top. Break your progress into steps.

Finally, this essay question asks how a particular program supports your goals. Admissions committees want to know why you've selected their school. That means you not only have to know, but also show, what's special about their program and how that relates specifically to your career aspirations.

(Hint: Many admissions officers say they can tell how much someone wants to go to their school by how well their essays are tailored to the offerings in their program.)

2. Theme: Extracurriculars and Social Interaction: our non-work side.

"What do you do for fun?"

"What are your principal interests outside of your job or school?"

"What leisure and/or community activities do you particularly enjoy? Please describe their importance in your life."

Translation:
Would we like to have you over for dinner? Do you know how to make friends? What are your special talents —the B-school Follies need help. Are you well balanced or are you going to freak out when you get here?

B-school is not just about business, case-studies, and careers. The best programs buzz with the energy of a student body that is talented and creative, and that has personality. You won't be spending all your time in the library.

Are you interesting? Would you contribute to the school's vitality? Are you the kind of person other MBAs would be happy to meet? Describe activities you're involved in that might add something to the B-school community.

Are you sociable? B-school is a very social experience. Much of the work is done in groups. Weekends are full of social gatherings. Will you participate? Initiate? Get along with others? Communicate that people, not just your job, are an important part of your life.

Can you perform at a high level without being a nerd?

B-school can be tough. It's important to know when to walk away and find some fun. Do you know how to play as hard as you work?

How well rounded are you? Business leaders have wide-angle perspectives; they take in the whole picture. How deep or broad are your interests?

(A warning: Don't just list what you've done. Explain how what you've done has made you unique.)

3. Theme: The Personal Statement

"Does this application provide the opportunity to present the real you?"

"The admissions committee would welcome any additional comments you may wish to provide in support of your application."

"What question should we have asked you?"

Translation:

What did we miss? Appeal to us in any way you want; this is your last chance. Be real.

If you have an experience or personal cause that says something interesting about you, and it hasn't found a place in any other essay, this is the time to stick it in. Keep in mind that you are hoping to present yourself as unique—so show some passion!

4. Theme: Whom You Most Admire

"If you were able to choose one person from the business world, past or present, to be your personal professor throughout the MBA program, who would this person be and why?"

"Describe the characteristics of an exceptional manager using an example of someone whom you have observed or with whom you have worked. Illustrate how his or her management style has influenced you."

Translation:

What are your values? What character traits do you admire?

This is the curve-ball question. The committee isn't looking to evaluate your judgment in selecting some famous, powerful person in your firm or in the world. What they're really after, which you reveal in your selection of the person, are the qualities, attributes, and strengths you value in others, as well as in yourself. Some important qualities to address: drive, discipline, vision, ethics, and leadership. As always, provide specific examples, and avoid choosing anyone too obvious.

Since whom you select is not as important as what you say about him or her, your choices can be more humble. You might write about a current boss, or business associate, or a friend. Bad choices are your mother or father.

If you like, it's perfectly fine to go for a famous figure. Indeed, there may be someone whose career and style you're passionate about. Make sure your essay explains why you find this person so compelling.

5. Theme: Ethics

"Describe an ethical dilemma you have experienced and discuss how you handled the situation."

"Can ethics be taught? How would you teach it?"

Translation:
Do you know what an ethical dilemma looks like? Are you a sleazeball? What kind of decisions and judgments might you make in your future practices as a business professional?

The last decade brought great attention to the ethics of the business world. In the aftermath of the BCCI, savings and loan, and insider trading scandals, B-schools don't want to turn out graduates who are fast into their suspenders, fast into a deal, and fast to swindle their clients and partners.

While the above two questions are not identical, they get at the same issues: your judgment and integrity. In the first question, it's important to present a real ethical dilemma. Applicants often write about the dilemma of obeying or not obeying a supervisor's orders because they knew a better way. But this is not an ethics problem (unless the order was improper or illegal). This is a management problem. Also, it doesn't showcase your sense of honor and conduct, which is what the essay is about.

Write about an ethical dilemma in which there was no easy course—one that entailed costs either way. For example, you sold a product to a client, and later discovered the product was faulty;

your employer wants you to keep mum. You've built your sales relationships on trust and personal attention, so you want to be forthcoming. What did you do?

The second question requires some imagination. Ethics is indeed tough to teach. And if you teach it, is it enough?

Like the essay above, this essay should communicate your sense of values. A lesson in ethics might include an exploration of the reasons behind business principles and practices. It might also include role-plays and simulations to tease out different perceptions of what's right and wrong.

SUMMARY
General Suggestions for the Essays

- In writing about your achievements, distinguish between those that are task-oriented and problem-oriented.

- Communicate that you're a proactive, can-do sort of person.

- Put yourself on ego-alert: stress what makes you unique, not what makes you great.

STRAIGHT TALK FROM ADMISSIONS OFFICERS:
Fifteen Sure-fire Ways to Torpedo Your Application

1. Write about the high-school glory days.

Unless you're right out of college or you've got a great story to tell, resist using your high-school experiences for the essays. What does it say about your maturity if all you can talk about is being editor of the yearbook or captain of the varsity team?

2. Submit essays that don't answer the questions.

An essay that does no more than restate your résumé frustrates the admissions committees. After reading 5,000 applications, they get irritated to see another long-winded evasive one.

Don't lose focus. Make sure your stories answer the question.

3. Fill essays with industry jargon and detail.

Many essays are burdened by business-speak and unnecessary detail. This clutters your story. Construct your essays with only enough detail about your job to frame your story and make your point. After that, put the emphasis on yourself—what you've accomplished and why you were successful.

4. Write about a failure that's too personal or inconsequential.

Refrain from using break-ups, divorces, and other romantic calamities as examples of failures. What may work on a confessional talk show is too personal for a business school essay.

Also, don't relate a "failure" like getting one "C" in college (out of an otherwise straight "A" average). It calls your perspective into question. Talk about a failure that matured your judgment or changed your outlook.

5. Reveal half-baked reasons for wanting the MBA.

Admission officers favor applicants who have well-defined goals. Because the school's reputation is tied to the performance of its graduates, those who know what they want are a safer investment.

If business school is just a pit stop on the great journey of life, admissions committees would prefer you make it elsewhere. However unsure you are about your future, it's critical that you demonstrate that you have a plan.

6. Exceed the recommended word limits.

Poundage is the not the measure of value here. Exceeding the recommended word limit suggests you don't know how to follow directions, operate within constraints, organize your thoughts, or all of the above.

Get to the crux of your story and make your points. You'll find the word limits adequate.

7. Submit an application full of typos and grammatical errors.

How you present yourself on the application is as important as what you present. While typos don't necessarily knock you out of the running, they suggest a sloppy attitude. Poor grammar is also a problem. It distracts from the clean lines of your story and advertises poor writing skills.

Present your application professionally—neatly typed, and proofed for typos and grammar. And forget gimmicks like a videotape. This isn't "America's Funniest Home Videos."

8. Send one school an essay intended for another— or forget to change the school name when using the same essay for several applications.

Double check before you send anything out. Admissions committees are (understandably) insulted when they see another school's name or forms.

9. Make whiny excuses for everything.

Admissions committees have heard it all—illness, marital difficulties, learning disabilities, test anxiety, bad grades, pink slips, putting oneself through school—anything and everything that has ever happened to anybody. Admissions officers have lived through these things, too. No one expects you to sail through life unscathed. What they do expect is that you own up to your shortcomings.

Avoid trite, predictable explanations. If your undergraduate experience was one long party, be honest. Discuss who you were then and who you've become today. Write confidently about your weaknesses and mistakes. Whatever the problem, it's important you show you can recover and move on.

10. Make the wrong choice of recommendors.

A top-notch application can be doomed by second-rate recommendations. This can happen because you misjudged the recommendors' estimation of you or you failed to give them direction and focus.

As we've said, recommendations from political figures, your uncle's CEO golfing buddy, and others with lifestyles of the rich and famous don't impress (and sometimes annoy) admissions folk—unless such recommendors really know you or built the school's library.

11. Letting the recommendor miss the deadline.

Most recommendors are busy. They require plenty of lead time to write and send in their recommendation. Even with advance notice, a well-meaning but forgetful person can drop the ball.

It's your job to remind them of the deadlines. Do what you have to do to make sure they get there on time.

12. Be impersonal in the personal statement.

Each school has its own version of the, "Use this space to tell us anything else about yourself . . ." personal statement question. Yet many applicants avoid the word "personal" like the plague. Instead of talking about how putting themselves through school lowered their GPA, they talk about the rising cost of tuition in America.

The personal statement is your chance to make yourself different from the other applicants, further show a personal side, or explain a problem. Take a chance and be genuine; admissions officers prefer sincerity to a song and dance.

13. Make too many generalizations.

Many applicants approach the essays as though they were writing a newspaper editorial. They make policy statements and deliver platitudes about life without giving any supporting examples from their own experiences.

Granted, these may be the kind of hot-air essays that the application appears to ask for, and probably deserves. But admissions officers dislike essays that don't say anything. An essay full of generalizations is a giveaway that you don't have anything to say, don't know what to say, or just don't know how to say whatever it is you want to say.

14. Neglect to communicate that you've researched the program and you belong there.

B-schools take enormous pride in their programs. The rankings make them even more conscious of their academic turf and differences. While all promise an MBA, they don't all deliver it the same way. The schools have unique offerings and specialities.

Applicants need to convince the committee that the school's programs meet their needs. It's not good enough to declare prestige as the primary reason for selecting a school (even though this is the basis for many applicant's choice).

15. Fail to be courteous to employees in the admissions office.

No doubt, many admissions offices operate with the efficiency of sludge. But no matter what the problem, you need to keep your frustration in check.

If you become a pest or complainer this may become part of your applicant profile. An offended office worker may share his/her ill feelings about you with the boss—that admissions officer you've been trying so hard to impress.

CHAPTER SEVEN

Essays That Work:
Writing Your Way into Business School

Case Examples:
Admissions Officers Critique Winning Essays

To show you how some applicants have answered the essay questions, we asked the B-schools for samples of "winning" essays. To show you what worked, we also asked the admissions officers to provide a critique.

As you read through the essays, keep in mind that each was but one of several submitted by an applicant for admission. Moreover, they were part of a package that included other important components. One essay did not "win" anybody admission.

One other reminder. The purpose of including essays in this book is to give you a nudge in the right direction, not to provide you with a script or template for your own work. It would be a mistake to use them this way.

Obviously, this collection is by no means all-encompassing. There are thousands of winning essays out there; we just couldn't include them all.

A final note: Because Harvard features a whopping ten-essay application, we especially wanted it in this section. Harvard declined our request. So to access what apparently is guarded as closely as FBI files, we contacted the students and grads directly. To our delight, everyone was eager to supply an essay. We selected those we believe the admissions officers would also have considered "winning."

BOSTON UNIVERSITY

Essay #1:

Imagine a straight line of infinite length, stretching out of sight in two directions. Assuming the line represents time, one can stand at any present moment and simultaneously look back at past experience and project one's sight into the future.

The time line is an assumption that makes planning possible. Though it may someday be proven a false, or at least incomplete, model, it can be useful for both personal and professional planning. For this essay, I'll limit myself to the latter.

Where I Stand

Looking back at what I have done, and ahead to what I'd like to do, I can find great sense in beginning a graduate management program.

I have: a foundation of experience in the administration of educational and cultural institutions. Past jobs have ranged from directing a college admissions office to promoting an opera company, to managing a modern dance company, to running a day care center, to editing a weekly newspaper.

I have: an understanding of how groups function, what makes an organization healthy, and various ways people can organize to accomplish a goal. This has come from work experience as well as graduate study in organization theory and design at Harvard and at M.I.T.

I have: dreams and plans for a range of jobs and enterprises that extend ahead through my life.

From Here to There

Among many goals, I would like to direct a major cultural institution. I would also like to head a major educational institution, run a major foundation, and start and run my own cultural or educational organization—not necessarily all at the same time.

To achieve the above, there are skills and arenas of knowledge and experience that I'd like to have in my grasp. Some of these are presently out of reach, others are at my fingertips, but none are firmly in hand.

Financial management is, for me, perhaps the largest arena of knowledge in which I want, but do not have, agility. A course of study that refreshes my quantitative skills and teaches me principles of economics, fiscal planning and other financial management skills would be very useful.

Another such arena includes management information systems and computer programming. I presently work on word processing equipment with comfort and joy. I hope, with time and guidance, to do the same with other systems at an even deeper level.

I would also like more personal contact with professional peers, particularly in the Boston and New England region. The public management program appears to offer that.

Some of my more obvious strengths and weaknesses should be evident from the above. I have confidence in myself. I have a great deal of curiosity. I generate ideas and I develop interests, and can usually turn these into realistic, well-organized and flexible plans. These I consider strengths.

I can also stretch myself too thin, which can be a problem. Though I realize taking on the new demands some letting go of the old, I also believe experience increases capacity. There seems to me a need for more trained generalists to protect against over-specialization and fragmentation.

One great tool for that kind of protection is humor. My own sense of the comic can be quite dry and subtle, or broad and bizarre. Regardless of the form in which it spills out, it provides me perspective, balance and spontaneity.

Cooperation, too, is a central motivation for me, and I am glad to see it stressed in the public management literature.

Arrivals

To accept two accomplishments and label [sic] these significant runs counter to my way of assessing substance. I try to resist measuring my achievement by individual moments of arrival. Still, when pressed, I can come up with a few.

Performing professional theater at the age of 17 is an accomplishment that seems more significant now than it did at the time. Being appointed a college admissions director at 23 seems similarly significant. Both provided a sense of competence at a young age, and both provided a peer experience with people older and more experienced than myself.

Doing well in a graduate program at Harvard feels notable in that the school was an environment very different from any in which I had worked before. The program became a test of adaptability as well as intellect. Other accomplishments might include a few backpacking ventures taken in severe conditions, some of which became life threatening. These provided dramatic tests of my reserves, and gave me confidence in my capacity for survival.

Less, dramatic, and not quite finished, is a quilting project that I have worked on for more than six years. I have just completed the top sheet, a multi-pieced pattern in fabric. Still ahead is the quilting process itself, stitching the top sheet to a sturdy backing, with a layer of batting between the two. When done, the quilt takes on an identity greater than the sum of its many parts.

The work on this piece has been a teacher of patience and harmony. The quilt, with its assortment of shapes and fabric, can serve as a model for the organization of one's life and the people and activities in it.

Now, imagine a fine thread of infinite length weaving in and out of all those pieces.

Critique: Admissions officers review several hundreds or thousands of applications each year. Due to this high volume, any given applicant should formulate a creative approach in composing the essay to attract attention to its quality and content. Unfortunately, many applicants write essays that are similar to a detailed résumé or cover letter. This not only discourages a thorough review, but also eliminates the opportunity for the individual to express his or her own uniqueness. The admissions officers are also usually interested in how an applicant responds to a specific question, rather than a general statement.

This essay creatively suggests the applicant's general outlook on his life, what he hopes to achieve, and how he will do it. He does not go into great detail about any of these issues but allows what he does say to have a powerful impact. Reading this essay gives the evaluator the opportunity to get to know the values as well as interests and accomplishments the candidate has. This is particularly helpful when applying to a school that does not have evaluative interviews as part of the application process.

The essay is also brief and concise and makes an effort to link all the topics mentioned in the essay to create a well-defined image. The use of subtitles introduces the outline and scope of the essay.

BRIGHAM YOUNG UNIVERSITY

Essay #1

Donald J. Buehner
January 23, 1991

MBA Admissions Committee
640 TNRB
Brigham Young University
Provo, UT 84602

Dear Members of the BYU MBA Admissions Committee:

In response to your request, I am writing to inform you of my intentions for this coming year as well as to describe my employment experience acquired during the past year.

I plan to attend the MBA program commencing in September, 1991. You should have already received my Bishops Form.

During the past year I have had extensive international and national work experience. In February of 1990 I was promoted by Franklin International Institute Inc. to assist in opening a European Distribution Center in England. My specific assignment was to establish and manage the order entry and customer service departments as well as to hire and train British employees in the various operational functions. Inclusive with this training assignment was to implement the corporate values, philosophies, and quality, and to instill in our employees the high standards of excellence and consumer satisfaction for which the Franklin International Institute strives. During my six-month assignment, I worked under pressured time constraints.

The international exposure in Europe during historic times as Britain and the other eleven continental countries prepare for the economic union in 1992 was extremely beneficial for me. Combined with my work experience in Japan and my mission to South Africa, as well as my ability to speak Japanese, Dutch and Afrikaans, working in the British Isles increased my confidence and desire to pursue a career in international business.

My next promotion came in September last year, which was to help open and manage the first Franklin Day Planner Retail Center to be situated in a mall. This opportunity is providing me with more valuable experience in hiring, training, and management skills, as well as useful retail understanding including sales, stock control, and profit and loss flows. Working with the extremely qualified and professional upper management of Franklin International has been valuable in shaping my career goals.

Regarding my decision to defer attendance at Brigham Young for one year, I believe Dr. Pete Clarke's counsel that additional exposure in the work force would only enhance my graduate experience was wise advice. I feel better prepared to both learn from and be a progressive participant in the Master of Business Administration program at Brigham Young University. I request admittance for the fall of 1991.

Essay #2

Dean of the Business School
Brigham Young University
Provo, Utah 84601

Dear Sir,

In preparation for a career as an International Businessman, I am seeking entrance into the graduate program at Brigham Young University. This letter will provide the requested information regarding my wish to study at BYU.

My family experience has significantly influenced my preparation for a career in business administration. As the youngest of six children I have shared family responsibilities of managing our 45 acre farm. Because my father worked full-time, my brothers and I learned at a young age to operate the farm. At fourteen, being the only son left at home, I learned to creatively utilize my resources and to seek expert advice from local farmers in managing the farm. I learned other important business principles such as hard work, commitment, and honesty. I also learned frugality by saving a portion of my earnings in order to attend University and in addition, support myself for two years as a volunteer missionary in South Africa.

I have actively sought for balance by being involved in school plays, learning to play the trumpet and the guitar, and to sing. I have sought excellence in athletics: baseball, football, track and field, and swimming. I was actively involved in scouting and obtained the Eagle Scout award and the Order of the Arrow, an award earned through leadership, service and courage. Such activities taught me self-discipline and team unity.

At sixteen, I was selected to go for one year as a High School Rotary International Exchange student to South Africa. My responsibility was to represent America while there, and then upon returning home, to be an ambassador for South Africa to enhance world peace and understanding. In this effort, I made presentations about America to business clubs, high schools, and social groups. I also became immersed in South African culture by learning to speak Afrikaans, play their sports, enjoy their food, and listen carefully to their interesting and unique perspectives. From this experience in such a diverse land, I learned to respect foreign cultures, and I feel I developed a special talent to communicate with and relate to a wide variety of people.

As a missionary to South Africa, I served as a district and Zone leader, and Assistant to the President. As an Assistant, I became responsible for the mission's 52 car fleet, the supply and distribution of mission products, and the transportation arrangements for over 130 missionaries. Working both in an intimate and business level in a foreign country was exciting and challenging. On my mission I decided I could best serve my fellow men as an international businessman. This decision was based on my passion for South Africa and my ability to relate with and influence a variety of people for good.

During the summer of my sophomore year at Brigham Young University, I decided to enhance my international marketability by going to Japan and learning Japanese. After arriving in Japan, I negotiated to establish and to teach at an English program to an expanding Japanese company. Through this experience, I became excited and confident in my ability to learn languages, and to conduct business in foreign cultures by being understanding and alert to their traditions and values.

One of my major accomplishments has been financing and completing a college education. In this pursuit, I demonstrated creativity in my capacity to see business opportunities and make them profitable. For example, I installed security door-viewers in apartment complexes in exchange for rent by discovering existing trends of vacancy of various apartments, as well as installing door-viewers in a cost effective manner. While working ten to thirty hours a week , I maintained an average of fifteen credit hours, and achieved an overall 3.61 GPA with a 3.74 GPA in my major. I feel this reflects my commitment to achieving excellence under challenging situations.

In addition to the university curriculum I have had valuable experience in the work field. As a salesman for an insulation company in San Francisco, I succeeded at and learned to love honest sales by being competent in my service and by discovering the true needs of the people. My marketing experience as a sales rotator for Karl Lagerfeld products in Utah, included direct selling as well as overseeing advertising displays in department stores such as Nordstrom's.

As a full-time employee of Franklin International, I have demonstrated total commitment. I have also sought creative ways to better the company through my organizational behavior training at BYU. Recently, I helped restructure the leadership responsibilities in my department in order for more on-going training and less busy-work. As a result of the confidence of my superiors, I have been offered positions of trust and leadership. In March until August, I will be establishing the customer service/order entry department for our company in England. My responsibilities will include hiring, training, and managing a British team of fifteen employees.

I am extremely enthusiastic about the future of international business administration. I believe there are major breakthroughs yet to be made in the field. After completing an MBA, I hope to gain practical experience and exposure with a major international business firm. Eventually, I intend to establish resorts, clinics and camps in which to motivate and train people of all cultures to incorporate values and thought patterns conducive to healthier, happier and more productive life styles. Such training would include a physical appreciation of body and environment, as well as a spiritual appreciation of fundamental values such as honesty and integrity. I envision training focused at salvaging youth from drug abuse and inspiring them to become producers. I believe this personal passion can best be accomplished as a professional and competent businessman.

I want to attend the graduate program at BYU for many reasons. I understand the working relationship between local corporations and the business school is conducive to consistent business exposure and experience combined with serious academic study. I desire a top quality accredited program that incorporates high moral values as part of the curriculum. I am also impressed with the close working association with professors and students at the Business School. I look forward to a challenging and stimulating relationship with professors and peers and feel my unique exposure to business in South Africa, Japan, England and America, will allow me to contribute interesting insights and comparisons.

Thank you for your consideration.

Critique: What the Admissions Committee Looks for in Letter of Intent at Brigham Young University's Marriott School of Management

A Complete Individual

Don's letter of intent gives us a picture of a well-rounded human being. He talks about his preparation in terms of his work experience as a youth as well as an adult, his high school activities in music, sports, and travel, his community experience in scouting and service to his church, as well as his academic preparation.

International Experience

Since 85 percent of our students speak second languages and 35 percent speak third, we are interested in international experiences which enrich the class. Don mentions four experiences of significance.

The first was his high school exchange student experience in South Africa. He not only explains how he presented information about America to business clubs and social groups, he also talks about what he has learned individually in playing South African sports, learning Afrikaans, and relating to people of different cultures.

The second experience was Don's voluntary mission for the Church of Jesus Christ of Latter-day Saints to South Africa. The admissions committee is well aware of the growth and maturity which occurs on a mission, but Don chose to elaborate by explaining his specific responsibilities as a leader and manager for the mission's fleet of cars.

The third was a choice Don made as a college student to learn Japanese and Japanese ways. He explains his work with a Japanese company in helping to expand their English program.

The fourth experience was Don's assignment in England to open a new branch of The Franklin International (now Franklin Quest) office.

Work Experience

Don shows valuable work experience from his youth. He supports his assertion that he learned how to work early with specifics about being in charge of a farm at 14 because his brothers had grown up, looking to neighboring farmers for advice, and saving his earnings for his own future plans.

Don financed his own college education. He mentions a creative part-time work—installing door-viewers.

After college Don gained marketing and sales experience with some well known companies before he joined Franklin International and was promoted to management positions.

Leadership

Evidence of Don's leadership skills is shown in his experience as District and Zone Leaders and eventually Assistant to the President on his church mission in South Africa.

Future Plans

Don has some definite ideas about what he would like to do in international business administration. He presents his plan to establish resorts and camps to train people. This information gives the admissions committee some idea about whether our program can contribute to what he has in mind.

Good Writing Skills

Don's writing indicates an ability to express himself well and reflects on his undergraduate preparation. He frames his letter in the first paragraph by telling us what the letter is about and he concludes in the final paragraph by pulling together the reasons the Marriott School of Management is attractive to him. This indicates he has done his homework to find out what our program is about. Within the framing are clear paragraphs explaining Don's experiences which make him a viable candidate.

What the Student Brings to the Class

Don shows he has something to contribute to his peers. He shows diversity in his experiences, a teachableness, some definite goals, and an ability to work hard. His international experiences show an ability to cooperate and get along with people and demonstrate good problem solving skills.

This area is very important. The Admissions Committee works at building a class with diversity in backgrounds and educational experiences which will enrich and contribute to the whole class.

UNIVERSITY OF CALIFORNIA—BERKELEY

Question #1: *What seminal influences, broadly defined, have especially contributed to your personal development? What correlation, if any, has your personal development to your professional goals? In your response to this question, please do not discuss the influence of members of your immediate family, athletic endeavors, or professional experiences.*

Essay #1:

Bangkok, Vientiane, Malaysia, Singapore, Tokyo, Washington DC., Manhattan, Boston, Camden, and San Francisco are the places where I have grown up. My father was a diplomat, my mother a teacher , and I am the youngest of four children. Together, my family moved every two or three years to a new city. Growing up was an adventure: as children, my brothers, sister, and I did not choose to move so frequently, but we became accustomed to it. We learned to assimilate quickly, make new friends, adjust to unfamiliar customs, even speak foreign languages.

The diverse cultural experiences that are part of my childhood have shaped the way I think about the world and my purpose in it. Living abroad cultivated my curiosity in politics and international relations, and moving frequently developed my interpersonal skills and created a strong personal motivation to make the best of a new situation.

Living abroad and moving frequently influenced who I am today, yet they are facts about my life that I have had little control over. When I think about who I am today, I focus on the choices I have made, the actions I have taken, and the guidance I have received from relatives and friends through various struggles. One choice I made stands out as an important influence because it resulted in challenges that stretched me in new directions and dramatically changed my perspective.

*   *   *   *

Following high school graduation, I worked as a roustabout out on an offshore oil rig in the Gulf of Mexico, 125 miles off the coast of Louisiana. For graduation, my family had pitched in for a round trip plane ticket to Europe. I had been preparing for a trip across the continent when my oldest brother called about a job opportunity on an oil rig. I opted for the job because it was both an adventure and an opportunity to earn a lot of money for college (my savings amounted to one year at Harvard).

Within a week I was in a helicopter heading for Block 352, an oil field leased from the government by Chevron. I have several lasting impressions of the experience. The first is primarily sensory as I recall the physical conditions under which we lived and worked. The incessant noise of power generators and welding machines hummed in our ears day and night. Every species of dirt and grime thrived on the rig. The platform was characterized by its oppressive heat, magnified by the flames from the acetylene torches and welding rods and by the exhaust from the welding machines. The only activity we looked forward to was mealtime in an air-conditioned bunkhouse.

The work was dangerous, and if it were not for luck and the other hands who kept a close eye on me, I certainly would have been injured. That summer seven people died in Block 352, four in a helicopter accident, two in a crane accident; the seventh was a close friend of mine. At twenty-one, Eric was the closest person to my age. When I first started, he and I worked closely together and he explained everything he knew about work on the rig. Eric was related in one way or another to many of the people in our crew, and as Eric's friend, I became one of the clan. Most of the older hands looked out for me as they did for Eric.

One day Eric was hurrying around a corner when he tripped on the extra slack of his torch line and he fell through a hole he had just cut in the deck. He fell 200 plus feet, hit the structure before landing, and drowned, taken swiftly under either by the current or the barracuda that circle below waiting for kitchen trash.

The lawyers and the search party came and went, and work began as usual the next morning. I was struck by two reactions to Eric's death. The first was that the other hands barely spoke of it. It was as though the danger of the job was something they had all accepted and put behind them so they could carry on. I will never know if I could have helped Eric if I were there, but I still wonder why it wasn't me. The other response was an unusual step taken by our foreman that morning: someone still needed to descend through the hole that Eric had fallen through and climb out to the very end of the structure to attach a cable. Without a word, our foreman joined us, climbed through the hole, attached the cable, and was back before we realized the spell was broken. His action made me realize that to earn respect as a leader, never ask another person to attempt what you might not try yourself.

Another lasting impression I have of work on the rig, in direct contrast to the harsh conditions, is the strong personal relationships that made the experience memorable. The men I worked with from 5:00 a.m. to 10:00 p.m. were an extraordinary crew, all Cajuns from southern Louisiana, all hard working, all part of a team. On my first day, one of the hands later told me, they thought I was an engineer because I came dressed with a new Chevron hard-hat, clean Levi's, and clean T-shirt. Far from an engineer, I was worse than a 'worm' (someone new on a rig) because I had no training. As a young kid from Maine who did not know how to cut, weld, fit, grind, or stack steel pipe, I had a lot of ground to cover. The interests that had been a strong part of my identity in high school: student athlete, leader, etc. were suddenly irrelevant. Where I had come from and where I was going at the end of the summer had no bearing in the context of working offshore. All that mattered was what I could accomplish during that summer. The way to join this crew was straightforward: work hard, learn quickly, and interact during mealtime.

Initially I was a 'rigger,' someone who supports welders by hauling steel and creating safe, makeshift platforms for welders to stand on as they weld. Early in the summer I asked our foreman, Henry Calais, if I could learn to weld. I did not know about the months of training it takes to become a certified pipe welder, but Henry was kind and offered instead to have me work with Charlie Reitenger as his assistant. Charlie was the crew's 'fitter' and, after Henry, was the most experienced person on the platform. A fitter measures and cuts pipe to length so that when the ends of two sections meet, they are adjacent, plumb, and square.

Charlie never wore a shirt, just a jeans jacket with cut off sleeves. Charlie was an intense man with a subtle sense of humor; on the morning of our first day working together, immediately after a healthy breakfast (at an unhealthy 5:00 a.m.) Charlie opened his first can of Skoal Long cut, pinched a lip-full of tobacco, and then offered me the can. We were hanging mid-air, about 200 feet above the water, and descending rapidly toward the workboat below as the crane operator lowered us. I smiled declining: 'Thanks, no, maybe after a second cup of coffee.' This exchange became a morning routine with us.

Charlie and I did not start off with a lot in common. I was not sure how to create common ground between us, but I began by showing interest in what he had to teach me. For the first week I hauled steel all over the platform for Charlie to measure and cut. Over time Charlie taught me everything there is to know about cutting and fitting pipe, and I, in turn, taught him some of the basic concepts of trigonometry. I was less successful with physics. One day I was trying to calculate how high we were above the water by dropping a welding rod and counting how many seconds it took to reach the water. For a moment Charlie thought that I was an idiot: He argued that my methodology was flawed because a heavier object would fall faster.

I tried to explain that gravity exerts the same force on all objects, but as our discussion progressed other hands took an interest, and Charlie prevailed by the sheer weight of popular opinion. Galileo would have been empathetic; we eventually conducted an experiment from the heliport, which is the highest level on the rig. We dropped several objects of varying mass before the debate was finally resolved and a basic law of physics restored. It was quite a revelation, and I was surprised by how it consumed the conversation that evening, interrupting the usual ribald dinner talk.

The summer spent offshore was unique preparation for college and for life. I still have not taken a summer off to travel in Europe, but I have never regretted passing up that opportunity to work on the oil rig. The experience exposed me to the human drama of a working class that I had not had contact with. The extreme working conditions and contact with a much older group of peers accelerated a period of growth and maturity for me. Working on the rig gave me an opportunity to reexamine what I wanted to accomplish in college and who I wanted to become. When the summer was over I felt like a completely changed person. In the helicopter heading back to Morgan City, Louisiana, I realized how fortunate I was to have the opportunity to go to college.

Critique: In reviewing Haas MBA application essays, the admissions committee places considerable weight on intellectual performance and potential; a sense of purposiveness; evidence of ethical character; and skill in the development, organization, and presentation of thoughts and ideas. We seek candidates who demonstrated initiative, creativity, thoughtfulness, receptiveness, and resourcefulness in the conduct of their personal and professional lives. We look for individuals who can provide a satisfactory account of who they are, what they have accomplished within the context of their own experiences and opportunities, and what they intend to accomplish during graduate school and beyond. Most compelling are those candidates whose reflections on their experiences and on their record of accomplishments, however defined, suggest an ability to make significant contributions to their class and to the Haas School.

The previous essay ostensibly describes a summer job following graduation from high school. Although the nature of the job may be unusual by MBA-application standards, it is not merely the novelty or drama of the situation that makes this essay successful. Its principal strengths are the degree of thought and writing skill the author exhibits in his composition. The essay is compelling because the author imparts with deep insight, wry humor, and seemly modesty an ability to work successfully with people of widely differing backgrounds, education, and cultures to the mutual benefit of all concerned. It is exceptional because while the author suggests that he was the principal beneficiary of that summer job on an oil rig in the Gulf, it is clear that his account is as instructive to the reader as his participation was to his colleagues.

CASE WESTERN RESERVE UNIVERSITY

Question#1: *Describe the most difficult personal or professional challenge that you have faced in the past five years. What did you learn from that experience?*

Essay #1:

In 1990, I formed my own company, Asian Profiles, Inc., to conduct research on the automotive industry, focusing primarily on East Asian markets. The compiled research is stored in a computer database system which allows me to analyze the data and forecast future automotive trends. Through the evaluation of automotive markets, I am able to construct "profiles" of East Asian nations and determine their relative potential as manufacturing sites and/or consumer markets for American automobile manufacturers and suppliers. My position as a research consultant and president of the company has given me the opportunity to test my professional and personal strengths as well as verify my leadership abilities.

Asian Profiles, Inc. has created a multitude of professional challenges for me. Running a small business of any kind requires a great deal of resourcefulness and ingenuity. When I started my business, my company had a database system with zero information. Four of the major management decisions I was confronted with at the time were: assessing the type of information my clients required, determining the availability of such information, selecting appropriate sources for the information, and choosing the methods for retrieving such information. I take pleasure in the fact that my company now has an extensive operating database. However, I am still faced with the above management decisions in addition to the daily challenge of determining the speed at which I need to retrieve information and the price I am willing to pay for it. I have to constantly ask myself, "is there a better, quicker, more cost-effective way to find this information?" Often the answer is yes, and I have found that local resources can offer more practical means of information retrieval than other sophisticated sources such as computer network systems and expensive publications. Ultimately, though, I have come to realize that people are the most valuable resource in business. Since incorporating my company, I have carefully developed useful contacts whom I can call upon for professional advice. (To date) my company has enjoyed great success primarily because I have learned when to seek advice, when to give it, and when to solve a problem on my own. During this period I have learned that networking is an important part any successful business career.

Being self-employed is a true test of ones personal character. When I first made the decision to go into business for myself, many questions ran through my mind. I wondered where I was going to find reliable data, how I was going to compile it, and when I would find time to learn new computer programs. One thing I never questioned, though, was whether I was capable of attaining my goals. From the outset I understood that being self-employed would require incredible self-discipline and emotional maturity. Because I did not have the years of work experience behind me, I have had to learn to rely on my own judgment. For example, soon after incorporating Asian Profiles, Inc., I was faced with the challenge of negotiating business contracts, setting up the company's finances, and deciding which computer system to purchase. With advice from experts and personal research, I found that lack of experience did not have to be a stumbling block to success but, rather, was a challenge to overcome. As company president, I have had to become my own supervisor and supporter, which has been the most challenging aspect of the position. Employing a healthy level of self-judgment has allowed me to improve my job performance by acknowledging and working with my strengths and weaknesses.

In addition to the professional challenges Asian Profiles, Inc. has created for me, it has also given me the opportunity to test my leadership abilities. Although I perform all the research and manage the company myself, I am fortunate to have the support of two secretaries. Being a manager has been a novel and rewarding experience for me. I have learned that in any working relationship, being a good manager is more about leading people and less about being a boss. I have worked hard to establish a consistent and professional management style for dealing with my clients and employees. With the personal and professional responsibilities required of a small business manager, I have had the opportunity to realistically assess my leadership capabilities. I am confident that I do possess leadership potential, but I recognize the need for expanded experience and new challenges. Asian Profiles, Inc. has fostered in me a tremendous amount of self-reliance and business know-how which I will continue to draw upon in my future endeavors.

Critique: We gave this essay high marks on the following dimensions:

Style: Well-constructed essay; gave succinct, but sufficient background information about the experience, then described the challenge, how she met the challenge, and what she learned. Tone of the essay was honest and eminently readable.

Content: Situation was unique and interesting to the reader. Descriptions provided specifics, which made the challenge more believable. Cause and effect between the situation and the learning process were made clear.

Reader would have liked to have seen reference to any measurable success resulting from meeting the challenge and learning from the experience.

DARTMOUTH

Question #1: *Discuss your career progression to date. What factors have influenced your decision to seek a general management education? Based on what you know about yourself at this time, how do you envision your career progressing after receiving the MBA degree? Please state your professional goals, and describe your plans to achieve them.*

Essay #1:

As a senior, my initial goal was to gain a thorough education in finance, which I could than apply in a field related to my personal interest in the outdoors. The most efficient way to achieve this education was as an analyst at a major investment bank. Most of the available positions were in New York. Although I was offered an analyst position there, I realized that I was unwilling to sacrifice my personal interest in order to move into the city. Instead I headed West and dedicated a year to fulfillment of these interest before beginning my professional career.

I spent the summer and fall as a professional river guide on the Snake River in Wyoming. Guiding over 2,000 people in Class IV white water rafting and fly-fishing trips taught me to interact comfortably with clients and to effectively promote myself and my abilities. I often draw upon these marketing skills in my current career when soliciting new clients. I then spent the following winter and spring in California managing a cross-country ski touring center. In this position, I gained valuable experience managing people and an appreciation for the numerous responsibilities of running a business, regardless of its size and purpose. More importantly, both experiences instilled within me an appreciation for our natural environment and an obligation to help preserve it.

Shortly thereafter, I began my professional career at Drexel Burnham Lambert in San Francisco. I was one of the first junior members to join its innovative debt restructuring group. The culture was highly entrepreneurial. Since we were the first group on Wall Street to enter the debt restructuring field, we had no standard operating procedures to rely on and therefore created our own. Our success has been a function of our creativity in developing innovative restructuring techniques as well as our cooperative group dynamics. All members of the team are encouraged to contribute to the creative process, regardless of their position. I performed well in this environment and was rewarded with a promotion from analyst to associate, a position usually reserved for MBA graduates. As the business flourished and the group expanded, I had the opportunity train and manage several second and third year associates who were new to the group and therefore junior to me in experience. When Drexel entered bankruptcy in early 1990, I was the only one out of ten junior members invited to join the senior group in their move to another investment bank, Smith Barney. Our group's continued success at Smith Barney has allowed me to further expand my responsibilities. We recently closed the largest public debt restructuring ever completed, which resulted in the sale of one of America's oldest and largest publishing companies. In this transaction I led our team of ten associates and analysts from Smith Barney and two other investment banks representing the buyer in a comprehensive financial review and valuation of our client. In collaborating with senior team members, I presented these analyses to our client's Board of Directors, who relied upon them in determining the viability of the offer.

In the last four and a half years, I have gained a solid background in finance, experience in line management, and strong negotiating skills by executing numerous transactions in a wide variety of industries. Clearly, I have surpassed the original goal I set as a senior in college. I now plan to pursue other professional goals that I have developed during my tenure at Drexel and Smith Barney.

My next professional goal is to combine my desire to run my own business with my passion for mountaineering, as a manufacturer of outdoor recreational equipment. Mountaineering has advanced at such a rapid pace that athletes in several technical disciplines have exceeded the limits of the equipment available to them. Modern technologies have only been applied to improve the equipment in such recently popular areas as technical rock climbing where sufficient demand has justified the cost of implementation. My focus would be on product development through technology-based innovation in other areas of mountaineering that are gaining popularity, such as back country skiing. I believe that the increased costs of such technology can be offset by more efficient production management. For example, back country ski boots are still made of leather, which freezes when wet and must be hand-stitched. A lightweight plastic boot with a removable synthetic liner, however, would not only improve performance but reduce production costs as well through automation of the manufacturing process. I plan to enter the outdoor recreational equipment market with a product innovation such as this one and then expand into other product lines through a) additional technological innovations, b) joint ventures with or acquisitions of other specialty manufacturers, and c) leveraging my brand recognition to promote related clothing and accessories which typically yield a higher profit margin.

Clearly my goal is not to run a Fortune 500 company. I believe the future of American manufacturing lies in small, highly specialized companies that can not only quickly respond to technological change but also help direct the public's shifting values regarding our natural environment. To create this type of enterprise, I plan to assemble a small team of individuals with diverse skills but common interests. The structure of this enterprise will combine the many positive organizational aspects of my current organization. I will create a "meritocracy" in which personal and professional growth will be rewarded with increased responsibility. All members of the team will be encouraged to contribute to the creative process regardless of their position. Compensation will be based strictly on performance rather than tenure, so that all members who share the responsibilities may also share the profits. Personal profit, however, will not be the sole motivation. The team will also be motivated by a common interest in environmental protection.

My mentor in the outdoor is Yvon Chouinard, founder of Patagonia, a leading manufacturer of outdoor equipment and clothing. Through product innovation he has advanced the sport of mountaineering and achieved a position at the forefront of the outdoor industry. As an industry leader, he has become a vocal proponent of "sustainable development," which encourages managers to balance economic growth with environmental concerns. I agree with his thesis that our country's current business practices are generally not sustainable. In the past several years, I have witnessed the effects of irresponsible growth at Drexel and at many of its clients' that I helped restructure. Currently we are all witnessing the effects of irresponsible growth on our natural environment. Through the success of my own company, I could fulfill the obligation to the environment I developed years ago as a river guide. As an industry leader, I would be in a position to promote responsible and sustainable growth at all levels—by example within my own organization and industry, by communication with other industry leaders, and by volunteering my time and skills to increase public awareness of the need to protect the wilderness areas on which my industry and interests depend.

I understand that, in order to pursue my entrepreneurial interest in manufacturing, I will need the skills to manage across an entire organization, from finance and production to sales and marketing. I have developed strong financial skills and gained experience in line management in my current career. An MBA education is clearly not a perfect substitute for experience, but I believe it would provide me with the framework necessary for effective decision-making in these areas. An MBA program would also allow me to further research my business ideas through the experiences of my peers, independent study, and related summer employment. Education and experience may not change my goals, but they may well change the means by which I achieve them. Finally, since I will not be able to create this organization alone, I look forward to the opportunity to meet other individuals who share my interests in entrepreneurship, manufacturing and sustainable development.

Critique: The admissions essay is a critical component in an application to the Amos Tuck School's MBA program. Throughout the process of reviewing an application, which includes careful reading of essays, the admissions committee will seek compelling reasons to admit the applicant. Although writing an excellent essay will not guarantee an applicant admission into Tuck, submitting a poorly organized or badly written essay as part of an otherwise good application will significantly reduce his or her chances for acceptance.

In addition to meeting our more immediate and obvious expectations of a well-organized, articulate presentation of his candidacy, the applicant who wrote our example essay offers (1) compelling reasons for the admissions committee to accept him and (2) convincing evidence that he would both thrive in, and contribute to, the academic and social environment at Tuck. In evaluating any essay, however, keep in mind that we judge neither the experiences nor the goals an applicant presents. Instead, we judge (1) how well the applicant presents these experiences and goals, (2) how well the applicant's accomplishments support his long-term goals, and (3) how the applicant's rationale for wanting an MBA fits into his or her overall career plan.

There are a number of indicators throughout the example essay that the writer possesses attributes that Tuck seeks: (1) the types of experiences and interests that demonstrate sufficient intellectual preparation for a rigorous curriculum of professional study, (2) a high motivational level for achievement, (3) a creative approach to problem solving, (4) a blend of leadership skills to successfully manage multiple aspects of an organization, (5) the interpersonal skills needed to work successfully with diverse groups of people, and (6) an appreciation of the need to balance one's professional and personal lives.

The applicant demonstrates these attributes in describing his career progress, relating each stage to long-term goals. He explains why general management training, central to Tuck's educational mission, is essential for implementing the next stage of his plan toward reaching those goals. The applicant knows what he wants—skills to manage an R&D-based manufacturing operation in close proximity to the great outdoors—and has a clear-cut idea of how to get it. In his essay, he indicates that he made a steady progression of conscious choices that supported his long-term goals by strategically identifying: (1) Where to live and work (on a river in Wyoming, near a ski area in California, then in a major financial center in California), (2) What types of industries were most valuable to gain experience in for his personal and professional interests (an outdoor excursions outfit, a customer service oriented sports operation, an investment banking firm), (3) What roles would prove useful for the future (leader of white-water rafting trips, general manager of a cross-country ski touring center, member of a team in an investment bank's new debt-restructuring group), and (4) Which issues to monitor (the environmental consequences of commercial land development, growth pattern of technological innovations in the sports-equipment industry, how manufacturing factors into the overall national economy).

The applicant asserts that he is management material and backs up this assertion in describing how his superiors at Drexel Burnham Lambert promoted him to a level of responsibility normally reserved for MBAs. He also demonstrates familiarity with current consequences of a slow economy by showing successful adjustment to a new position in another company after his own employer went bankrupt. This flexibility, along with his varied experiences, will enable him to offer an interesting perspective in class discussions.

In conclusion, this particular applicant's attitude, experience, goals, and interests all provided a close match with what Tuck seeks in prospective MBAs. The admissions committee was confident that his interests and abilities provided a close fit with our requirements and that he would be happy in the type of environment that Tuck offers: a rural, residential lifestyle; small classes emphasizing cooperative, highly interactive group learning; a close-knit and cohesive community that welcomes people from diverse backgrounds; and the ability to take full advantage of the career placement services and connections one would expect from an Ivy League business school.

HARVARD

Question #1: *Discuss a change you would make in your work environment and how would you implement that change.*

Essay #1:

The Gillette Personal Care Division is in financial difficulty having severely missed its *profit* objectives in the last half of 1989. The Division responded to its profitability problems by giving the sales force a more aggressive *sales* quota. To control escalating costs, the corporate Controller took over P&L responsibility from the divisional Marketing department.

I feel the above divisional and corporate responses to raising profitability were ill-considered and create new problems. First, the way in which a Sales Representative will respond to an aggressive new sales quota can, ironically, exacerbate the profitability problem. To achieve the aggressive new sales quota, the sales force will push high volume brands (i.e. White Rain) that contribute little to profit. This short term volume increase comes at the expense of the field's promoting and building smaller, high margin brands.

Second, the Controller cut out advertising and field discretionary funds showing his insensitivity to market considerations and trade issues; an immediate spike in profits comes at the expense of future consumer pickup.

The change I propose is to make the field more responsible for Divisional profitability. This can be done by giving the Sales Reps new Business Development Funds and more profit "accountability." With the funds, the Reps would be better able to respond to opportunities to develop and build the brands.

However, "accountability" would present implementation problems. How do you define and enforce accountability? The field cannot control many of the variables that impact on profitability: production costs, advertising commitments, price increases, and the size of trade allowances. Nor can the field break out different regions on a P&L basis because developing or maintaining some accounts will be more expensive than others. It might cost more to develop more promising markets where P&G, for example, is also trying to make inroads.

The best solution for field profit accountability is a dual quota system: by sales and by brand. A brand quota would force the Rep to promote a more profitable mix of product regardless of whether he understood the profitability concerns. With the Business Development Fund, he would be able to build the profitable brands emphasized in the new brand quota.

These funds would encourage the Rep to be much more entrepreneurial. The Rep could design trade push and consumer pull programs that best suit his territory. Sales Planning would represent the interests of the sales force in determining fair brand quotas with the marketing department. Ultimately, this change would help balance Divisional and Corporate needs. With the Business Development funds, Reps would better be able to respond to local opportunities. With brand quotas, Corporate could better control product profit mix.

The downside is that the trade will come to expect these additional allowances and give little incremental promotional support. Further, career Reps might not adapt well to the new entrepreneurial demands and may develop ineffective programs. While the immediate solution would be to give the Business Development funds to the Reps who could use the funds most effectively, this would create resentment. The longer term solution is to recruit and build a sales force of entrepreneurial Reps who could run their own "franchises."

Question #2: *Describe your avocations and hobbies.*

Essay #2:

My most passionate non-academic pursuit is athletics. I have learned invaluable lessons through playing on the Harvard Varsity Water-polo and Squash teams. As goalie in the Water-polo team, I learned the importance of teamwork. During a fast paced game, a goalie must be able to quickly identify potential problems and solve them in an effective manner. Collective responsibility is integral to teamwork. One cannot lay the blame on another player without jeopardizing team unity.

Squash taught me that progress can only be achieved through diligence and patience. Hitting a small black ball thousands of times for hundreds of hours in a small room can be perceived as a meaningless pursuit—or a disciplined process of developing precision and control. There are no shortcuts to improvement in the game of squash.

I have found these valuable lessons of teamwork and discipline to be easily transferable to other areas. Working with others in a competitive and tense environment can only be successfully achieved through proper teamwork. The discipline which I developed on the squash court has (similarly) enabled me to focus in other pursuits with equal determination.

Question #3: *Describe your most substantial accomplishments and explain why you view them as such.*

Essay #3:

1) Last spring I exported nearly $100,000 worth of exercise equipment to Japan. This shipment saved my company over $250,000 due to the price discrepancies between the United States and Japan. I was solely responsible for selecting the equipment, negotiating the price, arranging the insurance, and packing and shipping of the equipment to Japan. The first step of the process of selecting the equipment and the company involved inspecting manufacturing facilities based in California, Maryland, Texas, Vermont, and Colorado. I researched the legitimacy of the companies by calling their previous clients, checking credit records, and calling the Better Business Bureau. After exporting the equipment to Japan, I flew to Japan to facilitate the import process. This involved meeting with Japanese customs, as well as assisting in the domestic transportation and installation of the equipment.

I consider this a major accomplishment for three reasons. Firstly, I was solely responsible for the entire project. Secondly, it was a complicated process which involved many unrelated details. Finally, and not least of all, the fact that it was successful also contributes to my sense of pride.

2) When the Japanese company opened its third health club in Japan in July, 1988, it was a great sense of personal satisfaction. Two summers ago, I participated in the planning and design of this club. I saw many of my substantive recommendations implemented, including the installation of a racquetball court system which has movable glass walls to allow squash, racquetball, basketball, and volleyball to be played on the same court. My idea more effectively utilizes very limited and costly space and also provides greater recreational variety for the users. I have previously discussed my export deal that provided over half of the equipment for the club, which was another source personal satisfaction. In addition to helping design the club, I was actively involved in sales and marketing. I also conducted club tours for prospective members, and designed a new marketing strategy targeting foreigners living in the area. My combined efforts resulted in over 150 new members.

These accomplishments demonstrate my ability to work successfully in a large group setting as well as in an entirely different language and culture. In addition to the satisfaction of seeing my design recommendations actually implemented, I also enjoyed the challenges of sales and marketing.

3) I am currently co-teaching a Harvard college freshman seminar focusing on the economic development of Japan with Professor X. As a teacher, I had to design a reading list which would provide sufficient information without overwhelming the freshmen who have had no back-ground on the topic. A reading list has to have an overall argument with weekly topics to provide specific examples. Teaching in a seminar format presents a tremendous intellectual challenge of stimulating and guiding a discussion. I try to give only directive or stimulative comments rather than to lecture. In this manner students will ask questions and I will try to steer the discussion so that the student is able to answer his/her own question.

Teaching the Seminar represents the cumulative total of my academic career. My studies have largely revolved around Japanese economics and Japanese history. In addition, my practical experience of working in a

Japanese company in Japan complements my academic understanding and has further enhanced my abilities as a teacher.

UNIVERSITY OF MARYLAND

Essay #1:

My multi-page application answered the question, "Who am I?" Now it is time to answer another one— "Why am I here, in the pool of applicants to the Maryland MBA program?" That's a question many people have asked me.

My friends' confusion is understandable—why would a graduate student who enjoys doing research and teaching, with an expertise in a politically important part of the world and who allegedly would be able to get full funding in any school if he chose go to all the way to Ph.D. in political science, want to change his career to take an unknown road in business? Quite a legitimate question. Let me explain why I chose to apply to the Maryland MBA Program and not to do something else, first revisit my life history.

In 1990 I joined the analytical division of a trading firm in Moscow— International Secondary Resources Exchange. I discovered consulting as a career and developed an interest in assessment of market potential, including a degree of political risk. At the time, Russia and other former communist countries were opening their markets and it was fascinating, but also very important to try to predict how promising the Russian market was. So I decided to get my master's in political science in order to be able to competently assess such important categories for estimating market potential as government capacity, public administration competence, political risk (legal and other obstacles to foreign investment), entrepreneurial culture and economic training of the population.

Still working on projects with the Exchange, I started a graduate program with concentration in international relations, comparative politics (Europe), and economics. It has been an important part of my education, given the importance of the political situation and, therefore, political forecasting for the business future of the former communist world.

My education now has to enter its most critical stage - actual study of business. This would let me have a deep understanding, as I hope, of financial and other market structures, competitiveness, and other factors that a consultant needs to take into account when recommending whether to conduct business in a foreign country.

Taking advantage of my bi-cultural background, long study of international relations and foreign languages, and business experience, I plan to pursue a career as an international business consultant. The UMCP certainly has a focus on global business. I am attracted by the Center for International Business Education and Research—I work for CIBER at the University of Utah and my colleagues spoke highly of the Maryland Program. At the same time the School offers a strong general management program—something I need, coming from a country with no free market traditions.

These are the "career" reasons to apply to Maryland. But there is also a "character" reason. It is critically important for me to be challenged. Only when sufficiently challenged, can I work at full capacity and deliver results. Without doubt, Maryland provides enough challenge, without mentioning that an application process itself is very stimulating.

Business schools' quality criteria are no secret. From these I pay special attention to location. The Washington-Baltimore metropolitan area is a perfect location for somebody interested in an international business career. It is also the place to be for a person, who, coming from Utah, is just hungry for student body diversity and cultural attractions. I visited the area on two occasions during my first year in this country and just fell in love with the place.

Add to these advantages a critical one for me—generous financial aid options. Unfortunately, without financial aid, I will not be able to attend school.

The Program's diverse environment is of special importance for me. I appreciate diversity and think I could add something myself to the already culturally rich Maryland MBA Program—after two years in the U.S. I am a walking example of cultural interaction. I picked up a lot of American practices, keeping at the same time some of my old ones. I do not protest any more when my friends take me out dinner around my birthday, but on my birthday itself I, as the Russian tradition goes, have them over for dinner. I try not to go with the flow and never say "how are you?" when I do not care and "nice to meet you" when I do not mean it, but sometimes I am supposed to say these meaningless phrases. I still pass with my face, rather than my back, to people sitting in a theater. I use Kleenex tissues, but still have a handkerchief in my pocket just in case. I kept my main dining habit—never putting down a knife when having salad and a main course. I changed, on the other hand, the way I approach desert, when I dine by myself; I still eat it with a spoon, as the Russians do. And I drink both hot tea and coke.

From my Russian background I keep moral integrity, industriousness, strong attachment to my family, self-reliance, cooperative spirit, sense of humor, strong interest in spending time with children, and my three other hobbies—movies, soccer, and travel. My American present made me friendly, punctual, conscientious, self-disciplined, law-abiding, determined to help people who are less lucky than I am (first of all, my fellow Russians), and two more pastimes—basketball and hiking. I hope that a person combining two cultures will be a good addition to the School's environment.

I believe that the Maryland MBA Program will provide me with a training I need and enough challenges to launch me to a new intellectual orbit. And, also, it would just be nice to be back East.

Critique: One important way MBA programs strengthen their international focus is by attracting talented students from different parts of the world. Indeed, a priority of the Maryland Business School is actively to recruit such students because they increase both the breadth and depth of the school's international perspective.

In addition to fulfilling the basic requirement of every application's essay section—i.e., *answer the questions asked* (a surprising number of people fail to do this)—"Andrei's" statement also provided the admissions director with a vivid glimpse into his personality. And though English is obviously not his first language, his command of "Americanisms" is impressive and his sense of humor engaging. He comes across as a bright, self-motivated, high-energy individual. Just the type for Maryland.

He also did his homework. For instance, he mentions Maryland's Center for International Business Education and Research and the fact that the university is located in the culturally rich Washington, D.C., area. To the admissions director, this means he is serious about his application to the program; that he is not using the shotgun approach in applying to graduate school.

Had he wanted to make an even stronger impression, however, "Andrei" should have asked a native English speaker to read over his essay. Or two native speakers, for that matter. They would have helped him smooth out some of his sentences with proper punctuation and usage. For though his message is clear to the reader, his occasional lapses into fractured English somewhat detract from his many fine qualities.

UNIVERSITY OF MICHIGAN

Question #1: *During your years of study in the Michigan MBA program, you will be part of a diverse multi-cultural, multi-ethnic community within both the Business School and the larger University. What rewards and challenges do you anticipate in this campus environment, and how do you expect this experience to prepare you for a culturally diverse business world?*

Essay #1:

High return on investment...

One quality I have always admired is independent thinking. I always strive to be different and befriend those who share this same goal. I see conformity as a moral deficiency. "Group think" is the enemy of creativity and innovation. In contrast, diversity in thought is the key to any successful endeavor. I want to be a part of creative concepts proposed from a wide array of sources. These creative concepts can only be reached by assembling individuals with discordant views and from varying backgrounds. For this reason, I find the growing diversity of Michigan's student body to be one of its greatest selling points. I feel that understanding a wide range of views, opinions, and judgments on a variety of subject matter broadens the base of experience from which effective solutions may be derived. Therefore, learning, sharing, and growing within the context of diverse individuals is an avenue for developing a successful manager.

While there will be rewards from this melting pot, there is always the potential for difficulty when assembling people with divergent views and from different cultures. As a member of an international exchange program, in both training and travel, I was able to witness the glaring problems of cultural bias, prejudice, and close-mindedness. One thing I learned through this experience is that nobody is above prejudice of some kind, myself included. Everyone has some innate sense that they are superior to other individuals in some manner. When people feel superior because of their intellect, we call them arrogant. When people feel superior because of their nationality or culture, we call them elitists. And when people feel superior because of their race, we call them racists. The first step in understanding each other is to better understand ourselves and develop an understanding of our own prejudices. This will be the challenge facing every student in the melting pot. For some this challenge will be great and for some it may be overcome easily, but in either case I feel that the rewards from integration of people and ideas provide a great return on the time and energy invested to make it so.

Beyond the hallowed halls...
I expect my time at Michigan to enhance my understanding and appreciation of the benefits of mixing ideas and opinions among people from different backgrounds. The business community I will enter is a global, multi-national, multi-cultural based body. Any business manager willing to shun certain peoples or ideas because they are foreign will be injuring his company. And yet, I have every reason to believe that I will inevitably encounter these types of individuals.

While universities are taking the lead in cultural and ethnic diversification, the business world is somewhat behind. The reasons for this are twofold: those people who are fearful of new ideas tend to fight diversity, while those individuals in favor of diversity often find developing it a daunting task. For this reason, many companies concede to the status quo, to the old way of doing business. Yet there are firms willing to shift paradigms of current thinking. These are the companies that will prosper in the future. The company that takes the initiative to broaden its personnel base will find that any short term expenses it may incur in this diversification process are easily offset by the long term benefits of having a dynamic, progressive, and enterprising staff. This is the type of firm I would like to associate with. Just as I expect to do at Michigan, I hope in the business community to be an active part of the melting pot of ideas, developing creative concepts, and forcing new paths by engaging divergent viewpoints.

Critique: Originality, insight, and graceful writing immediately capture the reader for this essay. Tackling the topic directly and substantively, the author effectively relates the subject to past personal experiences and future career aspirations. The writer avoids the platitudes that slide all too easily into application essays. With admirable honesty, he acknowledges the challenges posed by a multi-cultural environment, admits the prejudices he has felt, and identifies the personal rewards of being part of the Michigan community.

The essay goes beyond any superficial treatment of the issue and reveals how the author thinks. Indeed, the independent thinking admired by the writer emerges from the piece. The reader finds clear evidence of the analytical reasoning skills so critical to success and leadership in management. Finally, the writing style, characterized by flowing, balanced prose and apt word choice, is eloquent. The essay convinces the reader that this is someone whose thinking and ability to convey thoughts will enrich the learning process in and out of the classroom.

UNIVERSITY OF NOTRE DAME

Question #1: *As a Notre Dame student, what contributions would you make to the life of the program, both inside and outside the classroom? How will an MBA from Notre Dame help you achieve your short-term career goals and your long-term professional aspirations?*

Essay #1:

As a Notre Dame M.B.A. student there are many contributions I will make to enhance the excellence of the program. These contributions include attributes such as professional insight, an inquisitive mind, and innovative ideas along with high moral and ethical standards.

My two years' experience with Sikorsky Aircraft has given me a good understanding of multi-functional disciplines within American aerospace firms. I have grown from these experiences, and I will bring them to the classroom in the form of anecdotes. My job has helped me to gain a good perception of some of the best and worst ways to run a business. These experiences are ones you could never pick up from a textbook, but they will enhance the lessons found in one.

To the classroom I also bring an inquisitive mind. I am never satisfied with the statements of "that's the way it is" or "if it's not broke don't fix it." I feel that if you do not ask why or try to completely appreciate a theory or technique you may never truly understand it. There is always an alternative to any method or theory, and questioning is a way of developing new understandings.

Outside the classroom I bring innovation. I enjoy adding to the competitiveness of the organization of which I am a part, and I am always willing to try new things. For example, while at Michigan State I assisted in developing the first annual Materials and Logistics student/faculty retreat. This retreat is now an event supported by both the University and the professional world. In the same respect, as an intern at Sikorsky Aircraft, I worked in our Overhaul and Repair facility (O&R). One of my first observations was that O&R had no definitive way of tracking our suppliers' performance. Every individual department had a different tracking system. I combined the best attributes of each system to form a consolidated tracking run which is now used throughout the entire 600-person facility.

Two other contributions I will bring to Notre Dame cannot be labeled either inside or outside of the classroom because they pertain to both. Number one, I am a good team player. I have a good disposition which helps me not only get along with many different types of people but to enjoy working with them. Number two, through my business trips and experience of serving on M.S.U.'s Anti-Discrimination Judicial Board I have developed a unique appreciation of others' cultures and beliefs. I enjoy learning about other people and what makes them tick.

A Notre Dame M.B.A. will help me to obtain my short-term and long-term goals by providing a solid foundation and set a direction from which I can build. Before choosing the M.B.A. programs to which I would apply, I sat down with a former professor to obtain his insight into this decision. He told me that when choosing an M.B.A. program, I am choosing a label to carry with me throughout my career. This label aligns me with beliefs and practices of my M.B.A. institution. I chose to apply to Notre Dame because of the school's strong stand on ethics and the International Market. At Notre Dame I will be exposed to people not only from the Midwest but from around the world. This will further help me to broaden my horizons and understanding of people.

My long-term professional aspiration is to enter into the field of management consulting. An M.B.A. from Notre Dame in Interdisciplinary Studies will enhance my understanding of all aspects of business. This will contribute significantly to becoming effective in the consulting profession.

In conclusion, as a Notre Dame M.B.A. candidate I will bring a sincere attitude to succeed in the classroom, high ethical standards, and the willingness to go the extra mile. Upon graduation from Notre Dame, I will represent the University as a sign of the excellence a Notre Dame M.B.A. portrays in the professional world.

Critique: We chose Ed's essay because it was clearly and concisely written, using examples from college and career to make his points. For example, he used his experience in O&R at his current employment to highlight his technical and analytical abilities with the establishment of a tracking system now used throughout the facility. He backed up his claim for being innovative by citing his assistance in developing the first faculty and student retreat in his college department.

He dealt with both the short-term and long-term orientation of the program. In seeking advice from his professor, he showed seriousness about making his choice of schools. He wanted an international thrust to his studies and chose Notre Dame because of its reputation in that area as well as its commitment to ethics in business. That fit in nicely with what he learned from his experience on the Anti-Discrimination Judicial Board of his university. And his choice of Interdisciplinary Studies reinforces Notre Dame's focus on preparing students for General Management. Finally, his choice of consulting for a career flows naturally from his prior experiences and his curricular choices.

We like Ed's essay because it was to the point, responded to the essay question, and in a subtle but concrete way "sold" the candidate to the admissions committee. Ed managed to weave in accomplishments on the job with commitments he planned to make to the Notre Dame program. He demonstrated college leadership in a large, public, "anonymous" kind of school in which students often get lost. Based on his experience, his career goals and aspirations appear to be realistic. While he has high ideals, they do not seem to be "pie in the sky" notions and he displayed a certain kind of maturity and sensitivity which we liked.

STANFORD UNIVERSITY

Question #1: *Tell us about those influences that have significantly shaped who you are today.*

Essay #1:

I am a descendent of a long line of Quaker business people. My family, the ...., have been Quaker since 1630. The common punch line about this group, at gatherings of Friends, is that Quaker business people set out to do good and ended up doing very well. I am just beginning to emerge as a Quaker in business.

Relating some background about my Quaker heritage should help to illustrate how values of the Religious Society of Friends (the official name of "Quakers") have shaped my sense of who I am. Quakers have particular ethics which I try to develop in myself and live out. Quakers believe there is that of God in every person—they often call it the "Inner Light"—and that all people, regardless of rank and position, should be treated with dignity and integrity. This vision has helped me to see the potential in other people, even those who may be difficult to work with. It has also helped me to relate comfortably to people of every rank; in my current job, I enjoy friendships with everyone from secretaries to the president. In addition, a belief in my own Inner Light has helped my self-confidence, especially in those situations where intuition must complement facts and objective measures in making decisions.

This faith in the Inner Light has many other implications, of course, but two of the most important ones involve how group decisions should be made, and the equality of women.

As a way of doing business, Quakers believe in consensus decision-making; in fact they don't believe in hiring or paying ministers. All administration for Quaker Meeting is done by voluntary committees. From participating in consensus decision-making, I have learned to work with diverse groups of people, to negotiate between individual agendas, and to build effective teamwork between people. Consensus decision-making gives everyone a chance to contribute, and helps all members of the group to understand and articulate both the problem and solution.

Because of the Quaker belief that all people possess an Inner Light, they have traditionally believed in the full equality of men and women. In fact, Quakers held separate business meetings for men and women until about 50 years ago, because it was felt that otherwise women would be overshadowed by the men. This separation allowed Quaker women to develop leadership skills in speaking and administration. Strong Quaker women like Lucretia

Mott, a leader in the movement to abolish slavery, and Elizabeth Cady Stanton, a leader among the suffragettes, were products of this culture.

Several other characteristic Quaker beliefs are placing a high value on simplicity, and on speaking and living the truth. For example, Quakers refuse to swear to anything, even at a trial or for a marriage license, because it implies that at other times one might not tell the truth. Being practical and "grounded" are Quaker values that discourage otherworldy or naive thinking. As a general rule, Quakers don't proselytize or even talk very much about their religion. They believe that their lives should speak of their convictions.

Quaker values can interact with business priorities in many ways, mostly positive, but some potentially negative as well. For example, because Quakers didn't limit their business contacts to the highest social echelon, they found opportunities for more customers and a wider circle of business associates. As Quaker women developed leadership skills, their ingenuity contributed to the success of Quaker businesses. Quaker businesses put a high value on providing products that truly add value for consumers, rather than devising ways to trick them into buying something. In the days before Consumer Reports, people saw many advantages to doing business with Quakers, because it was widely known that they wouldn't cheat you. Since Quakers were known to try to speak the truth regardless of the cost to themselves or whether the news was welcome, their word was trusted. Of course, being honest didn't prevent Quakers from being shrewd business people.

But although Quakers tend to be highly ethical, they can also be somewhat naive. Consensus decision-making can be far too slow and unwieldy for some decisions, and it runs a risk that people will feel coerced by the group into settling for less than they want. Rather than making everyone responsible, it can end up making no one responsible. Even people with an Inner Light can behave badly. "Speaking truth to power," to use the common catch-phrase for Quakers, can either increase long-run credibility, or can be a cover for venting harsh feelings at inappropriate times.

My mother has told me that she married my father partially because he had been raised Quaker and was comfortable with strong, independent women. During my senior year of college, I was disheartened to find that many men of my own age found me intimidating. It was also a time when my mother was diagnosed with serious and potentially life-threatening breast cancer. Now I'm happily married, and my mother has at least survived the chemotherapy, but I still keep and re-read a letter I received from my father that year about the strong women in my family. Here's an excerpt [sic]

"Let's start with this generalization: Highly articulate, handsome, intelligent women are not terribly rare. No doubt you yourself have many friends that would easily fit such categorization. But if you add two further adjectival phrases, then such women are very rare indeed. Namely, "passionate commitment" and "courageous." (I'm willing to concede that these may even be redundant ... they, in your case, certainly go together.) Obviously these same characteristics are very rare in men too.

"The problem arises primarily for women. These characteristics scare the bejabers out of others ... they may be admired by some, vilified by others, and wholly misunderstood by the majority. But even those that admire them generally want to do it at a safe distance. Let's face it—sparks are given off by such people. The prudent man usually decides that the warmth and excitement isn't worth the high risk of being consumed in a conflagration set off by so many sparks.

"You are the fourth in a line of such women."

I am enclosing a photocopy of this letter with application (Attachment I) because it illuminates the way Quakers like my father can support and encourage women in leadership. Also, it provides some insight into my family.

Another important influence is my new husband, Timothy .... We were married July 6 of this year. Tim is the managing editor of the Journal of Economic Perspectives, which is based at Stanford. My husband's background in economics informs and counterbalances my perspectives.

My career has forced me to balance the idealistic qualities of Quakerism with real-life experience, where the rubber meets the road. My first job out of college was as editor and then executive director for a non-profit foundation called Fellowship in Prayer (FIP), whose purpose was to "encourage the practice of prayer or meditation among people of all faiths." This non-profit was a rare one: it actually had an endowment that grew from $2.7 to 3.5 million during my three-year tenure. My job was to organize the programs and facilities from complete chaos to something more effective and methodical. I managed the budgets so that operating expenditures came only from the interest on the endowment, not from the capital. I also learned some lessons that went well beyond business. I was sexually harassed by two members of the Board of Trustees, and had to face the problem of other Board members stealing from the endowment.

Perhaps my biggest lesson from Fellowship in Prayer was that systems—the way information is transferred, decisions are made and reporting relationships defined—largely determine the effectiveness of the organization. When I started working there, the organization had no functioning systems in place, and no objectives or strategies beyond the general mission statement quoted a moment ago. I had previously looked on things like standard operating procedures and methods of reporting and accountability as necessary evils. But I found that it's not nearly enough to have an operating budget and some staff. An organization also needs definite goals, strategies for achieving them, and ways of measuring success. While working at FIP, I came to understand that structure is enabling: without it, people spend too much time wondering what they are supposed to be doing or reinventing the wheel. Now I appreciate the need to organize structures, and the significance when such systems work well.

My position as Executive Director at FIP forced me to learn a wide range of business skills and responsibilities. I wrote the annual budget and the annual report, and oversaw expenditures. I bought a $300,000 property for the headquarters of the foundation (previously, it had rented space), arranged for $20,000 of structural repairs and another $20,000 for redecorating and furnishing, and moved the office. I edited the bi-monthly magazine for nine months, until I became Executive Director. I supervised other staff. I tried to create a counterbalance to the power of the Board of Trustees, some of whom had been stealing from the foundation, by recruiting a lawyer with financial expertise to the Board. I also formed an advisory board composed of Christians, Jews, Baha'is, Buddhists, a Mohawk Chief, and others to improve the programs and create a balance of power with the Board of Trustees. Also, this group helped in generating ideas for programs, like lectures and retreats.

I also worked on developing my own speaking and writing skills; I gave lectures, workshops, and retreats myself. I have continued to pursue my interest in designing programs and giving talks that help people deepen their spirituality and fulfill their potential. During the past few years, for example, I have led retreats at the Quaker center in Ben Lomond, California, and for Faith at Work, a national ecumenical group with which I continue to do volunteer work. With my application, I have enclosed some flyers publicizing these retreats (Attachment II). I wrote the ones for Quaker Center.

Critique: *General Guidelines*—The strongest essays give us a real sense of who the applicant is. Because we do not offer interviews, this is the applicants' only opportunity to provide insight into who they are; in a way, it is like an interview on paper. But it should be more personal and less résumé-like. Ideally, after reading the essay, we should have a good idea of what this person would like to discuss if we (hypothetically) met over coffee. We're looking for *who* someone is rather than *what* he or she has done. *This is the fundamental distinction we make*: we want to get to know the person behind the grades, scores, and job accomplishments—what are his or her passions, values, interests, and goals? We expect applicants to get beyond the standard "I did this, I did that" model to share with us what they care about and what has shaped them. We look for an honest and natural tone, hoping to find essays that are engaging and immediate rather than dry and distant—ideally, a conversation on paper.

Evaluation of This Essay: For this student, being Quaker has been the most significant influence in her life. She does a good job of focusing deeply on that single influence, extracting specific insight from its effect on her. She ties it in to her values (simplicity, truthful living, living one's convictions), her social/emotional experiences (dating, equality of women), and even her philosophy of business (consensus decision-making, honesty). For her, being Quaker is more than a religious faith; it is a life choice, and by explaining its influences on her she provides insight into who she is and why she developed that way.

This essay is honest and immediate; she opens up about personal matters in a way that allows us to get to know the real her; for example, she shares a personal and emotional letter her father sent her during a difficult time for her family. She has analyzed the positives and negatives that her Quaker upbringing has fostered, further showing intelligent self-analysis and thoughtfulness. Overall, she presents a picture of a smart, committed woman who has thought hard about who she is, and is able (and willing) to communicate what she cares about and why.

Toward the end of the essay she shifts from the personal to the professional (from the "who" to the "what"), but does so relatively effectively. We learn how she puts her passions into action, as well as some key lessons she has learned from her initial work experiences. There is a bit too much "I did this, I did that" at the end of the essay; it would have been stronger had she let her résumé tell us her accomplishments, focusing here only on personal introspection. However, as a whole the essay is strong because some of that introspection is present, and even the "what" section tells us something about her.

TULANE UNIVERSITY— A. B. FREEMAN SCHOOL OF BUSINESS

Question #1: *Why are you seeking a Tulane MBA at this time? In your answer, please include critical academic and professional experiences that led to your decision, a self-assessment of your suitability for graduate management school, your career goals and your specific interest in the Freeman School.*

Essay #1:

I am seeking a Tulane MBA because the curriculum and international programs offered by the A. B. Freeman School of Business at Tulane University will expand my knowledge of core business concepts while allowing me to focus on the area in which I plan to make my career: international business. As the national accounts officer at ABC Bank, I serve as the account handling officer for the bank's national and multinational corporate customers, such as General Motors Acceptance Corporation, Anheuser-Busch, and Westinghouse Electric. In working with these firms, both now as an officer and previously as a credit card analyst, I have observed that many of them plan to increase their international presence, especially in Mexico and Europe. My career objective is to work for a multinational firm for several years to gain the experience needed to ultimately establish my own international service-related firm. The knowledge needed and experience offered by the programs at the Freeman School will help me achieve this goal.

After working at ABC Bank for three years, I have decided that I need more academic training in order to pursue a more challenging career. The will and drive to succeed has characterized my tenure at ABC Bank. I attribute my success to two of my personal strengths that will be equally important in future careers: persistence and interpersonal skills.

After graduating from the University of XYZ in August of 1986, my goal was to secure a credit analyst position with ABC Bank. I believed the analyst position would help me build a foundation for making credit decisions as a lender, as well as allow me to study the operations of many industries. Upon applying for the position, however, I was told that no analyst positions were available and that the bank preferred to hire internally for such jobs. With this guideline in mind, I asked for any available job at the bank. I was offered a commercial vault teller position and accepted it. Although the work of processing commercial deposits for eight hours a day was monotonous, I kept my strategy in mind: perform my teller duties well, be persistent with credit management, and thereby earn the credit analyst job. After nine months in the vault, my determination was rewarded; the credit manager offered me the position that I sought. As an analyst, I was responsible for writing detailed analyses of a firm's operations to assist the commercial lenders with credit decisions. After working only eleven months in the credit area (the normal tenure is eighteen to twenty-four months,) I was elected national accounts officer, thus becoming the bank's youngest officer. Although I wrote very good credit reviews, I was not promoted for this reason; there were several other analysts who also wrote good reviews. I was promoted largely because of my strong interpersonal and communications skills since the National Accounts position requires an officer who can work well with both current and prospective customers. The National Accounts position entails handling the lending and cash management needs of the bank's national customers.

At ABC Bank, I have moved from a teller to an officer position in a short time. I have used my intelligence, persistence, and interpersonal skills to move up rapidly and now I wish to pursue a more challenging career. I am ready to use my past experience, combined with my strengths that I have discussed above, to obtain a graduate management degree and then excel in the area of international business.

Goal: Career in International Business
I want to build on my three years of banking experience and my travels, literally around the world, in preparation for an international management position either within the U.S. or abroad. My travels to Australia, Latin America, and South Africa on behalf of my family's cattle ranch first stimulated my interest in international business and trade. This interest has subsequently evolved during my three years in the banking business.

While I was a credit analyst, I learned much more about the international direction in which many firms are increasingly moving. Some of the firms that I reviewed are aggressively pursuing opportunities in Mexico because of their proximity to the border, the probable free trade agreement between the United States and Mexico, and the burgeoning maquiladora industry along the international border. The common denominator among these firms is a desire to take advantage of Mexico's abundance of labor and natural resources. I believe these two resources, coupled with Mexico's progressive government and an increasing interest in Mexico by U.S. businesses, will provide great opportunity in this emerging area of trade.

In addition, the National Accounts position has afforded me the opportunity to travel nationwide to call on my customers' home office, and, in the course of conducting the bank's affairs, inquire about each firm's international operations. Although noting the obstacles, political and economic, many customers have eagerly outlined their plans to expand into Latin America, Eastern Europe, and China. They made it clear to me that trends such as the movement toward common markets and the increasing capability of long distance communication via satellite will further encourage foreign trade. Furthermore, most noted their company's need to employ more personnel in the international area; the general consensus among my contacts is that there will be an increasing demand for international managers in the next decade.

At present, I am undecided as to which career path I will choose in international business. Some possibilities that I have considered are finance-related and should capitalize on my lending and cash management experience with a multinational bank. Another option I am considering is to establish a firm that provides translation services to companies wishing to conduct business abroad. As more firms enter the international market, the language barrier could be an obstacle to many U.S. businesses. A translation service would overcome this problem and innovations such as video teleconferencing makes this idea quite feasible.

Why a Tulane MBA?

Clearly, there are a number of options available to someone pursuing a career in international management, but I realize that I first need a more substantive grasp of the basics of management and the specifics of international business in order to be an effective manager. The Freeman School's curriculum provides the opportunity for me to obtain this knowledge.

The program's first year of required core courses, such as Financial Accounting and Marketing Management, followed by a flexible course schedule in the second year appeals to my desire to expand my knowledge in the areas of finance and accounting, and then focus on international topics. I also hope to take advantage of the school's international internship program or the study abroad program. It is important that I take advantage of one of these programs since I believe one should have a sense of the culture and economic climate of a region if she or he hopes to conduct business in that area.

Since I will spend almost two years in a Masters program and the school I choose could well determine my career options, I have treated the selection of schools to which I will apply with great care. I am quite aware of the Freeman School's outstanding reputation for international studies. Furthermore, since New Orleans is one of the nation's largest ports, I will have the opportunity to obtain firsthand knowledge about international commerce. Finally, several of the school's alumni have highly recommended the Freeman School to me due to its significant global focus.

In summary, the combination of my three years of banking experience, international travels, and completion of the MBA program at Tulane should prepare me quite well to succeed as an international manager. As you can see, I have demonstrated both motivation and initiative during my tenure at ABC Bank. I realize that my grade point average is below the published median 3.1 for a recent entering class. I attribute my relatively low GPA to lack of career focus and immaturity during my undergraduate years. I want to assert my belief, however, that I have as much character, determination and will to succeed as any student in the MBA program. I might note that there are several credit analysts who obtained their jobs before I did mainly due to higher GPA's; most of these analysts are still in the credit department writing reviews while I travel nationwide representing the bank. I can successfully complete the MBA program at Tulane and would certainly like the opportunity to do so.

Critique: Our admissions committee felt that this was an extremely strong essay. Many applicants have the tendency to treat this as an open-ended "Tell us about yourself . . ." kind of question, and write very general essays that elaborate on their backgrounds without providing adequate rationale regarding their suitability for MBA studies, an outline of their goals, or how a Freeman MBA can help them attain these goals. Although often cleverly written, such essays do not help the committee in making an admissions decision.

This essay is well structured, well written, and gives us a clear picture of the applicant as an individual who is both motivated and focused. The description of his rapid progression at ABC bank from commercial vault teller to credit analyst (his initial goal) to national accounts officer clearly shows that the applicant is able to assess his options, set goals and successfully develop and execute a strategy to reach them. These characteristics we seek in our MBA students. The essay also shows that the applicant has gained important knowledge and insights along the way which have helped him formulate his goals for the future. Those goals include a Freeman MBA and a career in international business.

Although this applicant confesses that he is still weighing two options in the area of international business (rather refreshing, since many of the very specific career goals we read about are obviously contrived or not well supported in the essay), he makes a convincing case for his interest in the field. He also explains his interest in the Freeman School well, citing our global focus, location in one of the nation's largest port cities, and some of our specific international programs. The applicant shows a strong interest in the Freeman MBA program. He has researched the program and has clearly taken the time to speak with alumni.

Finally, the applicant acknowledges a weakness (his GPA), and, without making excuses, emphasizes the characteristics he has which he believes will make him a strong candidate for our program. These characteristics were amply demonstrated throughout the essay, but he does a nice job of summarizing them and "closing the sale" at the end.

UNIVERSITY OF VIRGINIA

Question #1: *What is the most difficult ethical dilemma you have faced in your professional life? Articulate the nature of the difficulty. Upon present reflection, would you have resolved this dilemma in a different manner?*

Essay #1:

Upon graduation from college, my sense of adventure and quest for learning continued when I accepted a non-traditional position with the Bank of Credit and Commerce International (BCCI). I accepted a position with BCCI with the understanding that overseas placements were the requirement given the bank's limited US presence. BCCI was founded in 1972 by Pakistani financier Agha Hasan Abedi whose goal was to create the first multinational bank for the Third World. Its shareholders were rich Middle Eastern oil sheiks. Healthy growth fueled by increased international trade helped BCCI expand to $20 billion in assets that circled the globe in a 70 country branch network.

After completing BCCI's international trade finance training program with distinction at Pace University in New York, I received my first placement in London, England working as a trainee in bank branch operations and special country analysis projects. After quickly completing my London assignment in three months, BCCI management promoted me to a marketing role at their main offices in the United Arab Emirates (UAE). The ruling sheiks of each of the emirates were BCCI's major stockholders and had enormous international political and economic clout.

By quickly absorbing the local culture and the basics of the Arabic language, I earned the respect of my peers at the bank and in the local business community. Through my efforts, I marketed and received commitments for trade financing and investing from many multinational businesses operating in the UAE.

It was right after my third month working in the UAE that I was faced with a major ethical dilemma. During my search for new business, I learned from a contact at the government ministry of trade that a European sportswear manufacturer had applied for permission to start up a business in the UAE. (An application to do business is required of all foreigners along with the requirement to find a local partner.) I immediately informed bank management of the prospect and began my research into the company. After an initial meeting with the company in the UAE a few weeks later, I learned that the firm required a $30 million line facility. I requested the necessary financial information from the company and began my analysis of the company to assess its creditworthiness. My recommendation to bank management was not to proceed any further with the company given its losses over the past three years and very high leverage. The risks posed by the company's profile were too great.

My manager, who had always valued my credit skills, mysteriously ignored my recommendations and ordered me to negotiate a loan facility with the company. I was puzzled by my manager's action, especially since he offered no explanation. I structured a smaller facility at a premium interest rate with adequate primary and secondary fallback collateral to protect the bank from any credit risks. After presenting the new proposal to my bank manager, he dismissed it without comment and made the necessary arrangements to grant the company a $30 million unsecured line of credit at an interest rate reserved for the bank's highest creditworthy clients. A new provision was added though. A finder's fee of one percent of the loan ($300,000) was due. Even though the fee was paid, there existed no mention of it in the loan documents. Through a search of the bank's accounting records, I learned that the fee was transferred out of the UAE to my manager's personal account abroad. I was naive to think that the manager did not have his contacts in the bank who would report my inquiring.

My manager explained that the fee was not to be considered extorted funds, rather it was his finder's fee. Further, he explained that this was a customary practice. In fact, to show goodwill, he offered to share this fee with me and suggested $50,000. The only stipulation was that I had to keep the matter quiet from "jealous" employees.

My dilemma was whether to accept part of my manager's illegally obtained funds and keep quiet or to report the matter to a higher level of bank management. Being only 23 years of age and in a foreign country 8,000 miles away from home, I was scared. If this was a customary practice and the branch was covering up for him, then my reporting this incident would put my job in jeopardy as well as my life. I was always taught by my family to practice high ethical and moral standards and to obey the law. This was my guiding principle in refusing the illegal funds and notifying the bank's London headquarters of this serious matter. Immediately, I was transferred back to London within 48 hours; and no mention of the incident was ever made to me either in the UAE or in London. My newly assigned job in London was non-marketing related and consisted of counting checks in a windowless basement room. Even though it felt like BCCI management was punishing me for good ethical conduct, I still believed that my decision was right. I resigned from the bank one month later and returned to the U.S. where I obtained a banking job with an organization that, I can feel proud to state, has never presented me with the choice of compromising my ethics and moral standards.

If, in the future, I am unfortunately presented with an ethical dilemma of any degree, I feel confident in holding my ethical and moral standards as a priority.

Critique: What makes an application to the Darden School stand out from among the thousands received each year? One important key is well-written essays. As with many business school applications, the essay portion is the applicant's chance to showcase his or her writing talents while at the same time communicating a lot of explicit (and sometimes implicit) information to the admissions committee.

Many B-schools offer the first year student traditional courses in such functional areas as accounting, marketing, and operations, but Darden was one of the first to include required, graded courses in both communications and ethics. Nowhere at Darden do these two disciplines dovetail more perfectly than in Essay #4 of Darden's application, which asks: "What is the most difficult ethical dilemma you have faced in your professional life? Articulate the nature of the difficulty. Upon present reflection, would you have resolved this dilemma in a different manner?"

While this essay question often prompts the most reflection and introspection on the part of the applicant, it is also often the least understood. The admissions committee is looking not necessarily to judge the nature of the dilemma but rather the candidate's ability to articulate an often personal and complex decision-making process. The key to an effective Essay #4 is in dissecting the terms *ethical* and *dilemma*. Too often, themes reflected in this essay are of a legal nature: Should I disagree with my boss? Should I turn a co-worker in who's stealing office supplies? Should I break the law? And many situations do not accurately present a true dilemma in which there is no clear right or wrong answer but two or more possible solutions, none of which are necessarily better than another.

The essay above serves as an outstanding example by setting the scene, explaining clearly the nature of the dilemma and summing up the candidate's experience in a concise and well-written essay. The admissions committee was particularly impressed by the author's honest approach and engaging writing style. The firm does not have to be well-known, in this case BCCI, nor must the dilemma involve large sums of money or shady characters. Rather, the essay should reflect the candidate's personal and professional commitment to ethics, a commitment that also underlies the foundation of The Darden School.

CHAPTER EIGHT

Schools Rated by Category

About These "Rankings"

Now before you say, "Hey, wait a minute! I thought this book wasn't going to rank schools," let us explain. Surveying 10,000 business school students is no easy task. In fact, it practically killed several staff members. But among the fruits of our labors—a reward that made our task seem worthwhile—were the fascinating numbers we came up with. We wanted to present those numbers to you in an informative and slightly less-than-serious way. The following rankings cannot and must not be considered objective. These lists are based entirely upon student opinion. So when our list rates a campus location, for example, we didn't use any scientific formula based on cost of living, climate, crime rate, etc. We simply listed the schools at which students raved about the location most, or complained about it most. So focus on the categories that are important to you, and make of these opinions what you will.

And remember, every one of the schools profiled in this book is a top-notch institution.

ACADEMICS

STUDENTS DEVELOP STRONG GENERAL MANAGEMENT SKILLS
Dartmouth College
University of Virginia
Georgetown University
Yale University
Harvard University
Wake Forest University
Stanford University
University of North Carolina/Chapel Hill
University of Michigan
Duke University

WEAK GENERAL MANAGEMENT SKILLS
Pennsylvania State University
City University of New York/Baruch College
University of Kentucky
Syracuse University
Georgia Institute of Technology
Massachusetts Institute of Technology
University of Rochester
University of Georgia
Loyola University/Chicago
University of Utah

QUANT JOCKS
(students develop strong quantitative skills)
Carnegie Mellon University
Massachusetts Institute of Technology
University of Chicago
Purdue University
University of Rochester
Yale University
University of Pennsylvania
University of Maryland
Rice University
Columbia University

POETS
(weak quantitative skills)
Harvard University
University of California/Los Angeles
Syracuse University
Boston University
Cornell University
Claremont Graduate School
Hofstra University
University of Minnesota/Twin Cities
Brigham Young University
Penn State University

STUDENTS DEVELOP STRONG INTERPERSONAL SKILLS
Georgetown University
University of Tennessee/Knoxville
Northwestern University
University of Virginia
Dartmouth College
Stanford University
Texas Christian University
Yale University
Southern Methodist University
University of Southern California

WEAK INTERPERSONAL SKILLS
University of Kentucky
Loyola University/Chicago
Syracuse University
City University of New York/Baruch College
University of Washington
University of California/Los Angeles
Georgia Institute of Technology
Washington University
Boston University
University of Wyoming

STUDENTS DEVELOP STRONG COMMUNICATION SKILLS
Texas Christian University
University of Tennessee/Knoxville
Southern Methodist University
Tulane University
Georgetown University
Duke University
Dartmouth College
College of William & Mary
Purdue University
University of Connecticut

WEAK COMMUNICATION SKILLS
Washington University
University of Kentucky
Loyola University/Chicago
University of California/Los Angeles
Syracuse University
University of Washington
Harvard University
University of Massachusetts/Amherst
Cornell University
Babson College

STUDENTS DEVELOP STRONG TEAMWORK SKILLS
Dartmouth College
Georgetown University
Northwestern University
Duke University
University of Tennessee/Knoxville
Yale University
University of Minnesota/Twin Cities
University of North Carolina/Chapel Hill
Stanford University
University of Virginia

NOT MUCH TEAMWORK
Harvard University
University of Kentucky
Loyola University/Chicago
University of California/Los Angeles
City University of New York/Baruch College
University of Texas/Arlington
University of Wyoming
Syracuse University
Pennsylvania State University
Wahington University

STUDENTS DEVELOP STRONG OPERATIONS SKILLS
Carnegie-Mellon University
Georgetown University
Massachusetts Institute of Technology
University of Virginia
Purdue University
University of Maryland
Washington University
University of Southern California
University of Minnesota/Twin Cities
Southern Methodist University

OPERATIONS NOT A STRONG POINT
Cornell University
Northwestern University
University of Kentucky
Syracuse University
University of Massachusetts/Amherst
Rice University
SUNY Buffalo
Hofstra University
Claremont Graduate School
University of Texas/Arlington

STUDENTS DEVELOP STRONG ACCOUNTING SKILLS
University of Maryland
University of Chicago
University of Southern California
Yale University
University of Pennsylvania
University of Texas/Austin
Dartmouth College
University of Washington
Rice University
Georgetown University

WHAT'S A SPREAD SHEET?
Pennsylvania State University
Babson College
Ohio State University
University of Tennessee/Knoxville
Hofstra University
Syracuse University
University of Iowa
Harvard University
University of Kentucky
University of Arizona

FINANCE WHIZZES
(students develop strong finance skills)
University of Chicago
University of Pennsylvania
Yale University
Columbia University
New York University
University of Rochester
Massachusetts Institute of Technology
University of Virginia
Rice University
Wake Forest University

HAVE TROUBLE MAKING CORRECT CHANGE
(weak finance skills)
University of Kentucky
Pennsylvania State University
University of Tennessee/Knoxville
College of William & Mary
Syracuse University
University of Georgia
Washington University
SUNY Buffalo
Texas A&M University
Boston University

STUDENTS DEVELOP STRONG MARKETING SKILLS
University of Maryland
Georgetown University
Northwestern University
University of Tennessee/Knoxville
Dartmouth College
Wake Forest University
Rice University
University of Southern California
University of Michigan
University of California/Berkeley

WEAK MARKETING SKILLS
Syracuse University
University of Rochester
City University of New York/Baruch College
Brigham Young University
Boston University
Washington University
Northeastern University
University of Washington
Rensselaer Polytechnic Institute
University of Georgia

COMPUTER GENIUSES
(students comfortable with computers and managing data)

Carnegie Mellon University
Massachusetts Institute of Technology
Wake Forest University
Duke University
Southern Methodist University
Purdue University
University of Illinois/Champaign-Urbana
Texas Christian University
Georgia Institute of Technology
Tulane University

HOW DO I TURN THIS THING ON?
(students uncomfortable with computers)

Harvard University
Loyola University/Chicago
University of Kentucky
Claremont Graduate School
Boston University
Hofstra University
Cornell University
Pennsylvania State University
Syracuse University
Northwestern University

BEST OVERALL SKILLS
(in the functional areas)

Georgetown University
Southern Methodist University
Wake Forest University
Dartmouth College
University of Virginia
Carnegie Mellon University
Yale University
University of Maryland
Purdue University
Duke University

WEAKEST OVERALL SKILLS
(in the functional areas)

University of Kentucky
Syracuse University
Loyola University/Chicago
City University of New York/Baruch College
Pennsylvania State University
University of California/Los Angeles
Boston University
Harvard University
Washington University
Hofstra University

PRESSURE

OVERALL MELLOW
Stanford University
Yale University
Northwestern University
Emory University
University of California/Berkeley
University of Wyoming
Dartmouth College
University of Washington
Cornell University
Case Western Reserve University

GOOD SAMARITANS
(non-competitive students)
Stanford University
Yale University
Northwestern University
University of California/Berkeley
University of Washington
Georgetown University
Case Western Reserve University
Emory University
Duke University
Cornell University

UP ALL NIGHT
(heavy work load)
Carnegie Mellon University
University of Virginia
Massachusetts Institute of Technology
Georgetown University
Purdue University
University of Southern California
Dartmouth College
Rice University
University of Pittsburgh
Rensselaer Polytechnic Institute

OVERALL TENSE
University of Alabama/Tuscaloosa
University of Oregon
University of Texas/ Arlington
Northeastern University
University of Southern California
Purdue University
University of Utah
New York University
University of Pittsburgh
Harvard University

BACK-STABBERS
(competitive students)
University of Alabama/Tuscaloosa
Arizona State University
Northeastern University
New York University
University of Connecticut
Purdue University
Rice University
Rensselaer Polytechnic Institute
University of Texas/Austin
University of Denver

LIGHT WORK LOAD
Emory University
Loyola University/Chicago
University of Kentucky
University of Wyoming
Boston University
Northwestern University
University of California/Los Angeles
University of California/Berkeley
University of Denver
Texas Christian University

SOCIAL LIFE & FELLOW STUDENTS

"SHINY, HAPPY MBAs"
(best quality of life)
Stanford University
Georgetown University
Dartmouth College
University of North Carolina/Chapel Hill
Southern Methodist University
University of Texas/Austin
Northwestern University
Columbia University
University of Virginia
University of California Berkeley

YOUR BROKERAGE OR MINE?
(students date often)
University of Denver
Southern Methodist University
University of North Carolina/Chapel Hill
Brigham Young University
Wake Forest University
University of California/Berkeley
Tulane University
University of Maryland
Ohio State University
Pennsylvania State University

STUDENTS LOVE TO HANG OUT TOGETHER
Dartmouth College
Yale University
Georgetown University
Stanford University
Southern Methodist University
University of Maryland
Northwestern University
University of Southern California
University of Virginia
Columbia University

SCHOOL OF THE LIVING DEAD
(worst quality of life)
Hofstra University
Rensselaer Polytechnic Institute
Syracuse University
University of Rochester
University of Utah
City University of New York/Baruch College
SUNY Buffalo
University of Connecticut
University of Texas/Arlington
Texas A&M University

WELCOME TO THE MONASTERY
(students don't date)
University of Minnesota/Twin Cities
University of Arizona
Indiana University/Bloomington
University of Rochester
University of Utah
Washington University
City University of New York/Baruch College
Massachusetts Institute of Technology
Cornell University
Carnegie Mellon University

STUDENTS DON'T HANG OUT TOGETHER
University of Kentucky
SUNY Buffalo
Boston University
Loyola University/Chicago
City University of New York/Baruch College
University of Utah
Hofstra University
Pennsylvania State University
Syracuse University
Texas A&M University

SOCIAL BUTTERFLIES
(active social lives)
Stanford University
Dartmouth College
Northwestern University
Georgetown University
Wake Forest University
University of California/Berkeley
University of North Carolina/Chapel Hill
Southern Methodist University
Duke University
Tulane University

THE HEART IS A LONELY BROKER
(moribund social lives)
University of Utah
City University of New York/Baruch College
University of Texas/Arlington
SUNY Buffalo
University of Arizona
Rensselaer Polytechnic Institute
University of Rochester
Washington University
University of Kentucky
Boston University

HERE'S MY CARD
(students will keep in touch)
Georgetown University
Dartmouth College
Stanford University
University of Virginia
Yale University
University of Southern California
Southern Methodist University
Northwestern University
Columbia University
University of Maryland

WHAT'S NETWORKING?
(students won't stay in touch)
University of Kentucky
Pennsylvania State University
SUNY Buffalo
Hofstra University
Loyola University/Chicago
University of Texas/Arlington
Syracuse University
University of Wyoming
Boston University
Texas A&M University

MULTICULTURAL SMORGASBORD
(ethnic & racial diversity)
University of Michigan
Columbia University
Tulane University
University of Pennsylvania
University of California/Berkeley
University of Pittsburgh
Massachusetts Institute of Technology
Rensselaer Polytechnic Institute
City University of New York/Baruch College
Northeastern University

WHITE BREAD
(ethnic & racial homogeneity)
University of Utah
Brigham Young University
Southern Methodist University
College of William & Mary
Arizona State University
University of Alabama/Tuscaloosa
University of Minnesota/Twin Cities
Babson College
Dartmouth College
Rice University

STUDENTS ARE EAGER TO HELP OTHERS
Dartmouth College
Yale University
Georgetown University
Stanford University
University of Virginia
Southern Methodist University
University of California/Berkeley
Northwestern University
Duke University
Carnegie Mellon University

GENIUS FOLK
(students say classmates are smart)
Yale University
Stanford University
Dartmouth College
Massachusetts Institute Technology
Georgetown University
Duke University
University of Virginia
University of Pennsylvania
Rice University
Carnegie Mellon University

"BEEN THERE, DONE THAT"
(students have diverse work experience)
Yale University
University of California/Berkeley
Columbia University
University of Virginia
University of Maryland
University of Pennsylvania
Stanford University
Georgetown University
Northwestern University
Cornell University

ONLY IF YOU ASK
Pennsylvania State University
Hofstra University
Loyola University/Chicago
SUNY Buffalo
University of Kentucky
Boston University
University of Rochester
University of Utah
City University of New York/Baruch College
Washington University

NOT SO BRIGHT
(students say classmates are not smart)
Syracuse University
City University of New York/Baruch College
Pennsylvania State University
University of Houston
University of Kentucky
University of Illinois/Champaign-Urbana
Hofstra University
Loyola University/Chicago
Washington University
Boston University

DO YOU WANT FRIES WITH THAT?
(students' work experience NOT diverse)
Texas A&M University
University of Illinois/Champaign-Urbana
University of Wyoming
SUNY Buffalo
Brigham Young University
University of Kentucky
Pennsylvania State University
University of Iowa
University of Kansas
Syracuse University

FACILITIES

ON-CAMPUS HOUSING GOOD
Dartmouth College
Wake Forest University
Babson College
University of Notre Dame
Southern Methodist University
Stanford University
University of Virginia
Purdue University
University of Texas /Austin
Cornell University

LOUSY
University of Chicago
University of California/Berkeley
University of Pennsylvania
Georgia Institute of Technology
Yale University
University of Georgia
SUNY Buffalo
University of Pittsburgh
University of Rochester
University of California/Los Angeles

MAXIMUM PUMPITUDE
(gym facilities excellent)
Harvard University
Vanderbilt University
Tulane University
University of Alabama/Tuscaloosa
Arizona State University
Purdue University
University of Texas/Austin
University of Virginia
Wake Forest University
University of Notre Dame

"WIMPY, WIMPY, WIMPY"
(like maybe a jump rope or something)
City University of New York/Baruch College
Columbia University
Massachusetts Institute of Technology
Carnegie Mellon University
Duke University
Claremont Graduate School
Cornell University
University of Pennsylvania
Boston University
Loyola University/Chicago

SCHOOL TOWN IS PARADISE
University of Minnesota/Twin Cities
University of Texas/Austin
University of Washington
Emory University
University of North Carolina/Chapel Hill
Columbia University
Southern Methodist University
University of Colorado/Boulder
Georgetown University
Stanford University

SCHOOL TOWN A PIT
Hofstra University
Rensselaer Polytechnic Institute
University of Pennsylvania
University of Rochester
University of Connecticut
University of Notre Dame
Yale University
Syracuse University
Texas A&M University
Purdue University

SO MUCH TO DO
(lots of school clubs & activities)
Northwestern University
Harvard University
Stanford University
Columbia University
University of Virginia
University of Texas/Austin
Georgetown University
University of Pennsylvania
Duke University
Vanderbilt University

BOOOOOORING
(not many school activities)
Loyola University/Chicago
University of Utah
City University of New York/Baruch College
University of Kentucky
Claremont Graduate School
Boston University
University of Massachusetts/Amherst
Hofstra University
University of Texas/Arlington
Northeastern University

A FIVE-STAR LIBRARY
University of Michigan
University of Maryland
Stanford University
Dartmouth College
Harvard University
University of Illinois/Champaign-Urbana
University of Texas/Austin
Vanderbilt University
Southern Methodist University
University of Tennessee/Knox

SOMEONE LOST THE BOOK
Georgia Institute of Technology
Case Western Reserve University
Texas A&M University
University of Utah
University of Kentucky
University of Iowa
University of Southern California
Columbia University
Ohio State University
College of William & Mary

PLACEMENT & FACILITIES

RECRUITING
(quality, range, & number of companies recruiting on-campus)

University of Pennsylvania
Columbia University
Stanford University
University of Chicago
Northwestern University
Harvard University
Dartmouth College
University of Virginia
Indiana University/Bloomington
Purdue University

RECRUITING
(not satisfactory)

City University of New York/Baruch College
University of Wyoming
SUNY Buffalo
University of Arizona
University of Utah
University of Kentucky
Claremont Graduate School
University of Massachusetts/Amherst
Loyola University/Chicago
Emory University

WE GOT JOBS
(placement office very effective)

University of Maryland
University of Pennsylvania
Stanford University
Harvard University
Dartmouth College
University of Chicago
Rice University
Purdue University
University of Southern California
Vanderbilt University

ARE YOU HIRING?
(placement office not so great)

City University of New York/Baruch College
University of Illinois/Champaign-Urbana
University of Wyoming
University of Colorado at Boulder
SUNY Buffalo
Cornell University
University of Georgia
University of Massachusetts/Amherst
Texas A&M University
University of Tennessee/Knox

CHAPTER NINE

Profiles
of
the
Best
Business
Schools

UNIVERSITY OF ALABAMA: MANDERSON GRADUATE SCHOOL OF BUSINESS

ADMISSIONS FACTS

Type of school   Public

Demographics

No. of men	134
No. of women	35
No. of minorities	1
No. of int'l students	13

EQUAL TREATMENT GRAPH

Women

Minorities

0   2   4 (GPA)

▨ Student Opinion ■ National Average

Admissions Statistics

Avg. GMAT	572
Avg. undergraduate GPA	3.11
Avg. age at entry	25
No. of applicants	195
No. accepted	137
No. enrolled	79

Deadlines and Notifications

Regular application	7/01
Regular notification	within 4 weeks

Focus of Curriculum

Specialized

Academic Specialties

Finance, Accounting

Joint Degrees

MBA/JD, The Three/Two Program, Executive MBA Program

Special Programs

The Three/Two Program, Executive MBA Program

FINANCIAL FACTS

In-state tuition	$2,068
Out-of-state tuition	$5,166
On-campus housing	$3,288

ACADEMICS

If you've postponed or avoided getting an MBA because of the high tuition, The University of Alabama offers one of the most low-cost, sought-after MBAs.

But this doesn't come at the cost of academics. One student raved, "The standards are very high." Enthused another, "the program is insightful and targeted towards today's business needs." First-year students take core courses in a "lock-step" sequence. Translation: courses are sequenced in a pre-set order and the sixty-five entering students take them all together. Quantitative methods are front-loaded in the first semester so that students have these skills at their disposal for the remainder of the program. Second-year students select a concentration in either finance/accounting, international business, human resources management, marketing, or production/operations management. Wrote one student, "I've found the Strategic Management and Human Resources programs very strong." Beyond the basic curriculum, students are enrolled in a year-long professional development program that could easily pass for a finishing school. The topics include: interviewing skills, etiquette, ethics, business entertaining, wine tasting, art appreciation, dressing for success, and theater appreciation. Another unique feature of the program is the Executive-On-Campus series, which provides students up close and personal attention from visiting execs.

Students we surveyed gave their professors above average marks for their teaching and after-class accessibility. Wrote one, "Professors are helpful and friendly. They don't act superior or intimidating." Students are equally pleased with the administration. Indeed, Alabama is among only a dozen or so schools where students are satisfied with the way the school is run. Alabama has tried hard to win its students' respect. Chief among their efforts is the new, high-tech B-school building. They've also integrated more computer and team assignments into the curriculum. And they score well on the basics, too: it's a cinch to get into popular courses.

As one might expect, with a $5,000 price tag for out-of-state residents, and $2,000 for natives, the overwhelming majority of students say this program is well worth the investment. Adds one MBA, "Alabama offers over a century of tradition and a very strong alumni network and support."

PLACEMENT AND RECRUITING

The Alabama Placement Office shares services and staff with the undergraduate program. One student told us, "the placement office needs to operate as a separate entity from the college. This would enhance our ability to achieve top tier status." Sensing student resentment with this "sharing" arrangement, the administration has added a part-time staff person to focus on MBA placement. Alabama has also joined several other schools in participating in the Southeastern MBA Consortium, a shared recruiting day. MBAs are still disappointed with the overall capabilities of the placement office. In particular, they'd like a broader and deeper range of companies to visit campus. Sixty-three percent of 1993 MBAs had been placed within three months of graduating.

UNIVERSITY OF ALABAMA: MANDERSON GRADUATE SCHOOL OF BUSINESS

STUDENT LIFE/CAMPUS

The workload at Alabama is at its heaviest during the first year. The majority of students report spending an average of fifteen to twenty-five hours a week preparing for class, although this is light by top B-school standards. Almost everyone works in a study group. By the second year, students know the shortcuts and relax a bit.

Students are very competitive, but not into backstabbing. In such a small program, the emphasis is on cooperation and mutual support. Most students claim their closest friends are found within the B-school. Judging by the responses to our survey, they expect these relationships to continue long after the program has ended. Students are impressed by the depth and range of professional experiences that their peers bring to the program. They're even more impressed by their smarts which they describe as "sharp."

The majority of students live off-campus in nearby apartments. Parking isn't great. Consider living within walking distance. Or bring a bike. Back on campus, students work out in a fully equipped, high-tech gym. They also enjoy Alabama's top-ranked athletic teams. Wrote one MBA, "We have a kick ass football team." For those who want to do more than watch football, the MBA Association sponsors a wide range of professional and social events including MBA Week. This features a golf tournament with both MBAs and local entertainers as players.

ADMISSIONS

The admissions office considers your college GPA to be most important; after that, in descending order, they consider your GMAT scores, work experience, essays, letters or recommendation, extracurricular activities, and interview.

According to the school, "The undergraduate record, from a good school, is the first step to successful admission since it demonstrates motivation. GPAs of less than 3.0 (out of a 4.0) should be explained in depth. The GMAT score should be at least 500, although no cut-off is used. Work experience is always a plus. You should take the short essay very seriously. This reflects upon your writing skills and ability to proof your materials." Decisions are made on a rolling admissions basis. Applicants are notified of a decision within approximately one month after the application has been received. Waitlisted applicants are notified of a spot by April 15th. Admitted applicants may defer admission for up to one year.

STUDENT'S OVERVIEW BOX

FACULTY RATING

HITS AND MISSES

HITS
Gym
Helping other students
Accounting dept.

MISSES
Placement
Ethnic & racial diversity
Marketing dept.

APPLICANTS ALSO LOOK AT
(not available)

FOR MORE INFORMATION, CONTACT:
Manderson School of Business
P.O. Box 870223
Tuscaloosa, AL 35487
(205) 348-8935

UNIVERSITY OF ARIZONA: KARL ELLER GRADUATE SCHOOL OF MANAGEMENT

ADMISSIONS FACTS

Type of school	Public

Demographics

No. of men	106
No. of women	47
No. of minorities	21
No. of int'l students	19

EQUAL TREATMENT GRAPH

Women

Minorities

0   2   4 (GPA)

▨ Student Opinion   ☐ National Average

Admissions Statistics

Avg. GMAT	598
Avg. undergraduate GPA	3.24
Avg. age at entry	27
No. of applicants	380
No. accepted	201
No. enrolled	77

Deadlines and Notifications

Regular application	4/15
Regular notification	within 4 weeks
Special dates	12/01 (transfers)

Focus of Curriculum

General Management

Academic Specialties

Marketing, MIS, Entrepreneurship, Finance

Joint Degrees

JD/MBA, MBA/Masters in International Management

Special Programs

Accelerated Three/Two program with the College of Arts and Science

FINANCIAL FACTS

In-state tuition	$1,580
Out-of-state tuition	$6,996
On-campus housing	$2,436

ACADEMICS

Where can you find a first-rate Management Information Systems Department, a resort-like campus, gorgeous weather, and bargain-basement tuition? At the University of Arizona (U of A), which not only boasts a nationally renowned MIS department, but a technological environment consistently supported by large grants from some of America's premier technology companies: IBM, Apple Computer, and Hewlett Packard. Interested in the development of new business ventures? Then U of A is also a natural choice. Students can study in the Berger Entrepreneurship Program in the Eller Center for the Study of the Private Market Economy, which was cited as a model program by the U.S. Association for Small Business in 1989. Here students get hands-on experience in workshops and two-person projects presented in a Business Plans Competition judged by local Arizonians. Other strong departments include marketing and finance.

U of A offers a basic, meat-and-potatoes MBA, but with a heavy quantitative slant. During the first year, a broad management education is emphasized with ten core courses. Four of these are "integrative" to introduce students to multi-disciplinary approaches. All first-years participate in a competitive business simulation game. To balance out the emphasis on quantitative analysis, students also receive special training in communication and presentation skills. Beginning during the second semester, students select nine electives in several areas: accounting, decision sciences, entrepreneurship, finance, health care administration, human resources, MIS, marketing, reliability and quality engineering, and quality management. Unsurprisingly, students in our survey reported feeling well-prepared by their training in presentation and communication skills. They also felt confident of their finance and general management skills. A surprising miss—close to fifty percent of students surveyed said they're only moderately confident of their operations skills, the school's power subject. Overall, students are unanimous—the U of A MBA is worth the investment of time and money. But not everyone agrees that it's meeting their academic expectations.

PLACEMENT AND RECRUITING

The Eller School operates its own placement office in addition to collaborating with the U of A Career Services Center which serves the entire university. Among the services offered MBAs are workshops on everything from preparing resumes to conducting job search campaigns. Each year a permanent position resume book is distributed to 300 national and local firms. A summer internship resume book is mailed to 150 firms. Prospective employers may also access an "electronic resume book" on diskette. According to the school, during 1991-1992, over 100 companies recruited on-campus for B-school students. According to students, this wasn't enough. Students say they're very disappointed by the range of companies recruiting and the efforts of a less-than-aggressive placement office. U of A boasted a ninety-two percent placement rate in 1993.

UNIVERSITY OF ARIZONA: KARL ELLER GRADUATE SCHOOL OF MANAGEMENT

STUDENT LIFE/CAMPUS

Students here study an average of twenty-five to thirty-five hours a week, and report an intense first-year workload. By the second year, both the workload and pressure lighten up. Still, like other B-school students, many U of A MBAs say they do assignments selectively—skimming and skipping—to lighten the load. They also collaborate on assignments in study groups. Bonus points go to the school for proactively preparing students for the demands of the program in two ways: quantexcel learning sessions and a four-week summer prep session offered to all first-years. Classes are small and held Monday through Thursday. Class-less Fridays are reserved for activities such as on-site business visits and the quantexcel workshops.

U of A students agree classmates are smart and professionally diverse. As for their competitiveness, it depends on whom you ask. While the majority of students say U of A MBAs are very competitive, a not insignificant number say they're laid back. Perhaps because many students choose U of A because it's close to home, the on-campus social scene is not as happening as it is at other B-schools. Nor are MBA friendships. While a large number of students say they like to hang out with fellow classmates, an almost equal number say they don't. Social and professional activities are organized by the student-run Master of Business Administration Student Association.

The U of A campus is beautiful and everyone seems to like the town of Tucson, although it's hardly a hopping metropolis. A few hours' drive away is Phoenix, the Grand Canyon, or even a Mexican beach. Students get most pumped about the gym, which is reportedly amazing. The majority of students live off-campus in surrounding neighborhoods. Housing is easy to find and considered extremely affordable and attractive.

ADMISSIONS

The admissions department considers work experience most important, followed by undergraduate course work, undergraduate GPA, GMAT scores, essays, and recommendations.

STUDENT'S OVERVIEW BOX

Overall Happiness

Academic Satisfaction

50   75   100%

Student Opinion   National Average

FACULTY RATING

Student Opinion   National Average

HITS AND MISSES

HITS
Gym
Classmates are smart
Finance dept.
Innovative curriculum
Tuition
Diverse work experience
Tucson

MISSES
Recruiting
Social life
Accounting dept.
Placement
Competitive classmates

APPLICANTS ALSO LOOK AT
(not available)

FOR MORE INFORMATION, CONTACT:
Karl Eller Graduate School of Business
Tucson, AZ 85721
(602) 621-2566

ARIZONA STATE UNIVERSITY COLLEGE OF BUSINESS

ADMISSIONS FACTS

Type of school   Public

Demographics

No. of men   98
No. of women   47
No. of minorities   18
No. of int'l students   17

EQUAL TREATMENT GRAPH

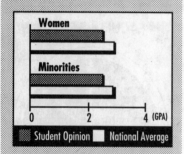

Admissions Statistics

Avg. GMAT   604
Avg. undergraduate GPA   3.31
Avg. age at entry   26
No. of applicants   514
No. accepted   142
No. enrolled   75

Deadlines and Notifications

Regular application   5/2
Regular notification   N/A
Special dates   N/A

Focus of Curriculum

General Management

Academic Specialties

Marketing, Accounting, Finance,
Purchasing and Logistics

Special Programs

PepsiCo Minority Scholarship Program

FINANCIAL FACTS

In-state tuition $1,600
Out-of-state tuition $6,994
On-campus housing $4,110

ACADEMICS

The Arizona State University (ASU) B-school does a good job of living up to the reputation it has created. Students say it offers first-rate academics, an innovative learning environment, and excellent value. One told us, "ASU is an up-and-coming school that is extremely student-oriented and aggressive in its pursuit of a quality education." Thoroughness is the operative game plan here. ASU's program builds strength in every conceivable area: 1) core knowledge—technical and analytical skills in the major business disciplines of business; 2) basic skills—computing, writing, speaking, time management, and teamwork; and 3) managerial abilities—ethics, diversity issues, global business, and quality in service and products. But the program doesn't stop here. To aid team formation, students are given psychological tests during orientation. As part of the emphasis on cooperative learning, students with previous coursework no longer "opt out" of core courses; they take the class and mentor other students and serve as discussion leaders. During the first semester, students are expected to a participate in a "one-time" volunteer activity such as renovating a shelter. As for the basic program, year one is extremely structured. Year two is extremely flexible. Students specialize or take a cross-functional sequence of electives. These may be taken at the B-school itself, in other parts of the university, or at the nearby American Graduate School of International Business (Thunderbird). Many courses feature field projects with employers such as PepsiCo and Motorola.

To judge by the responses to our survey, the administration is responsive to student needs. Reported one student, "They restructured the core course offerings to limit the days we are in class—at the student's request!" A significant number feel there are still major kinks in the system. Explained one MBA, "A lot of new ideas are being implemented, which will be fine once the details are ironed out." Of the faculty, the reviews are mixed. Many are considered stellar teachers. Many are not. Professors receive higher marks for their after-class accessibility and "desire to help." Overall, students report that taking time off to get an ASU MBA is well worth it. Summed up one: "I couldn't have picked a better school to attend."

PLACEMENT AND RECRUITING

The B-school has its own Director of Placement for MBA students, but not its own stand-alone Career Services Office. This is shared with a central university placement center. According to ASU, approximately 100 recruiters come on campus annually for MBA hiring. Of the graduating class, seventy-eight percent are placed within three months after graduation from the program. Apparently, the numbers don't tell the whole story. The vast majority say career placement services need to improve dramatically. They also want to see a wider range of companies recruiting on campus.

ARIZONA STATE UNIVERSITY COLLEGE OF BUSINESS

STUDENT LIFE/CAMPUS

The first-year workload is heavy, intense, demanding—that pretty much sums it up. Students spend roughly thirty to forty hours a week chugging through it. Classes are small and feature group assignments. To bolster communication and interpersonal skills, many of these involve oral presentations to an audience of peers and faculty. Observes one MBA, "Working in teams allows us to achieve higher quality work than if we individually competed with each other on a bell curve." But outside of teamwork, students here are very competitive.

They're also interested in helping each other, but not as much as one might expect at such a teamwork-driven school. This may have something to do with how classmates feel about each other. While the majority report they like each other and expect to continue their friendships after school, a sizeable number are more lukewarm about each other. Students agree, however, that the student body is professionally diverse and "bright."

ASU boasts great libraries and state-of-the-art facilities. It's also located in Tempe, rated "one of the top ten college towns in America." The climate and dramatic desert setting make it a great place to go to school. Several students told us they weren't sure if they came here for the sun or the MBA. Perhaps they came for ASU's own eighteen-hole, 160-acre golf course. Maybe they came for the gym, which students said was as good as you'll find at any five-star resort. As for student life, popular extracurriculars involve any activity in the great outdoors. Students annually organize a trip to one of Arizona's scenic destinations such as the Grand Canyon. Career clubs organize events related to professional development.

ADMISSIONS

According to the admissions department, your work experience/résumé is weighted most heavily. Then in descending order, your GMAT score, college GPA, "a personal statement reflecting on maturity, strength of purpose, academic potential and ability to communicate clearly," letters of recommendation, extracurricular activities, and the interview. Applications are reviewed in rounds. The deadlines for each round are December 15, March 1, and May 2. It is advisable to apply in round one or two. Joint degree programs include: MBA/MIM with Thunderbird; MBA/Masters in Architecture; MBA/Masters in Health Services; and MBA/JD. Scholarships and assistanceships are available, including the PepsiCo Minority Scholarship Program. Applicants to Arizona State often apply to the University of Arizona and Thunderbird as well.

STUDENT'S OVERVIEW BOX

FACULTY RATING

HITS AND MISSES

HITS
Gym
Diverse work experience
Marketing dept.
Tempe

MISSES
Off-campus housing

APPLICANTS ALSO LOOK AT
UC Los Angeles
Rice U.
U Arizona

FOR MORE INFORMATION, CONTACT:
School of Business
Tempe, AZ 85287
(602) 965-3331

BABSON COLLEGE GRADUATE SCHOOL OF BUSINESS

ADMISSIONS FACTS

Type of school	Private

Demographics

No. of men	204
No. of women	131
No. of minorities	16
No. of int'l students	98

EQUAL TREATMENT GRAPH

Women

Minorities

0   2   4 (GPA)

▨ Student Opinion   ▢ National Average

Admissions Statistics

Avg. GMAT	576
Avg. undergraduate GPA	3.1
Avg. age at entry	26
No. of applicants	690
No. accepted	338
No. enrolled	153

Deadlines and Notifications

Regular application	5/15
Regular notification	within 4 weeks
Special dates	N/A

Focus of Curriculum

General Management, option to specialize

Academic Specialties

Entrepreneurial Management, International Business

Joint Degrees

Two-year MBA, One-Year MBA for Business graduates, Evening MBA

Special Programs

International Management Program (IMP), Management Consulting Field Experience (MCFE), International Study Programs

FINANCIAL FACTS

In-state tuition	$16,050
Out-of-state tuition	N/A
On-campus housing	$7,080

ACADEMICS

Babson has re-tooled its curriculum to reflect the latest trends in business education today. Individual courses specific to each of the business functional areas have been scrapped in favor of cross-functional, multidisciplinary "modules," which are taken during the first year. Subthemes of each module are "values and ethics, innovation, quality, entrepreneurship, global thinking, and leadership." This teaching concept is a big draw for students; several wrote they picked Babson because of the "new curriculum."

But Babson is probably best known for its entrepreneurial and international focus. Considered one of the top two B-schools in the nation in entrepreneurship studies, Babson offers more learning and networking opportunities for would-be entrepreneurs than almost any other program. In addition to serious courses on the subject, such as managing business growth, there's the Entrepreneurial Exchange, a network, and Academy of Entrepreneurs.

One student wrote he "chose this school because of its global and international perspective." Notes the school, "In an expanding and dynamic global business environment, managers need to understand the subtleties of working across cultural boundaries." Cross-cultural experiences are strongly encouraged and a formal concentration in International Business is available. All Babson students must complete a rigorous cross-cultural requirement. This may be met taking a summer-long international internship, spending a semester abroad, or taking an intensive three-week international course. The Center for Language and Culture conducts orientation programs for students heading off to foreign lands for their internship which includes pre-departure language training and readings on local culture. They also offer non-credit undergraduate courses to increase language proficiency.

PLACEMENT AND RECRUITING

Among the many services offered by the career placement office are one-on-one counseling, videotaped mock interviews, and résumé/cover letter assistance. All students are required to participate in the Career Management Program, which takes a marketing-oriented approach to job seeking and helps students plan one-of-a-kind job searches. Particularly noteworthy is Career Search, "an automated data base of more than 183,000 employers around the U.S." The program allows students to "identify the parameters of their search (industry, location, company size, and specialty), generate a written report for networking and research purposes, and download to a disk for mail merging." In addition, students may submit their resume, for inclusion in the MBA Résumé Book, and they may attend the Greater Boston MBA Consortium Job Fair, which provides access to over 300 employers. In 1992, sixty-one percent of all students had accepted positions by commencement. Over seventy companies recruited on campus. Leading recruiters were Johnson and Johnson, Proctor and Gamble, Union Bank of Switzerland, GTE, Merck and Co., and Fidelity Investments.

BABSON COLLEGE GRADUATE SCHOOL OF BUSINESS

STUDENT LIFE/CAMPUS

An attractive aspect of life at Babson is the sense of community, fostered by its size and location. Wrote one student: "very small, very personal, very far from Boston!" Located on a secluded, 450-acre wooded site in Wellesley, Massachusetts, the Babson Campus offers students an idyllic, country-inn atmosphere. Most students enjoy the tranquility of the campus; however, it can feel isolated. Popular events include the Spring Cruise, the Fall and Spring Formals, and "The Buffoonery"—the annual spring talent show in which students spoof their profs (who serve as judges for the event). Because many students live on campus, dorm parties are common. One-third of the student body is foreign, so many of these have international themes. Trips are organized to Martha's Vineyard, Montreal (for skiing), and Boston (for sports events).

Babson offers a small and intimate program—plenty of up-close and personal contact with both faculty and students. One student wrote that the program is "small enough to encourage participation by all." Agreed another, "the school has an attitude of intimacy and is team-oriented." Class size is limited to a maximum of forty-two students. All students are assigned to study sections with a group of thirty-five to forty other students. Students are competitive, but not overly so. They rated themselves as friendly and willing to help each other out. Students are happy with the laid back atmosphere. Wrote one enthusiastic student, "I love it! Students are REALISTIC, so are the profs. No Harvard-type weenies here."

ADMISSIONS

The Babson admissions office ranks your work experience as most important, and then in descending order, GMAT scores, college GPA, essays, the interview (required), letters of recommendation. According to the school, though, "the ranking of these criteria will vary by candidate."

Wrote the school: "At Babson, we consider each candidate as an individual, and look at the entire package, not simply at test scores and GPAs. Accordingly, we require an interview for all full time students. This personal approach provides both Babson and our candidates an opportunity to determine whether there is a 'fit' within the Babson community. We look for goal-oriented individuals with an entrepreneurial spirit, a global mindset, and an ability to grapple with the ambiguities of managing change in a dynamic business world. We also want 'team players' because the success of Babson's integrated approach to management education is predicated upon enthusiastic cooperation among all students."

For the one-year program, applicants must have an undergraduate degree in business administration. Babson batches applications by rounds. There are three rounds for the two-year program and two rounds for the one-year program. Students may defer admission for up to one year.

STUDENT'S OVERVIEW BOX

Overall Happiness

Academic Satisfaction

50   75   100%

Student Opinion   National Average

FACULTY RATING

Student Opinion   National Average

HITS AND MISSES

HITS
Finance dept.
Helping other students
On-campus housing
Gym
Small classes
Entrepreneurship
Mentoring program

MISSES
Accounting dept.
Ethnic & racial diversity
Placement

APPLICANTS ALSO LOOK AT
Penn State U.
Northeastern U.
Boston U.
Boston College

FOR MORE INFORMATION, CONTACT:
Graduate School of Business
Office of Graduate Admission
Babson Park, MA 02157
(617) 235-1200
(800) 488-4512

BOSTON UNIVERSITY SCHOOL OF MANAGEMENT

ADMISSIONS FACTS

Type of school   Private

Demographics
No. of men   350
No. of women   206
No. of minorities   7
No. of int'l students   32

EQUAL TREATMENT GRAPH

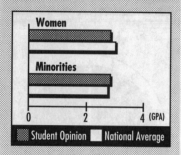

Student Opinion ▪ National Average

Admissions Statistics
Avg. GMAT   585
Avg. undergraduate GPA   3.1
Avg. age at entry   26
No. of applicants   1,127
No. accepted   541
No. enrolled   184

Deadlines and Notifications
Regular application   5/01
Regular notification   within 4 weeks
Special dates   4/01 (int'l students)

Focus of Curriculum
Specialized

Academic Specialties
Operations, MIS, Non-profit Management

Joint Degrees
MBA/JD; MBA/JD with concentration in Health Care Management; MBA/MA in Economics, International Relations, and Medical Sciences; MBA/MS in Management Information Systems, Manufacturing Engineering, and Broadcast Administration.

Special Programs
Leadership, Careers, and Self Assessment Program; Kobe, Japan Program; The Asian Management Field Seminar; International Study in England.

FINANCIAL FACTS

In-state tuition $16,590
Out-of-state tuition   N/A
On-campus housing $6,000

ACADEMICS

The Boston University School of Management is best known for its specialized programs/concentrations. A sizeable number of students come to study in one of the school's many dual degree programs. First-year MBA students take the standard fare of core courses in which faculty utilize theory, case analysis, group projects, and field experiences. These are followed by concentrations in areas such as finance and economics, marketing, management policy, operations, and organizational behavior. Wrote one student, "I came here because of the very good operations department." Praised another MBA, "The MIS department is exceptionally strong." Other stand-out concentrations are Information Systems Management, Health Care Systems, and Public and Not-for-Profit Management. Each of these involves unique coursework and field experiences. Overall, students told us they feel well-prepared by their training in finance, accounting, operations, and general management. The vast majority of students feel less confident about their quantitative and computer skills.

Professors received good grades for their accessibility and teaching, although some students complained that the quality of teaching is uneven. Wrote one disgruntled MBA, "Fifty percent of faculty are excellent, fifty percent are average."

Complaints also extended to BU's administration. Griped one student, "The program is well-designed and specialized programs are great, but the MBA program as a whole gets bogged down in the red tape typical of a large university." Several students told us, "The school focuses too much on its own profit," and that "the tuition is too high in comparison to quality and overall benefits." But help may be on the way. According to one student, "The school is undertaking a Total Quality Management approach and is going to improve much in the near future." Students overwhelmingly said prestige was the most important factor in choosing BU's program. After that, in a three-way tie, students say they chose the school because of the faculty, it was the best school to which they were accepted, and its proximity to home. Students also mentioned the health care management program, operations department, real estate program, and the Boston area as strong drawing cards.

PLACEMENT AND RECRUITING

Like most B-school placement offices, BU's Career Center provides students a variety of workshops on interviewing and job search strategies. An exciting new service is Career Search. According to the school, this "state-of-the-art database covers nearly 180,000 companies with customized retrieval capabilities and allows users to swiftly identify companies that match their interests and experience." Approximately eighty-five companies recruit on campus annually. By graduation, eighty-two percent of the second-year students have accepted a position.

Despite the school's strong placement rate, BU students say they're disappointed with the efforts of the Career Center and range of companies recruiting. On the upside, students are happy with the responsiveness of the alumni, whom the majority contacted for help in their job search.

BOSTON UNIVERSITY SCHOOL OF MANAGEMENT

STUDENT LIFE/CAMPUS

Entering full-time students are divided into sections of roughly fifty students each and take first semester courses together. The sections foster the formation of study groups and help develop camaraderie. The mood here is noncompetitive, relaxed, and cooperative. This may be due in part to the moderate workload. The vast majority of students report they spend roughly twenty hours a week studying/preparing for class, a light schedule by most B-school standards. This leaves plenty of time for extracurriculars, of which there are many. Thursday nights, students hang out at the B.U. Pub; faculty tend to congregate there, too. Favorite activities include student government, ski trips, outings to Boston events, and golf and tennis tournaments. A big crowd turns out for the volleyball matches against Wharton and MIT. One-third of the student body is foreign, which leads to many international social events and "dining" nights. A popular on-campus spot is "The Lounge," a newly built area for MBAs to study and relax. The lounge contains wall size U.S. and world maps with pins designating each student's hometown. Big news: the Computer Club is setting up a BU on-line network, so that students and professors can e-mail each other.

Student relations at BU seem most affected by the mix of full- and part-time students in the same program. Described one MBA, "Students are generally apathetic, probably because most are part-time." Agreed another, "This isn't a place where students hang out with each other." Advised one disgruntled MBA, "the school needs more daytime classes, full-time students, and clubs and activities."

Still another area of complaint was about the poor condition of the school's physical structures and equipment. Wrote one MBA, "Horrible physical facilities. Classrooms have windows that don't close, falling ceilings. Because the building is on a busy street, classrooms are extremely noisy when windows are open (and there's no A/C)." Reported another, "No business school library." Of BU's home city, students are not only complaint-free, but uncharacteristically positive. Raved one, "It combines the best aspects of a college town with a modern urban area. There's tons to do." Summed up one student, "I like preppy people."

ADMISSIONS

The admissions selection process places equal importance on all credentials—essays, college GPA, GMAT score, work experience, letters of recommendation. Interviews are *not* part of the process. Advises the school, "Work experience is strongly preferred. The essay should elaborate on that experience as well as provide the kind of information that could be gained in an interview. BU is interested in attracting a high level of diversity in the classroom—in work experience, ethnicity, nationality, and gender." Decisions are made on a rolling basis in four "cycles," beginning in February for the September cycle (full- and part-time). The Spring cycle is for part-time only. Applicants are advised to apply early and are notified of a decision within three to four weeks of receipt of the completed application. Students may defer admission up to one year.

STUDENT'S OVERVIEW BOX

FACULTY RATING

HITS AND MISSES

HITS
Accounting dept.
Ethnic & racial diversity
Boston

MISSES
Marketing dept.
Don't like classmates
Gym

APPLICANTS ALSO LOOK AT
Boston College
Northeastern U.
Babson College
Syracuse U.
Bentley College

FOR MORE INFORMATION, CONTACT:
Graduate School of Business
685 Commonwealth Ave.
Boston, MA 02215
(617) 353-2673

BRIGHAM YOUNG UNIVERSITY: MARRIOTT SCHOOL OF MANAGEMENT

ADMISSIONS FACTS

Type of school	Private

Demographics

No. of men	200
No. of women	23
No. of minorities	1
No. of int'l students	38

EQUAL TREATMENT GRAPH

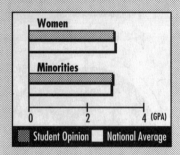

Women

Minorities

0   2   4 (GPA)

Student Opinion   National Average

Admissions Statistics

Avg. GMAT	589
Avg. undergraduate GPA	3.42
Avg. age at entry	26
No. of applicants	281
No. accepted	158
No. enrolled	125

Deadlines and Notifications

Regular application	5/15
Regular notification	within 2 weeks
Special dates	N/A

Focus of Curriculum

General Management

Joint Degrees

General Management, Accounting, Finance

Special Programs

The Executive Lecture Series, Entrepreneurship Lecture Series, International Business Series, Computer Summer Prep

FINANCIAL FACTS

In-state tuition	$4,020
Out-of-state tuition	$6,030
On-campus housing	$5,000

ACADEMICS

Brigham Young University is the official school of the Church of Latter Day Saints (Mormons). According to the school, two slogans greet BYU visitors as they enter the campus: "Enter to Learn; Go Forth to Serve" and "The World is Our Campus." This sets the tone for what is easily one of the most ethics-oriented and spiritual B-schools in the nation. There's a dress code. Students are expected to abstain from drugs, alcohol, and tobacco. In the classroom, ethics and the moral responsibilities of leadership are emphasized. A byproduct of the Mormon affiliation, which requires service in a foreign country, is that over eighty percent of the student body has had one to two years of foreign work experience; eighty-five percent speak a second language, thirty percent a third. The high level of cross-cultural knowledge enhances the study of international business.

BYU features a progressive curriculum. In almost all of the core courses, several professors share the podium, team-teaching cases from a cross-functional perspective. This approach doesn't please everyone, however, as one student griped, "Over emphasis on case method. I feel I'm not getting the practical skills that will be valuable in the short-term."

There are only 120 or so students in each entering MBA class, and during the first year, students take roughly ten core courses in the functional areas. But here's where things get strange: MBA students share the core courses with students from the Master of Organizational Behavior, Master of Accountancy, and Master of Administration Programs. The school lumps *all* the first-year business masters students together and then divides them into more manageable sections of seventy-five students each.

In the second year, there are only two required courses: Ethics and Business Policy. After that, students have twelve electives enabling them to specialize in an area. A popular offering is Management Consulting and Projects where Utah businesses pay students to consult in their organization.

Overall, students say BYU is meeting their academic expectations. Students judged their teamwork, presentation, accounting, general management, and finance skills as strong. But students felt they had weak spots in marketing, operations, quantitative methods, and computers.

PLACEMENT AND RECRUITING

The B-school uses both its own placement personnel and that of the University placement center to assist students in their job search. Workshops are offered on networking, résumés, cover letters, interviewing and negotiations. Individual counseling sessions are also available. Students are entered in a database from which recruiters select candidates for positions. In addition the school compiles a résumé book and intern résumé packets for employers. In 1992, ninety-three percent of the class had a job within three months of graduation. Like many B-school students, BYU MBAs told us they were not entirely satisfied with the efforts of the placement office. They felt a whole lot better about the school's alumni, with whom the school has close ties. Wrote one student, "the network of alumni is large, helpful, and well-respected in their companies."

BRIGHAM YOUNG UNIVERSITY: MARRIOTT SCHOOL OF MANAGEMENT

STUDENT LIFE/CAMPUS

Students report a heavy workload. They crack the books an average of twenty to thirty hours a week. Not surprisingly, they say it's important to do all the required reading. Teamwork is heavily promoted which results in what students report as "a strong camaraderie among the MBA students." Students say they're competitive, but—you know the answer here—most eager to help a fellow classmate out.

Life at a Mormon school can be interesting for a single person. At what is known as "Breed-em Young" University, dating (especially among undergrads) is geared towards finding a mate. Indeed, several B-school students told us they chose BYU to do just this. (Not that we want to get in the personals business, but each was looking for a wife.) Further hindering the social scene is the school honor code which doesn't permit drinking or smoking on campus. Extracurriculars here are devoted to church, family life, informal get-togethers, and outdoor activities in the nearby mountains. The MBA Association sponsors many events, including community service projects such as reading to the blind, and helping foreign students with English. There's even a Vice-President for Community Service. The Mormon community is divided into "wards" of 100 or so families who plan social activities. Non-Mormons are welcome to attend. There's also an active "Spouse Association" that organizes dinners and outings. According to one student, "Single housing is great. Married housing is terrible (old apartments that are expensive)." The majority of students opt to live in suburban-style garden apartments off-campus in the foothills of the Wasatch mountains.

As for diversity: forget it. The majority of students here are Mormons. They're conservative. They're white. Of the student body, seventy percent are married—many have two or more children. Non-Mormons do attend school here. But the only part of the honor code they're exempted from is mandatory church attendance.

ADMISSIONS

According to the admissions office, your GMAT score is considered most important. After that, in descending order, your college GPA, letter of intent, letters of recommendation, language spoken, work experience, and leadership activities are considered. Writes the school, "Though we look carefully at GMAT and GPA qualifications, we also look at the person behind the numbers. The letter of intent and letters of recommendations are valuable resources in getting acquainted with the person. We strongly suggest prerequisites in Accounting, Economics, and Statistics, as well as computer skills. Because of the international emphasis in our MBA program we look at favorably at applicants who speak a second and third language. We like to look at what the student brings to the program. As a result we encourage any undergraduate major except business, and we also encourage some work experience." Brigham Young utilizes a rolling admissions process. Applicants are notified of a decision within two weeks of receipt of their completed application. Students may defer admission for up to one year for either a mission or specialized work.

STUDENT'S OVERVIEW BOX

FACULTY RATING

HITS AND MISSES

HITS
Finance dept.
Classmates are smart
On-campus housing
Family

MISSES
Marketing dept.
Ethnic & racial diversity
Recruiting

APPLICANTS ALSO LOOK AT
(not available)

FOR MORE INFORMATION, CONTACT:
Marriott School of Management
730 Tanner Building
Provo, UT 84602
(801) 378-4121

UNIVERSITY OF BUFFALO—STATE UNIVERSITY OF NEW YORK

ADMISSIONS FACTS

Type of school	Public

Demographics

No. of men	264
No. of women	127
No. of minorities	tktk
No. of int'l students	tktk

EQUAL TREATMENT GRAPH

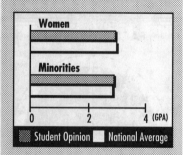

Women

Minorities

0   2   4 (GPA)

▨ Student Opinion   ☐ National Average

Admissions Statistics

Avg. GMAT	573
Avg. undergraduate GPA	3.00
Avg. age at entry	26
No. of applicants	1,454
No. accepted	541
No. enrolled	290

Deadlines and Notifications

Regular application	7/15
Regular notification	5/01
Special dates	N/A

Focus of Curriculum

Generalized, with specialization

Academic Specialties

Accounting, Finance, Marketing, General Management

Joint Degrees

JD/MBA, MBA/MA in Asian Studies, MBA/MPH

FINANCIAL FACTS

In-state tuition	$3,200
Out-of-state tuition	$6,516
On-campus housing	N/A

ACADEMICS

Why do students go to the University of Buffalo (UB) B-school? Because "the state school tuition is cheap," UB provides the "best education for the money," "it's close to home," and it offers the "3-2 program," the latter of which permits undergraduates to submatriculate into the B-school without work experience and complete their degrees in five years. But this is where the complaints begin. As one student put it, "The 3-2 program is the school's largest drawback. There are as many 3-2 students as there are those with job experience. They fail to bring experiences into the classroom that enhance the learning process or elevate us to a great B-school." Overall, student discontent at UB runs deep and wide, although one exasperated student wrote, "A lot of people go to UB because they live in Buffalo or because it's affordable...then they complain about it!" Yes, they do—in buckets. The quality of faculty is another point of discontent. While the majority agree, "The faculty are well-versed in their respective fields, and are interested in and accessible to students," a not insignificant minority feel differently. Griped one, "The teachers have really cushy, high-paying jobs, but don't provide insights beyond the textbook." Complained others "the profs are rude," "they're more concerned with publication than teaching," and "classes are boring." Even more damning, "Teachers are extremely lazy, they force the students to teach the class with constant presentations." On the upside, students said registration for classes is very easy compared to the whole university, the accounting program is tops, teamwork is emphasized, and "the administration is trying hard to make UB a better place." They better hurry.

UB offers students a basic two-year, generalist MBA with a concentration in one or more functional areas. Students take thirteen required core courses over the four-semester program. During the second year students use up to eight electives to tailor their students to career interests. The basic teaching methodology is lecture/discussion, but students report, "The school is moving more to case study." Professors utilize simulated business games, group projects, report writing, and role-playing. One student describes a unique platform for learning: "Local industry provides insightful guest lecturers both in class and in career activities like workshops." Writes another, "UB is very good at securing internships." Students spend one to two days a week at the sponsoring company. Summed up one student, "It is possible to get an excellent education here, but the student has to work hard and go beyond the classroom experience."

PLACEMENT AND RECRUITING

UB has its own B-school placement office. Résumé writing and job-search skills workshops are available, as are one-on-one counseling sessions with placement staff. According to the school, the mean salary for graduates with two or more years of work experience is "more than twenty-five percent above the reported national average."

Sounds good. But UB MBAs still sound off: "The job placement service is one of the areas that definitely needs improvement." Students say they need more and a wider range of companies recruiting on-campus. Griped another, "Alumni are not utilized at all."

UNIVERSITY OF BUFFALO–STATE UNIVERSITY OF NEW YORK

STUDENT LIFE/CAMPUS

Students here grind through a heavy workload, and bury themselves in their books an average of twenty to thirty hours per week. The majority find their study groups helpful, but still report a fair amount of pressure. Students wish more of the work was substantive and challenging. In particular, one student said, "There is way too much group work just for the sake of group work." There is an average of twenty-five to thirty students in each class.

They're not the note-burning type, but they are very competitive. Still, with all the emphasis on teamwork, UB MBAs are just as interested in helping fellow classmates out. Confirmed one, "Very friendly atmosphere." But according to the students in our survey, they're not too interested in being friends. So it's not surprising that the majority of students also told us they don't intend to stay in touch after graduation. Remember, though, many students chose this school because it's close to home. This tends to hinder on-campus social life/friendships. Also, those 3-2 students seem to annoy everyone. As for racial and ethnic diversity, several students say this school has got to do a better job. Wrote one, "For a black person, this school is silently hostile."

According to students, specialized clubs (Finance, Marketing, etc.) provide career-related extracurriculars. The Graduate Management Association sponsors mixers, and other get-togethers. Of course, you can always join the Precision Briefcase Marching Drill Team, the goofiest activity around. Sports are big. Wrote one student, "The UB basketball and football teams are now Division one." Reported another MBA, "The new student union is now completed, as well as a commons area with several stores." Buffalo's a decent town, and the housing off-campus is much better than the so-so on-campus accommodations. However, parking is terrible and the winter is loooong.

ADMISSIONS

Although Buffalo has rather modest application standards, the disproportionate size of its applicant pool keeps the process competitive. After grades and GMAT scores, Buffalo takes work experience into account. Only then do personal statements, recommendations and undergraduate course work come into play. On the academic front, Buffalo's admissions committee looks for candidates with strong math skills.

STUDENT'S OVERVIEW BOX

FACULTY RATING

HITS AND MISSES

HITS
Safety
Accounting dept.
Ethnically and racially diverse

MISSES
Diverse work experience
Social life
Placement

APPLICANTS ALSO LOOK AT
(not available)

FOR MORE INFORMATION, CONTACT:
School of Management
206 Jacobs Management Center
Buffalo, NY 14260
(716) 645-3204

UNIVERSITY OF CALIFORNIA–BERKELEY: WALTER A. HAAS SCHOOL OF BUSINESS

ADMISSIONS FACTS

Type of school	Public

Demographics

No. of men	299
No. of women	130
No. of minorities	67
No. of int'l students	135

EQUAL TREATMENT GRAPH

Women

Minorities

0   2   4 (GPA)

▓ Student Opinion ▢ National Average

Admissions Statistics

Avg. GMAT	636
Avg. undergraduate GPA	3.28
Avg. age at entry	27
No. of applicants	2,090
No. accepted	505
No. enrolled	224

Deadlines and Notifications

Regular application	3/01
Regular notification	within 6 weeks
Special dates	11/15 (early adm.)

Focus of Curriculum

General Management

Academic Specialties

International Business, Management of Technology, Innovation and Entrepreneurship, Real Estate

Joint Degrees

JD/MBA, MBA/MA in Asian Studies, MBA/MPH

Special Programs

International summer internships, Language workshops, Partners in Entrepreneurial Leadership (PEL)

FINANCIAL FACTS

In-state tuition	$2,918
Out-of-state tuition	$10,617
On-campus housing	$4,359

ACADEMICS

By any yardstick, Berkeley is one of the nation's best public B-schools. First-years take a minimum of seven out of ten required courses. These provide a foundation of analytical tools and basic skills. Second-years choose from over 195 electives offered both within and outside the B-school. Two joint curriculum programs, one in Management of Technology, with the College of Engineering and the other in Real Estate Development, with both the Department of City and Regional Planning and the Center for Real Estate and Urban Economics, are among the country's most respected.

Of equal renown is the school's international focus. Faculty have integrated international content into virtually every MBA course. Students wrote, "Berkeley is a great place for an international perspective." And, "Berkeley has a large percentage of the student population from overseas or with foreign job experience." Several students wrote they selected Berkeley because of its entrepreneurship studies. Commented one would-be entrepreneur, "Outstanding training—enough to get anyone launched." Partners in Entrepreneurial Leadership (PEL) offers training programs for aspiring entrepreneurs. Students complete a "residency" with a high-growth company for seven months. As part of the program, interns attend biweekly classes on entrepreneurial management.

Overall, students said they chose Haas because of its value, prestige, geographic location, and access to the biotech industry and firms in Silicon Valley. One student summed it up this way: "High quality, low cost, diverse students, and the beautiful Bay Area." Still another added, "When one looks at the whole Berkeley package of value relative to costs for a B-school, Haas comes out at the very top." Of the first-rate faculty, students said forty to sixty percent of their professors are recognized leaders in their field. They also gave them high marks for their teaching abilities. Explained one, "Faculty are very vigorous and energetic in their teaching, as well as in their research. They like being at Haas, that's why."

PLACEMENT AND RECRUITING

Berkeley's Career Center helps students secure international summer internships. Many of these are underwritten by corporations. To further prepare students for global careers, Berkeley offers language workshops. MBAs also make yearly pilgrimages to businesses abroad. Annual destinations are Japan and other Pacific Rim countries, Eastern Europe/St. Petersburg, and Mexico/Latin America. Berkeley is also a member of the MBA Enterprise Corps, which matches recent grads to Eastern European companies.

The Career Center brings in over 150 employers for on-campus interviews. Despite these efforts, students find career center services lacking. One wrote, "The Career Center is gradually improving and should be a great resource in a couple of years." Alumni are considered key in the job search; almost all students contacted someone and said he/she was helpful. Eighty-five percent of the Haas MBA class of '92 had been placed three months after graduation.

UNIVERSITY OF CALIFORNIA–BERKELEY: WALTER A. HAAS SCHOOL OF BUSINESS

STUDENT LIFE/CAMPUS

Everyone agrees, the physical structures at Berkeley—classrooms, study lounges, library, and computer center—are in bad shape. A typical complaint was, "outstanding school, lousy facilities." Thanks to a $24 million donation from the Haas family of Levi Strauss & Co., a new state-of-the-art structure and 200,000 square-foot campus will be completed in 1994. A majority of students live off-campus in apartments in the Berkeley/Oakland area. Students wrote they love the college-town atmosphere of Berkeley, the ambiance of the Bay Area and its proximity to Napa Valley. Three hours away, Tahoe provides opportunities for skiing. Reported one student, "Haas is the best combination of city and nature."

Students at Berkeley like each other. They describe a "splendid social life." They date, they go out in groups, they "know how to have fun." Extracurriculars include intramural sports, student-run clubs and—no surprise here—student government. This may be because Berkeley encourages students to have a say in just about everything—classes, administration, and policy. Many programs are student initiated and run. An annual event is the Serv-A-Thon (a weekend of volunteer work). Favorite watering holes are the Triple Rock and Bison micro-breweries. For burgers and blues, students head to Larry Blake's. A final note: students agree that the student body is ethnically and socially diverse.

The Haas School is a small program of 440 MBA students, seventy-five full-time faculty, and fifty visiting professors/lecturers in the midst of a huge (31,000 students) university. MBA students share a sense of community fostered by the small size of the program. Students are competitive, but not sharks. The learning environment is cooperative; classmates go out of their way to help each other. "Everyone takes time to explain concepts and issues to others," shared one student. But alas, someone longed for a bit of blood—one student complained, "Students could be a bit more aggressive." Classmates rated each other as smart. Raved one, "The people at Berkeley really make this program stand out!"

ADMISSIONS

The admissions office reports that it accepts applications during one long "continuous cycle" which goes from November to March. Students are notified of a decision generally within six weeks of a file's completion, except for the final deadline. One-year deferments are granted on a case-by-case basis only for extraordinary circumstances, (death, illness, etc.) According to Berkeley, "The admissions committee reviews files and makes decisions continuously. Applicants who apply prior to the final deadline have a stronger chance of being admitted."

The following criteria is considered in descending order of importance: the essays, work experience, GMAT score, letters of recommendation, extracurricular activities.

STUDENT'S OVERVIEW BOX

FACULTY RATING

HITS AND MISSES

HITS
Marketing dept.
Diverse work experience
School clubs
Global study
Tuition
Alumni mentors
The Bay area

MISSES
Accounting dept.
On-campus housing
Facilities
Library

APPLICANTS ALSO LOOK AT
Mass. Inst. of Tech.
Dartmouth College
Columbia U.
Northwestern U.
New York University
Cornell U.
UNC Chapel Hill
U Southern CA

FOR MORE INFORMATION, CONTACT:
Walter A. Haas School of Business
MBA Programs, 350 Barrows Hall
Berkeley, CA 94720
(510) 642-1405

UNIVERSITY OF CALIFORNIA–LOS ANGELES: JOHN E. ANDERSON GRADUATE SCHOOL OF MANAGEMENT

ADMISSIONS FACTS

Type of school	Public

Demographics

No. of men	249
No. of women	101
No. of minorities	66
No. of int'l students	66

EQUAL TREATMENT GRAPH

Women

Minorities

0   2   4 (GPA)

▦ Student Opinion ■ National Average

Admissions Statistics

Avg. GMAT	640
Avg. undergraduate GPA	3.5
Avg. age at entry	27
No. of applicants	3,700
No. accepted	700
No. enrolled	370

Deadlines and Notifications

Regular application	3/24
Regular notification	rolling
Special dates	N/A

Focus of Curriculum

General Management

Academic Specialties

Entrepreneurial Studies, Finance, Marketing, MIS, Arts Management

Joint Degrees

JD/MBA, MBA/MA in Latin American Studies, MBA/MA in Urban Planning

Special Programs

The Center for International Business, Education & Research, The Center for Finance & Real Estate, The Center for Technology Management

FINANCIAL FACTS

In-state tuition	N/A
Out-of-state tuition	N/A
On-campus housing	N/A

ACADEMICS

The Anderson School of Business places great emphasis on the balance between theory and practice. Classroom learning is supplemented with internships, consulting projects and other off-campus programs in what the school calls the "laboratory of Los Angeles." There are three main components to the curriculum: the management core, advanced electives, and field study. Students can take electives in other departments at the university to build an interdisciplinary area of strength. Two of the most popular areas are arts management, and entertainment management. Students run to take electives in the graduate school of film, where they get a taste of Hollywood in Peter Guber's "The Development Process in Feature Film Productions" course. One happy student wrote, "Anderson's program caters to individual needs." Anderson's "capstone" experience, the management field study, offers teams of students experiential instruction in companies such as Disney, the L.A. Dodgers, and Bugle Boy.

The hottest area of study at Anderson is Entrepreneurship. In 1991, the Association of Collegiate Entrepreneurs designated Anderson's entrepreneurial program the best in the U.S. It offers an incomparable array of experiences: mentoring, small-business consulting, a venture proposal competition, visiting entrepreneur series, and assistance with placement in venture capital and portfolio companies. An equally exciting program is the International Management Fellows (IMF) Program, which offers an immersion in international business, culture, and language. It runs concurrently with the regular MBA program, takes twenty-four months to complete, and involves a total of nine months outside the U.S., as well as intensive language/cultural instruction. Japanese, French, German, and Spanish tracks are available. In addition to the newcomer specialties of international business and entrepreneurship, UCLA is well known for its outstanding finance department.

All in all, the majority of students say that taking time off to pursue an Anderson MBA is well worth it. Students we surveyed rated their general management skills as very strong. Students also doled out high marks for their marketing, finance, and accounting finesse. They judged themselves to be weaker in operations, quantitative methods, and computer skills. Another disappointment: the faculty. The school has brilliant, though not necessarily eloquent teachers. Problems with teaching quality are most evident in the core courses. Electives profs are among students' favorites.

PLACEMENT AND RECRUITING

Approximately 200 companies recruit for permanent positions on-campus annually. In 1992, eighty-six percent of the class had accepted an offer by the end of the academic year. According to the school, four percent had no offers. The remainder were not seeking employment, or were undecided with their career plans. Despite these figures, students told us they were moderately satisfied with the efforts of the placement office. Students were much more pleased with the school's alumni, whom they contacted in their job search and found very helpful.

University of California–Los Angeles: John E. Anderson Graduate School of Management

Student Life/Campus

Students report a manageable workload, spending roughly twenty to thirty hours a week studying. To encourage student bonding, the entering class of 360 is divided into sections of approximately sixty each. Each semester students are rotated into a new cohort; by the end of the year, you've been shuffled in the deck so much, you've met everyone in your class.

The B-school is housed in one high-rise building in which undergrads also take classes. A new seven-building B-school complex is in the process of being built, and should go a long way toward enhancing student life and fostering a strong school identity. UCLA is located in West L.A., adjacent to Westwood Village, a trendy neighborhood of shops and restaurants catering to the college crowd. The majority of students opt to live off-campus in nearby Brentwood and Santa Monica, or further out in the Hermosa and Long Beach communities.

Along with their sunglasses and tans, Anderson students sport a laid back attitude. They're competitive, but not out to demolish each other. Classroom dynamics don't require it. Unlike case study classes at Harvard and Darden, classes here rarely place students in the hot seat. Professors are more likely to open a case with a "softball" (a question that guides the student to the answer) than a hard cold call. Students also report there is a great deal of camaraderie. Much of student life revolves around the activities of the student run clubs. Every Thursday a "Beer Bust" is held, on the outdoor patio, of course, after which everyone heads to the bar of the week. Especially popular are intramural sports and volleyball on the beach. Student involvement is also important. After the L.A. riots in the spring of 1992, students went out in the community to pitch in and clean up. Several work in a mentor program with ex-gang members.

One student paid this compliment to fellow classmates: "Anderson has quality students with quality backgrounds (career and education)." Added another, "We also have the best looking undergrads."

Admissions

Writes the admissions office, "In evaluating applications for admission, the school looks for evidence of exceptional academic ability and managerial potential. An applicant's leadership qualities, interpersonal skills, personal values and unique character are especially important to us. On average, an application is read by two to three individuals. Included is the input of a number of readers (faculty, admission officers, second year students alumni.)" A special effort is made to recruit minority students. Notes the school, "Our minority graduate advisors (Black, Latino, and Asian MBA students at Anderson) play an important role in providing information and counseling for prospective minority applicants. Advisors assist in arranging visits to the campus and annually organize an MBA Information Day for minority applicants." Decisions are made on a rolling admissions basis although applications are batched in rounds. It is advisable to apply in the earlier rounds.

STUDENT'S OVERVIEW BOX

Overall Happiness

Academic Satisfaction

50 75 100%

Student Opinion ■ National Average

FACULTY RATING

Student Opinion ■ National Average

HITS AND MISSES

HITS
Finance
Internationalization
Diverse work experience
Teamwork
Alumni recruiting

MISSES
Marketing
On-campus housing
Campus safety

APPLICANTS ALSO LOOK AT
Northwestern U.
UNC Chapel Hill
New York University
Harvard
U Michigan
Claremont Graduate School

FOR MORE INFORMATION, CONTACT:
John E. Anderson Graduate School of
Management at UCLA
405 Hilgard Avenue
Los Angeles, CA 90024-1448
(310) 825-7982

CARNEGIE MELLON UNIVERSITY GRADUATE SCHOOL OF INDUSTRIAL ADMINISTRATION

ADMISSIONS FACTS

Type of school	Private

Demographics

No. of men	323
No. of women	72
No. of minorities	32
No. of int'l students	103

EQUAL TREATMENT GRAPH

Women

Minorities

0   2   4 (GPA)

Student Opinion   National Average

Admissions Statistics

Avg. GMAT	638
Avg. undergraduate GPA	3.12
Avg. age at entry	25
No. of applicants	1,316
No. accepted	445
No. enrolled	189

Deadlines and Notifications

Regular application	3/15
Regular notification	4/15

Focus of Curriculum

Specialized

Academic Specialties

Management Information Systems, Entrepreneurship, Production/Operations Management

Joint Degrees

MS in Information Networking, JD/MSIA, Joint Master's Program with the Engineering College, Collaborative program with the School of Urban and Public Affairs

Special Programs

Exchange programs in Europe, Japan & Mexico, Total Quality Management University Challenge, Program in Financial Analysis and Security Training

FINANCIAL FACTS

In-state tuition	$18,500
Out-of-state tuition	$18,500
On-campus housing	$5,670

ACADEMICS

Carnegie Mellon offers the Master of Science in Industrial Administration (MSIA), which is similar to an MBA. Don't worry, the program is accredited as a graduate B-school by the American Association of Collegiate Schools of Business. Carnegie Mellon is particularly renowned for its innovative breakthroughs in both education and research. In fact, there are too many to list here. Let's just say if you go to school here you'll study among Nobel-prize winning faculty who are expanding the frontiers of business. True to their emphasis on innovation, the Graduate School of Industrial Administration (GSIA) has scrapped the traditional fall/spring semester. In its place, four seven-and-a-half week long mini-semesters make up the school year. Students appreciate the school's trailblazing. Wrote one, "When I talk with friends at other B-schools, I always find GSIA is in the forefront of teaching techniques." Raves another, "The school is a leader; take a look at the research that comes out of here."

Particularly noteworthy is the "Management Game," a computer simulation of a consumer products company, which students are required to take in the final semester. "Game" teams meet with a board of directors (four of whom are corporate executives), negotiate mock contracts with actual representatives from unions, secure "financing" through Pittsburgh banks, and obtain legal advice from third-year law students.

GSIA has a reputation as a quantitative, technical school. But one student wrote, "GSIA's curriculum is frequently misunderstood by applicants. The school is technical, but this doesn't mean you won't become a strong generalist. GSIA emphasizes a generalist education while exposing you to the technical and theoretical business functions." But one student complained, "The school needs to tone down on the quant stuff. If you're not comfortable with numbers don't come here." Happily, students said the school is strong in other areas. For example, thirty to forty percent of all graduates are entrepreneurs. They rate the entrepreneurial classes as excellent. And a recent one million dollar gift from Pittsburgh entrepreneur Donald H. Jones will go a long ways towards further establishing an entrepreneurship center at the school. Students also give high marks to the finance department. Wrote one, "GSIA is the best-kept finance secret of the top twenty B-schools."

PLACEMENT AND RECRUITING

The Career Opportunities Center (C.O.C.) strongly encourages first-years to pursue summer internships. Thirty to thirty-five percent of students are offered permanent positions through summer internships.

According to the school, in 1991–1992, the C.O.C handled 2,815 on-campus interviews. Despite all this, students were only moderately satisfied with the C.O.C. Wrote one, "My primary complaint—C.O.C. isn't too swift. Companies are attracted to the quality of the school; they're not here because of C.O.C.'s efforts." Said another, "Recruiting could be better."

CARNEGIE MELLON UNIVERSITY GRADUATE SCHOOL OF INDUSTRIAL ADMINISTRATION

STUDENT LIFE/CAMPUS

First-year students report a killer, barely survivable workload. This is compounded by the acceleration of the mini-semester schedule and up-all-night number crunching assignments. According to our survey, this is a source of great stress. Fortunately, many courses are structured around team projects and most students rely on help from their study groups. MBAs at GSIA get to know each other quickly. A total student body of 400 fosters a "close-knit group of people." Students rated their classmates as very smart, interested in helping each other and competitive, but not out for blood. Wrote one, "Students are high caliber and hard working." But one student reported, "There's a wide variance in student abilities."

Again and again students told us the "new building and facilities are great." Indeed, new additions recently doubled the physical size of the B-school. The campus is located in the Oakland section of Pittsburgh which has college-town characteristics. The immediate neighborhood is tree-lined and residential. Indeed, because on-campus housing is not available, many students live in the nearby communities of Shadyside, Oakland, and Squirrel Hill, which are among Pittsburgh's trendiest. As for Pittsburgh, well, your ideas about it are wrong. Consistently rated one of America's most livable cities, it's clean, modern, and teeming with cultural events. Back on campus, the volunteer GSIA social committee organizes many school events; picnics, holiday parties, boat cruises, and talent shows are all regular events. But students say their social life is hindered by the ultra-heavy workload. Weekends are spent at informal get-togethers at student's homes. Of the student body, students agree that their classmates are ethnically and racially diverse. As for types, one student told us there are "a lot of conservative geeks." But you know the saying—it takes one to know one.

ADMISSIONS

According to the admissions office, the following criteria are weighted equally: essays, college GPA, letters of recommendation, extracurricular activities, work experience, interview (required), and GMAT score. Notes the school, "When we evaluate an application, we try to understand that person as an individual. For example, we examine the entire academic record—grade trends, the major, the school extracurriculars, and part-time work, if any." Applications are batched in rounds. The admissions office suggests applying in round two.

STUDENT'S OVERVIEW BOX

FACULTY RATING

HITS AND MISSES

HITS
Quant skills
Classmates are smart
Pittsburgh
Innovative curriculum
Consulting projects

MISSES
Accounting dept.
Administration
Social life
Gym

APPLICANTS ALSO LOOK AT

Cornell U.
Mass. Inst. of Tech.
UNC Charlotte
U Chicago
U Michigan
U Rochester
New York University
Boston College

FOR MORE INFORMATION, CONTACT:
Graduate School of Industrial
Administration
Schenley Park
Pittsburgh, PA 15213-3890
(412) 268-2272

CASE WESTERN RESERVE: WEATHERHEAD SCHOOL OF MANAGEMENT

ADMISSIONS FACTS

Type of school	Private

Demographics

No. of men	212
No. of women	111
No. of minorities	41
No. of int'l students	73

EQUAL TREATMENT GRAPH

Women

Minorities

0   2   4 (GPA)

Student Opinion   National Average

Admissions Statistics

Avg. GMAT	590
Avg. undergraduate GPA	3.22
Avg. age at entry	27
No. of applicants	664
No. accepted	399
No. enrolled	152

Deadlines and Notifications

Regular application	4/01
Regular notification	rolling
Special dates	N/A

Focus of Curriculum

General Management

Academic Specialties

Industrial Marketing, Commercial Banking, MIS, Health Systems Management, Entrepreneurship, Operations Management.

Joint Degrees

JD/MBA, MBA/MS in Management Science, MBA/MS in Nursing

Special Programs

The Weatherhead Mentor Program, International Exchange Programs, the 42 Credit-Hour Accelerated Curriculum

FINANCIAL FACTS

In-state tuition	$15,900
Out-of-state tuition	$15,900
On-campus housing	$4,900

ACADEMICS

The Weatherhead School of Management (WSOM) takes an almost liberal arts approach to business education. Entering students participate in a Management Assessment and Development Exercise to diagnose strengths and weaknesses, and develop a competency-based learning plan. At the close of the exercise, students list the academic and extracurricular activities—courses, internships, mentorships—they'll need to complete their learning plan. Faculty advisors check that it meets degree requirements, and their self-styled MBA program is launched. Of course, MBAs still take the prescribed set of core courses. In addition, they take two team-taught, interdisciplinary Perspectives Courses, which focus on global management, industrial development, or technology management. According to one student, these courses "bring students in touch with how they and others think." Particularly impressive are all the opportunities outside the classroom. Notes the school, "Approximately twenty-five percent of courses require field projects in which students work with local companies and nonprofit organizations for their research." During the second year, students take six electives to complete their learning plan and specialize. Grading goes by an old-fashioned A, B, C, D—there's no forced curve. But this doesn't mean that the academic environment isn't challenging or demanding. According to students, there have been expensive trade-offs associated with the eclectic, participatory model of learning. Wrote one student, "The school's intense focus on the qualitative approach has led to quantitative disciplines being almost completely ignored. I feel sorry for any students coming from a liberal arts background. Should these students enter positions requiring quantitative skills, I suspect the learning curve will resemble the North Face of the Eiger—very steep and very difficult to climb."

PLACEMENT AND RECRUITING

The Office of Career Planning and Placement (OCP&P) hosts recruiter receptions and career forums in addition to requisite services. A résumé book is made available to recruiters who may not come to campus. Students may attend the MBA Placement Consortium in Chicago, a cooperative interviewing day with several other B-schools.

In 1992, over 105 companies recruited on campus. An impressive ninety-five percent of the graduating class had a job within three months of graduation. The major recruiters: Ernst and Young, The Cleveland Clinic Foundation, Coca-Cola, Bank One, Anderson Consulting, and Ford Motor company. Although the OCP&P recently moved into new and larger facilities and added a second director to its staff, students were disappointed with the services of the placement office. Wrote one, "While improvements have been made in the placement office, much more effort in this area is needed in the future." On the upside of things, students were extremely happy with the role alumni played in their career search. The majority of students surveyed contacted alumni and found their counsel useful.

CASE WESTERN RESERVE: WEATHERHEAD SCHOOL OF MANAGEMENT

STUDENT LIFE/CAMPUS

A total student body of 250, small classes, lots of student/faculty interaction—as one student put it, "One of the best advantages of WSOM is its size." Students here are among the least competitive of all the B-schools we surveyed. There's pressure to succeed, and under the new curriculum, students report a moderately heavy workload. Students spend about thirty-five to forty-five hours a week studying and completing group assignments.

Case Western's hometown is Cleveland—a livable city that boasts the third largest number of Fortune 500 industrial corporate headquarters in America. For an urban school, Case Western is surprisingly campus-like, with wide open spaces and plenty of greenery. The school's management computer laboratory was the first to provide a fully integrated network of PCs for MBAs. But as modern as the computer center is, the library is a dinosaur. Griped one MBA, "Business info is either difficult to obtain or unavailable." However, the school is considering the construction of a new library in the next five years.

According to students, both on- or off-campus housing is terrific. Most students prefer apartment living in divided homes in the tree-lined streets of Cleveland Heights or Shaker Heights, a short walk away from campus. The social scene is dominated by the Graduate Student Association, which organizes activities like intramural sports, parties, and the survival series happy hour, although one student said this organization is "limited." Thursday nights, everyone heads to the designated bar of the week. Favorites are the Euclid Tavern and Knotty Pine.

Almost fifty percent of the students are from Cleveland. Otherwise, this school seriously values diversity. Thirty-four of the student population is international. An above average number of women are enrolled: forty-one percent. Although only ten percent of the students are minorities, the general atmosphere is one of acceptance. It wouldn't be a stretch to call WSOM a progressive institution.

ADMISSIONS

According to the admissions office, your college GPA is most important, and then in descending order, work experience, GMAT score, the interview, essays, letters of recommendation, and extracurricular activities. Personal interviews are recommended for admission. Students may defer admission for up to one year. College seniors are admitted with a mandatory deferral of two years.

STUDENT'S OVERVIEW BOX

Overall Happiness

Academic Satisfaction

50   75   100%

Student Opinion   National Average

FACULTY RATING

Student Opinion   National Average

HITS AND MISSES

HITS
Accounting dept.
Diverse work experience
Ethnic & racial diversity
School clubs

MISSES
Quant skills
Library

APPLICANTS ALSO LOOK AT
U Iowa
Indiana U.-Bloom.
Ohio State U.

FOR MORE INFORMATION, CONTACT:
Weatherhead School of Management
310 Enterprise Hall
10900 Euclid Avenue
Cleveland, OH 44106-7235
(216) 368-2030/2069

UNIVERSITY OF CHICAGO GRADUATE SCHOOL OF BUSINESS

ADMISSIONS FACTS

Type of school	Private

Demographics

No. of men	850
No. of women	264
No. of minorities	144
No. of int'l students	286

EQUAL TREATMENT GRAPH

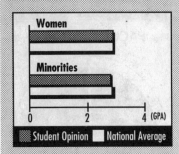

Women

Minorities

0   2   4 (GPA)

▨ Student Opinion ▢ National Average

Admissions Statistics

Avg. GMAT	637
Avg. undergraduate GPA	3.3
Avg. age at entry	26
No. of applicants	2,752
No. accepted	995
No. enrolled	452

Deadlines and Notifications

Regular application	4/01
Regular notification	within 6 weeks
Special dates	N/A

Focus of Curriculum

General Management

Academic Specialties

Accounting, Economics, Finance, Total Quality Management

FINANCIAL FACTS

In-state tuition	$19,250
Out-of-state tuition	$19,250
On-campus housing	$9,000

ACADEMICS

The University of Chicago has a lot to boast about. For starters, it's the first B-school to boast a Nobel laureate on its faculty. It's also the first to publish a scholarly business journal and initiate a Ph.D. program. But Chicago hasn't chosen to rest on its laurels. As one student put it, "This school is continuously trying to improve itself. There are so many innovative opportunities here, it's sometimes hard to concentrate." Chief among them is LEAD, a first-year mandatory leadership program that students—not faculty—design and reformulate each year. Raved one Chicago MBA, "Mention our revolutionary approach to business education: LEAD—a student-driven program of interpersonal and multicultural learning, and teamwork." But the innovation doesn't stop here. An equally exciting program is Chicago's New Product Laboratory, through which teams of students consult to major corporations. But this is no ordinary fieldwork. Students are brought in at a high enough level that they're asked to sign confidentiality agreements. Still another stand-out program is the Argonne Chicago Development Corporation. Budding entrepreneurs get a chance to commercialize the scientific inventions of Chicago's faculty and of scientists at Argonne National Laboratory. Summed up one enthusiastic student, "Chicago is brilliant theoretically, and more applications-oriented than ever."

As for the basic two-year curriculum, students declare it's "the single most flexible around." Other than the non-credit, year-long LEAD program, there are no specifically required courses. Students can waive out of every core course if they've mastered the material before. Confirmed one MBA, "You can pretty much take whatever class you want." Students specialize by bundling four courses in one discipline. A unique area of study is Total Quality Management; the school has designated this up and coming field as true concentration.

Chicago is probably best-known for its quantitative, economics, and finance departments. But "Chicago is not for everyone," claims one student; "it's extremely numbers-heavy. And not every department is equally strong." According to our survey, two departments in which students feel their skills are subpar in relation to their other skills are marketing and operations. However, they feel Chicago's faculty is "not just excellent, but brilliant." Exclaimed one student, "The faculty is both world-class from a research standpoint and outstandingly able to convey complex concepts in a sensible manner." A few flaws in this academic Eden: students say there should be more casework as well as a global focus in curriculum. They also say the facilities—athletic, placement, and classrooms—need a facelift.

PLACEMENT AND RECRUITING

Amazing—a groups of students who say they're satisfied with their career placement office. We're not surprised. In 1992, 230 companies recruited on campus for both summer internships and full-time positions. Another 400 listed job openings by mail/phone. Ninety-five percent of the second year class had a job by graduation. Top employers of Chicago MBAs are Deloitte and Touche, McKinsey, J.P. Morgan & Company, Hewlett-Packard, and Proctor and Gamble. As for 1993, the school writes, "We are seeing an eighteen percent increase in interviews this year."

UNIVERSITY OF CHICAGO GRADUATE SCHOOL OF BUSINESS

STUDENT LIFE/CAMPUS

As one student put it, "The pressure here is subjective, although certainly the workload is substantial." The most pressure seems to come from trying to juggle a job search with academics. Complained one MBA, "This place would deliver a better business education if there were less conflict with full-time job searching. Ask people how many pass/fail classes they take." The majority of students work in study groups. Classes tend to be large, and it can be difficult to get into the most popular ones. As for the classes themselves, one student wrote, "Some are mostly problem sets and exams, some are mostly papers and presentations, and some are both."

Over and over, students told us they were "pleasantly surprised" by the "attitudes of the other students." Explained one student, "Classmates are more inclined to help each other out, rather than stab each other in the back." Reported another, "Students are competitive, but collegial, too." Of the professionally diverse student body, most are "extremely bright, intense, and ambitious." Reported another, "The caliber of students here is first rate, yet there aren't many 'attitudes' coming from New York City types." Still, there were a few complaints. One student wrote, "Anal retentiveness is rampant!" Added another, "Students are not well-rounded; they're too focused on business."

The school is located on a beautiful campus in the Hyde Park section of Chicago, not one of the city's safest spots. But students say housing, either on- or off-campus is considered safe, affordable, and attractive. Students also told us that "the B-school exists in a separate world from the rest of the University." As for the social scene, it's teeming with activity. There are plenty of planned activities, both professional and social. Wrote one student, "For those of us who like to party, there are plenty of events at least three nights a week. I really feel like I'm back in college." As for students whose partners plan on joining the Student Spouse group, one student warned, "They're extremely patronizing to working spouses. They offer cooking lessons and decorating tips. Ridiculous."

ADMISSIONS

According to the admissions office, your GMAT scores, work experience, essays, college GPA, letters of recommendation, and extracurricular activities are all considered equally. The interview is recommended, but not required. Decisions are made on a rolling admissions basis, but are batched in rounds. Applicants are notified of a decision within approximately six weeks of receipt of the completed application. Students may defer admission for up to two years for a professional opportunity or personal needs.

STUDENT'S OVERVIEW BOX

Overall Happiness

Academic Satisfaction

50   75   100%

Student Opinion   National Average

FACULTY RATING

Student Opinion   National Average

HITS AND MISSES

HITS
Accounting dept.
Finance dept.
Diverse work experience
Placement & recruiting
Classmates are smart

MISSES
Marketing dept.
On-campus housing
Hyde Park

APPLICANTS ALSO LOOK AT
Stanford U.
U Pennsylvania
Northwestern U.
Cornell U.

FOR MORE INFORMATION, CONTACT:
Graduate School of Business
1101 East 58th Street
Chicago, IL 60637
(312) 702-7369

CLAREMONT GRADUATE SCHOOL: THE PETER F. DRUCKER GRADUATE MANAGEMENT CENTER

ADMISSIONS FACTS

Type of school	Private

Demographics

No. of men	132
No. of women	88
No. of int'l students	44
No. of minorities	44

EQUAL TREATMENT GRAPH

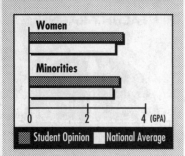

Women

Minorities

0   2   4 (GPA)

▨ Student Opinion ☐ National Average

Admissions Statistics

Avg. GMAT	578
Avg. undergraduate GPA	3.2
Avg. age at entry	26
No. of applicants	281
No. accepted	106
No. enrolled	58

Deadlines and Notifications

Regular application	5/30
Regular notification	within 3 weeks
Special dates	N/A

Focus of Curriculum

General Management

Academic Specialties

Strategic Management, Managing People

Special Programs

Strategic Management

FINANCIAL FACTS

In-state tuition	$5,397
Out-of-state tuition	$10,470
On-campus housing	$3,100

ACADEMICS

The Claremont Graduate School has "brand recognition" due to Peter F. Drucker, a professor at the school since 1971, and the world's most widely read author on the subject of management. But the talent pool isn't limited to Drucker. As one student put it, "The faculty has become increasingly top tier with the addition of highly recognized leaders in their respective fields." You can study here with former Harvard professors Dick Ellsworth, Vijay Sathe, Christine Hekman, and Robin Cooper, the latter of whom is one of the originators of activity-based accounting and was among Harvard's most popular teachers. But these are obviously some of the best. Writes one student, "It's hit or miss with the quality of teaching. Profs are either great or disappointing. No in-between." Adds another, "I would rate fifty percent of the professors here absolutely fantastic and the rest just good."

According to the school, "The Drucker Center offers a distinctive educational experience. The educational philosophy emphasizes an understanding of global forces affecting markets, recognizes the growing importance of information technology, and focuses on individual leadership skills." Although the program features a generalist perspective, students have the option of specializing in one of eight areas. The integrated curriculum "stresses an interplay between the real world and the classroom." One of the most popular courses is "The Human Component," in which student teams perform an analysis of an industry and then present conclusions to real-life players. This past year, Rob Kohler, head of a TRW subsidiary, provided feedback to students on their analyses.

Another unique feature at Claremont is the mentor program, which places full/part-time MBA students in mentoring relationships with senior managers in the Executive Education Program. As for the way this school is run, students rave about the personal attention: "Each and every person employed here—faculty, administration—goes out of their way to make sure the students are happy." Adds this MBA: "They're concerned about your needs. I haven't had so much as a minor fluctuation in my blood pressure here." One sour note: students feel the tuition is too high, diminishing their bang for the buck. Still, one student's comments typified the prevalent feeling here: "It has met and actually exceeded my academic expectations. This is a high caliber program."

PLACEMENT AND RECRUITING

It's kind of hard to run a full-fledged placement office when fifty percent of your students already have jobs. Moreover, companies like to recruit at schools where they can yield the greatest number of hires. Simply put, Claremont is too small to reel in large numbers of major on-campus recruiters. Nonetheless, in 1992, eighty-five percent of those seeking a new position were placed by July. The average starting salary was $51,000.

CLAREMONT GRADUATE SCHOOL: THE PETER F. DRUCKER GRADUATE MANAGEMENT CENTER

STUDENT LIFE/CAMPUS

According to our survey, students have a moderate workload. Nights and days are not pressure-filled. Of the one hundred students in each entering class, approximately fifty are part-timers. These two groups take courses together. The average class size is twenty-six students. Claremont MBAs work in study groups, but as one student put it, "Because so many are here part-time, it's a little more difficult to form study groups and have a 'full' student life experience." Added another, "Interaction among students is limited." Students are non-competitive and interested in helping each other out. There is a strong teamwork ethic. Several students raved, "A great place for international students!"

Claremont is located in Southern California, about a forty-minute drive away from L.A. and the beach. But the setting is all California: palm trees, red-tiled roofs, and the San Gabriel Mountains as a backdrop. Half of all full-timers live on campus, the other half rent apartments off-campus in Claremont, Upland, and Montclair. Housing is plentiful and affordable. Everyone joins the Graduate Management Association, which sponsors everything from corporate speaker series to social events like the annual spring formal and barbeques.

ADMISSIONS

According to the admissions office, college GPA and GMAT score are considered most important. Then, in descending order of importance, work experience, letters of recommendation and essays, interview, and extracurricular activities. Adds the school, "Extracurriculars and work experience are not required, but are considered. Interviews are recommended." Admissions decisions are made on a rolling decisions basis. Students may defer admission for up to one to year.

STUDENT'S OVERVIEW BOX

Happiness

Satisfaction

50   75   100%

Student Opinion   National Average

FACULTY RATING

Student Opinion   National Average

HITS
Accounting dept.
Finance dept.
Diverse work experience
Placement & recruiting
Classmates are smart

MISSES
Marketing dept.
On-campus housing
Hyde Park

APPLICANTS ALSO LOOK AT
UC Los Angeles
U Southern CA
Loyola Marymount

FOR MORE INFORMATION CONTACT:
Peter F. Drucker
Graduate Management Center
925 N. Dartmouth Ave
Claremont, CA 91711-6189
(909) 621-8073

UNIVERSITY OF COLORADO AT BOULDER GRADUATE SCHOOL OF BUSINESS ADMINISTRATION

ADMISSIONS FACTS

Type of school   Public

Demographics

No. of men	175
No. of women	89
No. of minorities	21
No. of int'l students	40

EQUAL TREATMENT GRAPH

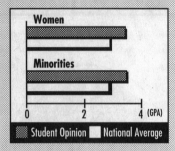

Women

Minorities

0   2   4 (GPA)

▨ Student Opinion   ☐ National Average

Admissions Statistics

Avg. GMAT	560
Avg. undergraduate GPA	3.1
Avg. age at entry	27
No. of applicants	430
No. accepted	184
No. enrolled	89

Deadlines and Notifications

Regular application	3/01
Regular notification	N/A
Special dates	N/A

Focus of Curriculum

Specialized

Academic Specialties

Technology and Innovation, Finance, Marketing

FINANCIAL FACTS

In-state tuition	$3,244
Out-of-state tuition	$11,070
On-campus housing	$3,540

ACADEMICS

There are plenty of students whose primary reason for attending the University of Colorado (UC) is summed up by the one who wrote, "I'm here for the Boulder experience." Plenty wrote, "I wanted to get my MBA in a state where I would live." Of course, many students also mentioned academic reputation as a strong drawing card. But it's really the best of both worlds—students agree they're getting a top-notch education in an extremely pleasing environment. That education includes a newly created "lock-step" program whereby one hundred entering students are divided into two cohorts of fifty students and take core courses together. Explained one MBA, "This is the first year of the new program. Although the kinks need to be worked out, the potential for real-world management training is excellent. Teamwork and communication are main themes." Wrote another, "The program is excellent in term of team assignments—all students, regardless of their academic background get to work together." The first year is filled with courses in the functional areas and features a quantitative slant. It also integrates global themes which are enhanced by a student body that is one-quarter international. Second-year students major in finance, marketing, organization management, or technology and innovation management. Unique to UC is the option to pursue a self-designed major. For example, a student with an engineering background might design an interdisciplinary telecommunications major and take classes in the engineering school.

As for teaching, there is a high degree of variability. Wrote one student, "Some professors are fantastic. Others are barely tolerable." Complained another, "UC's focus and resources should be on getting top-notch professors and not on a gimmick 'lock-step' program that is attracting a lesser quality of student." Professors receive better grades for their after-class accessibility which is considered above average. All in all, the majority of students say this program offers very high value/low cost, especially with the low in-state tuition factored in.

PLACEMENT AND RECRUITING

No matter where you go, students are unhappy with their career development office. UC students are not the exception. One MBA sounded off: "The placement center is hopelessly bogged down in red tape." Another griped, "They don't do much." Perhaps. This may explain why UC compiles no placement statistics. Nevertheless, the roster of companies recruiting on this campus is impressive—and notably blue chip.

UNIVERSITY OF COLORADO AT BOULDER GRADUATE SCHOOL OF BUSINESS ADMINISTRATION

STUDENT LIFE/CAMPUS

As a function of the new lock-step system, students are assigned to study groups which are organized around student members' strengths and weaknesses. During the first year, the workload is especially heavy. Wrote one student, "It's tough, but good." Students spend an average of twenty-five to thirty-five hours a week in study group and/or preparing for class. Partly because of the competitive grading system, students feel a lot of pressure. There is a targeted grade distribution—thirty percent of the class get A's, sixty percent B's, ten percent C's. UC MBAs need a solid B average to graduate, and B- doesn't cut it. In most courses, class participation, grades, and papers count equally toward the grade.

As one might expect, students are fairly competitive. But this is kept in check by the cohort system. In addition, students are happy to extend a helping hand and are friendly. UC MBAs say classmates are smart, but not as professionally diverse as they'd like them to be. Griped one, "Four years' work experience was suggested, but not mandatory; it should have been."

"If you're the outdoorsy type," wrote one MBA, "this is the school to go to." One student's comments seemed to say it all: "I love to ski." Boulder is beautiful, but expensive. Students who opt to live off-campus (which most do), find inexpensive housing outside of town. Public transportation is great—students get free metro bus passes. Social and professional activities are sponsored by the Graduate Students Business Association (GSBA) and include weekly Thursday night get-togethers (no class on Friday), a faculty/student softball game, and what you'd expect—plenty of ski trips. Raved one MBA, "Without the GSBA, this would be like any other school."

A final note: there are a variety of student-run specialized clubs for women and ethnically diverse students including the Black Business Students Coalition and the Hispanic Business Students Association. Unfortunately, there are few minority students to join them.

ADMISSIONS

According to the admissions office, your work experience is considered most important. After that, in descending order, your GMAT score, college GPA, interview, essays, letters of recommendation, and extracurricular activities. Domestic ethnic minorities receive special consideration. Decisions are made on a rolling basis. Applicants are notified of a decision six to eight weeks after a completed application has been received. Waitlisted applicants are notified of a spot by July 1st.

STUDENT'S OVERVIEW BOX

FACULTY RATING

HITS AND MISSES

HITS
Finance dept.
Diverse work experience
Boulder

MISSES
Marketing dept.
Ethnic & racial diversity
Placement

APPLICANTS ALSO LOOK AT

Case Western Res U.
Stanford U.
U Arizona
U Denver

FOR MORE INFORMATION, CONTACT:
Graduate School of Business
Administration Box 419
Boulder, CO 80309-0419
(303) 492-1831

COLUMBIA UNIVERSITY: COLUMBIA GRADUATE SCHOOL OF BUSINESS

ADMISSIONS FACTS

Type of school	Private

Demographics
No. of men	939
No. of women	402
No. of minorities	308
No. of int'l students	389

EQUAL TREATMENT GRAPH

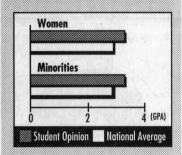

Women

Minorities

0   2   4 (GPA)

Student Opinion   National Average

Admissions Statistics
Avg. GMAT	630
Avg. undergraduate GPA	3.3
Avg. age at entry	27
No. of applicants	2,800
No. accepted	800
No. enrolled	450

Deadlines and Notifications
Regular application	4/20
Regular notification	within 6 weeks
Special dates	N/A

Focus of Curriculum
General Management, specialization required

Academic Specialties
Finance, International Business

FINANCIAL FACTS

In-state tuition	$19,000
Out-of-state tuition	$19,000
On-campus housing	$9,000

ACADEMICS

The Columbia Business School (CBS) is considered one of the finest MBA programs in the nation. Like many B-schools, CBS has just introduced a new curriculum and is currently in a state of transition. Wrote one student, "The school recently implemented a required core based on globalization, ethics, total quality management, and human resources management." These themes are now integrated across the traditional disciplines of business. An unchanged aspect of the program is the emphasis on a required concentration. Students choose from among twelve. The newest one is Management of Information, Communications, and Media. Students agree, "Finance is an outstanding department here." Several also told us, "Resources and programs at the school are very strong for those interested in international careers." Columbia has a math requirement which can be satisfied by previous coursework, passing an exemption exam, or by attending the popular summer "math camp." To bolster skills in school, review sessions are held for all quantitative core courses and some upper-level electives on class-less Fridays. Students who need extra help can work one-on-one with a peer tutor. Another unique feature of the program is that students can begin school in any one of three terms—September, January, or May. If they choose to, students can go straight through and graduate in sixteen months.

As one student put it, "Columbia has had some operational and customer service problems." According to students, these are now "being addressed by the administration and are improving." Explained one MBA, "The Dean and faculty are trying to build a strong student community and take the academic program in the right direction." To promote camaraderie, they've implemented "clusters"—sectioning first-year students into "homeroom" groups of roughly fifty-five each. Still, this is Columbia. This is New York. Translation: students like to complain. One student griped, "Bottom ten percent of the class shouldn't be here," although a recent surge in applications may change this. According to the school, "Only one in four students are now admitted."

PLACEMENT AND RECRUITING

The Office of Career Services offers the standard fare: counseling sessions, résumé writing workshops, and seminars on job search strategies. But what puts Columbia on top—you guessed it—is its New York location. Over 10,000 Columbia alumni live or work in New York. Chided one MBA, "You are nuts to go outside of NYC for your MBA. You have to be here to make contacts. It's that simple." Advised another, "Columbia is ideal for someone who wants to work on Wall Street."

Here are the quick and dirty stats: In 1992, ninety percent placement. One student's comments typified the state of affairs here: "Columbia tends to focus on large investment banks, consulting firms, and product management companies (i.e. Procter and Gamble) almost exclusively. But I believe the school is actively trying to solicit smaller/diverse companies." Adds another: "Alumni/professor contacts critical to getting a job."

COLUMBIA UNIVERSITY: COLUMBIA GRADUATE SCHOOL OF BUSINESS

STUDENT LIFE/CAMPUS

The majority of first-year students describe an up-all-night workload and hit the books an average of thirty-five to forty hours a week. One student explained it this way: "Because we have a shorter academic year (by about six weeks compared to other B-schools), yet cover the same amount of material, our courseload is intense." Shorter year or not, academics are rigorous and demanding. Unsurprisingly, students say it's important to do all or most of the work. The wise ones form study groups to get through it.

Has Columbia changed from a cutthroat to team-oriented school? It's heading in that direction. Wrote one MBA, "CBS is no longer a pressure cooker where people sabotage each other's homework." Agreed another, "Students go out of their way to help one another; the backstabbing that was described to me certainly doesn't happen here." Students seem to like and want to hang out with each other, too. They also said they'll continue their friendships post-graduation. Even so, some sharp elbows remain. Several students said, "Columbia can be very competitive," and "Lots of students go their own way." Summed up one MBA, "Columbia is in many ways a microcosm of New York City. The energy and motivation required to succeed in NYC are also necessary to succeed here."

Most students would agree, "Going to school in New York has its good points and bad points." The good points have to do with being located in what one student terms "the financial and media mecca of the world." Another location plus—Columbia gets a lion's share of visiting business luminaries, from Henry Kravis to Warren Buffet. Confirmed one student, "Through the Distinguished Lecture Series, power-hitters are constantly on campus." Another plus: Columbia brings in NYC business professionals as adjunct professors. The bad points have to do with what one student calls the "tight New York space factor." Simply put, Columbia's one-building schoolhouse doesn't offer enough room or ambiance. The immediate neighborhood isn't "Camelot" but is fairly yuppified, due to the presence of Columbia/Barnard. The majority of students live off-campus in apartments around the campus or further downtown. For extracurricular activities, students choose from over fifty student-run clubs. Thursday nights, they kick off their weekend with a happy hour in the school's eatery.

ADMISSIONS

According to the admissions department, your work experience is considered most important. After that, in descending order: your extracurricular activities, college GPA, essays, interview/letters of recommendation, and GMAT score. Notes the school, "Applicants are evaluated in three categories listed in order of importance: professional promise, personal characteristics, and academic credentials." Alumni children/spouses receive special consideration. Decisions are made on a rolling basis.

STUDENT'S OVERVIEW BOX

FACULTY RATING

HITS AND MISSES

HITS
Finance dept.
Diverse work experience
New York City
Adjunct professors
Visiting executives

MISSES
Marketing dept.
Helping other students
Gym
Facilities

APPLICANTS ALSO LOOK AT
Harvard
Dartmouth College
Yale U.
U Penn.
New York University

FOR MORE INFORMATION, CONTACT:
Graduate School of Business
Uris Hall
New York, NY 10027
(212) 854-5567

UNIVERSITY OF CONNECTICUT SCHOOL OF BUSINESS ADMINISTRATION

ADMISSIONS FACTS

Type of school	Public

Demographics

No. of men	147
No. of women	83
No. of minorities	15
No. of int'l students	19

EQUAL TREATMENT GRAPH

Admissions Statistics

Avg. GMAT	540
Avg. undergraduate GPA	3.2
Avg. age at entry	26
No. of applicants	550
No. accepted	227
No. enrolled	109

Deadlines and Notifications

Regular application	rolling
Regular notification	rolling
Special dates	N/A

Focus of Curriculum

Specialized

Academic Specialties

Accounting, Finance, Real Estate

Special Programs

Foreign Study in France, Germany, and the Netherlands.

FINANCIAL FACTS

In-state tuition	$4,580
Out-of-state tuition	$10,798
On-campus housing	$4,850

ACADEMICS

As several students told us, the best things about the University of Connecticut (UConn), are the low-cost/high-value education, the accounting department, and the Center for Real Estate Studies. An added benefit is that the school maintains strong ties with the local business community. Students have frequent contact with visiting business professionals from the region. Students say academics at UConn are both challenging and rigorous. "The majority of coursework deals with applying business theory to real-life situations," said one student. MBAs take six electives to concentrate in one of nine areas. The program has started to develop an international focus. Reported one student, "About twenty percent of the students are from foreign countries, which truly gives an international flair to class discussions as well as enhances social tolerance outside the classroom." In addition, all students must take an international studies course.

Over and over, students told us that collaboration is heavily emphasized. Wrote one student, "There is a strong focus on teamwork and presentations, but with individual accountability. Good combination." Other students told us it's too much. Griped one unhappy teammate, "UConn enforces group projects. They're a part of every class. It's overdone and takes time away from studying." As for the professors, one student's comments typified the prevalent feeling here: "Overall, faculty are a little inconsistent. But we have some outstanding teachers." The majority agreed with this UConn MBA, "Most professors are genuinely concerned and very accessible." Although the administration is considered "helpful and responsive," more than fifty percent of the students surveyed said the school needs some fine tuning. Problems and complaints: "The director of the program caves in on the side of professors or lack of money when students are unhappy with a professor," and "We are not financially supported by the state of Connecticut—the physical plant is deteriorating, electives are being reduced," and "The future of the program is uncertain." All in all, students say this program is well worth the investment of time and money. For the majority, it has exceeded academic expectations.

PLACEMENT AND RECRUITING

As one student put it, "This school prepares students well for employment." Among their services are a two-day Career Interview Conference and résumé book. Wrote one pleased customer, "I have competed against students from the top five B-Schools for positions and have found that my skills are as good or better." Raved another, "I've received three job offers at top public accounting firms after interviewing with eleven companies." Granted, UConn does tend to do well with placement in its star academic areas. But more than fifty percent of the students surveyed told us they're disappointed with the range/caliber of companies recruiting on campus. The majority take matters into their own hands and contact alumni, who are generally responsive. In 1993, seventy-eight percent of new UConn MBAs had been placed by August.

UNIVERSITY OF CONNECTICUT SCHOOL OF BUSINESS ADMINISTRATION

STUDENT LIFE/CAMPUS

As one student put it, "Many activities go on on-campus, but the workload is so heavy, you don't usually have time to participate and enjoy yourself."

Students are bogged down in schoolwork an average of twenty-five to thirty-five hours a week. The vast majority report it's important to do all or more of the assigned reading. Study groups help students synthesize their ideas, but there's still a lot of pressure. Things lighten up during the second year.

As one student put it, "The program has a total of 260 students. The smallness gives UConn a sense of 'family.'" Raved another, "Very strong *esprit de corps*." Students are competitive, but not into one-upmanship. Student here help each other. They also hang out with each other. Students feel classmates "are not only smart, but have great character." The majority reported that the student body is both ethnically and professionally diverse. One complaint: "Too many cocky students straight out of undergraduate school." Over and over, we heard "getting involved is the key." Advised one UConn MBA, "Anyone who comes here and sits back will not gain much." Reported another, "There are many opportunities for the ambitious student to stand out." The be-all and end-all extracurricular is the student-run Graduate Business Association, which UConn MBAs rave about. As one student put it, "It supplements the MBA office and placement with professional development exercises, networking, recruiting, etc. A lot of the gaps in the program are filled in by the Graduate Business Association." It also organizes social activities at favorite watering holes such as Ted's and Husky's. Of the students, 60 percent live off-campus, but housing can be pricey. Also, you'll need a car. On-campus housing is a decent bet for single student. UConn is located in Storrs, a rural area about a one-and-a-half hour train ride from New York City and forty-five minutes from Hartford.

ADMISSIONS

According to the admissions office, the following three criteria are considered most important and weighted equally: your GMAT score, work experience, and college GPA. Then your essays, letters of recommendation, and extracurriculars. Writes the school, "Each application is considered on its own merits, as a whole. We do not use cut-offs for GMAT scores or GPA. Evidence of high promise in one area can offset average accomplishment in another." Admissions decisions are made on a rolling basis throughout the year. There are no deadlines—until the class has filled up. Students typically receive a decision within one month of completion of their file. They may defer admission for up to one year depending on the circumstances.

STUDENT'S OVERVIEW BOX

FACULTY RATING

HITS AND MISSES

HITS
Finance dept.
Classmates are smart
On-campus housing

MISSES
Marketing dept.
Social life
Location

APPLICANTS ALSO LOOK AT
Dartmouth College
U Pennsylvania
New York University
Boston College
Boston University

FOR MORE INFORMATION, CONTACT
School of Business Administration
368 Fairfield Road, U-41D
Storrs, CT 06269-2041
(203) 486-2872

CORNELL UNIVERSITY: JOHNSON GRADUATE SCHOOL OF MANAGEMENT

ADMISSIONS FACTS

Type of school	Private

Demographics

No. of men	371
No. of women	150
No. of minorities	28
No. of int'l students	166

EQUAL TREATMENT GRAPH

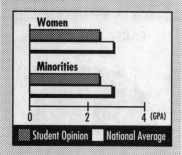

Women

Minorities

0   2   4 (GPA)

[░] Student Opinion [ ] National Average

Admissions Statistics

Avg. GMAT	635
Avg. undergraduate GPA	3.09
Avg. age at entry	27
No. of applicants	1,758
No. accepted	645
No. enrolled	261

Deadlines and Notifications

Regular application	3/01
Regular notification	within 4 weeks
Special dates	N/A

Focus of Curriculum

General Management, specializations

Academic Specialties

International Business, Asian & European Business Studies, Finance

Special Programs

International Business, Asian and European Business Studies, Finance

FINANCIAL FACTS

In-state tuition	$18,500
Out-of-state tuition	$18,500
On-campus housing	$6,150

ACADEMICS

International electives and foreign study options overflow the Cornell course catalog. The students we spoke to repeatedly emphasized three innovative programs: FALCON (Full-year Asian Language Concentration), designed for students who have never spoken a word of Japanese; the MBA concentration in Japanese business; and the joint MBA/MA in Asian studies. In the past, students have interned with the Industrial Bank of Japan and Nippon Telegraph and Telephone. Beyond the study of Japanese business, concentrations are available in international economics and trade, international public policies, and international management.

As for the MBA program itself, Cornell is not very different from others included in this book. The first year is filled with core courses. During the second year, students use electives which are organized into "maps" to pursue a broad or specialized course of study. What distinguishes Cornell is the flexibility students have in taking electives in other University schools (like the Cornell School of Hotel Management; the College of Art, Architecture, and Planning; and the School of Industrial and Labor Relations). One student reports, "The Johnson school relies heavily on other parts of Cornell to provide a full range of classes. But this is both a weakness and a strength." Cornell has also been known to turn out an entrepreneur or two. Most of these are students who have taken Entrepreneurship and Enterprise, one of the most popular electives.

Professors here receive good, though not stellar, grades for their teaching. More impressive, given the emphasis on research, is that professors are considered extremely accessible. This is a school where it's not uncommon for professors to give out their home phone number, take students on a field trip, or have them over for dinner. But a serious flaw in this academic Utopia is that for a distinguished management program, students report it's surprisingly mismanaged. Among their complaints: it's often difficult to get into popular courses, classes are large, the facilities need renovation (a new B-school is being built) and the Career Placement Office is the pits. While the majority agreed, "Cornell is more than I expected and all that I needed," a sizeable minority felt less certain. Explained one disappointed MBA, "Some classes are excellent, some are a nightmare. Many fall in between."

PLACEMENT AND RECRUITING

As one student put it, "The Career Services office does a better job of showing people techniques for getting a job than they do getting companies to the campus." Explained another, "The remote location and small size make independent job searches more important." One satisfied MBA reported, "Cornell has made my career transition into money management very successful." Most students in our survey sought out alumni for career advice. Reported one job-seeker, "Alumni (not limited to the Johnson School) are generally very loyal and supportive in job search efforts." In 1992, eighty-three percent of the class had offers by graduation.

CORNELL UNIVERSITY: JOHNSON GRADUATE SCHOOL OF MANAGEMENT

STUDENT LIFE/CAMPUS

The Cornell program stresses teamwork and oral and written communications skills. Reported one MBA, "There are many learning opportunities through frequent guest speakers." There are also a large number of out-of-class experiences: a Community Weekend in September, a retreat for first-years led by second-years, winter break trips to Japan and Russia, and week-long Outward-Bound-like summer leadership programs in rugged locales like the Hurricane Islands, Adirondacks, and the Rockies. Students report only a moderately heavy workload. The pressure is manageable. Students hit the books an average of twenty-five to thirty-five hours a week, hardly killer by top B-school standards. Perhaps because of all that's going on outside of class, a sizeable number told us it's not important to do all of the assigned reading.

The defining characteristic of life here seems to be the tight-knit community of students. Wrote one student, "The school is better than I expected, people are very friendly and helpful." Added another, "You get to know everyone in your classes." Students are congenial, not back-stabbingly competitive. Students also report classmates are smart and professionally diverse. As for the campus itself, it's beautiful. Students agreed, "Ithaca is a great place to live in," although the weather is often incredibly dreary. According to our survey, both on- and off-campus housing is considered excellent. Because of its remote location, on-campus activities prevail. One of the most unusual is the Frozen Assets Hockey Team, a group of all female MBAs who compete against Tuck in an annual tournament.

ADMISSIONS

According to the admissions office your interview is considered *most important,* and then in descending order, the type of undergrad institution attended, your GMAT scores, work experience, essays, college GPA, letters of recommendation, and extracurricular activities. Adds the school, "we prefer liberal arts majors." They also write, "We work to attract minority and women applicants, as well as disabled applicants." It pays to be a child or relative of an alum. "All things being equal," notes the admissions office, "sometimes" these applicants receive extra consideration. Decisions are made on a rolling admissions basis. Students are notified of a decision within one month of receipt of the completed file. The final deadline is March 1st. Some advice from the school: "The earlier you apply, the better your chances. Send in part one of the application ASAP so we can arrange an alumni interview for competitive applicant." Deferrals are granted to students on a case-by-case basis.

STUDENT'S OVERVIEW BOX

FACULTY RATING

HITS AND MISSES

HITS
Accounting
Diverse work experience
On-campus housing
International business

MISSES
Quantitative skills
Placement
Facilities

APPLICANTS ALSO LOOK AT
Stanford U.
Columbia U.
Carnegie Mellon U.
Harvard
MIT

FOR MORE INFORMATION, CONTACT:
Johnson Graduate School of
Management, Malott Hall
Ithaca, NY 14853
(607) 255-2327
(800) 847-2082

CUNY Baruch College School of Business and Public Administration

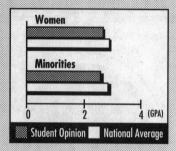
ACADEMICS

Most students would agree with the individual who wrote "For the money you get a quality education and star faculty." The "star" is a reference to a Nobel prize-winning finance professor, several others in the same department, and Professor Yoshiro Tsurumi, a Harvard Ph.D. who is a top scholar on U.S./Japanese relations. It was Tsurumi who the national media turned to for his in-depth analysis of former President Bush's notorious trip to Japan. Other standout faculty include the school's accounting professors. Indeed, Baruch boasts it is "rated first in the nation for the number of candidates with advanced degrees who successfully take the CPA exam." Baruch's only possible shortcoming may be its low national profile. As one student put it, "Although Baruch is relatively well known in New York, it is unknown throughout the rest of the country."

Baruch is basically a part-time, go-at-your-own-pace program. The majority of students take only a small number of courses per semester and create their own academic schedule while working full time. It can take up to four years to complete the program. The first half of the program is devoted to the standard core curriculum; the latter half covers an area of specialization including accounting, business administration, computer systems, economics, finance and investments, health care administration, industrial psychology, international business, management, marketing, operations research, statistics, and taxation.

Students reported feeling well-prepared by their studies in the school's power subjects—accounting and finance. As one might expect, Baruch boasts strong quantitative skills. Students felt less confident of their skills in marketing, operations, and communication skills suggesting that the path to specialized study falls short on providing a foundation in the basics. Also in the complaint department: getting into any course, even a required class, is a nightmare. Planning a course of study is equally frustrating. Moaned one MBA, "First, figuring out what you need to take to graduate is impossible. Everything must be done with consultation with an advisor. Then getting an appointment to set up a program is *impossible*." Other trouble spots: the library and the placement office. On the upside, the vast majority of students agree that pursuing a Baruch MBA is well worth the time and money. They expect the degree will provide them long-term career leverage.

PLACEMENT AND RECRUITING

The Office of Career Services serves the entire school of business which encompasses an undergraduate population of 13,000 students. In the best of economic times, over 400 companies recruit on-campus each year. More recently, the number has dropped to 250 companies.

CUNY BARUCH COLLEGE SCHOOL OF BUSINESS AND PUBLIC ADMINISTRATION

STUDENT LIFE/CAMPUS

Baruch is one of the largest B-schools in the nation, packing in upwards of 2,500 students into its two-year program. Surprisingly, this doesn't affect class size which is kept to an average of thirty-five to forty-five in the core courses, half that in the electives. In almost all classes, exams count most heavily toward the grade, then papers. The workload is manageable, the pressure moderate to light. Students report they only study an average of fifteen to twenty-five hours a week, a cakewalk by most B-school's standards.

Students rate themselves only moderately competitive, but this isn't the result of a cozy, all-for-one student community. Indeed, the student community is basically non-existent. Baruch's large size, and "commuter" characteristics, make it rough to bond and build camaraderie. This extends to the social scene which students also rated as below that of almost all B-schools profiled in this book. This doesn't mean students don't have a life. They do, it's just not at the B-school. To redirect students back on campus and foster strong school relationships, the administration plans on introducing a cohort system and more planned activities. As for the student body, Baruch MBAs agree, classmates are both professionally and racially diverse. There's a large contingent of foreign and minority students.

Baruch is located in the Gramercy Park section of mid-town Manhattan, in what students term the "heart of New York City." The campus is safe, public transportation extremely accessible. Students live all around the city and its neighboring areas.

ADMISSIONS

According to the admissions board, your college GPA and GMAT scores are considered most important. After that the board considers, in descending order, your essays, letters of recommendation, and work experience. Admissions decisions are made on a rolling basis. Students applying in the spring (June 1) Round should take the March GMAT prior to submitting their application.

STUDENT'S OVERVIEW BOX

FACULTY RATING

HITS AND MISSES

HITS
Accounting dept.
New York City
Tuition
Diversity

MISSES
Marketing dept.
Gym
Off-campus housing
Social life

APPLICANTS ALSO LOOK AT
St. John U.
New York U
Fordham
Columbia

FOR MORE INFORMATION, CONTACT:
Office of Graduate Admissions
17 Lexington Ave. Box 276
Baruch College/CUNY
New York, NY 10010
(212) 447-3920

DARTMOUTH COLLEGE: THE AMOS TUCK SCHOOL OF BUSINESS ADMINISTRATION

ADMISSIONS FACTS

Type of school	Private
Demographics	
No. of men	249
No. of women	94
No. of minorities	32
No. of int'l students	75

EQUAL TREATMENT GRAPH

Women

Minorities

0   2   4 (GPA)

▨ Student Opinion ■ National Average

Admissions Statistics

Avg. GMAT	651
Avg. undergraduate GPA	3.34
Avg. age at entry	26.2
No. of applicants	2,162
No. accepted	422
No. enrolled	185

Deadlines and Notifications

Regular application	4/12
Regular notification	within 3 weeks
Special dates	N/A

Focus of Curriculum

General Management

Academic Specialties

General Management

Joint Degrees

MBA/MALD in International Affairs, MBA/MS in Engineering, MBA/MD

Special Programs

Executive-in-Residence Program (EIR)

FINANCIAL FACTS

In-state tuition	$18,750
Out-of-state tuition	$18,750
On-campus housing	$3,500

ACADEMICS

Founded in 1900, Amos Tuck was the first graduate school of management in the world and the only top U.S. business school that offers only the MBA degree. This means Tuck focuses *all* of its resources on its MBA students. Tuck has a reputation for developing talented general managers through rigorous, quantitatively demanding academics. By any standards, the workload is heavy and the curriculum very structured.

First-years take a set of thirteen required core courses to introduce them to concepts and skills in the key functional areas of business. Second-years choose from over fifty electives to specialize or build breadth, but don't have to select a major. Indeed, the emphasis here is on a general management education. The curriculum is integrated so that students learn how one functional area impacts on another. The curriculum at Tuck also stresses a "theory into practice" understanding of business. Students learn practical, hands-on solutions to problems. Several enthusiastic students told us about Tuck's first-year, three-day business simulation game, TY-COON. Student teams start with assets of $25 million with which to purchase and then manage a company. Professors impose "surprise" conditions and disasters upon different worlds—from floods to labor strikes. Students also raved about the Executive-in-Residence Program. Explained one, "CEO's and other high-ranking executives visit campus for several days to lecture and, more importantly, personally meet with interested students."

Tuck features a learning environment that is personal and intimate. Wrote one student about the school's small size "it allows individuals to be individuals, not just another number." An unusually low student/faculty ratio of nine to one means Tuck professors are accessible to students. According to students, they're also off-the-Richter scale terrific teachers. Raved one Tuckie, "Profs are one of the best things about Tuck." More cooperative than competitive, Tuckies are a all-for-one and one-for-all bunch. Wrote a typical booster, "Tuck is nothing like other B-schools. The peer pressure is completely against back-stabbing." Explained another, "Students enjoy the experience. It's not something to 'get through'." But one realist wrote, "For fear of making Tuck sound like a summer camp— I'll be honest. I worked harder than I've ever worked in my life."

PLACEMENT AND RECRUITING

Career Planning arranges seventy yearly "company briefings." One hundred companies interview on-campus, fifty for summer intern positions. In addition to the on-campus process, 300 companies contact Tuck with job listings each year. Career planning also helps students ferret out one-of-a-kind jobs off-campus. Tuck alumni further provide students even more contacts. One student reported, "Recruiters are impressed with the quality of students as smart, sociable, and team players." Another student wrote he expects to find "excellent career prospects after graduating from Tuck." By graduation in June of 1992, eighty-eight percent of the class was placed. Three months after graduation, ninety-six percent of the class was placed.

DARTMOUTH COLLEGE: THE AMOS TUCK SCHOOL OF BUSINESS ADMINISTRATION

STUDENT LIFE/CAMPUS

Tuckies, as they like to call themselves, gave their school the highest quality of life ratings. Whether they were married with children or single, in their mid-thirties or a few years out of college, dozens of students wrote, "I LOVE TUCK!" In fact, the survey results suggest a veritable lovefest! Tuckies are extremely happy. Many raved, "Best two years of my life," and "I've made friends that will last a lifetime." Almost all first-year students live in Tuck dorms, making it a very cozy, residential experience. (Married students and their spouses can live in Sachem Village.) But because the school is so small, students can get "over-exposed" or quickly develop a "reputation." One Tuckie warns, "Tuck is too involved a place if you're simply looking to get your MBA stamp."

Many describe the campus as "beautiful" and the rural, outdoorsy setting as "perfect." Located in the quaint town of Hanover, students at Tuck have access to many outdoor activities. Wrote one enthusiast, "There's skiing, cross-country, canoeing, hiking and biking!" Adds the school, "Most students look forward to winter; the biggest sports here are ice hockey and skiing." The Tuck Tripods are novice hockey players. Skiing is available at Killington, Stowe, and Dartmouth's Skiway. And Tuck hosts Winter Carnival, an invitational slalom race, each year, complete with serious après-ski partying. Tuckies also enjoy an active social life, in which spouses/partners are merrily included. "Partying, dancing, and late nights," are common. So are intramural sporting events, talent nights and student club activities. But Tuck is also family-oriented; the campus is crawling with babies and puppies. Declared one student dramatically, "Tuck is a true American MBA experience." But they agree theirs is not a diverse community; a meager eight percent are minority. About forty students are foreign.

ADMISSIONS

The admissions office reports that "although the GMAT, GPA, and work experience are very important, we look for well-roundedness in our candidates. Tuck's admissions process is based on the belief that every applicant is an individual; a formula is not used to determine admission. We look for applicants with different qualities who will add value to our classrooms and community." Beyond the undergrad record and test scores, the committee looks for accomplishment in the workplace. Within the parameters of work, Tuck looks for applicants who exhibit leadership, creativity, and a strong foundation of business skills and experiences that will bring diversity to classroom discussions. Teamwork, management potential, and developed career goals for the future are other significant factors. "An applicant's appreciation for cultural diversity in all its forms as well as an awareness of workforce issues is also essential."

Tuck goes by "rounds" and writes it is advisable to apply "within the first three."

STUDENT'S OVERVIEW BOX

Overall Happiness

Academic Satisfaction

50   75   100%

Student Opinion   National Average

FACULTY RATING

Student Opinion   National Average

HITS AND MISSES

HITS
Marketing
Faculty
Student community
Classmates are smart
Hanover

MISSES
Finance dept.
Ethnic & racial diversity
Gym

APPLICANTS ALSO LOOK AT
Stanford U.
U Pennsylvania
Duke U.
Columbia U.
Harvard

FOR MORE INFORMATION, CONTACT
The Amos Tuck School of Business
Administration
Tuck Drive
Hanover, NH 03755
(603) 646-3162

UNIVERSITY OF DENVER GRADUATE SCHOOL OF BUSINESS

ADMISSIONS FACTS

Type of school	Private

Demographics

No. of men	N/A
No. of women	N/A
No. of minorities	N/A
No. of int'l students	N/A

EQUAL TREATMENT GRAPH

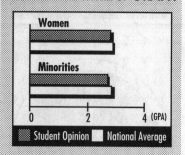

Admissions Statistics

Avg. GMAT	N/A
Avg. undergraduate GPA	N/A
Avg. age at entry	N/A
No. of applicants	N/A
No. accepted	N/A
No. enrolled	N/A

Deadlines and Notifications

Regular application	6/01
Regular notification	within 3 weeks
Special dates	N/A

Focus of Curriculum

Generalized

Joint Degrees

Masters in International Management, Masters in Domestic and International Tourism, JD/MBA

FINANCIAL FACTS

In-state tuition	$12,852
Out-of-state tuition	$12,852
On-campus housing	$4,857

ACADEMICS

Students looking for a progressive academic curriculum and an outdoorsy lifestyle, look no further; the University of Denver (U of D) offers both. This generalist program provides MBAs traditional nuts-and-bolts skills, as well as exposure to critical '90s issues: leadership, team-building, negotiation and communication, gender and cultural diversity. The program also features many experiential components—an Outward-Bound leadership and team building training, a community service project, and an "integrative challenge which brings all the program elements together in a practical business application." Wrote one MBA, "The recently revised MBA curriculum offers a variety of courses and electives that are very pertinent to today's business issues." The newly opened Center for Managerial Communication provides students the facilities and resources to work on presentation, communication and group dynamics skills. U of D also offers a Masters in International Management, which makes the school home to a strong international studies program.

Overall, U of D students report they feel well prepared by their studies in finance, accounting, and general management. Due to the emphasis on soft skills, they report a high level of confidence in their teamwork, interpersonal, and presentation abilities. But students say their skills need bolstering in marketing and computers. Although the vast majority of students told us taking time off to pursue a U of D MBA is worth it, they disagreed on the value of their education relative to its cost. Students were unanimous–U of D's low tuition is a draw. But several students agreed with the one who wrote, "Value of education received in terms of dollars is a little low." Complained another, "The tuition is high, given that the school facilities are below average." Students also griped about the difficulty of getting into popular courses.

PLACEMENT AND RECRUITING

Wrote one student, "There are good job opportunities and networking here." But the majority said their job placement office needs to work harder. They also complained about the range and number of companies recruiting on campus. Nevertheless, over eighty-eight percent of MBAs were placed within three months of graduation in 1992.

UNIVERSITY OF DENVER GRADUATE SCHOOL OF BUSINESS

STUDENT LIFE/CAMPUS

According to one MBA, "Course workloads usually include a good mixture of exams, research projects (individual and group), and class participation."

Classes are small, many with twenty to twenty-five students in each. The workload is average, although it's heavier during the first year. The majority of students study an average of fifteen to twenty-five hours a week; several diehards report they hit the books thirty to forty hours a week. As for the academic pressure, students are split. Half say it's intense, the other half say it's barely there.

Students agree, fellow classmates are smart, racially diverse, and bring a range of professional experiences to the classroom. But U of D MBAs aren't killer-competitive. They're more oriented towards cooperation. One student's comments typified the prevalent feeling here "people are very helpful and friendly." Because the school is so small, the tight-knit student body tends to hang out with and enjoy each other. Unsurprisingly, they also report an active social life. Three hundred days of sunshine a year and the nearby mountains provide students unsurpassed recreational opportunities. Favorite extracurriculars include anything to do with the great outdoors: whitewater rafting, rock climbing, mountain biking, fishing. The B-School organizes frequent skiing trips. Also popular are trips to Central City for Vegas-style gambling. As for they city of Denver, students think it's great. The majority of MBAs opt to live off-campus in apartments within walking distance of school.

ADMISSIONS

According to the admissions office, your college GPA is considered most important. After that, in descending order, your GMAT score, essays, letters of recommendation, issues of diversity (minority, female, international), work experience, and extra-curricular activities. Notes the school, "U of D is the eighth oldest school of business in the nation, and has been AACSB accredited since 1923. We offer the following degrees: Masters of Business in administration, international management, real estate and construction management, taxation, a Masters of Science in domestic and international tourism, and accountancy." Decisions are made on a rolling basis. Students are notified of a decision three weeks after the completed application has been submitted. Waitlisted students are notified of a spot by August first.

STUDENT'S OVERVIEW BOX

Overall Happiness

Academic Satisfaction

50   75   100%

Student Opinion   National Average

FACULTY RATING

Student Opinion   National Average

HITS AND MISSES

HITS
Finance
Safety
Classmates are smart
Social life

MISSES
Marketing
Off-campus housing
Competitive classmates

APPLICANTS ALSO LOOK AT
U Colorado-Boulder
U Colorado-Denver
Colorado State
U Texas-Austin

FOR MORE INFORMATION, CONTACT:
Graduate Business School
Admission Office
2020 South Rice
Denver, CO 80208
(303) 871-3416

DUKE UNIVERSITY: FUQUA SCHOOL OF BUSINESS

ADMISSIONS FACTS

Type of school   Private

Demographics

No. of men	456
No. of women	161
No. of minorities	69
No. of int'l students	92

EQUAL TREATMENT GRAPH

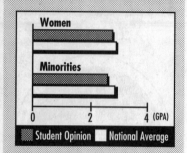

| Women | |
| Minorities | |

0   2   4 (GPA)

▨ Student Opinion   ▢ National Average

Admissions Statistics

Avg. GMAT	631
Avg. undergraduate GPA	3.31
Avg. age at entry	26
No. of applicants	2,315
No. accepted	696
No. enrolled	330

Deadlines and Notifications

Regular application	3/15
Regular notification	within 8 weeks
Special dates	N/A

Focus of Curriculum

General Management

Academic Specialties

General Management, Accounting, Finance, Marketing

Joint Degrees

MBA-AM in Public Policy Studies, MBA/JD, MBA/MF in Forestry or Environmental Management, MBA/MS in Engineering

Special Programs

International Study Opportunities, The MBA Enterprise Corps

FINANCIAL FACTS

In-state tuition	$18,500
Out-of-state tuition	$18,500
On-campus housing	N/A

ACADEMICS

From marketing to finance, from quant skills to teamwork, Fuqua's departments are solid across the board. Distinct to the school is a hot, new experiential program called Integrative Learning Experience (ILE). Four one-week-long seminars embrace the trendy topics of the '90s—diversity, internationalization, etc.—and provide students an opportunity to learn by doing. Each ILE precedes a semester of traditional classroom instruction. Over the two year program, students take four ILEs: Team building and leadership; Managing Quality and Diversity; Competitive Business Strategy, and Complex Management Programs. The last two are the "capstone" experiences in that they involve business simulation games and team competitions. Wrote one student, "Fuqua's addition of the Integrative Learning Experiences has been very successful." Raved another, "Fuqua's updated curriculum is on top of market trends."

First-years squeeze in a whopping fourteen core courses and have room for two electives. As one student put it, "It moves so fast, there's no time to fall behind. Good time management skills are essential." A prereq for the program is a working knowledge of calculus. Advised one student, "Liberal arts majors with no experience in business courses should be prepared to hit the ground running." Second-year students take only one required course, the International Environment, and have up to eleven electives to pursue more individualized study. Four of these may be taken in other schools or departments at Duke University. As for the faculty, one student wrote, "Profs all have open-door policies. They know your name." Although students say professors are good teachers, overall they don't compare favorably with the teachers at other competitive schools. Some of the problem seems to be that Fuqua's profs who teach core courses are young and inexperienced.

From the Dean of the school to the maintenance department, staff are trained in the techniques of TQM (Total Quality Management) and aim to provide customer satisfaction. It must be working. As one student put it, "More than any other school, Fuqua treats its students like a customer— we're paying a lot and getting our money's worth." Agreed another, "Excellent school. I'm very satisfied, even at $20,000 a year."

PLACEMENT AND RECRUITING

In 1992, 140 companies interviewed on-campus, and there were 3,063 interviews scheduled. Over ninety percent of the graduating class had jobs by commencement. According to the respondents in our survey, the placement office is doing a decent job, but could stand improvement. One student explains, "Fuqua offers a terrific education in great surroundings, but it's not New York or Chicago. The placement office should be working twice as hard to bring companies to campus." Students were most satisfied with the *number* of companies recruiting on campus. Almost every student contacted an alumni in their job search and found them very helpful.

DUKE UNIVERSITY: FUQUA SCHOOL OF BUSINESS

STUDENT LIFE/CAMPUS

Students reported that "Fuqua is seriously outgrowing its facilities." This is because the program continues to fill every spot; at 330 students per entering class, Fuqua is at its max and students feel the pinch. But don't expect them to expand facilities soon. The modern B-school building was just completed in 1983 and boasts state-of-the-art facilities.

As for the campus itself, Duke's is one of the nation's most beautiful—complete with Gothic architecture and sweeping lawns. A mile of woodlands divides the campus in two. Fuqua is perched on the edge of Duke Forest on Duke's West Campus. Most students opt to live off-campus in small groups in apartment complexes nearby. Housing, both on- and off-campus, is good and very affordable, about $500-$750 for a two-bedroom apartment. Most students bring a car. But parking is a nightmare at peak times.

Although students report an above average social life, dating hardly figures into this. As for extracurriculars, there are plenty. Reported one MBA, "Students work hard, but like to have fun too—kegs every Friday at 5:30." There's a Fuquavisions show every other month (like a "Saturday Night Live" video), and a Winter Gala Black Tie party. Favorite hang-outs include Satisfaction Pizza and the Hideaway. Intramural sports are big. Student clubs play a big part in campus life as well. The Black MBA Organization hosts a Wall Street panel. The Entrepreneurship Club hosts a two-day seminar.

One student's remarks typified the prevalent feeling here: "I have never been involved with a more outstanding and bright group of people! The term teamwork does not do justice to the genuine concern the students have for one another's performance—help is always available."

ADMISSIONS

According to the admissions office, "We encourage, but do not require, evaluative interviews. We feel that the interview is an important component of the application process." Other components include the GMAT score, college GPA, essays, work experience, letters or recommendation, and extracurricular activities. Decisions are made on a rolling admissions basis. Applicants are notified of a decision six to eight weeks after the admissions office has received a completed application. Accepted applicants may defer admission for up to two years for health issues or special job opportunities. Fuqua may also offer college seniors a two-year deferred admission with the expectation that there will be appropriate work experience in the interim.

STUDENT'S OVERVIEW BOX

Overall Happiness

Academic Satisfaction

50   75   100%

Student Opinion   National Average

FACULTY RATING

Student Opinion   National Average

HITS AND MISSES

HITS
Finance dept.
Classmates are smart
School community
Facilities
Placement

MISSES
Ethnic & racial diversity
Gym
Crowd control

APPLICANTS ALSO LOOK AT
Northwestern U.
U Pennsylvania
U Virginia
Dartmouth College
Harvard

FOR MORE INFORMATION, CONTACT:
Fuqua School of Business
Towerview Drive
Durham, NC 27706
(919) 660-7705

EMORY BUSINESS SCHOOL

ADMISSIONS FACTS

Type of school	Private

Demographics

No. of men	181
No. of women	79
No. of minorities	29
No. of int'l students	41

EQUAL TREATMENT GRAPH

Admissions Statistics

Avg. GMAT	615
Avg. undergraduate GPA	3.2
Avg. age at entry	26
No. of applicants	716
No. accepted	247
No. enrolled	122

Deadlines and Notifications

Regular application	4/15
Regular notification	within 6 weeks
Special dates	N/A

Focus of Curriculum

General Management

Academic Specialties

International Finance, International Business, General Management

Special Programs

Emory's Customer Development Track (CDBT), Student Exchange Programs, The Center for Leadership and Career Studies

FINANCIAL FACTS

In-state tuition	$16,950
Out-of-state tuition	$16,950
On-campus housing	$3,000

ACADEMICS

Emory is highly regarded for its progressive curriculum, international studies program, and dedicated faculty. The latest teaching methodologies are used, such as field projects and computer simulations. One of its greatest strengths is that it provides unique opportunities for individualized study which make Emory "excellent for self-starters." It's also excellent for non-quant types. According to the school, "There is a balanced emphasis on quantitative and qualitative approaches." For those who need a little help, the school runs an optional three-day course in computer application prior to orientation.

The first-year curriculum is prescribed. Students take eleven core courses (a few are minis) in the functional areas of business. A unique requirement is the Communication Skills Workshop in which students participate in a communications lab.

The second year, as one student put it, "is flexible to individual student needs." Students take up to nine electives. In addition, students take classes in other University departments such as Law, Political Science and Foreign Language. Particularly noteworthy is the Directed Study Elective, which allows students to do their own thing, under the direction of a faculty member, of course. Unique "fieldwork" courses involve students in the community or place them in top national and international firms.

Overall, students say taking the time off to pursue an Emory MBA is worth it, although several students told us, "It's too expensive." Emory MBAs judged their skills in marketing, accounting, teamwork, presentation, and especially general management to be strong. Weaker areas were finance, computer, and quantitative skills.

PLACEMENT AND RECRUITING

Among the many services offered by the Office of Career Services are: a visiting speakers panel, workshops on communication skills and job search tactics such as networking and negotiating salaries. In addition, they run a mini-internship program: During the first two weeks in January, selected companies invite MBA students to participate in day-to-day operations. Over seventy-five companies came to recruit on campus in 1992, which didn't impress students very much. Students uniformly agree, the job placement office is not one of Emory's strong suits. "I thought I would get some more help in my job search than I am getting," seems to be the common refrain among students. Still, many others feel, "It's poor now, but very much improving." Students are enthusiastic about the alumni. The majority of students surveyed told us they contacted an alumni in their job search and found them helpful. Many relationships are developed in the Emory Mentor Program, which matches current students with local alumni.

EMORY BUSINESS SCHOOL

STUDENT LIFE/CAMPUS

Emory provides its students with the best of both worlds: an expansive, beautiful campus, and the city of Atlanta, a thriving southern metropolis. Students told us, "The quality of life can't be beat." Over 450 Fortune 500 companies are either headquartered or have an office in Atlanta. Students also told us, "The B-school is actively involved with the business community in Atlanta. This gives students the opportunity to expand upon the knowledge gained in the classroom."

Students note they "need a new B-school library." A new state-of-the-art structure should go a long way to restoring on-campus spirit and providing the necessary facilities. Time outside the classroom is spent doing community service projects, although students also find plenty of time to hit the town—together.

The students at Emory really like each other and made a point of telling us that their classmates are a great, smart group of people: "The student body is strong, aware, and very versatile." With only 115 students in each entering class, and an average of thirty-five in the classroom, students describe "a warm, congenial environment." Emory's student body is pretty homogeneous. However, most students share this second-year student's opinion: "Emory is an excellent choice if you like an intimate atmosphere where both students and professors are supportive and interested in seeing that you get the most out of the program."

Students often skip readings (a shortcut almost universally applied by B-school students). Still, Emory MBAs hit the books an average of twenty to thirty hours per week. Competition is against the grade, not fellow students.

ADMISSIONS

According to the admissions office, your work experience is considered most important. After that, in descending order, your GMAT scores, interview, college GPA, letters of recommendation, essays, and extracurricular activities are considered. Notes the school "Interviews are strongly encouraged. Candidates are also encouraged to visit a class with one of our current students."

Emory recommends that applicants have completed one semester of college calculus and be computer literate. Decisions are made on a rolling admissions basis. The school may allow applicants to defer admission for up to two years; this is decided on a case by case basis.

STUDENT'S OVERVIEW BOX

FACULTY RATING

HITS AND MISSES

HITS
Marketing dept.
Diverse work experience
Atlanta

MISSES
Quantitative skills
Don't like classmates
Recruiting

APPLICANTS ALSO LOOK AT

Duke U.
U Texas-Austin
UNC Chapel Hill
U Georgia
Vanderbilt U.

FOR MORE INFORMATION, CONTACT:
Emory Business School
1602 Mizell Drive
Atlanta, GA 30322
(404) 727-6311

GEORGETOWN UNIVERSITY SCHOOL OF BUSINESS ADMINISTRATION

ADMISSIONS FACTS

Type of school	Private

Demographics

No. of men	250
No. of women	99
No. of minorities	33
No. of int'l students	82

EQUAL TREATMENT GRAPH

Women

Minorities

0   2   4 (GPA)

Student Opinion   National Average

Admissions Statistics

Avg. GMAT	608
Avg. undergraduate GPA	3.16
Avg. age at entry	26
No. of applicants	1,112
No. accepted	487
No. enrolled	163

Deadlines and Notifications

Regular application	5/01
Regular notification	within 6 weeks
Special dates	N/A

Focus of Curriculum

General Management, Option to specialize, International Business, Business and Government, Public Policy

Academic Specialties

Int'l Business, Business and Government, Public Policy

Joint Degrees

JD/MBA

Special Programs

The International Business Diplomacy Certificate, Summer Study Abroad Opportunities, International Exchange Opportunities, Summer Pre-Enrollment "Prep".

FINANCIAL FACTS

In-state tuition	$17,460
Out-of-state tuition	$17,460
On-campus housing	$7,000

ACADEMICS

At Georgetown, academics are challenging, and coursework is relevant to what's going on in the real world. "What the University of Chicago talks about in its LEAD program," wrote one student, "we actually *do*." Particularly impressive is the focus on international business which students praised: "The international flavor is high—30 percent international students and everyone else has lived/worked abroad and speaks a second language."

In many classes, teamwork counts for up to twenty-five percent of the grade and class participation counts for another forty to sixty percent. The first-year curriculum consists of ten required courses. The second year program provides great academic diversity and flexibility. Although there are four required courses— Ethics, Public Policy, and Business I and II—students have six electives which they may take in any number of ways. They can specialize in one of three areas: international affairs, government, or public policy. Students can take electives in other graduate schools at Georgetown. And because Georgetown is part of the University Consortium System in the DC area, they can take them at consortium schools. Finally, to further pursue an interest in global business, students can get elective credit for courses taken in Area Studies Programs. Students may also apply to receive an area studies certificate. This involves choosing a geographic area of the world to study, taking all six electives in that area, and demonstrating proficiency in the native language. Area studies regions are African, Arab, Asian, Latin American, Russian, and German.

Across the board, students reported Georgetown has provided them excellent training in general management, marketing, accounting, operations management, and interpersonal/presentation skills. According to students, the school's only major weaknesses are due to its youth, resulting in lack of a national reputation, small library collection, limited alumni base, and lackluster placement services. However, students feel that "in ten years we will be tops!"

PLACEMENT AND RECRUITING

Georgetown's Career Management Office has several services and workshops. First-years have the option of enrolling in a non-credit career seminar during the first semester. Students have the option of participating in a videotaped mock interview. Both first- and second-year students are asked to submit résumés for Georgetown's résumé book, which is published and distributed to several hundred employers. According to the school, "Many initial job contacts and invitations to interview, on- and off-campus, result from the résumé books." In 1992, approximately fifty companies recruited on-campus. Ninety percent of the class of '93 had been placed within three months of graduating.

Perhaps as a function of being only a ten-year-old program, Georgetown students said they were only moderately satisfied with the services of the Career Management Office. A note for international students: job opportunities are limited by the type of visa that is held.

GEORGETOWN UNIVERSITY SCHOOL OF BUSINESS ADMINISTRATION

STUDENT LIFE/CAMPUS

With only 320 students, Georgetown offers an intimate, cooperative learning environment which students enjoy: "Classes are small, and students develop close relationships with each other, the faculty, and administration." Almost everyone works in a study group. Not surprisingly, students are extremely friendly and supportive. In fact, students strongly advised, "This is not a school for cutthroats." This camaraderie extends into the social life and students claim, "MBAs go out together every weekend, tight group."

Located on the main campus, B-school students share an undergrad campus that comprises 104 acres and sixty buildings—many of them historic landmarks—and the athletic fields you'd expect of sports powerhouse. As for the seat of government itself, one student wrote, "The Washington, D.C. location provides students access to government and business facilities," and most share this opinion. What really impressed us, however, was the students' high regard for their fellows: "The school attracts a special set of people who are genuinely interested in making a difference in the business world."

ADMISSIONS

According to the admissions office, your work experience and college GPA are considered most important. After that your essays and GMAT scores are considered. Then, in descending order or importance, your letters of recommendation and extracurricular activities. Writes the school, "The admissions committee generally numbers twelve individuals, and includes both first- and second-year MBA students, faculty, and administrators. Each applicant's file is reviewed and discussed by the Committee. General considerations are professional experience, academic performance and potential, and personal interests, qualities, and skills. International experience and community involvement are of particular interest to the admissions committee, as are positions of leadership held in academic, professional, or community organizations." Decisions are made on a rolling admissions basis. Applicants are notified of a decision four to six weeks after the completed application has been received.

STUDENT'S OVERVIEW BOX

FACULTY RATING

HITS AND MISSES

HITS
Marketing dept.
Faculty
Student Community
Washington, D.C.

MISSES
Quantitative skills
Ethnic & racial diversity
Job placement
Library

APPLICANTS ALSO LOOK AT
Duke
Emory U.
U Virginia
UNC Chapel Hill
U Michigan

FOR MORE INFORMATION, CONTACT:
School of Business Administration
Graduate Business Admissions
105 Old North Building
Washington, DC 20057-1008
(202) 687-4200

UNIVERSITY OF GEORGIA GRADUATE SCHOOL OF BUSINESS

ADMISSIONS FACTS

Type of school   Public

Demographics

No. of men	125
No. of women	39
No. of minorities	9
No. of int'l students	19

EQUAL TREATMENT GRAPH

Women

Minorities

0   2   4 (GPA)

▓ Student Opinion   ▢ National Average

Admissions Statistics

Avg. GMAT	615
Avg. undergraduate GPA	3.2
Avg. age at entry	26
No. of applicants	734
No. accepted	224
No. enrolled	106

Deadlines and Notifications

Regular application	rolling
Regular notification	rolling
Special dates	N/A

Focus of Curriculum

General Management

Academic Specialties

Accounting, Real Estate

FINANCIAL FACTS

In-state tuition	$2,175
Out-of-state tuition	$5,757
On-campus housing	$4,160

ACADEMICS

The University of Georgia–Athens (UGA) offers students either a one-year accelerated MBA or a two-year program. The one-year MBA is designed for students with an undergrad degree in business. Much of the required coursework is based on individual weaknesses in the student's background. In the regular two-year program, students spend the first year studying the basics. During the second year, students choose two "sequences" from among twenty to develop a specialization. Sequences are unique to UGA— three pre-selected courses are packaged to guarantee expertise in an area. According to students, some of the best ones—pharmacy care management, media organization management, and textile management—involve study in other university departments. Within the school, stand-out sequences are found in the accounting and real estate departments. The most interesting component of the program is the year-long professional development series which focuses on teamwork, leadership, and presentation skills. Students take part in a range of activities—from a two-day outward bound-type exercise, to a cultural diversity workshop, to a wine education seminar conducted by *Wine and Spirits* magazine—in order to supplement their classroom instruction. A highlight of the series (besides the wine tasting) is Super Saturday, in which six corporate heavyweights conduct workshops on hot topics.

Despite all these innovations, many students feel there's a lot of window dressing at UGA. Wrote one student, "They offer a lot of hype and not enough substance." Almost fifty percent of the students surveyed said UGA is not meeting their academic expectations, suggesting that the school needs to revisit its academic strategy. One MBA said, "The program needs to be more academically challenging." Students also told us the school needs its own B-school library. According to one student, "The program is going through a transition and the administration is making improvements. Bugs will be worked out in due time."

PLACEMENT AND RECRUITING

UGA's Career Services Office offers the typical fare—sessions on résumé writing and interviewing, a résumé book sent to prospective employers. One distinctive program is the Executive Breakfast Club, which invites senior management to breakfast with students. UGA has also been working on a new recruiting event, the Southeastern MBA Consortium, which will be held for the first time in January, 1994. The school already participates in the MBA Employment Conference and MBA Consortium in Chicago.

Like many B-school students, UGA MBAs report they're unhappy with career services and the range of companies recruiting. Writes one MBA, "Due to hard economic times, I'm more critical of the placement facilities." Adds another, "The school's main weakness is its inability to market the value of the program to future employers." Despite these criticisms, UGA's placement office boasts a ninety-five percent placement rate as of 1992.

UNIVERSITY OF GEORGIA GRADUATE SCHOOL OF BUSINESS

STUDENT LIFE/CAMPUS

First-year UGA students report a heavy workload and spend an average of twenty to thirty hours a week prepping for class. The pressure is intensified by the quarterly academic schedule, which causes courses to fly by. In particular, students told us there are many reading assignments during the first quarter—a mix of case studies, articles, and textbook—and students say it's important to do all or most of them. The majority of UGA MBAs utilize study groups and divvy up the load. By the second year, things have lightened up considerably.

UGA MBAs are competitive, but not overly so. Students are more interested in lending a helping hand, a by-product of the emphasis on teamwork and being part of a small MBA class (only 106 per entering class). Although students rate their classmates as extremely smart, a sizeable number indicate they don't intend to keep in touch with them after B-school.

UGA is located in Athens, a small city with a college-town feel. For road trips, Atlanta is just seventy miles away. According to students, housing is attractive/affordable either on- or off-campus. Students usually opt for off-campus living in apartments. The Graduate Business Association sponsors social, professional, and athletic activities. Especially popular are intramural sports teams of all types. Weekly happy hours provide relief from a diet of regression analysis.

ADMISSIONS

UGA weighs your GMAT score, work experience, and college GPA most heavily. After that, they weigh your letters or recommendation, extracurricular activities, and essays equally. Writes the school, "We are not looking for those attributes and experiences that make you identical to other candidates, but for those which differentiate you from the masses. While most admitted candidates will have obvious similarities, your effort should be on trying to present those things that make you unique. Don't try to isolate the 'right' answer; there are none." The school has a modified rolling admissions process—if an application is received by February 15th, the notification goes out by March 23rd. After February 15th, applicants receive a decision within twenty to thirty days of receipt of the application. On a case-by-case basis, the school permits students to defer admission for up to one year.

STUDENT'S OVERVIEW BOX

FACULTY RATING

HITS AND MISSES

HITS
Quantitative skills
Athens
Classmates are smart

MISSES
Marketing dept.
Placement
Don't like classmates

APPLICANTS ALSO LOOK AT
UNC Chapel Hill
U Texas-Austin
Georgia Inst Tech.
Duke U.
U Tennessee-Knox
Emory U.
U Alabama-Tuscaloosa

FOR MORE INFORMATION, CONTACT:
College of Business
335 Brooks Hall
Athens, GA 30602
(706) 542-5671

GEORGIA INSTITUTE OF TECHNOLOGY: IVAN ALLEN COLLEGE OF MGMT, POLICY AND INT. AFFAIRS

ADMISSIONS FACTS

Type of school	Public

Demographics

No. of men	143
No. of women	59
No. of minorities	18
No. of int'l students	34

EQUAL TREATMENT GRAPH

Women

Minorities

0   2   4 (GPA)

▨ Student Opinion   ☐ National Average

Admissions Statistics

Avg. GMAT	624
Avg. undergraduate GPA	3.2
Avg. age at entry	26
No. of applicants	540
No. accepted	205
No. enrolled	105

Deadlines and Notifications

Regular application	6/01
Regular notification	rolling
Special dates	3/01 (int'l students)

Focus of Curriculum

Specialized

Academic Specialties

Finance, Accounting, Operations, Computers

FINANCIAL FACTS

In-state tuition	$2205
Out-of-state tuition	$6531
On-campus housing	N/A

ACADEMICS

Georgia Tech offers a master of science in management (MSM) degree, and is accredited by the American Assembly of Collegiate Schools of Business. Because of its technological orientation, the school focuses on and excels in providing students with strong technical, analytical, and computer skills. According to the students we surveyed, it also offers excellent training in accounting, finance, and operations. The first-year curriculum consists of traditional core coursework. Two of the required courses—Quantitative Methods I and II—place a heavy emphasis on statistics. Two computer labs bolster Macintosh and IBM PC computing skills. During the second year, students design their own program of study through a specialization or through a combination of courses taken in the program and other university departments. Popular concentrations include: accounting, computer-integrated manufacturing systems, and management of technology. According to the school, "The MSM curriculum, both the core and many elective offerings, build on our strong technological roots and reflect the growth of the international business sector." Although one student told us, "The program is working hard to improve its international focus," another said this is just lip service: "There is a very low international orientation."

Indeed, it's unclear how satisfied students are with this school. While many say Georgia Tech is meeting their academic expectations, a not-insignificant number say it's not. The most common gripe is about professors who "seem more interested in their own research than in teaching courses." Professors fare better when it comes to their accessibility. Other complaints are about a lack of "practice-oriented courses with fieldwork," and "courses in communication skills." One student added, "The library needs better management and business resources." Still one student is satisfied: "This school provides a stronger foundation than many top twenty schools." And everyone agreed, "GT provides a great bang for the buck."

PLACEMENT AND RECRUITING

The Office of Management Career Services offers students all the typical services: a career seminar series, workshops on résumé writing, and two résumé books. According to the school, "The résumé book is the principle means by which corporations learn about the current MSM class." GT is also a member of the MBA Consortium which hosts a joint recruiting event with other B-schools. Each year more than 700 companies interview students at the placement center, but many of these companies come for the undergraduates.

Judging by the responses to our survey, students are not happy with the office of career services. Complained one student, "More emphasis is needed on bringing a wide range of employers to campus for recruiting." Another griped that too many recruiters look for engineers. One student suggested, "We need better alumni ties for job placement." Eighty-five percent of '93 Tech MBAs were placed within three months of graduation.

GEORGIA INSTITUTE OF TECHNOLOGY: IVAN ALLEN COLLEGE OF MGMT, POLICY AND INT. AFFAIRS

STUDENT LIFE/CAMPUS

GT boasts a rigorous and demanding curriculum. During the first year, this translates into a substantial workload. To keep up with it, students prepare for class an average of twenty to thirty hours a week. They also form study groups to divide and conquer assignments. The pressure, while not killer, can heat up quickly. Class participation counts heavily towards the grade. But students don't have to worry about facing a huge sea of faces; classes average twenty-five to forty students.

There's some debate over how competitive students are here. The majority said "very." The remainder said "somewhat." One student's comments resolve the issue best: "While there's competition, we work together and support one another. It's not cutthroat here." Added another, "very friendly and unstuffy atmosphere." Of the professionally diverse student body, students also said they're extremely bright. Confided one student, "Much more than I expected." A final point: students are subject to an honor code and expected to sign a pledge on exams/individual assignments stating they have "neither given nor received help."

GT boasts modern classroom and computer facilities. A unique set-up is found in "Classroom 2000," which is fully equipped with Macintosh II computers. Software allows the instructor to control any student's computer, as well as project individual screens for the entire class. Very cool. As for GT's hometown of Atlanta, it consistently rates as one of the most livable cities in the nation. As you might expect, the majority of students opt to live off-campus in apartments and say housing is great. On campus, they especially like the gym—a multi-purpose athletic monument to sweat. Leisure time is spent on outdoor activities—barbecues, golf tournaments, and intramural sports.

ADMISSIONS

If you're thinking of applying to GT straight out of college, reconsider. The vast majority of Ivan Allen students have at least two years of work experience under their belts. Also of great concern to the admissions committee is your GMAT score: The average GMAT score of accepted applicants was a smashing 614—way up in the 85th percentile. Also considered are undergraduate GPA, essays, and letters of recommendation.

STUDENT'S OVERVIEW BOX

FACULTY RATING

HITS AND MISSES

HITS
Accounting dept.
Atlanta
Classmates are smart

MISSES
Finance dept.
Library
Don't like classmates

APPLICANTS ALSO LOOK AT
U Georgia
Emory U.
Georgia State U.

FOR MORE INFORMATION, CONTACT:
Ivan Allen College
212 School of Management
Atlanta, GA 30332
(404) 894-2604

HARVARD UNIVERSITY GRADUATE SCHOOL OF BUSINESS ADMINISTRATION

ADMISSIONS FACTS

Type of school   Private

Demographics

No. of men	1,163
No. of women	475
No. of minorities	229
No. of int'l students	410

EQUAL TREATMENT GRAPH

Women

Minorities

0   2   4 (GPA)

▓ Student Opinion   ☐ National Average

Admissions Statistics

Avg. GMAT	N/A
Avg. undergraduate GPA	3.4
Avg. age at entry	26
No. of applicants	5,700
No. accepted	4,959
No. enrolled	812

Deadlines and Notifications

Regular application	3/01
Regular notification	within 10 weeks
Special dates	N/A

Focus of Curriculum

General Management

Academic Specialties

General Management, Finance, Operations, Service Management

FINANCIAL FACTS

In-state tuition	$18,550
Out-of-state tuition	$18,550
On-campus housing	$6,700

ACADEMICS

Harvard Business School (HBS) is indisputably the nation's most famous business school. According to our research, it's also the unofficial yardstick by which other B-schools measure their own programs. Over and over, we heard students and administrators compare their programs to HBS's: "We're not Harvard, but . . ." or "Our students are as smart as Harvard's . . . ." Further evidence of Harvard's unique standing is that it is the only B-school that doesn't require the GMAT. Unsurprisingly, the prevalent feeling here is summed up by one student's remarks: "If you're going to do an MBA, don't mess around. Come to the best B-school in the world."

How did Harvard come to occupy such an august position in the minds of so many students and businesses? First, as one of the oldest B-schools in the nation (it was founded in 1916), it got a head start on all the other programs. Second, as the biggest B-school—graduating roughly 800 MBAs per year—it's built a network of more than 58,000 alumni worldwide. HBS also boasts more CEO alums than any other program, a nationally renowned faculty, and authorship of ninety percent of the case materials used worldwide.

Harvard Business School (HBS) is renowned for how well it integrates all the aspects of general management and for its comprehensive coverage of the functional areas of business. During their second year, students may choose to specialize. In keeping with Harvard's emphasis on general management, courses are sequenced to "integrate the lessons of each functional area with others." Every course is taught exclusively through case analysis. Although general management is considered the cornerstone of the program, accounting, marketing, finance, entrepreneurship, and production and operations management are also strong.

In the complaint department: students feel HBS does not feature enough of an international orientation in its curriculum. Also, HBS's strict meat-and-potatoes program features little teamwork, student consulting, or other innovative learning experiences now characteristic of B-school education at other top-tier schools. Some students feel HBS has not been responsive to changes in the marketplace, and that the program's rigidity has put the school's leading-edge reputation at risk. But change is in the air. The usually self-assured Harvard has recently begun a stem-to-stern appraisal and overhaul.

PLACEMENT AND RECRUITING

HBS students get an average of two job offers each. Over eighty-five percent have a job by graduation. Twenty-six percent go into consulting, sixteen into investment banking, twenty-six into manufacturing, the remaining thirty-two percent into the non-manufacturing sector. On average, Harvard students earn the highest starting salaries, and also experience the greatest "differential factor"—the difference in salary between what they come in with and what they come out with. Needless to say, most students are quite pleased.

HARVARD UNIVERSITY GRADUATE SCHOOL OF BUSINESS ADMINISTRATION

STUDENT LIFE/CAMPUS

Harvard boasts one of the most beautiful, well-manicured campuses in the nation. Over and over, students described its "country club" ambiance and told us about groundskeepers obsessed with sod and shrubbery. "A plant died here last week," one student told us. "They replaced it within three days. And they use a snowblower to clear leaves." Students rave about the ever-popular Shad Hall, Harvard's Gym, which is a veritable temple to sweat: "Shad is worth the tuition alone."

Harvard MBAs enjoy an active social life, although one noted, "There is no such thing as dating at HBS. Local undergrads aren't bad if you hide the fact that you go to Harvard." Over fifty-five student clubs keep students fully engaged. Many of the clubs sponsor black-tie affairs such as the well-known Predator's Ball. Favorite spots for section gatherings are The Border Cafe and The Boat House. On warm days, students can be found hanging out on the sun-drenched patios of Kresge, an on-campus eatery.

Harvard divides its 800 incoming students into sections of ninety; each section takes an entire year of prescribed courses together. Wrote one MBA, "Section life is a great experience. You develop great camaraderie with classmates from diverse cultural and professional backgrounds." Most of the first-year social life revolves around the section, which schedules dozens of section events to insure you get to know those ninety classmates well. The school highly recommends forming study groups. During orientation and the first week of class, students generally seek out classmates with whom to form a group. It's not uncommon for overanxious types to begin doing this in the summer, to lock-in someone smart.

Harvard's reputation for intensity and competitiveness is well earned. The first four months are the most difficult. As one student explained, "It ramps up quickly. Students who know zero about accounting and stats get left behind." The pressure to succeed is formidable. A forced grading curve causes roughly ten percent of the students in each course to fail, which is known as "looping." In fact, about seventy percent of the first-year students loop at least one class. Too many loops, however, and the board evaluates whether you need to take a year or two off. Not to worry, though: Class participation counts so heavily toward your grade, students say if you participate in class it is very unlikely that you will fail.

ADMISSIONS

The admissions board at Harvard considers the following criteria (not ranked in order of importance): college GPA/transcripts, essays, letters of recommendation, and extracurricular activities. Harvard does not consider the GMAT. The essays are considered extremely important. Applicants are interviewed at Harvard's discretion only to further evaluate the student's candidacy. Applications are batched in one of four rounds, ending Nov. 9th, Dec. 9th, Jan. 4th, and March 4th. Applicants who apply as college seniors may be admitted with a mandatory deferral. For all other applicants, admissions deferrals are rarely granted.

STUDENT'S OVERVIEW BOX

FACULTY RATING

HITS AND MISSES

HITS
Teaching
Library
Gym

MISSES
Operational skills
Computer skills
Off-campus housing

APPLICANTS ALSO LOOK AT
Northwestern U.
MIT
U Virginia
Columbia U.
U Michigan
Stanford
U Chicago
U Penn

FOR MORE INFORMATION, CONTACT:
M.B.A. Admissions
Harvard Business School
Boston, MA 02163
(617) 495-6127

HOFSTRA UNIVERSITY SCHOOL OF BUSINESS

ADMISSIONS FACTS

Type of school	Private

Demographics

No. of men	122
No. of women	78
No. of minorities	19
No. of int'l students	35

EQUAL TREATMENT GRAPH

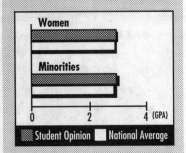

Admissions Statistics

Avg. GMAT	586
Avg. undergraduate GPA	3.2
Avg. age at entry	26
Avg. of applicants	637
Avg. accepted	350
Avg. enrolled	110

Deadlines and Notifications

Regular application	4/30
Regular notification	within 6 weeks
Special dates	N/A

Focus of Curriculum

Specialized

Academic Specialties

Accounting, Finance, Information Systems

Joint Degrees

JD/MBA

Special Programs

The Hofstra Univ. Consulting Group, The Assoc. of Students of Economics and International Commerce (ASEIC), Beta Gamma Sigma, The Long Island Venture Group, The Retail Management Institute

FINANCIAL FACTS

In-state tuition	$10,000
Out-of-state tuition	$10,000
On-campus housing	$5,000

ACADEMICS

One of Hofstra's strengths is that it tailors its program to the individual needs of a student by tailoring each program based on prior education, graduate degree objectives, and a common body of knowledge. Business undergrads, for example, might be required to take fewer courses. They can also pursue the MBA full-time and complete degree requirements in only one calendar year by attending both summer sessions and the January session as well as the fall and spring semesters.

The MBA program consists of four components: prerequisite courses for students who lack an undergrad business degree or specific course work, core courses that cover common business knowledge, specialization electives that allow a student to concentrate in an area of business, and the option of either a master's thesis or graduate research seminar. The thesis or research seminar trains students in research design and in the preparation of sophisticated business reports. Seven areas of concentration are offered. Students who select the non-thesis option take four specialization electives in one of these areas. The thesis option requires three specialization electives. Students are exposed to traditional learning experiences as well as innovative exercises and simulated business situations. Particularly noteworthy is the program's emphasis on hands-on computer learning which is enhanced by Hofstra's state-of-the-art computer facilities. Hofstra is also "one of only a few non-doctoral programs which subscribes to the Center for Research in Security Prices (CRSP) database" and makes this data available to students. The database provides "daily and monthly information for over 8,000 firms" and is considered "essential for conducting financial event and market efficiency studies." A unique opportunity is found in the school's Small Business Management Institute whereby students serve as consultants to small businesses who have sought assistance from the fed's Small Business Administration (SBA). The SBA provides small stipends to this group which helps the businesses avoid defaulting on their SBA loans.

PLACEMENT AND RECRUITING

The Career Development Office offers students assistance with résumé preparation, interviewing skills, and job search strategies. Students may access this help in one-on-one counseling sessions or in one of the MBA Career Planning Seminars. Students may also place their résumé in Hofstra's MBA Résumé book which is distributed to Fortune 500 firms and smaller financial institutions in the New York City area.

In 1992, sixty-eight companies recruited on campus. Of all the students, eighty-five percent had a job within three months of graduation (four percent go on for additional education). Despite these stats, students said they're not satisfied with the range of companies recruiting nor the efforts of the placement office. One student even felt that "the placement office stats are unrealistic." But he might have been down on his luck. Students felt a lot better about the schools alumni. At least half of the respondents in our survey chose to contact an alumni for help in their job search and found them helpful.

HOFSTRA UNIVERSITY SCHOOL OF BUSINESS

STUDENT LIFE/CAMPUS

Hofstra is located in Hempstead, New York, twenty-five miles from New York City. Situated right on the Hempstead Turnpike, the campus itself is lovely—tree-lined and dotted with sculpture. It even houses an arboretum. Less lovely is the parking situation, which students say can be next to impossible. This is a daily headache since the school is dominated by Long Island commuters (a small number live on-campus in the modern high-rise dorms). Classes are small, with an average of ten to twenty-five students in each. Students rate themselves as competitive, but hardly the type to mow someone down. Instead, there is a sense of camaraderie and students solve problems in a team environment. Hofstra MBAs bring diverse and interesting work perspectives to the classroom experience. They also bring their smarts. But according to our survey, students don't necessarily like to hang out with or intend to keep each other as long-term buddies. Indeed, the social scene is subdued here because students commute and aren't around on weekends. School spirit is largely absent. However, students agree that Hofstra is well-run. Wrote one student, "The administration is accessible, including the Dean of the school." However, there are many school activities. There's an active seminar program, and lots of "Career Forums" to attend. Students also organize tailgate parties before Hofstra football games, a spring picnic, and a graduate cruise around Manhattan. A newsletter keeps everyone connected to campus. Although this school tends to be attended by Long Island commuters, a small number live in the hi-rise dorms.

ADMISSIONS

According to the admissions office, the following is considered most important in your application: leadership, communication skills, and levels of increasing professional responsibility. After that, in descending order of importance, are your work experience, college GPA, GMAT score, letters of recommendation, extracurricular activities, and interview. "Admission processes," writes the school, "tend to be very similar to the selective to highly selective schools in the United States. All (application) materials are evaluated carefully by a committee comprised of faculty and administrators. We offer perhaps one of the more timely application turnarounds among the group of selective schools; once an application is complete, we generally notify the applicant of a decision within four weeks." Members of American minority groups, e.g. African-Americans, receive special consideration.

Applicants may defer admission up to one year for medical reasons or to accrue additional work experience. There is an admission deferment program for college seniors.

STUDENT'S OVERVIEW BOX

FACULTY RATING

HITS AND MISSES

HITS
Marketing dept.
Computer facilities
Students professionally diverse
Small classes

MISSES
Hempstead
School spirit

APPLICANTS ALSO LOOK AT
New York University
St. John's U.
Columbia U.
USC
U Maryland

FOR MORE INFORMATION, CONTACT:
School of Business
1000 Fulton Avenue
Hempstead, NY 11550
(516) 463- 5683

UNIV. OF ILLINOIS AT URBANA-CHAMPAIGN COLL. OF COMMERCE AND BUSINESS ADMINISTRATION

ADMISSIONS FACTS

Type of school	Public

Demographics

No. of men	473
No. of women	153
No. of minorities	30
No. of int'l students	162

EQUAL TREATMENT GRAPH

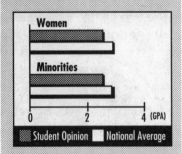

Admissions Statistics

Avg. GMAT	590
Avg. undergraduate GPA	4.25
Avg. age at entry	25
Avg. of applicants	813
Avg. accepted	587
Avg. enrolled	297

Deadlines and Notifications

Regular application	5/01
Regular notification	within 10 days
Special dates	N/A

Focus of Curriculum

General Management

Academic Specialties

Marketing, Finance

Special Programs

Chief Financial Officer Lecture Series, Business Advisory Council, Executive in Residence Program

FINANCIAL FACTS

In-state tuition	$3,988
Out-of-state tuition	$9,620
On-campus housing	$4,000

ACADEMICS

The curriculum at the University of Illinois (UI) B-school consists of three components: foundations, managerial functions, and professional concentrations. Six first-year courses provide a basic foundation—statistics, quantitative methods, production and operation management, organizational behavior, and micro and macro economics. Another six introduce students to the functional areas—marketing, managerial accounting, financial management, business law, and strategic management. During the second year, students take a capstone course that integrates and applies previous coursework. Specifically, it teaches corporate strategy from a CEO's point of view. Electives are used to create areas of specialization. The three newest are: Health Care Management, Agribusiness Management, and the Management of Technology. Students may also take electives in other university departments. Wrote one student, "The MBA program is very flexible in terms of elective coursework, unlike other schools which force you to take a track of courses." For those who need to juice up their computer skills, a required computer competency course gets students cranking through spreadsheets, database management, and business graphics.

The majority of MBAs report they feel well prepared in the following areas: general management, marketing, finance, teamwork, quantitative methods, and computing. A sizeable number feel less confident about their accounting and operations skills. As for the faculty, students told us teaching at IU can be spotty. There are some amazing professors and some not-so amazing professors. Professors do garner rave reviews for their after-class accessibility. Although some students told us UI is not meeting their academic expectations, the majority said taking time off to get an UI MBA is worth it. Several students said they chose this program because of its "high value/low cost." Enthused one student, "Great school. Overshadowed because Northwestern and Chicago are so close."

PLACEMENT AND RECRUITING

The Placement Office is common property here, shared by both undergrads and MBAs in the College of Commerce and Business Administration. However, they provide special services to MBAs. For example, a summer internship and full-time résumé book is distributed to hundreds of firms, and over 300 companies recruit on-campus annually. A program that distinguishes UI is CAREERLINE, a database of alumni grouped by geographic location, industry, and job title, who have made themselves available to field questions about their industries. Still, students aren't satisfied with what they perceive to be as a less-than-aggressive MBA placement office. In particular, they'd like the school to beef up on the range and number of companies recruiting from outside the Chicago area. But according to one student, "Career placement is improving. The resources are there, it just takes some digging." Of 1992 MBAs, sixty-seven percent had been placed within forty-five days of graduation.

UNIV. OF ILLINOIS AT URBANA-CHAMPAIGN COLL. OF COMMERCE AND BUSINESS ADMINISTRATION

STUDENT LIFE/CAMPUS

Students report a heavy first-year workload and spend roughly twenty to thirty hours a week preparing for class. Although many students skim or blow off an occasional case, the majority feel it's necessary to read all or most of it. Wrote one student, "The case load may be intense, but it gives the school its strong academic reputation." To maintain their sanity, students look to their pre-assigned study groups for help. Said one, "The study group concept enhances interpersonal skills" as well. In terms of competitiveness, students observe there are some sharks, and there are some helpers. Overall, teamwork and a supportive learning environment prevails. As one student put it, "I was apprehensive about the competitive nature of B-schools. But my fears have been put to rest. The maturity and diversity of my classmates foster a cooperative spirit throughout this program." Another student, though, doesn't think much of IU MBAs: "I have the feeling that some students came here merely because they couldn't find a job, not necessarily because they definitely wanted to get an MBA."

One student's comments typified the prevalent feeling here: "IU boasts excellent facilities. The library is the third largest in the nation." In particular, IU MBAs are big fans of the athletic facilities—which house four entire gymnasia—a monument to sweat. Students report both on- and off-campus housing is plentiful and attractive, although the majority opt to live off-campus in apartments. Social events are orchestrated through the MBA Association. They direct activities such as career forums, the annual spring banquet, and barbecues on football weekends

ADMISSIONS

The admissions office considers your GMAT scores to be most important. After that, in descending order, they consider your college GPA, essays, and letters of recommendation. Work experience and extracurricular activities are "preferred" but not required. Because of the quantitative components of the curriculum, applicants are advised to have completed a college-level calculus course. Writes the school, "The admissions program is client-oriented. An applicant can track his/her application through a 1-800-MBA-UIUC number."

Decisions are made on a rolling admissions basis. Applicants are notified of a decision ten days from receipt of the completed application. Waitlisted students are notified of a spot by June 15th.

STUDENT'S OVERVIEW BOX

Overall Happiness

Academic Satisfaction

50   75   100%

Student Opinion   National Average

FACULTY RATING

Student Opinion   National Average

HITS AND MISSES

HITS
Quantitative skills
Library
Ethnic & racial diversity

MISSES
Accounting dept.
Placement
Lack diverse work experience

APPLICANTS ALSO LOOK AT
Northwestern U.
U Iowa
Indiana U-Bloom.
U Texas-Austin
U Wisconsin-Madison

FOR MORE INFORMATION, CONTACT:
College of Commerce and Business
Administration
1206 South 6th St. 260 Comm West
Champaign, IL 61820
(217) 333-4555

INDIANA UNIVERSITY GRADUATE SCHOOL OF BUSINESS

ADMISSIONS FACTS

Type of school	Public

Demographics

No. of men	404
No. of women	140
No. of minorities	65
No. of int'l students	91

EQUAL TREATMENT GRAPH

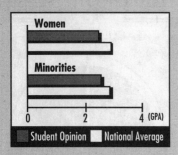

Admissions Statistics

Avg. GMAT	605
Avg. undergraduate GPA	3.2
Avg. age at entry	27
Avg. of applicants	1,674
Avg. accepted	642
Avg. enrolled	227

Deadlines and Notifications

Regular application	3/15
Regular notification	within 6 weeks
Special dates	N/A

Focus of Curriculum

Specialized

Academic Specialties

Finance, Marketing, Human Resources Management, International Business

Joint Degrees

MBA/JD

Special Programs

Deloitte-Touche and Procter and Gamble sponsored and judged case analysis competition, Foreign Study in eight foreign countries.

FINANCIAL FACTS

In-state tuition	$6,000
Out-of-state tuition	$12,000
On-campus housing	$3,300

ACADEMICS

One of the best B-schools in the nation, Indiana University has enhanced its reputation with a thorough overhaul of its curriculum. The new program incorporates modern-day themes such as cross-functional learning, globalization, social values, teamwork, leadership, and multi-culturalism. In an unusual break from tradition, the first-year courses are grouped in "cores." During the first semester there is a foundations core, a professional core, and a week-long "immersion" seminar on total quality management. During the second semester, there is a functional core and an immersion seminar on an industry analysis. The most novel innovation is that students receive only two grades in the first semester—one for each of the cores, and one for the remaining core in the second semester. The second year is devoted to an area of specialization. To further enhance teamwork, IU divides its entering class into cohorts of sixty-five students each. Cohorts take first semester courses together and are then reshuffled to introduce students to as many classmates as possible. Four faculty members oversee each core, creating a personal learning environment. But their involvement with the students extends beyond class. Students unanimously praise professors for their generous accessibility. The vast majority of students also praise them for their fine teaching.

Although the program is only a year old, students already reported, "The new program is a great success." Added another, "The new curriculum is well thought out and offers a great team learning experience." Overall, students reported they felt well-prepared in accounting, finance, and general management. Given the emphasis on collaborative learning, it's not surprising that students rate their teamwork and interpersonal skills as extremely strong. But there are weak spots: students feel less confident about their skills in marketing, operations, and computing. Although some MBAs seemed to agree with the student who told us, "The administration is very customer-oriented," a sizeable number say the school might be better run. For example, it can be difficult to get into popular courses.

PLACEMENT AND RECRUITING

The Business Placement Office (BPO) offers students every modern placement service, from workshops on job search strategies to résumé books and career nights with visiting execs. What's most impressive about this office is its volume of offerings. According to the school, in 1991–1992, the BPO "sponsored over 100 corporate presentations, arranged for more than 50 companies to conduct more than 1,100 interviews for summer internships," and brought over 300 companies on campus for graduating students. Although the school claims that firms from every region recruit at IU, more than 50 percent of the students we surveyed said the school needs to do more to attract a wider range of companies. Wrote one student, "This is a Midwest school with a majority of job recruiters coming from Midwest companies [including Chicago]."

INDIANA UNIVERSITY GRADUATE SCHOOL OF BUSINESS

STUDENT LIFE/CAMPUS

Students agree that during the first year, the pace and breadth of learning at IU can be frightening. Indeed, an "extremely demanding workload" requires students to study/prepare an average of thirty-five to forty hours each week. Few corners can be cut; the majority of students report it's important to do all or most assigned reading. Since the professionally diverse student body is also intelligent, they're well equipped to make it through the program. Still, one IU MBA said the trick is to learn how to "master balancing the demands of the program and your social life, so that you can enjoy the experience immensely." Good advice. According to students we surveyed, there's plenty to enjoy at IU. Students are laid-back and friendly. Explained one MBA, "IU is an extremely cooperative place. Students are not cut-throat or too competitive." Students say they go out a lot, but in groups, not on dates. A favorite destination on Thursday nights (there's no class on Friday) is the designated bar of the week. Organized social events are also popular—picnics, barbecues, and the Spring Banquet. The majority of students become involved in the student-run career clubs, such as the Graduate Women of Business or Finance Club.

As for IU's hometown of Bloomington, writes the school, it's a "little like a mix of Ann Arbor, Berkeley, and Cambridge with a dash of Main Street, USA thrown in." Agreed one student, "Bloomington is a wonderful town." Students report that housing, whether on- or off-campus, is cost-effective and extremely attractive. The majority opt to live off-campus in apartments in Bloomington or surrounding neighborhoods. Public transportation is easily accessible. A car is helpful if you want to go exploring on the weekend, but according to students, parking is the pits.

ADMISSIONS

According to the school, Indiana does not prioritize its admissions criteria, "but weighs GMAT scores, the undergraduate record, and work experience most heavily. There are not cut-offs for GMAT scores or GPAs. Leadership experience is also an important factor." An interview is recommended, but not required. Applicants to Indiana University must have completed a course in calculus and received a grade of "C" or better. The school does not review applications on either a rolling admissions or rounds basis. There is one final deadline—March 15th. All applicants are notified of a decision during the first two weeks of April. Students may request a deferments for up to two years.

STUDENT'S OVERVIEW BOX

FACULTY RATING

HITS AND MISSES

HITS
Finance dept.
Bloomington
Helping other students

MISSES
Marketing dept.
Off-campus housing
Ethnic & racial diversity

APPLICANTS ALSO LOOK AT
U Michigan
UNC Chapel Hill
Duke U.
Northwestern U.

FOR MORE INFORMATION, CONTACT:
Bryan Hall Rm 333 10 & Fee Lane
Bloomington, IN 47405
(812) 855-8006

University of Iowa: Iowa Business School

ACADEMICS

As one student puts it, "The Iowa MBA program is in transition and is still making adjustments in order to educate efficiently." Indeed, the school is instituting many changes to secure its position as one of the nation's best. One notable change is the new state-of-the-art building, which, according to MBAs, "will have one of the best libraries and computer labs on campus." But students also hope that Iowa "establishes firmer ties with area corporations for classroom study, not just placement" and "introduces personal development skills (time management, diversity, and etiquette)."

Certain components of the MBA program are already in place. Chief among them are a commitment to first-rate academics and a general management education. Students described Iowa as a "gem in the rough" with "top-twenty potential." The first year consists of a highly structured sequence of core courses and has a quantitative bent. However, students explain "the curriculum during the second year allows students to choose the majority of their classes. Many students pursue joint degrees in law, hospital administration, MIS, or accounting." One unique program, according to Iowa MBAs, is the Emerging Free Market Economy Program, which sends teams of MBAs to act as consultants in Eastern Europe during the summer. Shares another MBA, "Iowa is a place that welcomes student involvement and lets you build a portfolio of skills. The IMPACT program is a wonderful example. It starts during orientation week with an Outward Bound-like course and continues with workshops on communications skills, etc."

Professors garner high marks for their accessibility, but get mixed reviews for their teaching. One MBA told us, "There are excellent professors in the finance and management departments." Enthused another, "Profs are wonderful; I'll keep in touch with them long after I leave." But a sizeable number of students had complaints. Griped one, "Some faculty are more concerned with their research than teaching. Also, not enough have had serious business experience before becoming a prof." Overall, students say this program is worth the investment of time and money, but is not yet meeting all of their academic expectations. Stay tuned, the upgraded, high-tech facilities should go a long way toward bolstering academics here.

PLACEMENT AND RECRUITING

Seventy-six companies recruit on-campus annually. Eighty-one percent of graduating students are placed within three months of commencement. Leading recruiters are Aegon USA, Andersen Consulting, Ford Motor Company, Kimberly Clark, Merck, and Proctor and Gamble. Writes the school, "It is quite common for recruiters to comment on the strong work ethic and resourcefulness exhibited by Iowa students. When our graduates bring this level of commitment to their employing companies, they begin making meaningful contributions very quickly."

But students told us this is one of the departments in transition and rapidly improving. As of now, students feel this office is not doing enough to attract new companies and build a national reputation.

UNIVERSITY OF IOWA: IOWA BUSINESS SCHOOL

STUDENT LIFE/CAMPUS

Students report a moderately heavy workload and spend an average of fifteen to twenty-five hours a week preparing for class. Core classes have roughly fifty students per class, electives twenty-five to thirty. The majority of students work in a study group. As one MBA put it, "One of the best things about this school is its small size. Only 120 students in each entering class, so you get to know everyone!" Students report a "FANTASTIC student community," and an "unbelievable amount of school pride." As one might expect in this kind of environment, students are competitive, but in a spirited way. The vast majority say classmates are very interested in helping others. As for the student body, Iowa MBAs say there are an "interesting cross-section of non-business types with good insights." But another gripes, "Since there is no work requirement for this school, the average student is young with little or no experience. So the diversity is not what it should be."

At the center of all extracurriculars is the MBA Association. It orchestrates everything from educational programs to faculty/student mixers. Highlights are once-a-semester trips to cities like Chicago, St. Paul/Minneapolis for corporate site visits. Community Service is also popular—Iowa MBAs volunteer to Habitat for Humanity. Every Thursday night they head to Fitzpatricks, the unofficial MBA pub. Iowa offers civilized city living, although with a population of 50,000 this pace feels more like a small town. MBAs live off-campus in apartments in Iowa City and Coralville. The bus system is good, but most students bring a car.

ADMISSIONS

According to the admissions office, the following components are all weighed equally: essays, college GPA, letters of recommendation, extracurriculars, work experience, and GMAT scores. The school advises, however, "Applicants are encouraged to pay particular attention to the essay component of the application process. In addition to considering quantitative factors such as GMAT scores and the undergraduate transcript, we look at prior work experience (responsibilities, not just titles) career focus and ambition, maturity, and individuality. Our understanding of those attributes is derived from essay responses." Admissions decisions are made on a rolling basis until the final deadline of April 15th. Students may defer admission for up to one year. Roughly forty percent of all applicants are admitted.

STUDENT'S OVERVIEW BOX

FACULTY RATING

HITS AND MISSES

HITS
Quantitative skills
On-campus housing
Helping other students

MISSES
Accounting dept.
Recruiting
Don't like classmates

APPLICANTS ALSO LOOK AT
Ohio State U.
U Texas-Austin
U Illinois-C.U.
Michigan State U.
U Wisconsin-Madison

FOR MORE INFORMATION, CONTACT:
121 Phillips Hall
Iowa City, IA 52242
(319) 335-0862

UNIVERSITY OF KANSAS SCHOOL OF BUSINESS

ADMISSIONS FACTS

Type of school	Public

Demographics

No. of men	114
No. of women	57
No. of minorities	8
No. of int'l students	27

EQUAL TREATMENT GRAPH

■ Student Opinion	□ National Average

Admissions Statistics

Avg. GMAT	554
Avg. undergraduate GPA	3.12
Avg. age at entry	25
Avg. of applicants	261
Avg. accepted	110
Avg. enrolled	73

Deadlines and Notifications

Regular application	rolling
Regular notification	within 3 weeks
Special dates	N/A

Focus of Curriculum

General Management

Academic Specialties

Accounting, Finance

FINANCIAL FACTS

In-state tuition	$2,176
Out-of-state tuition	$6,396
On-campus housing	$2,700

ACADEMICS

As one student put it, "The University of Kansas (KU) is thought to be the best school in the Big Eight." Students we surveyed repeatedly emphasized two themes: first, that "KU's MBA program provides low cost/high value," and second, that it "emphasizes what the business world wants—teamwork/interpersonal skills and total quality management (TQM)." Most students feel the school does an excellent job with both. KU offers a generalist perspective; students pursue a broad study of the major business disciplines. Coursework features a global slant and "a TQM people-as-assets mentality." Students elect to specialize in one of several areas, including international business and human resources. Stand-out departments include accounting and finance. Wrote one MBA, "Only one professor gives a course in production or operations, but it's excellent." A popular course is Total Quality Management, taught by Professor Dennis Karney, whose in-class theatrics entertain and delight. There's flexibility in first- and second-year course selection and sequencing. But scheduling creates snags. One MBA moaned, "Many of the courses that should be taken in the same semester often overlap in time, thus the student cannot take all of them."

Students described faculty as "extremely approachable and supportive," but said teaching is uneven. The majority are very good. The rest are average. Explained this MBA, "Faculty are very talented, but many need to work on their basic teaching skills. They're capable in the analytical areas of the field, yet have difficulty delivering a solid lecture." The administration also gets mixed reviews. According to one student, "They work closely with the students and have a good knowledge of student affairs." But the majority agreed, "There is too much emphasis on procedure, not enough on process."

Overall, students report they feel well trained by their studies in finance, accounting, quantitative methods, and particularly in the school's area of emphasis—teamwork. A sizeable minority say they feel less confident about their marketing, operations, and computer skills. Wrote one MBA, "The basics need to be strengthened." Still, the overwhelming majority say this program is worth the investment of time and money. Summed up one student, "The school has the potential to be tops if it can get away from state restrictions and improve its financial position."

PLACEMENT AND RECRUITING

The placement office publishes an electronic MBA résumé book and turns students on to jobs through a networking referral system. According to the school, over 175 national, regional and local firms recruit on campus, although these firms come as much for the undergraduates as they do for the MBAs. Wrote one student, "KU carries a lot of weight when searching for a job in the Kansas City area." But students feel the placement office isn't on the ball. Wrote one student, "Placement Center needs a new director and funds to go to work with. Basically, I got a job on my own." One student put out a bulletin: "The top thirty percent of this program are an undiscovered treasure. They have great overall skills, yet are willing to accept lower salaries because of the low cost of this program."

UNIVERSITY OF KANSAS SCHOOL OF BUSINESS

STUDENT LIFE/CAMPUS

The workload is heavy, the pressure can be intense. Students hit their books an average of twenty to thirty hours a week—sometimes more, sometimes less. Griped one student, "Every prof (with the exception of two) that I have had has assigned approximately two times the work that can be completed for the course." On the upside, students rave about the benefits of KU's small size. Wrote one enthusiastic student, "It's possible to get into all required courses and popular electives." Reported another, "Classes are small, especially in the electives—twenty to twenty-five students in each." As one might expect in a small program, "students are close and extremely helpful." Added another, "We are competitive in getting what we need to achieve, but don't step on each other to get there." The majority of students report a vibrant social life. As for the student body itself, MBAs describe a program filled with "bright, talented students who have a lot of ambition." Praised one, "KU has done a great job with international students and relations." But one intolerant type wrote, "Too many foreign students get special privileges in class because of their so-called lack of English."

According to KU MBAs, "Computer technology is antiquated, as is the access to network services." These are gradually being updated. As for UK's hometown, just ask any MBA about Lawrence and she/he'll tell you "it's a great place to go to school." It's small and civilized, and just a forty minute drive from the bright lights of Kansas City. One MBA observed, "The campus is beautiful and school spirit abounds (how 'bout them Hawks!)." But parking is difficult during sporting events, and in general, expensive. Most MBAs live off-campus in apartments and rental homes in Lawrence. The Graduate Business Council sponsors activities such as weekly beer busts, and twice a year, hosts a faculty roast and toast.

ADMISSIONS

According to the school, your college GPA, GMAT scores, letters of recommendation, and work experience are all weighted equally. Your extracurricular activities are also considered. Writes the admissions office, "There are no minimum scores for GPA/GMAT when considering candidates. The admissions board will also consider extra submissions, such as résumés and extra letters of recommendations." Decisions are made on a rolling admissions basis. Students are notified of a decision approximately three weeks after all application materials are received. Notes the school, "The application form, supplemental data form, and check for $40.00 must be received by the deadline. Other materials (GMAT, transcripts, letters of recommendation, TOEFL) can come in after the deadline, but a student will not be admitted without all. We have no auditing of classes for non-credit, no exceptions." Students may defer admission for up to one year with a written request.

STUDENT'S OVERVIEW BOX

Overall Happiness

Academic Satisfaction

50   75   100%

Student Opinion   National Average

FACULTY RATING

Student Opinion   National Average

HITS AND MISSES

HITS
Finance dept.
Lawrence
Helping other students

MISSES
Marketing dept.
Placement
Social life

APPLICANTS ALSO LOOK AT

U Texas-Austin
Wichita State U.
U Missouri-K.C.
Ohio State U.

FOR MORE INFORMATION, CONTACT:
School of Business
203 Summerfield Hall
Lawrence, KS 66045
(913) 864-4254

UNIVERSITY OF KENTUCKY COLLEGE OF BUSINESS AND ECONOMICS

ADMISSIONS FACTS

Type of school   Public

Demographics

No. of men	88
No. of women	60
No. of minorities	3
No. of int'l students	7

EQUAL TREATMENT GRAPH

Women

Minorities

0   2   4 (GPA)

■ Student Opinion   □ National Average

Admissions Statistics

Avg. GMAT	575
Avg. undergraduate GPA	3.09
Avg. age at entry	26.9
Avg. of applicants	230
Avg. accepted	133
No. enrolled	86

Deadlines and Notifications

Regular application	7/01
Regular notification	rolling
Special dates	N/A

Focus of Curriculum

General Management

Academic Specialties

General Management

Joint Degrees

MBA/JD

FINANCIAL FACTS

In-state tuition	$2,150
Out-of-state tuition	$5,838
On-campus housing	$3,200

ACADEMICS

If you're looking for a school where students are in accord about their B-school experience, the University of Kentucky (UK) is not for you. In almost every area, this school gets mixed reviews. Some consider it an "excellent school" of "high academic quality." Others complained, "Classes concentrate on plug-and-grind memorization," and "Elective offerings are limited." There's also a lack of consensus about faculty. While the majority of students agreed professors are "good" and "go out of their way to be available," an almost equal number say they're mediocre to bad. Complained one, "Most profs are not here to teach, they're here to do research." Griped another, "All graduate courses should be taught by professors." Some of the reported unevenness of UK's program can be explained by this MBA: "UK is currently experiencing budget cuts. The result is fewer professors and crowded classrooms. A real disappointment." It's even difficult to get into required and popular courses.

In terms of academics, UK is like other schools included in this book. The first year is devoted to a broad study of the functional areas of business. The second year permits students to concentrate their electives in one of several areas: decision science and information systems, finance and banking, health care, international business, and marketing. Electives may also be taken in other university departments. Although the marks students gave themselves for their academic preparedness were average in all the major disciplines—i.e., finance, marketing, accounting—the two highest were in general management and quantitative methods. Still, students should do well when they take the B-school's required four-hour comprehensive exam in their final semester. Reported one MBA, "About twenty percent of the class have 4.0 averages and no one has ever failed it." All in all, the majority of students say taking time off to get a UK MBA is worth it. And UK MBAs expect to be leveraging their degree long after that first job out of school.

PLACEMENT AND RECRUITING

Students are unanimous in their negative feelings about the placement center. Wrote one student, "The MBA Center is not the focal point it should be. Staff seem unprepared to help students with job seeking. The center does not help students find internships/co-op type employment." Students are also disappointed with the range of companies recruiting on campus. The school has recently asked the special assistant to the dean to pitch in, and things should pick up shortly. Most recent figures from the school show a ninety percent placement within three months of graduation.

UNIVERSITY OF KENTUCKY COLLEGE OF BUSINESS AND ECONOMICS

STUDENT LIFE/CAMPUS

The workload is moderate, the pressure is light. The majority of students report they hit the books an average of fifteen to twenty-five hours a week. In most courses, exams count heavily towards the grade. As for those overstuffed classes, one student griped that they are "too large to have any quality discussions."

According to one student, "The school's greatest asset is the range and depth of students." Again, it depends on whom you ask. Disagreed one MBA, "Too many students don't have enough work experience to make valuable contributions." What about competitiveness? No surprise—it depends on whom you ask. Some say yes, some say no, with most answers falling in between. As for the social scene, the majority say it's lacking. There's only one student club, the MBA Association, which sponsors activities like a Thursday night supper club and a few intramural sports, but not much more. On the upside, students say the gym is pretty good and the "business lab and new classrooms are excellent."

As for the town of Lexington, students like it. A short roadtrip away is the city of Louisville. International students tend to live in on-campus housing that is considered decent. The majority of MBAs opt for off-campus living in the town of Lexington. Parking is difficult. Most students drop their car at the football stadium and shuttlebus in.

ADMISSIONS

According to the admissions office, your GMAT score, college GPA/transcript, and university attended are considered most important. After that, in *descending* order, your letters of recommendation, work experience, essays, and extracurricular activities. Notes the office of admissions: "Undergraduate degrees in engineering or science are considered a plus. The one hundred best applications are accepted every year. Completed applications are reviewed within fifteen days of receipt and divided into three categories: accept, reject and hold. Those in the 'hold' category are placed in a pool and a decision on them is deferred until late spring."

STUDENT'S OVERVIEW BOX

Overall Happiness

Academic Satisfaction

50   75   100%

Student Opinion   National Average

FACULTY RATING

Student Opinion   National Average

HITS AND MISSES

HITS
Quantitative skills
On-campus housing
Classmates are smart

MISSES
Finance dept.
Placement
Don't stay in touch

APPLICANTS ALSO LOOK AT
U Tennessee-Knox
Indiana U.-Bloom.
U Cincinnati

FOR MORE INFORMATION, CONTACT:
College of Business and Economics
B and E Building
Lexington, KY 40506
(606) 257-8939

LOYOLA UNIVERSITY–CHICAGO GRADUATE SCHOOL OF BUSINESS

ADMISSIONS FACTS

Type of school	Private

Demographics

No. of men	91
No. of women	49
No. of minorities	12
No. of int'l students	24

EQUAL TREATMENT GRAPH

Women

Minorities

0   2   4 (GPA)

■ Student Opinion □ National Average

Admissions Statistics

Avg. GMAT	550
Avg. undergraduate GPA	3.2
Avg. age at entry	26
No. of applicants	322
No. accepted	209
No. enrolled	125

Deadlines and Notifications

Regular application	7/26
Regular notification	within 2 weeks
Special dates	N/A

Focus of Curriculum

Specialized

Academic Specialties

General Management, Accounting

Special Programs

Foreign Study at Loyola's Rome Center Campus, Multi-cultural advisors for minority students

FINANCIAL FACTS

In-state tuition	$10,620
Out-of-state tuition	$10,620
On-campus housing	N/A

ACADEMICS

Loyola University Chicago is a private university affiliated with the Roman Catholic Church. Although religion is not carried over into the classroom, the university describes itself as committed to the development of "socially responsible leadership." Most recently, the school retreaded its curriculum and added a required ethics course. According to the school, this "provides an analytical framework for integrating the personal values of the manager with the functional areas of business decision-making." Another new addition is an international business course. But beyond this, there's nothing especially different or innovative about this program. First-year students take a traditional lineup of eleven core courses. During the second year, students may specialize by taking three courses in one of the following fields: accounting, financial management, marketing management, personnel management, production and operations management, management science and computers. Any deviation from the prescribed course of study is met with rigid sequencing rules. You can't take certain courses before others, and no more than two electives may be taken in any field of study beyond the area of specialization. The majority of students surveyed report they feel well prepared in the areas of accounting, general management, and quantitative methods. Students feel their computer and presentation skills are far weaker.

Loyola students agree that the faculty are the backbone of this program. Professors are widely regarded as good teachers. Exclaimed one student, "Some profs are outstanding." In particular, professors are praised for their accessibility. Reported one Loyola MBA, "I have never had a T.A. here. Most of my professors are very accessible and even give out their phone numbers." As for how well this school is run, it depends on whom you ask. A number of students agree with the MBA who described the administration as "caring and responsive." An equal number of students agree with this MBA: "The administration leaves a bit to be desired." Other complaints were about the inadequate library hours, and difficulty of getting into popular courses. One of the biggest gripes was about the lack of class discussion, hardly a surprise given how little class participation counts toward the grade.

PLACEMENT AND RECRUITING

The Graduate School of Business has its own placement office. Advisors are available to help with résumé and cover letter writing, as well as career planning. Training workshops are held on subjects from interviewing techniques to salary negotiation. While the school stresses that students are responsible for securing their own jobs, the placement office does publish a résumé book and schedules on-campus interviews. Students are also encouraged to participate in career days and job fairs.

LOYOLA UNIVERSITY–CHICAGO GRADUATE SCHOOL OF BUSINESS

STUDENT LIFE

Loyola's program is especially designed for both full- and part-time students, and this pervades almost every aspect of the school. For example, classes meet one night a week for three hours. In addition, both full- and part-time students may begin the program at any of the four quarters during the year. One student wrote, "Moving between part-time and full-time is easy." Perhaps because almost eighty-five percent of students attending this program hold down a full-time job, the workload is manageable. The majority of students spend only ten to twenty hours on schoolwork. They don't even do all of it; Loyola MBAs reported it's only somewhat important to do all the assigned reading. As for competition, it depends on who's in your class. Half of the students surveyed rated classmates as very competitive; the other fifty percent said they're only moderately so. Students were in agreement, however, that their classmates are professionally diverse.

The overwhelming feel to this school is commuter. As one student put it, "There is not much of a school-related social life for full-time students. The majority come to school part-time and therefore are not very interested in socializing. The location in Chicago somewhat makes up for this." All MBA classes are held at the downtown Water Tower Campus.

ADMISSIONS

Despite its generous fifty percent acceptance rate, Loyola places some exacting demands on its applicants. Academic strength, GMAT scores, work experience, recommendations, quality of undergraduate institution and difficulty of major are considered in that order. These fairly ordinary criteria become somewhat more daunting when you consider that the average Loyola MBA candidate has *four* years of work experience before enrollment—twice that of most other schools' applicants.

STUDENT'S OVERVIEW BOX

FACULTY RATING

HITS AND MISSES

HITS
Accounting dept
Chicago
Diverse work experience

MISSES
Marketing dept.
Off-campus housing
Don't stay in touch

APPLICANTS ALSO LOOK AT
Northwestern U.
U Illinois-C.U.
U Chicago

FOR MORE INFORMATION, CONTACT:
Graduate School of Business
820 North Michigan Avenue
Chicago, IL 60611
(312) 915-6120

UNIVERSITY OF MARYLAND COLLEGE OF BUSINESS AND MANAGEMENT

ADMISSIONS FACTS

Type of school	Public

Demographics

No. of men	194
No. of women	104
No. of minorities	60
No. of int'l students	41

EQUAL TREATMENT GRAPH

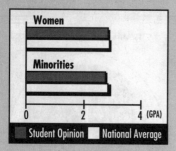

Women

Minorities

0   2   4 (GPA)

■ Student Opinion   □ National Average

Admissions Statistics

Avg. GMAT	605
Avg. undergraduate GPA	3.2
Avg. age at entry	25
No. of applicants	1,124
No. accepted	260
No. enrolled	138

Deadlines and Notifications

Regular application	5/17
Regular notification	within 8 weeks
Special dates	2/01

Focus of Curriculum

General Management

Academic Specialties

Entrepreneurship, Transportation and Logistics, International Business, Management Science

Joint Degrees

MBA/JD, MBA/Masters of Public Management

Special Programs

Part-time MBA program available

FINANCIAL FACTS

In-state tuition	$5,635
Out-of-state tuition	$9,536
On-campus housing	N/A

ACADEMICS

The University of Maryland (UM) MBA kicks off with an intensive orientation week. If you missed out on summer camp, or never learned to climb a rope, you've got one more chance in this Outward Bound-oriented program. Management skills seminars and get-to-know-you sessions with faculty and classmates are also held. With new relationships in hand, you're ready for B-school.

UM offers a generalist MBA. A highly structured first-year curriculum provides students a grounding in the functional areas. A global perspective is emphasized throughout the coursework. During the second year, students choose electives based on their interests. UM is part of a consortium of Washington universities, so students often take courses at member schools such as Georgetown and GW. Within the B-school, a popular option is the field study project. Students offer their consulting services to real organizations on actual projects. Another value-added feature is the "How-to" Management Workshops Series. Topics are generated by students and cover issues such as leadership, and communication skills. Participation is required. Students must also take one elective on international business. All in all, students say UM is well-worth the investment of time and money. Indeed, the vast majority of UM MBAs say it is meeting or exceeding their expectations. Backing this up, students report they feel well-prepared by their studies in marketing, accounting, finance, and general management. They also report a high level of confidence in their teamwork and quantitative skills. In only one area do a sizeable minority report average skills—computers. Professors are highly regarded for their excellent teaching and accessibility. As for the administration, the reviews are mixed. The vast majority of students say the school runs like a well-oiled gear and "the new dean has been a positive influence." But one third say it creaks and cranks. Shared one student, "The administration is feeling growing pains—new dean, new curriculum, new building." Of course things aren't that bad. Students say getting into popular courses is unusually easy. Summed up one student, "Maryland is a great MBA program for the price. It's not Harvard, but it doesn't charge Harvard's tuition."

PLACEMENT AND RECRUITING

The Office of MBA placement aggressively pursues opportunities for students. To put students in touch with prospective employers, they hold career forums with visiting execs/alumni, distribute a résumé book, and participate in the MBA Consortium held in Chicago.

The majority of students report they are satisfied with the placement office and the range of companies recruiting. Wrote one MBA, "The school has recently turned more of its attention to the placement department. The new placement staff are well seasoned and knowledgeable about recruiting MBAs." Still, a sizeable number of students can't wait until they get things going.

UNIVERSITY OF MARYLAND COLLEGE OF BUSINESS AND MANAGEMENT

STUDENT LIFE/CAMPUS

UM divides its entering class into sections of forty to forty-five students each, affording its students lots of personal attention. Sectionmates take all their required courses together and develop a support system early in the program when they need it most. The demanding first-year curriculum translates into twenty-five to thirty-five hours of work a week. Wrote one MBA, "The workload comes in waves." As one might expect with the case study method, the majority of students say it's important to do all or most of the assigned reading. Students say classmates are very smart. They also bring a wealth of work experience to their B-school studies. One student observed, "They need a more diverse ethnic and racial group."

Students are competitive. But cooperation, not confrontation, is the basic theme here. UM MBAs are interested in lending a helping hand. In fact, this is an extremely friendly group of students. They enjoy each other's company. They expect to stay friends long after graduation. And they report an active, involved social life. The B-school has just moved into brand spanking new, state-of-the-art facilities. As for the University of Maryland, it's huge—21,500 students. The B-school keeps to itself and maintains a small-school feel. There is almost no on-campus housing, but students say off-campus digs are attractive and affordable. A university shuttle bus will cart you on- and off-campus. The Social Committee fills up your calendar with weekly happy hours, football/lacrosse tailgate parties, and golf tournaments. A popular extracurricular is community service. One student says the D.C. location "provides access to a wealth of national educational/business resources."

ADMISSIONS

According to the admissions office, your GMAT score, college GPA, and work experience are considered "very important." Your essays, interview, letters of recommendation, and extracurricular activities are considered "important."

Decisions are made on a rolling admissions basis. Applicants are notified of a decision eight weeks after the completed application has been received. Accepted applicants may defer admission for up to one year.

STUDENT'S OVERVIEW BOX

FACULTY RATING

HITS AND MISSES

HITS
Marketing dept.
Library
Diverse work experience

MISSES
Finance dept.
On-campus housing
Social life

APPLICANTS ALSO LOOK AT
U Virginia
U Tennessee-Knox
UNC Chapel Hill
U Illinois-C.U.
Georgetown U.

FOR MORE INFORMATION, CONTACT:
Management and Business Affairs
Building, Room 2308
College Park, MD 20742
(301) 405-2278

UNIVERSITY OF MASSACHUSETTS–AMHERST SCHOOL OF MANAGEMENT

ADMISSIONS FACTS

Type of school	Public

Demographics

No. of men	N/A
No. of women	N/A
No. of minorities	N/A
No. of int'l students	N/A

EQUAL TREATMENT GRAPH

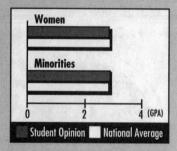

Admissions Statistics

Avg. GMAT	598
Avg. undergraduate GPA	3.2
Avg. age at entry	27
No. of applicants	N/A
No. accepted	N/A
No. enrolled	N/A

Deadlines and Notifications

Regular application	3/01
Regular notification	rolling
Special dates	

Focus of Curriculum

General Management

Academic Specialties

Accounting, Finance

FINANCIAL FACTS

In-state tuition	$3,522
Out-of-state tuition	$8,214
On-campus housing	$3,500

ACADEMICS

If getting to know fellow classmates is of prime importance, the University of Massachusetts School of Management (SOM) is the program for you. Only thirty-five students entered this year's class. In a day you can know everyone's name. SOM used to enroll ninety students a year, but this was dropped to the current thirty-five so the administration could perform a review of the program. There's no word on when they'll reinflate to their normal size.

The SOM trains its students to be general managers. During the first year, students take eight required courses in the functional areas of business and have one elective. During the second year, students have up to four electives to specialize in fields such as accounting, finance, marketing, human resources management, and management information systems. According to the school, "The course of study also emphasizes techniques of corporate management, including policy analysis, strategic planning, organization design, and control." Because courses emphasize quantitative methods, all students are expected to be proficient in math and to have previously taken a statistics and microeconomics course. In a unique program twist, students can supplement classwork with research and public service.

According to our survey, students report they feel well prepared in quantitative methods, accounting, and computer skills. Perhaps because teamwork is emphasized, or because the whole school is no bigger than an extended study group, students also said they possess strong teamwork skills. They feel less confident of their skills in operations. The vast majority say taking time off to pursue a U Mass MBA is worth it, especially when they factor in the program's low cost. Still, almost fifty percent of those students surveyed said the program is not meeting their academic expectations. Students wish there were more electives and that the school was run more efficiently. Indeed, if a program drops two thirds of its capacity to focus its energies on an overhaul, you can be sure the entering thirty-five are not going to be a top priority. On the other hand, students are guaranteed a high student to faculty ratio. And students here praise their professors for their teaching skills and accessibility.

PLACEMENT AND RECRUITING

The placement office conducts workshops on résumé preparation and interview skills, and hosts recruiters from over a hundred firms. According to the students in our survey, the placement office is one notch above the bottom of the barrel. Students are equally unhappy about the range of companies recruiting on campus. However, not all the blame can be shunted on the placement office. With only thirty-five students to pick from, most recruiters don't have the time or resources to visit this campus.

UNIVERSITY OF MASSACHUSETTS–AMHERST SCHOOL OF MANAGEMENT

STUDENT LIFE/CAMPUS

What it lacks in size, this school makes up for in academic rigor. A demanding and challenging curriculum keeps most students buried in their books an average of twenty to thirty hours a week. Although the majority of students say it's important to do all or most of the reading, a significant number regularly skip or skim assignments. But students are certainly up to the workload; their peers consider them "extremely intelligent" and "professionally very diverse."

As for competition, students are keen on doing well, but not at the expense of a classmate. In such a tightly knit group, aggressive behavior would be unseemly. Students are friendly and team-oriented. This intimacy breeds easy friendships that students expect to maintain long after graduation.

Amherst is located in a quintessential college town in suburban Massachusetts. Students report both on- and off-campus housing is more than adequate and affordable.

ADMISSIONS

The admissions office considers your work experience most important. After that, in *descending* order, your GMAT score, letters of recommendation, college GPA and essays. Extracurricular activities and interviews are not considered. It is recommended that applicants have completed course in microeconomics and statistics before applying. Writes the school, "We are willing to make a number of academically 'high-risk' admissions decisions if we feel an individual has the potential to make a significant contribution to the business community. The strength of our program lies in its small size. Each student receives a great deal of individual attention from faculty and administrators."

STUDENT'S OVERVIEW BOX

FACULTY RATING

HITS AND MISSES

HITS
Quantitative skills
Library
Diverse work experience

MISSES
Finance dept.
On-campus housing
Social life

APPLICANTS ALSO LOOK AT

Babson
Boston College
Boston U.
U Michigan
Yale
U Rochester

FOR MORE INFORMATION, CONTACT:
209 SOM Building
Amherst, MA 01003
(413) 545-5608

MASSACHUSETTS INSTITUTE OF TECH.: SLOAN SCHOOL OF MANAGEMENT

ADMISSIONS FACTS

Type of school	Private

Demographics

No. of men	387
No. of women	113
No. of minorities	64
No. of int'l students	162

EQUAL TREATMENT GRAPH

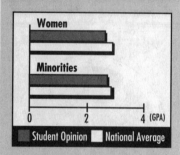

Admissions Statistics

Avg. GMAT	N/A
Avg. undergraduate GPA	3.4
Avg. age at entry	26.8
No. of applicants	1,707
No. accepted	354
No. enrolled	237

Deadlines and Notifications

Regular application	2/01
Regular notification	4/01
Special dates	N/A

Focus of Curriculum

Specialized

Academic Specialties

International Business, Manufacturing/ Production, Transportation Logistics, Finance, Management of Technology, Information Technology

Special Programs

The MIT-Japan Program in Science, Technology and Management

FINANCIAL FACTS

In-state tuition	$19,500
Out-of-state tuition	$19,500
On-campus housing	$5,400

ACADEMICS

While few schools want to be stereotyped, at MIT the "techie" stereotype not only fits, but is a badge worn with pride. The Sloan School has a well deserved international reputation for excellence in quantitative and technical disciplines. Wrote one student, "MIT typically attracts a specific type of student—science, math, and engineering types—which enhances the school's position as a niche player. For people who know what they want to get out of school and have a focus on what they want to do job-wise, this is a great place." Standout departments include finance and operations. In the latter area, students may participate in Leaders in Manufacturing, a twenty-four-month program whereby students earn a masters in both management and engineering. Here students spend six months interning with one of fourteen sponsoring industries, for example, Eastman Kodak or Boeing.

According to our survey, students report their strongest academic skills are consistent with Sloan's strengths: finance, operations, and computers. One notable find: students report stellar skills in marketing, a strength often overshadowed by Sloan's other programs.

Like many B-schools, Sloan recently restructured its masters program and delivery. Under the new program, students are placed in tightly structured cohorts for the first semester and take all core courses together. However, after the first semester, students enjoy unprecedented flexibility. As one student wrote, "The level of freedom to design one's program of study is outstanding." Specialized management tracks, such as the Product Development and Management track, have also been introduced, and all students must now take a leadership/team building seminar lead by second-years. Serious problems that still need to be addressed: teaching quality in the core is uneven, classrooms are crowded, the library needs improvement, and campus and learning facilities—from buildings to blackboards—are sub-standard. Some of the problems are due to the fact that the school has grown by thirty-five percent over the last seven years. To ease up crowded conditions, Sloan is building a new auditorium, classrooms, student lounge space, and a corporate information center.

PLACEMENT AND RECRUITING

Here's the bottom line: over ninety percent of all students have secured a position by graduation. Furthermore, Sloan's niche positioning has enabled students to command sky-high salaries, among the top five of B-schools surveyed in this book. Perhaps it's a matter of distorted expectations, but students are unhappy with the services of their career placement office. They report Sloan needs a greater diversity of companies recruiting on campus—consulting and I-banking dominate. True. But Sloan's placement stats still beat-out most other schools. On a happier note, the vast majority of students reported contacting an alum for help in the job search and found them happy to lend a hand.

MASSACHUSETTS INSTITUTE OF TECH.: SLOAN SCHOOL OF MANAGEMENT

STUDENT LIFE/CAMPUS

As one student put it, "Students tend to take many courses and overwork themselves." Self-imposed or not, Sloan students report a killer-heavy workload. They hit the books an average of thirty-five to forty-five hours per week, making them one of the most hard-working, driven groups of all those surveyed in this book. Although the majority of students report it's important to do most of the reading/assignments, a large number say taking shortcuts is the key to survival. As for the pressure, it depends on who you ask. Fifty percent said it's extremely intense, the other fifty percent said they can deal with it. Classes tend to be small. The majority of students work in study groups.

The often intense academic pressure does not corrupt an amiable atmosphere both in and out of the classroom. Sloan students rate themselves more cooperative than competitive. There are no fixed grading curves, no setting anyone apart for distinction based on grades alone. Wrote one "students can be difficult—but are basically laid back, warm and friendly." Claimed another, "Students here help each other out." Partly because the environment is friendly, and partly because classmates have a lot in common, Sloan students like to hang out with each other and expect to maintain their strong friendships after graduation. As for the student body, students describe it as off-the-richter-scale smart and very professionally diverse.

Students agree, Cambridge is a great town is to live in. But MIT itself is not located in a pretty or residential section. Located only a couple of miles from resort-styled Harvard, the aesthetics of this campus make it seem a distant cousin. New grad apartments have added to the on-campus housing capacity, but eighty percent of students live off-campus all over Boston and Cambridge. A nearby subway station provides access to the Boston area, although off-peak service is erratic and trains are slow. But they're safe. As for the social scene, it's dominated by the Graduate Management Society which sponsors barbecues, weekly "Consumption Functions," and lots of international theme parties. But according to our survey, students aren't overwhelmed by their social life.

ADMISSIONS

Incoming students are expected to have completed calculus and economic theory before matriculating. If you wind up taking these courses at MIT, as one student put it, expect "math hell!"

Gaining admission to MIT is no walk in the park. From an applicant pool of over 1,500, Sloan fills a class only 200+ strong. The admissions committee considers GMAT score, undergraduate GPA, quality of undergraduate school and coursework, recommendations, essays and interview. The interview is recommended, and the admissions committee will have a written record of the meeting. And, yes, successful applicants to the Massachusetts Institute of Technology MBA program must have two semesters of college-level calculus.

STUDENT'S OVERVIEW BOX

FACULTY RATING

HITS AND MISSES

HITS
Quantitative skills
School clubs
Classmates are smart

MISSES
Marketing dept.
Gym
Social life

APPLICANTS ALSO LOOK AT
Harvard
U Chicago
UNC Chapel Hill
Columbia U.
Stanford U.

FOR MORE INFORMATION, CONTACT:
Sloan School of Management
50 Memorial Drive, Room E52-112
Cambridge, MA 02139-1347
(617) 253-3730

University of Michigan: The Michigan Business School

ADMISSIONS FACTS

Type of school	Public

Demographics

No. of men	651
No. of women	207
No. of minorities	220
No. of int'l students	122

EQUAL TREATMENT GRAPH

Women

Minorities

0 2 4 (GPA)

■ Student Opinion □ National Average

Admissions Statistics

Avg. GMAT	621
Avg. undergraduate GPA	3.27
Avg. age at entry	26
No. of applicants	2,789
No. accepted	889
No. enrolled	420

Deadlines and Notifications

Regular application	3/01
Regular notification	within 8 weeks
Special dates	N/A

Focus of Curriculum

General Management

Academic Specialties

General Management, Finance, Marketing, Accounting

Joint Degrees

Available with nineteen minorities university departments/schools

Special Programs

Executive Skills, Workshops, International Studies, Center for International Business Education, International Exchange.

FINANCIAL FACTS

In-state tuition	$11,550
Out-of-state tuition	$18,200
On-campus housing	$5,000

Academics

The University of Michigan has a well-deserved reputation as one of the best B-schools in the nation, boasting strong academic programs across the board. But Michigan has decided to go one step further and teach students what they'll need to know in the coming decades. The result is a new and progressive curriculum that incorporates interdisciplinary approaches, team-teaching, action-based learning, and '90s themes like global business and citizenship. A cornerstone of the new program is the Multidisciplinary Action Project (MAP), a six-week business apprenticeship that puts first-year students to work for real-life companies. The mission of this program is to provide students an opportunity to learn by doing and "examine the processes by which businesses apply and integrate functional expertise." To judge by the comments in our survey, students are wild about MAP: "It offers the most excellent hands-on training I could ever conceive of." They're also wild about their dean, whom students credit with the forward direction of the school: "Michigan is incredibly innovative since Dean White came on board. His strong vision and high goals have produced many new programs that are making this school more competitive, attractive, and fun!"

The school year kicks-off with an orientation that emphasizes public service. Students take a field trip into Detroit to work on a community project. During the remainder of the year, students perform community work in teams. There are four academic "sessions" in the calendar year. These feature a blend of seven-week and fourteen-week courses. The shorter courses (and some mini's) are typically devoted to more topical issues. Classroom instruction is also supplemented with workshops on issues such as leadership and cultural diversity. During the second year, only one core course is required, the remainder are electives. Some of these may be taken in other university programs such as the Law School and School of Natural Resources. Students told us that Michigan had prepared them very well in the following areas: marketing, finance, accounting, general management, teamwork, and presentation skills. Students reported weaker skills in operations and computers.

Placement and Recruiting

Distinct to Michigan is a unique career tool called "M-Track." According to the school, "This is a state-of-the-art information and personal networking system that provides access (via computer) to listings of open positions, recruiter presentations, and student/faculty information."

In 1992: 133 companies recruited on-campus for summer internships, ninety-three percent of the first-year class worked in a professional position during the summer, 281 companies recruited on-campus for permanent positions, and 365 MBAs (out of 400) reported accepting a position by July 15th. Students received an average of two job offers each. "Located an outstanding job through the OCD," says an MBA who speaks for his classmates. Students who seek help from alumni find them responsive.

UNIVERSITY OF MICHIGAN: THE MICHIGAN BUSINESS SCHOOL

STUDENT LIFE/CAMPUS

The Michigan B-school boasts a sleek, modern, multi-building structure and amazing facilities. To foster strong academic and social relationships, Michigan sections the entering class of 400 into a more manageable size of six groups of roughly seventy students each. Students take all their first-year classes with their sectionmates, and travel in packs from classroom to classroom. Students report a heavy workload and spend an average of thirty to forty hours a week studying. Despite this academic intensity, students report an "unpretentious environment" and "a positive, humble attitude." Complained one, "There is a lot of busywork, which is unproductive. Team projects are time-consuming and can have minimal learning benefit." Students say their classmates are competitive, extremely smart, very friendly and genuinely interested in helping each other.

As for Michigan's home town of Ann Arbor, commonly referred to as A2, students told us "it's the best place to go." Wrote one married MBA, "It's great for a family." About the only drawback is that "winters here are dismal." You'd better like football and basketball. Or at least have some Michigan spirit. "GO BLUE!" appeared several times on our survey questionnaires. Always popular are the pre-game tailgate parties. In addition, students get involved in intramural sports such as football, racquetball, and soccer. Two favorite events are the B-school Faculty Auction and the Spring Swing formal.

Students say, "The school spirit really takes you by storm and you feel that this place is home." Students also told us they appreciate and benefit from Michigan's diversity. If you're looking to broaden your experiences and go to school with a diverse and happily integrated student body, this is the place. This school attracts more minorities than any other B-school profiled in this book.

ADMISSIONS

According to the admissions office, the following criteria are considered: essays, college GPA, letters of recommendation, extracurricular activities, work experience, interview, and GMAT score. A college-level calculus course must be completed before enrollment. Applicants are strongly encouraged to interview. The school asks applicants to note alumni ties in their applications, but does not reserve places in the class for those related to alumni. The school notes, "Each applicant is evaluated by several members of the admissions committee. We do not use any 'formulas' or numerical cut-offs in admitting students. Because we use rolling admissions, there is an advantage to applicants who apply well before the March 1 deadline." Applicants are notified of a decision within two to eight weeks. Applications past the deadline are considered on a space-available basis. Students may defer admissions for up to one year only for exceptional personal circumstances or joint degree enrollment. Some college seniors are admitted; others are admitted with a one- to two-year mandatory deferral. There is not a fixed allocation of space for in-state and out-of-state students. Tuition is somewhat lower for Michigan residents.

STUDENT'S OVERVIEW BOX

Overall Happiness

Academic Satisfaction

50   75   100%

Student Opinion   National Average

FACULTY RATING

Student Opinion   National Average

HITS AND MISSES

HITS
Accounting
Marketing
Finance
Ethnic & racial diversity
Facilities

MISSES
Confidence
Operational skills
Computer skills
Placement

APPLICANTS ALSO LOOK AT
Harvard
Stanford U.
Dartmouth College
UC Los Angeles
Cornell U.

FOR MORE INFORMATION, CONTACT:
The Michigan Business School
701 Tappan
Ann Arbor, MI 48109
(313) 763-5796

UNIVERSITY OF MINNESOTA: CURTIS L. CARLSON SCHOOL OF MANAGEMENT

ADMISSIONS FACTS

Type of school	Public

Demographics

No. of men	205
No. of women	81
No. of minorities	14
No. of int'l students	18

EQUAL TREATMENT GRAPH

Women

Minorities

0   2   4 (GPA)

Student Opinion ■ National Average

Admissions Statistics

Avg. GMAT	600
Avg. undergraduate GPA	3.4
Avg. age at entry	28
No. of applicants	1,020
No. accepted	567
No. enrolled	382

Deadlines and Notifications

Regular application	4/01
Regular notification	within 4 weeks
Special dates	3/15

Focus of Curriculum

General Management with specialization.

Academic Specialties

General Management, Information Systems

Special Programs

International Study in France, Germany, Sweden, Japan, Italy, Spain, Australia, International Management Exchange.

FINANCIAL FACTS

In-state tuition	$7,000
Out-of-state tuition	$11,200
On-campus housing	$4,000

ACADEMICS

A big advantage of going to the Carlson School of Management is that it has close ties with the local Minnesota business community—a veritable hive of Fortune 500 companies. Through internships, field projects, and executive forums, students have extraordinary opportunities to learn by doing. Indeed, so many courses feature field work, at any given time a Carlson MBA is likely to be applying his/her skills in a real-life corporate setting. This emphasis on both theory and real-life applications is one of the reasons the majority of students say taking off time to pursue a Carlson MBA is worth it. They also report Carlson has provided them a thorough and balanced B-school education. During the first year, students take an extremely structured series of courses in the basic functional areas. These are integrated to reflect a cross-functional perspective. In addition, they take a lab in Managerial Communications, which provides students with personalized assessments of their oral and written communications skills and focuses on business writing and presentations. In the second year, students take electives in a chosen field of study. Concentrations are available in finance, marketing and logistics management, operations and management science, strategic management and organization, and information and decision sciences, the latter of which boasts a nationally renowned faculty/department. They also take a fourteen-week field project—another chance to consult in one of those Minnesota companies.

The faculty here gets mixed reviews. Students give them good, but not outstanding marks. In addition, there's a downside to going to a school that produces cutting edge research—many professors are holed up in their ivory towers. Students wish they had more interaction with them. As for their business training, students told us they feel reasonably well-prepared by their courses in marketing, operations, MIS, finance, and accounting. They gave themselves sky-high marks for their teamwork skills, but felt somewhat less confident of their quantitative and computer skills. Next year, Carlson will join other the ranks of the other B-schools that have implemented a new, '90s curriculum.

PLACEMENT AND RECRUITING

The Career Planning and Placement Office offers students a range of workshops and services to help them find a job. You'll like one of them—toll-free national and international phonelines for MBAs to use to contact prospective employers. Two national job fairs, one in Chicago, the other on the West Coast, also put students in touch with recruiters who may not recruit on-campus.

With the exception of a few B-schools, no group of MBAs reported they are satisfied with the services of career placement. But Carlson MBAs are particularly disappointed. According to our survey, the overwhelming majority say the Career Placement office is the pits. They also indicate that the number and range of companies recruiting on-campus is inadequate. This won't be news to the school. They've already begun an internal audit and plan on making improvements soon.

UNIVERSITY OF MINNESOTA: CURTIS L. CARLSON SCHOOL OF MANAGEMENT

STUDENT LIFE/CAMPUS

Core courses have an average of fifty students each. Concentration courses are much smaller, fifteen to twenty per class. Currently, students report a very heavy workload. It is expected this will increase under the new curriculum which compresses more learning into the calendar year. Relief comes in the form of study groups, which provide students academic as well as social support, and in skipping some of the work. A sizeable number of students say it's not necessary to do all of the reading.

Like many small schools (roughly 115 in the entering class), Carlson provides its students a supportive learning environment. Students are non-competitive. They're extremely interested in helping each other. Perhaps because twenty-five percent of the student body is married, a not insignificant minority report they're not into hanging out with fellow MBAs. But this may just be the social climate here; fifty percent of the students we surveyed report a lackluster social scene. Of the professionally diverse student body, seventy percent have undergraduate degrees in areas other than business administration.

Currently the B-school is housed in several buildings shared with undergraduates and other departments. Students want improved facilities, as well as their own building. You ask—sometimes you get: Ground breaking for the new B-school is planned for 1994. As for residential housing, students say it's very affordable and very nice. Most opt for off-campus living in the nearby communities of Dinkytown and St. Paul. Many students share a duplex in one of the old divided homes on the lake. The MBA Association sponsors events such as intramural sports, barbecues, and a charity golf outing. Due to class-less Fridays, every other Thursday is TGIT night.

ADMISSIONS

The admissions office considers your GMAT score, work experience, and college GPA most important. Then in descending order, they consider your letters of recommendations, essays, and extracurricular activities. Applications are processed in semi-batches. According to the school, "Applications are reviewed when they become complete. Those not offered admission at the time at which they are received are reviewed again within six weeks of the April 1st deadline." Students may defer admission for one year.

STUDENT'S OVERVIEW BOX

Overall Happiness

Academic Satisfaction

50   75   100%

■ Student Opinion □ National Average

FACULTY RATING

■ Student Opinion □ National Average

HITS AND MISSES

HITS
Marketing dept.
Helping other students
Location

MISSES
Quantitative skills
Ethnic & racial diversity
Placement

APPLICANTS ALSO LOOK AT

U Texas-Austin
U Iowa
U Chicago
Northwestern U.
U Illinois-Chicago
U Wisc-Madison
U Illinois-C.U.

FOR MORE INFORMATION, CONTACT:
Curtis L. Carson School of Management
271 19th Avenue South
Minneapolis, MN 55455
(612) 624-0006

NEW YORK UNIVERSITY: LEONARD N. STERN SCHOOL OF BUSINESS

ADMISSIONS FACTS

Type of school	Private

Demographics

No. of men	733
No. of women	290
No. of minorities	137
No. of int'l students	296

EQUAL TREATMENT GRAPH

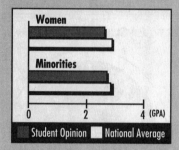

Women

Minorities

0   2   4 (GPA)

■ Student Opinion □ National Average

Admissions Statistics

Avg. GMAT	616
Avg. undergraduate GPA	3.15
Avg. age at entry	26
No. of applicants	2,293
No. accepted	740
No. enrolled	400

Deadlines and Notifications

Regular application	4/15
Regular notification	within 8 weeks
Special dates	N/A

Focus of Curriculum

General Management

Academic Specialties

International Management, Finance, Information Systems

Joint Degrees

JD/MBA, MBA/MA in French studies, MBA/MA in Journalism, MBA/MA in Politics.

FINANCIAL FACTS

In-state tuition	$17,200
Out-of-state tuition	$17,200
On-campus housing	$9,000

ACADEMICS

NYU's international management and finance departments are widely regarded as among the best in the country. With eighteen foreign exchange programs and international research centers of worldwide renown in their arsenal, the study of international business is especially strong. As for the finance department, one student wrote, "In interviews with financial services firms, a Stern finance major is on equal footing with students from Ivy League schools." But one student complained, "Finance is very good at NYU, but the other subjects are not taught as well." Griped another, "The school is too focused on churning out Wall Street finance types." However, one student advised, "NYU is ideal for someone with a liberal arts background in need of a formal quantitative base."

The first year consists of a prescribed program of eleven core courses in the functional areas of business. Because of the newly integrated curriculum, all have a global bent. Two mini-courses are mandatory: ethics and management communication. A year-end capstone course, in the form of a team project, pulls learning from all the core courses together. The second year is more flexible—only two required courses: Legal, Social and Ethical Aspects of Business, and Business Strategy. Students take eight electives and declare a major, or a double major, and even a co-major. For would-be-entrepreneurs, there are appealing courses from the Center for Entrepreneurial Studies. Particularly noteworthy is the Management Consulting Program, in which corporations such as Reebok, Campbell Soup, and IBM hire teams of students to do consulting work. Raved one student, "This is for course credit and a great real-life experience."

Equally impressive is the emphasis on environmental study. Several core marketing and product development courses integrate "environmental" concerns. The career placement office has even compiled a "green" directory of organizations looking for MBAs with an environmental orientation.

Overall, students we surveyed told us NYU had prepared them very well in the following areas: finance, accounting, general management, teamwork, and quantitative skills. Students reported weaker skills in marketing, operations, presentation/interpersonal, and computer skills. But students claim the marketing department is a rising star.

PLACEMENT AND RECRUITING

More than 250 corporations annually recruit Stern students both on- and off-campus. In all, more than 5,000 interviews were held at Stern in 1990." Their 1993 placement rate was around eighty-seven percent.

Still, students in our survey said they weren't satisfied with the efforts of OCD. Complained one student, "The Placement Center could be a *lot*, *lot* better." Many students feel the companies come for the school, not because of the efforts of the placement center. On a more positive note, students were enthusiastic about the school's alumni, whom the majority of them contacted and found responsive. Reported one Stern MBA, "Access to alumni is very easy and very helpful."

NEW YORK UNIVERSITY: LEONARD N. STERN SCHOOL OF BUSINESS

STUDENT LIFE/CAMPUS

NYU boasts one of the largest international enrollments among B-schools—thirty percent! Unfortunately, only seventeen percent of the students are female. But according to one student, "The women are so tough, they demand more attention and respect than any group of women I've ever encountered!" NYU divides the entering class into "blocks" of about sixty students each who spend the first two semesters together. This creates a school within a school and allows students to develop the academic and social bonds early on.

"NYU is a great place to combine the merits of an outstanding university and the excitement of a cosmopolitan city," writes one student. The social scene depends on the activities of the student-run clubs which organize parties and outings. This being New York, there are a million things to do. Students cluster in small groups and hit the town.

Students describe a heavy workload and spend an average of twenty to thirty hours a week studying. Classes tend to be large, with an average of fifty to sixty students in each. Several students complained: "Too big classes, too many people, too much irrelevant material." Stern MBAs rate themselves as fairly competitive, but also willing to help each other. As for congeniality, NYU doesn't win any awards. While the majority of students say they enjoy hanging out with fellow classmates, a surprisingly large number say they don't. The school is basically campusless, which causes students to feel detached from each other. Almost no one lives on-campus and school housing is in scant supply. Priority is given to foreign students. Most would do better to locate their own digs in nearby Greenwich Village, Chelsea, or Tribeca. NYU is primarily a commuter school. Compounding this commuter feeling is NYU's huge part-time program—1,800 students who can easily switch to full-time status or vice versa. The total effect is a lack of the *esprit de corps* that fires up so many of the other B-schools.

But the campus is not without its merits: As one student cited, "The new Management Education Center building has enhanced the school greatly. It has state-of-the-art presentation equipment, comfortable lecture halls, and small meeting rooms. The new uptown location creates a much friendlier and collegiate atmosphere." Although one student complained, "There is no adequate cafeteria on premises and no decent places to study in the building." This MBA should venture out of the facilities. Located in the heart of Greenwich Village, the immediate neighborhood boasts Chinese food, sushi, a street vendor's hot dog, pizza, and several diners.

ADMISSIONS

According to the admissions office, the following criteria are considered (in order of importance): essays, college GPA/transcript, letters of recommendation, extracurricular activities, work experience and GMAT scores. The interview is optional.

STUDENT'S OVERVIEW BOX

FACULTY RATING

HITS AND MISSES

HITS
Finance
Quantitative skills
Ethnic & racial diversity
New York City

MISSES
Marketing
Off-campus housing
Student community
Large classes

APPLICANTS ALSO LOOK AT
Columbia U.
Northwestern U.
Carnegie Mellon U.
U Connecticut

FOR MORE INFORMATION, CONTACT:
44 West 4th Street
New York, NY 10003
(212) 998-0900

UNIV. OF NORTH CAROLINA AT CHAPEL HILL: KENAN-FLAGLER BUSINESS SCHOOL

ADMISSIONS FACTS

Type of school	Public

Demographics

No. of men	284
No. of women	92
No. of minorities	41
No. of int'l students	35

EQUAL TREATMENT GRAPH

Women

Minorities

0   2   4 (GPA)

Student Opinion   National Average

Admissions Statistics

Avg. GMAT	620
Avg. undergraduate GPA	3.2
Avg. age at entry	27
No. of applicants	2,225
No. accepted	378
No. enrolled	194

Deadlines and Notifications

Regular application	3/01
Regular notification	within 8 weeks
Special dates	12/02 (int'l students)

Focus of Curriculum

General Management

Academic Specialities

General Management

Joint Degrees

JD/MBA, MBA/MRP in Real Estate Development and Urban Planning, Master of Accounting

Special Programs

The Board of Visitors, The MBA Enterprise Corps, International Exchange, The Washington Campus

FINANCIAL FACTS

In-state tuition	$2,129
Out-of-state tuition	$8,680
On-campus housing	$5,000

ACADEMICS

Kenan-Flagler (KFBS) is one of the nation's most highly regarded state B-schools. Its reputation is based on a rigorous program of academics, "designed to build broad-based knowledge rather than narrow expertise." Particularly impressive is KFBS's innovative curriculum, which teaches business from a cross-functional, integrated point of view. The curriculum is designed around seven-week modules ("mods"), four per year. Some core courses span more than one mod. Some span the entire year—as in the second-year, combo international business, regulation, and business policy course. The mod approach allows KFBS to offer a greater variety of topics—such as consulting or environmental issues—not possible under a semester system. Second-year students who want to specialize can take several mods in one area. Because the multi-functional courses cram so much learning into one program, students told us KFBS is not for lightweights. Wrote one, "We think our workload is heavier than that at most other top B-schools." However, one advised, "This school is great for people with non-business backgrounds."

As one student put it, "KFBS is very serious about teamwork." Indeed, they are. To begin with, students are pre-assigned mandatory study groups organized around members' experience and background. Even when people get into a major personality conflict, the teams must stay together and work it out. During Intro Week, (a ten-day orientation that includes a review of basic skills and math), ninety-eight percent of the class also participates in the optional MBA Adventure, an Outward Bound-style exercise designed to enhance the team approach to problem solving. Again, during the fall, a two-day "Time Out for Team Building" exercise is held. But according to one disgruntled MBA, "While the school touts diversity and teamwork, these are often forced on students; versus a genuine appreciation for these very important management skills."

Students raved about all the academic opportunities. Wrote one, "There are excellent opportunities to get in 'real' work situations—practicums, case development, consulting." For example, second-years participate in "The Art of Negotiation," a one-day workshop and role-play where students learn the three main approaches to negotiation. Bountiful electives feature student consulting projects to real companies. At less than $10,000 a year in tuition for out-of-state residents, happy KFBS students say this program offers "high value for the low $$$!" Summed up one, "If you're looking for a top ten public university in the south, this is it."

PLACEMENT AND RECRUITING

In 1992, ninety-three percent of grads had a position within three months of graduation. Over 110 companies recruited on-campus. In all, 2,050 interviews were scheduled. According to the school, "Corporate recruiters characterize our students as being assertive, yet not aggressive, and unpretentious, yet full of energy and enthusiasm." Indeed, students at this school are renown for their self-initiated, "phonothon" to massive numbers of alumni for job leads. The majority of students reported they were only moderately satisfied with the career placement office. As for the range of companies recruiting, the typical response was that it's okay, not great.

UNIV. OF NORTH CAROLINA AT CHAPEL HILL: KENAN-FLAGLER BUSINESS SCHOOL

STUDENT LIFE/CAMPUS

Core classes average sixty students per class, electives, thirty-five. Grading is based on a combination of tests, papers, class participation, and project-based work. As one student wrote, "UNC is about cooperation; the cutthroat tactics that exist at some schools are not seen here." Indeed, "The quality of your team can affect your grades." Students reported classmates are extremely smart and have varied and interesting work experiences. A typical comment was, "The people make this school outstanding." The most frequent complaint was about the sub-par B-school facilities. Fortunately, a new structure is being built. Otherwise students describe "an ideal college setting." UNC/ Chapel Hill boasts a stately, tree-lined campus, and buildings listed with the National Historic Register. The school enjoys proximity to the Research Triangle area, which is home to three major universities and companies such as GE, IBM, and Mitsubishi. Chapel Hill is a university town with extensive apartment developments. Students find it's a renters market. Public bus lines make off-campus living especially convenient.

Sports, particularly the Tarheel's basketball team, are popular. According to one student, "The golf is also good." Students describe an active student community. There's a "high level of participation, involvement in school functions, and a commitment to community service." The annual mini-biathlon sponsored by the MBA Student Association raises thousands of dollars for charities (most recently Habitat for Humanity), as does a student golf tournament at the prestigious Governor's Club course. The social scene is active and extends into town on the weekends. Franklin Street is the site of the major student hang-outs. He's Not Here, and Spanky's are favorite watering holes. A short road trip away are coastal beaches to the east, the Appalachian mountains to the north and west. A final note: "Diversity," wrote one, "is something the program needs to work on more."

ADMISSIONS

According to the admissions department, "evidence of strong leadership capabilities" is considered most important. After that the following criteria are weighed equally: essays, college GPA, GMAT scores, letters of recommendation, interview, and extracurricular activities. The admissions office notes that "because of our small class size and large applicant pool, applicants are strongly encouraged to apply as early as possible." Only seventeen percent of those who apply are accepted, establishing KFSB as one of the five most selective schools profiled in this book. Applicants are strongly encouraged to schedule an on-campus interview, sit in on classes, and meet with current MBA students. In addition, the school "places emphasis on an applicant's prior work experience, which shows the development of managerial and leadership abilities before joining the program. As such, a practical knowledge of the business world is an important criterion in admissions decisions. Approximately ninety-eight to ninety-nine percent of candidates in each class have at least two years practical work experience." Students may defer admission for up to two years for "work reasons."

STUDENT'S OVERVIEW BOX

FACULTY RATING

HITS AND MISSES

HITS
Quant skills
Diverse work experience
Chapel Hill
Tuition
People-matter culture

MISSES
Marketing
Ethnic & racial diversity
Facilities

APPLICANTS ALSO LOOK AT
Duke U.
U Virginia
U Penn
U Michigan

FOR MORE INFORMATION, CONTACT:
Kenan-Flagler Business School
Cb 3490, Carroll Hall
Chapel Hill, NC 27599
(919) 962-3232

NORTHEASTERN UNIV. GRADUATE SCHOOL OF BUSINESS ADMINISTRATION

ADMISSIONS FACTS

Type of school	Private

Demographics

No. of men	322
No. of women	138
No. of minorities	41
No. of int'l students	138

EQUAL TREATMENT GRAPH

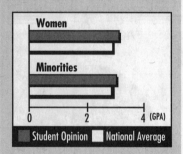

Women

Minorities

0 2 4 (GPA)

■ Student Opinion □ National Average

Admissions Statistics

Avg. GMAT	550
Avg. undergraduate GPA	3.2
Avg. age at entry	25
No. of applicants	742
No. accepted	428
No. enrolled	220

Deadlines and Notifications

Regular application	5/01
Regular notification	within 3 weeks
Special dates	N/A

Focus of Curriculum

General Management

Academic Specialties

Finance, Accounting

Special Programs

Part-time MBA Program; Executive MBA Program.

FINANCIAL FACTS

In-state tuition	$15,750
Out-of-state tuition	$15,750
On-campus housing	$6,500

ACADEMICS

Northeastern offers five different MBA programs: a part-time program, an Executive MBA, the two year full-time MBA, the Cooperative Education MBA, and the High Technology MBA. The High Tech MBA is the first of its kind in the nation. In this program, technical professionals take classes one night a week and on alternate Saturdays, and focus on management in the high-tech industry. The Cooperative Education MBA offers students an accelerated twenty-one-month program alternating coursework and paid work assignment. Raved one student "This is an excellent opportunity for those who continue straight from undergrad. I bolstered my résumé by gaining MBA level experience with a Fortune 500 Company!" Each MBA program offers a generalist perspective. All contain a traditional core which includes the study of accounting, finance, operations, management science, marketing, economics, organizational behavior, management of information systems, strategic management, and international business. Electives are used to broaden or deepen the course of study.

Apparently Northeastern's generalist formula works. The overwhelming majority of MBAs say this program is worth the investment of time and money. They also say it's meeting their academic expectations. Reported one, "The MBA program is excellent and very practical—coursework involves lots of 'real-life' examples and cases." Wrote another, "We are constantly reminded that there is a balance between *analysis* and good *instinct*, and *analysis* and *action*. We are better prepared to face the reality of business life than most Ivy-Leaguers!" Students feel well prepared by their studies in finance, accounting, general management, and quantitative methods. But close to fifty percent feel far less confident of their marketing and computer skills. Other weak spots—students say it can be difficult to get into popular courses. They also wish the school ran more efficiently and the faculty were better. Griped one, "Professors appear to do very little preparation for class. They seem to rely on Harvard case solutions." Students gave professors higher marks for their wide availability after class. The hottest topic: diversity. Although minority representation among the student body is unusually high for a B-school, one MBA claimed, "Professors are biased toward Caucasians who are presumed to be 'smarter'." Blasted another, "All professors and speakers are white only!" Overall, however, Northeastern earned high marks for its equitable treatment of minorities and women.

PLACEMENT AND RECRUITING

The Office of Career Development and Placement has lots of nice sounding programs including a job posting service and a résumé book. But students feel this office is long on talk and short on delivery. They criticize it for providing them minimal on-campus recruiting and almost no leads. Complained one job-seeker, "The career development center/placement office is weak, especially in comparison to the other B-schools in the area." Want a job? You'll have to find it on your own. Students suggest you head over to the university's main career office in Ryder Hall for some extra help.

NORTHEASTERN UNIV. GRADUATE SCHOOL OF BUSINESS ADMINISTRATION

STUDENT LIFE/CAMPUS

Northeastern relies on the case study method, which tends to produce late-night, intensive study sessions. Students here study an average of twenty-five to thirty-five hours a week. Observed one student, "Since this school is quarterly, the workload is quite heavier than at other schools which are semesterly (as compared to my friends in B-school elsewhere.) The vast majority report there are few corners to cut; it's important to do all or most of the assigned reading. Depending on the program you're in, the pressure ranges from manageable to formidable. Fortunately, study groups play an integral part in case preparation. Typically, students analyze cases on their own, then meet to share ideas and prepare comments for the next day's class. Class participation counts for twenty to forty percent of the grade. Classes are generally kept to twenty-five to fifty students.

Students are fairly competitive, but rarely into one-upmanship. Cooperation is the accepted mode of behavior. Northeastern MBAs say the student body is both professionally and racially diverse, a claim that most B-schools can't make. Wrote one student "I'm amazed by the diversity of the students, which has changed my opinion of B-schools for the better. This is how it should be." They also say fellow students are bright. However, a sizeable number report that classmates aren't the type of people they like to hang with. In all likelihood this has to do with the influx of part- and semi-full-time attendees who tend to be focused on their own thing. Still, the majority report an active social life.

B-school classes are held in Hayden Hall which features tiered, seating-in-the round classrooms perfect for spirited case discussion. A brand new facility will be unveiled in 1994 and provide students a new school building, state-of-the-art classrooms and computers, and a student lounge. As for Boston, everyone loves this preppy east coast city. But finding affordable housing is difficult and almost no one lives on campus. For extracurriculars, the MBA Association sponsors corporate speaker events, as well as barbecues. Students advise: "This is a great school if one gets involved."

ADMISSIONS

The admissions office considers the following criteria (in no particular order): essays, college GPA, letters of recommendation, work experience and GMAT scores. The office of admissions notes, "Decisions are made by small committees after an application has been read by at least three professionals who independently assess several factors: academic preparation (GMAT scores and transcripts), maturity, motivation, and direction (essays, recommendations and work experience). These factors are considered equally important."

STUDENT'S OVERVIEW BOX

FACULTY RATING

HITS AND MISSES

HITS
Accounting
Ethnic & racial diversity
Location
Small classes

MISSES
Marketing
Student community
Placement

APPLICANTS ALSO LOOK AT

New York University
Boston U.
Babson College
Suffolk U.

FOR MORE INFORMATION, CONTACT:
Graduate School of
Business Administration
360 Huntington Ave.
205 Hayden Hall
Boston, MA 02115
(617) 373-2714

NORTHWESTERN UNIV.: J.L. KELLOGG GRADUATE SCHOOL OF MANAGEMENT

ADMISSIONS FACTS

Type of school	Private

Demographics

No. of men	831
No. of women	307
No. of minorities	182
No. of int'l students	250

EQUAL TREATMENT GRAPH

Admissions Statistics

Avg. GMAT	635
Avg. undergraduate GPA	3.3
Avg. age at entry	27
No. of applicants	4393
No. accepted	890
No. enrolled	472

Deadlines and Notifications

Regular application	3/30
Regular notification	rolling
Special dates	1/17 (int'l students)

Focus of Curriculum

General Management, students may select a major(s)

Academic Specialties

General Management, Marketing, Non-profit Management, Transportation Management, Production Management.

Joint Degrees

MM/JD, MM/MD, MM/MS in nursing at Rush University, Master of Management in Manufacturing.

Special Programs

Pre-enrollment math "Prep"; Foreign study in nine countries.

FINANCIAL FACTS

In-state tuition	$18,780
Out-of-state tuition	$18,780
On-campus housing	$6,500

ACADEMICS

Kellogg offers the Master of Management (MM) degree. Students pursue a general management curriculum and "specialize in one or more of the professional fields: general business, public and nonprofit, health services, transportation, and real estate management." First-years take nine required core courses and three electives. Students who have completed prior study in a core course may apply for a waiver. Students with enough prior coursework may even complete their MBAs in one year. Group work dominates everything at Kellogg—studying, classwork, even social life—giving students their well-earned reputation as team players, although a common complaint was that the "teamwork thing" gets tiresome. While Kellogg has a seemingly unshakable reputation as a marketing school, the program actually has many strong suits, notably: transportation management, real estate management, public and nonprofit management, and manufacturing. Finance is big: it's the most frequently selected "major." Tons of international business courses and nine foreign study programs in Europe and Thailand make the study of international business a priority. And an exciting new area of formal study is entrepreneurship.

Kellogg has a reputation of being an easy school. Students describe the workload as only moderately heavy and the majority spend an average of twenty to thirty hours per week studying, a leisurely pace by top B-school standards. Claimed one student, "People complain that Kellogg is too easy, but it can be as challenging as you want it to be. I took several five-course loads and 'tube' classes and am planning to take only three a couple of times just to enjoy life." The academic year at Kellogg is divided into three quarters. Most classes are kept to twenty-five to fifty students. The first year kicks off with Conceptual Issues in Management (CIM), a week-long orientation organized by returning second years; CIM features get-to-know-you, teamwork exercises, but thankfully, no high anxiety ropes courses. Faculty and administration come out to press the flesh and offer words of encouragement about the next two years.

Overall, students said they were moderately satisfied with their quantitative and computer skills. But on the plus side, mentioned they "have a lot of say or control in how the school is run. This is very good—and unique." As for their profs, students rated them as good, but this rating falls well below the ratings faculty received at comparable schools. Most of the ineloquent teaching occurs in core courses, unsurprising given Kellog's emphasis on publish or perish. On a happier note, students said faculty are very accessible.

PLACEMENT AND RECRUITING

More than 300 companies recruit on-campus. Roughly 14,000 interviews are conducted both on- and off-campus. As for placement rates, in 1993 more than eighty-seven percent of the graduates had reported placement three months after graduation. Students are happy with the quality and number of companies recruiting on-campus, and moderately satisfied with the Office of Career Development itself.

NORTHWESTERN UNIV.: J.L. KELLOGG GRADUATE SCHOOL OF MANAGEMENT

STUDENT LIFE/CAMPUS

Like many schools, Kellogg uses sectioning to foster social and academic relationships. The 440 entering students are divided into eight sections, creating a "homeroom" of about fifty-five students each. This lasts for the fall quarter only. After that, disbanded section-mates keep in touch via numerous planned events. Much of the social scene revolves around activities successfully sponsored by the Graduate Management Association (GMA). These range from the academic (they compile quarterly teacher-course evaluations) to the social (weekly Friday afternoon beer bashes and parties like the Halloween Bash). The GMA also coordinates Kellogg's two largest social events: the Charity Ball in February and the Black Tie Spring Fling. The Northwestern campus itself is beautiful, located along a half-mile stretch of Lake Michigan, twelve miles from downtown Chicago in the suburb of Evanston. Evanston offers an array of museums, art galleries, and some of Chicago's finest restaurants. On-campus housing is fair, with space available to 250 single students and fifty apartments for the wedded. The HOTTEST topic among Kellogg respondents was diversity. Although students here claim classmates are ethnically and racially diverse, they're steamed about the concept of diversity for diversity's sake. They also claim that minority students tend to segregate themselves from the white mainstream. Not surprising, considering comments like these: "Regarding treatment of females/minorities/homos, all should be treated equal and not *special* as these groups are," "Minorities have better job opportunities than Caucasians—it's unfair," and "The drive for international students and women and minorities dilutes quality." However, students say, "Meeting people at Kellogg is an education in itself. People are amazingly friendly, helpful and smart." More than one enthusiastic student wrote "I love it here!" The atmosphere is midwestern laid back and students who enjoy the rigor of a competitive environment might be better off elsewhere. Then again, if they transferred they might not be able to say, "I'm having much more fun than my friends at Harvard Business School and have no fewer job offers."

ADMISSIONS

According to the Kellogg admissions office, your GPA, GMAT score, essays, work experience, extracurricular activities, recommendations and interviews (which are required) are all "equally important." GMAT scores of applicants are typically high, undergrad grades are strong, and applicants have several years of impressive work experience. Applications are reviewed in rounds. As for when to apply, applicants are advised, "The earlier the better." Admission deferrals are considered on a case-by-case basis, but professional circumstances may be considered.

STUDENT'S OVERVIEW BOX

FACULTY RATING

HITS AND MISSES

HITS
Finance
Marketing dept.
Diverse work experience
School clubs
Cozy student community
Teamwork

MISSES
Quant skills
Ethnic & racial diversity
Off-campus housing
Crowded classes

APPLICANTS ALSO LOOK AT
Harvard
U Pennsylvania
U Chicago
Duke U.
New York University

FOR MORE INFORMATION, CONTACT:
Leverone Hall
2001 Sheridan Road
Evanston, IL 60208
(708) 491-3308

UNIVERSITY OF NOTRE DAME COLLEGE OF BUSINESS ADMINISTRATION

ADMISSIONS FACTS

Type of school	Private

Demographics

No. of men	193
No. of women	58
No. of minorities	10
No. of int'l students	38

EQUAL TREATMENT GRAPH

Admissions Statistics

Avg. GMAT	590
Avg. undergraduate GPA	3.2
Avg. age at entry	25
No. of applicants	803
No. accepted	380
No. enrolled	190

Deadlines and Notifications

Regular application	5/01
Regular notification	rolling
Special dates	N/A

Focus of Curriculum

General Management, Students can specialize.

Academic Specialities

General Management

Joint Degrees

JD/MBA

Special Programs

The London and Santiago Program: Notre Dame has it's own campus and faculty in the heart of each city. The 3-Semester Taxation Program.

FINANCIAL FACTS

In-state tuition	$15,204
Out-of-state tuition	$15,204
On-campus housing	$4,000

ACADEMICS

Notre Dame offers two MBA programs: the traditional two-year program, and the accelerated three-semester MBA. The two-year program is "designed for students with little or no academic background in business." Students in this program must have completed a calculus and/or advanced algebra class prior to matriculation. First-years in this program take twelve required core courses. Second-years have flexibility and tailor coursework to their career goals.

The three-semester MBA is designed for students who hold an undergraduate degree in business. This program kicks off with a nine-week summer semester in which students attend review sessions of the courses in the first year of the two-year MBA program. After completing these sessions, which are graded, students join the second years in the other program. But this doesn't always work. Reported one student, "There are two flavors here—two-year and twelve-month. The school promotes them as one integrated program, but competition and animosity between the two can be high." A few students complained about the three-semester program itself: "The review sessions cram information down your throat. You don't learn—you survive." Still, many others were satisfied. Wrote one, "It provides an excellent opportunity to take time out from your profession and look at things from a new perspective. I would highly recommend the program."

Overall, students gave good marks to both programs for the rigor of academics. Professors are widely regarded as "excellent" and "accessible." Students appreciated the international focus in the curriculum, the opportunities for foreign study, and Notre Dame's intensive language classes. Over twenty percent of the student body is foreign, further promoting the international perspective. Group work is standard practice; team projects make up many of the class assignments. Given Notre Dame's Catholic tenor, a huge emphasis is on ethics which is featured in several stand-alone courses.

PLACEMENT AND RECRUITING

Ninety-five firms recruited on campus last year. As of June 1, 1993, sixty percent of all graduating students had secured a job. Leading recruiters were Arthur Anderson, Ford, Anderson Consulting, and Proctor and Gamble and tended to come from the midwest.

Students were fierce in their criticism of the placement center, firing off comments like, "Employers come for the undergraduates, not the MBAs!" and "They do nothing." Students are optimistic, however, that things will improve under new placement director Joyce Manthey. Said one student, "They've made great strides and are positioning themselves to do better." Students absolutely raved about the alumni network. "I have contacted a number of alumni in very senior positions and all of them have offered more help that I could ever have asked for. One student put it more bluntly, "Alumni are EVERYTHING; don't even bother going to the placement office."

UNIVERSITY OF NOTRE DAME COLLEGE OF BUSINESS ADMINISTRATION

STUDENT LIFE/CAMPUS

Like their undergrad counterparts, Notre Dame MBAs enjoy their football games and sports. Students write they have a great social life. Planned activities are organized by the MBA Student Association and include welcome back parties, football tailgaters, student/faculty mixers, the Christmas Dance and the Spring Formal. Community service projects, (a natural extracurricular at this ethics-heavy school) include the Urban Plunge, Big Brothers/Sister program, and a food drive at Thanksgiving. Students also enjoy the small school environment which boasts a student body of only 500 where "a family atmosphere pervades everything." Raved one MBA, "The environment is not competitive. Everyone helps each other through the program." However, complaints about the facilities and the administration were common. Respondents wrote, "The school's dedication to the B-school is suspect," "The MBA administration is pathetic," and "The administration focuses on undergrad hand-holding." There seems to be a link between the problems with the administration and a lack of improvement in problem areas. More than one student said the typical response to suggestions was, "We don't have the money" "no excuse—go get it" or "Wait for the new building" (completion date: 1995). Still, one student's remarks typified the prevalent attitude here: "I chose the school for where it's going and what it will become. A $50-million new building with library will create real confidence and a new identity." Help is on the way, but not soon enough for some students. In the meantime, though, students will continue to enjoy each other: "Things are intimate here; you really get to know your professors and classmates."

A note on housing: on-campus digs are available in a new modern graduate complex. There's a married student complex, but at present, demand is greater than supply. Most folks head off-campus where housing is more plentiful. Campus parking is available at a nominal fee.

ADMISSIONS

The admissions committee considers the following criteria, (not necessarily in order of importance) college GPA, GMAT scores, extracurricular activities, letters of recommendation. According to the admissions office, "Our criteria are not weighed. We prefer but do not require work experience. A undergraduate business degree is required for our three semester program, but there are no specific curricular requirements for our two year MBA. We highly recommend interviews; we conduct interviews at all the United States MBA Forum sites as well as schedule on-campus interviews, followed by a class and tour, if requested. Applicants should choose their recommenders carefully. Family, friends and colleagues should be avoided. Supervisors and managers are preferred for those applicants with work experience; if still in school, faculty members or supervisors from internships are appropriate." Students are advised to apply as early as possible and to take the GMAT in October.

STUDENT'S OVERVIEW BOX

FACULTY RATING

HITS AND MISSES

HITS
Profs are great teachers
Ethics count
Alumni
Students happy with each other
Cozy student community

MISSES
Administration
Facilities
Library

APPLICANTS ALSO LOOK AT

U Chicago
Vanderbilt U.
Dartmouth College
Georgetown U.
Ohio State U.
Syracuse U.
Wake Forest U.

FOR MORE INFORMATION, CONTACT:
College of Business Administration
110 Hayes–Healy Center
Notre Dame, IN 46556
(219) 631-8488

OHIO STATE UNIVERSITY COLLEGE OF BUSINESS

ADMISSIONS FACTS

Type of school   Public

Demographics
No. of men	193
No. of women	67
No. of minorities	36
No. of int'l students	54

EQUAL TREATMENT GRAPH

Admissions Statistics
Avg. GMAT	605
Avg. undergraduate GPA	3.23
Avg. age at entry	25
No. of applicants	962
No. accepted	344
No. enrolled	126

Deadlines and Notifications
Regular application	rolling
Regular notification	within 4 weeks
Special dates	4/01 (int'l students)

Focus of Curriculum
General Management

Academic Specialties
Finance, Real Estate, Transportation, Logistics

Special Programs
Business Solution Team (BST);Student Investment Management (SIM); Executive Luncheon Series; Foreign Study.

FINANCIAL FACTS

In-state tuition	$3,966
Out-of-state tuition	$10,278
On-campus housing	$3,500

ACADEMICS

Ohio State has a well-deserved reputation as one of the best B-schools in the country. To ensure that entering students begin on equal footing, a pre-enrollment program provides students a review of skills in accounting and quantitative methods. The school also offers students three computer literacy modules. The first of these take place a week before classes begin and focus on hardware, operating systems and word processing. The remainder take place during the fall and winter quarters.

The first-year core curriculum is highly structured. It consists of three phases: the basics, introduction to the functional areas, and a combined punch of practice and theory in the disciplines of management science. In true '90s style, all courses are tightly integrated and complement one another. They also feature group projects. But this is basically a rigorous, meat and potatoes program. The second year is extremely flexible and devoted to specialization. Operations and Logistics Management, Finance, and Real Estate are reportedly excellent departments. Wrote one student, "The first year provides a solid grounding in the fundamental concepts. The second year is more interesting and practical." Said another, "I will not be competent in all of the functional areas—but I will be competent in my areas of concentration." Apparently this is so for many students. Ohio MBAs report uneven skills in several areas. The overwhelming majority of students feel well-trained in finance, general management, and quantitative methods. This is evidenced by their success in running and managing five million dollars of the University's endowment. MBA's participating in the Student Investment Management Program, boast a portfolio growth of over $2 million in just two years. A sizeable number report they're less confident about their abilities in marketing.

Regardless of their own academic strengths and weaknesses, students give their professors good grades for their teaching. Still, this can be uneven. Like most programs, Ohio has its share of "incompetent teachers." Explained one MBA, "During the first year, half of the teachers are very good to stellar. During the second year, this increases to three fourths of the faculty." As for accessibility, with a student to faculty ratio of 8:1, students report they get plenty of individual attention from professors. According to one MBA, "They even participate in student events."

PLACEMENT AND RECRUITING

The Career Development Office works with other MBA placement offices to coordinate the Big Ten Job Fairs in major U.S. cities and participate in the MBA Consortium held in Chicago. Still, like the students at most B-schools, Ohio MBAs say it isn't enough. One student's comments seemed to typify the prevalent feeling here: "Career placement and the quality of companies recruiting on campus needs to improve. Most students do not or cannot find their jobs through this office." Still, students say there are opportunities to network: "The local business community is very receptive to student requests for participation in speeches and luncheons."

OHIO STATE UNIVERSITY COLLEGE OF BUSINESS

STUDENT LIFE/CAMPUS

Students report a heavy workload and moderate to high anxiety levels, although one MBA qualifies this: "A great deal of the pressure is self-imposed." Self-imposed or not, students here study hard. They hit their books an average of thirty to thirty-five hours a week and do all or most of the required reading. As one might expect, the result of this intensity is that students are fairly competitive. But according to our survey, they're also "team-oriented and friendly." Students want to succeed, but not at the expense of a classmate. As one student put it, "One of the benefits of going to a small school (only 130 students in each class), is everyone knows each other and there is a supportive atmosphere." This also extends to the social scene. Raved one MBA, "All the students are friends and go out together frequently."

A favorite watering hole is Street Scenes. Extracurricular activities include whitewater rafting and ski trips. One of the most popular events is an annual MBA/corporate golf day, in which a foursome of executives and students share a game of golf. Reported one student, "The golf facilities are excellent." Students are less pleased with the school's facilities. Most agreed with the MBA who said they're "horrible." But a new $62,000,000 B-school complex is in the works and should go a long way towards creating a campus befitting a top school. One student has even higher hopes: "Once the new facility is built, I expect the MBA program to be the best in the nation." Fortunately, students don't have to wait that long to find decent housing. Both on- and off-campus accommodations are affordable, available, and attractive. The majority of students opt to live off-campus in shared apartments in Columbus. Several students alluded to "a feeling of excitement here," and told us, "The program is on the move, trying to implement changes that will improve the program." Some of the changes may come in the form of a revamped curriculum, which is currently under review. Some of the changes may be administrative. Students said the school needs to be run more efficiently and the library needs a facelift.

ADMISSIONS

The admissions office at Ohio State considers your work experience most important. The school then considers, in descending order or importance, your GMAT scores, college GPA, essays, letters of recommendation, and extracurricular activities. Decisions are made on a rolling admissions basis. The school adds, "Our self-completing application allows the applicant to manage their file. Once they submit a completed application, an admission decision will be sent to them within two to four weeks. Early application completion is strongly recommended." The final deadline is July 1st, provided spots are still available.

STUDENT'S OVERVIEW BOX

Overall Happiness

Academic Satisfaction

50   75   100%

■ Student Opinion   □ National Average

FACULTY RATING

■ Student Opinion   □ National Average

HITS AND MISSES

HITS
Finance
Operations/logistic management
Ethnic & racial diversity
School clubs
Tuition
Student community

MISSES
Placement
Facilities

APPLICANTS ALSO LOOK AT
U Tennessee-Knox
U Pennsylvania
U Michigan
Indiana U.
U Texas-Austin

FOR MORE INFORMATION, CONTACT:
College of Business
112 Hagerty Hall, 1175 College Road
Columbus, OH 43210
(614) 292-2715

UNIVERSITY OF PENNSYLVANIA: THE WHARTON SCHOOL GRADUATE DIVISION

ADMISSIONS FACTS

Type of school   Private

Demographics

No. of men	549
No. of women	214
No. of minorities	92
No. of int'l students	224

EQUAL TREATMENT GRAPH

Admissions Statistics

Avg. GMAT	645
Avg. undergraduate GPA	3.4
Avg. age at entry	27
No. of applicants	6,022
No. accepted	1,218
No. enrolled	763

Deadlines and Notifications

Regular application	4/15
Regular notification	within 6 weeks
Special dates	N/A

Focus of Curriculum

Specialized, with a major declared

Academic Specialties

Finance, Marketing, Accounting

Joint Degrees

MBA/JD, MBA/MD, MBA/DMD-dental
MBA/MSE Engineering

Special Programs

Wharton's Sol C. Snider Entrepreneurial Center. The Lauder Institute's International Exch. Programs: Paid consulting available, Summer Pre-enrollment "Prep", Foreign Study.

FINANCIAL FACTS

In-state tuition	$17,000
Out-of-state tuition	$17,000
On-campus housing	$4,500

ACADEMICS

Long considered a bastion of finance, Wharton now boasts first-rate academics in general management, marketing, accounting, real estate, entrepreneurship, non-profit business management, insurance/risk management, and business law. Equally important is the emphasis on global study. This is supported by an international student body (almost thirty percent), international courses, two international joint-degree programs, and an international business simulation. Courses at Wharton contain a quantitative orientation and require well-developed math skills. Advised one student, "It helps if you were quantitative before coming to this program."

Wharton recently overhauled its MBA program to create a "curriculum for the twenty-first century." The traditional two-term academic year has been replaced with four intensive six-week modules. Single-discipline instruction has been scrapped for "team-taught courses and integrative case study projects which draw together cross-functional insights." Reported one student "Wharton is working very hard to change, incorporating leadership, teamwork, and increasing teaching quality through constant feedback." Entering first-years kick off with a four-week pre-term in August. Students are "prepped" in courses such as economics and statistics so that all first-years begin on equal footing. Although the new program has been in pilot stages, thus far students report a heavier workload, and more papers/exams due to the more compact schedule of modules.

First-years take nine core courses and must complete a Management Communications course, demonstrate proficiency in LOTUS and basic math before progressing to the second year. The second year offers students a choice of nearly thirty majors offered in ten departments. A dizzying collection of 200 electives offers opportunities for specialization or eclectic sampling. Here's some favorites: Innovation and Entrepreneurship, Geopolitics, Risk and Crisis Management, and Environment of the Firm.

A hot topic: teaching quality, which has reportedly been sub-par in the last few years. Here's what we found: superstars and duds walk the same hallways. Wrote one student "the best researchers don't mean the best teachers."

PLACEMENT AND RECRUITING

Students are quite happy with the quality, range, and number of companies recruiting on campus. Students also gave high marks to the career placement center itself, and rated the alumni network is vital and helpful. In 1990–1991, a total of 643 firms, representing over forty-five industries, made offers to Wharton graduates and summer interns. Despite this, Wharton's eighty-three percent placement rate (1992) is low by Ivy League standards.

Leading recruiters were financial and consulting heavyweights such as Booz Allen, McKinsey, Bankers Trust, and Goldman Sachs. But Proctor and Gamble stole away a fair number of hires as well. Average starting salaries were sky-high, among the top five of B-schools profiled in this book.

UNIVERSITY OF PENNSYLVANIA: THE WHARTON SCHOOL GRADUATE DIVISION

STUDENT LIFE/CAMPUS

Each fall, 750 students enter Wharton, making it the second largest MBA program in the nation. To create a more intimate environment, the entering class is now divided into "cohorts" of sixty students each who are named by alphabetical letter and remain together through the core courses. Classes are held in amphitheater-style rooms where students are identified by their name plates, known as "tents." An average class numbers forty to fifty. Students are competitive, but not out for blood. Indeed, given the school's emphasis on group work, competitive students are at a distinct advantage. Shark behavior is frowned on and pegs someone as undesirable for group projects. "The best part of Wharton is the student body," says a typical student. Exclaimed one student, "Great people here—much more helpful than I thought they would be." "They're bright, conscientious and interesting." Still, one student complained, "Wharton students like to complain."

Part of the University of Pennsylvania's 260 acre campus, Wharton is bordered by historic buildings and spacious lawns. The official Wharton building is Vance Hall, an outdated four-story structure. (Stay tuned—Vance should receive a face-lift in the near future.) The new Steinberg-Deitrich Hall is shared with (and really home to) Wharton undergrads. It's hard to characterize a Wharton type, but because of the finance department and the close proximity to New York City, Wharton has been described as a feeder to the financial community with more than its share of investment bankers. Despite the diverse student body, Wharton has an East Coast, ivy league feel. But that doesn't mean students don't know how to go crazy. There is a HUGE social scene here. Example: The Walnut Walk, in which students don boxer shorts and bar-hop down Philly's Walnut Street, cohort theme parties such as the "Kentucky Derby," weekly all-you-can-eat pizza nights at the pub, the Holiday Ball and Spring Ball, and "ding" night at Cavanaugh's where a rejection letter gets you free beer. In between are the Wharton Follies, intramural sports, and the activities of over nineteen student clubs. As for housing, married or single students can live in the Graduate Towers, in which twelve floors have been set aside for MBA students. Many students opt to live off-campus in Center City or West Philly (less safe) where apartments are plentiful and reasonably priced.

ADMISSIONS

The admissions office considers the following criteria (in no particular order): essays, GMAT score, college GPA, letters of recommendation, extracurricular activities and work experience. The interview is optional. Writes the school, "The admissions committee evaluates applicants individually. Selection of students is not driven by categories or quotas. Applicants should represent themselves as they truly are versus what they may feel Wharton wants to hear. Applicants should also help the committee fully understand any unusual or non-traditional aspects of their candidacy." It is advisable to apply earlier in the admissions period.

STUDENT'S OVERVIEW BOX

FACULTY RATING

HITS AND MISSES

HITS
Finance dept.
Diverse work experience
School clubs
Student smarts
Teamwork
Placement

MISSES
Marketing dept.
Banker types
On-campus housing

APPLICANTS ALSO LOOK AT
Dartmouth College
U Virginia
Duke U.
Harvard
Stanford U.

FOR MORE INFORMATION, CONTACT:
The Wharton School
102 Vance Hall
Philadelphia, PA 19104
(215) 898-3430

PENN STATE UNIV.: MARY JEAN AND FRANK P. SMEAL COLLEGE OF BUSINESS ADMINISTRATION

ADMISSIONS FACTS

Type of school	Public

Demographics

No. of men	191
No. of women	83
No. of minorities	55
No. of int'l students	34

EQUAL TREATMENT GRAPH

Women

Minorities

0   2   4 (GPA)

■ Student Opinion ■ National Average

Admissions Statistics

Avg. GMAT	n/a
Avg. undergraduate GPA	3.17
Avg. age at entry	26.3
No. of applicants	920
No. accepted	375
No. enrolled	138

Deadlines and Notifications

Regular application	6/01
Regular notification	within 6 weeks
Special dates	4/30 (int'l students)

Focus of Curriculum

Specialized

Academic Specialties

Transportation logistics

Special Programs

The Center for International Business Education and Research (CIBER), The Center for Finance and Real Estate, The Center for Technology Management, Class-less Fridays meant for internships.

FINANCIAL FACTS

In-state tuition	$5088
Out-of-state tuition	$10,176
On-campus housing	$3,700

ACADEMICS

The Smeal College of Business is highly regarded for its rigorous academics, team-building approach, emphasis on communication skills, and small, personal program. Not content to rest on their laurels, Smeal has revised its curriculum to reflect the latest in trendy B-school offerings: an international focus has been built into all the core courses, the semester has been regrouped into seven-week blocks, and team-teaching and the integration of functional areas has been introduced. Off-campus corporate experiences have become integral to the learning process. Wrote one student, "The changes in the course structure and program make Penn State an even better school."

Due in part to the new seven-week sessions, (there are four per academic year), first year students take a whopping nineteen core courses, and have room for one elective. But since some of these courses extend for all four of the seven-week sessions, they're really more like one epic course, rather than four minis. One of these is the Communications Skills for Managers Course which happens to be a hallmark of the program. According to Harold E. Edmondson, Vice President of Manufacturing at Hewlett-Packard Company, a leading employer of Smeal MBAs, "Penn State MBAs can talk to anybody about anything, thanks to the communication program." According to one Smeal MBA, "The program is not as well-known as some other Big Ten Schools, but we're just as good."

The core courses are offered in a predetermined schedule. Translation: you've got no flexibility here. During the second year, however, it's all electives. Some of these are used to pursue an area of emphasis such as accounting, insurance, international business, etc. According to the school, dual concentrations are popular. In addition, students can select electives from any of the 125 departments at the University.

Students in our survey judged their marketing, operations, quantitative, presentation, and teamwork skills to be particularly strong. Areas needing strengthening were finance, accounting, general management and computer skills.

PLACEMENT AND RECRUITING

Under the auspices of the MBA Association, students are provided workshops on goal clarification, time management, etc. Visiting executives discuss industry and career issues. The simulated interview program affords students an opportunity to have a mock interview with a corporate representative and receive valuable feedback. In addition, the MBA Association puts together both a Corporate Guide and Résumé book which it mails to more than 750 companies. According to the school, "The most intensive recruiting takes place during the Career Interview Program, organized and directed by second-year MBA candidates. In this program, interviews are assigned by computer through a mutual company/student selection process. More than 1,350 interviews are conducted in a two-day period." Between 150–170 companies recruit on campus annually.

PENN STATE UNIV.: MARY JEAN AND FRANK P. SMEAL COLLEGE OF BUSINESS ADMINISTRATION

STUDENT LIFE/CAMPUS

The total entering class of 160 students is divided into four sections of forty students each to create an intimate learning environment and afford students a low student-to-faculty ratio. The school utilizes a range of teaching methods: lectures, case studies, readings, management simulations, games, and role playing. Group work and team building are emphasized through the program. The majority of students work in study groups. In many of the courses, class participation is weighed most heavily in the grade. Students report a heavy, though not killer, workload. On average, they study twenty to thirty hours a week.

Students here say they're competitive, and despite a strong desire to help each other, students are ambivalent about whether their classmates are the type of people they'll want to stay in touch with after graduation. But this isn't due to a lack of scholarly appeal; students say their classmates are smart. A final note: Penn State sponsors the Executive Panel Presentation, a simulated business exercise that invites executives from a wide range of companies to participate as review panel members. Participants have included Malcom Forbes Jr.; Mark DuMars, president of Inglewood Associates; and John Rawley, assistant to the chairman of Hershey Foods. The exercise formally culminates thirty weeks of first-year instruction. The entire class is placed into small consulting groups to review a complex business case that calls on technical concepts learned in the first year. They have seventy-hours within which to arrive at solutions and make a presentation to faculty serving on the review board. Winning teams go on to present to the visiting executives.

ADMISSIONS

According to the admissions office, your work experience, GMAT score, and college GPA are considered most important, and then in descending order, your essays, extracurricular activities, and letters of recommendation. They note, "Interviews are encouraged and considered on a par with essays, but not required at present." Applications are handled in a rolling admissions basis. It generally takes two to six weeks "depending on the backlog" for a student to be notified of a decision after receiving the completed application. Students may defer admissions for up to two years for personal reasons.

STUDENT'S OVERVIEW BOX

FACULTY RATING

HITS AND MISSES

HITS
Marketing dept.
Social life
School clubs

MISSES
Accounting dept.
Stay in touch
Placement

APPLICANTS ALSO LOOK AT

Indiana U.-Bloom.
Duke U.
U Michigan
U Texas-Austin
U Pittsburgh
Emory U.
Cornell

FOR MORE INFORMATION, CONTACT:

Smeal College of Business Admn.
106 Business Admn. Building
University Park, PA 16802
(814) 863-0448

UNIV. OF PITTSBURGH: JOSEPH M. KATZ GRADUATE SCHOOL OF BUSINESS

ADMISSIONS FACTS

Type of school   Public

Demographics

No. of men	316
No. of women	139
No. of minorities	27
No. of int'l students	70

EQUAL TREATMENT GRAPH

Admissions Statistics

Avg. GMAT	603
Avg. undergraduate GPA	3.26
Avg. age at entry	26
No. of applicants	1,014
No. accepted	456
No. enrolled	300

Deadlines and Notifications

Regular application	5/15
Regular notification	within 6 weeks
Special dates	N/A

Focus of Curriculum

General Management with specialization in nine concentration areas

Academic Specialties

Finance, Int'l Business

Joint Degrees

MBA/MS in areas of specialization such as East Asia, Latin America, and Eastern Europe, MBA/Masters International Business, MBA/Information Systems

Special Programs

Foreign Study in Prague and Budapest; Intensive foreign language instruction.

FINANCIAL FACTS

In-state tuition	$12,345
Out-of-state tuition	$20,427
On-campus housing	$6,000

ACADEMICS

The Katz Graduate School of Business "offers an MBA program that is unique, enabling you to earn your MBA in eleven months, over three terms of study rather than in the two years usually required elsewhere." This is made possible by the program's pace and breadth of study, and integrated curriculum which prevents duplication of course material. The obvious advantages of an eleven month program are 1) you get quick re-entry into the working world, and 2) tuition and other costs are cut in half. The disadvantages are you miss out on a summer internship and have little time to digest what you've learned. To get students in and out in eleven months, Katz puts its students through intensive seven week modules that emphasize organizational, analytical, and interpersonal skills. The hyper-speed at which you race through the modules is also meant to reflect the "managerial reality in which you will be working." Required courses can be reduced by taking accelerated courses. A highlight of the program are Project Courses, company-sponsored electives which allow students to solve an actual corporate problem and see their solution implemented.

International content is integrated into a majority of the courses. Wrote one student, "Katz is very active in international business education, the professors incorporate new issues from the international business community into curriculum." All students take a "strategy envelope" of three courses: the Management Systems and Decision Making (MSDM), Planning and Control, and Management Policy. MSDM occupies the entire first week of the program and immerses students in "managing a business enterprise from a top management point of view." Students feel that "Katz does an outstanding job in getting the student to focus on and understand the entire business process—from functional management to HR and strategic management."

According to one student, "faculty genuinely care about students." Apparently so—students doled out high marks to their profs for spending quality time with them. As for their teaching abilities, the reviews were decidedly mixed. Complained one "Katz needs fewer professors who act as consultants and more who act as teachers."

PLACEMENT AND RECRUITING

According to students: "Katz's greatest disadvantage is that graduation occurs in the summer, causing less recruitment." To correct this problem, in a few years Katz will begin their program in the summer and end it in May to stay in sync with recruiting efforts at other schools.

Of last year's MBA class, seventy percent had a job by graduation, eighty-four percent forty-five days later, and over ninety percent, within six months. Twenty percent of students accepted positions in Pittsburgh and twenty percent in Pennsylvania. Leading recruiters were Ford, the Big Six CPA firms—Pittsburgh National Bank, National Bank of Detroit, AT&T, Merck, and Swiss Bank. Writes the school "We're also actively working with lots of small companies who need just two to three MBA hires per year." But one student advised "If you're looking to get into Wall Street, don't expect any campus recruitment."

UNIV. OF PITTSBURGH: JOSEPH M. KATZ GRADUATE SCHOOL OF BUSINESS

STUDENT LIFE/CAMPUS

Everything here is defined by the breakneck pace of the program which isn't comfortable. One student's remarks typified the prevalent feeling here: "Katz's one-year format makes the workload/pressure heavy most of the time. I'm not a virgin, but these seven-week courses are tough." Advised one, "Academics in some areas get compressed. People who really want to learn the subjects, e.g., economics, accounting, should consider another B-school. This one-year program is a great jumping board for people who just need a degree for the next job switch." Several MBAs said "the one-year MBA is fast and super-intense just like the real-world."

Students noted that their classmates are somewhat competitive, smart, and interested in helping fellow classmates: "Students are a big part of what makes Katz exceptional. This is definitely not the ultra-competitive cutthroat environment you might find at some MBA schools."

The campus itself is located in Oakland, a small, college-townsy part of Pittsburgh. Hard to believe, but Pittsburgh is consistently ranked as one of the most livable cities in the U.S. Students say it's so—clean, safe, and full of things city folk love to do such as attending the annual Three Rivers Shakespeare Festival. Favorite on-campus activities include weekly happy hours, intramural sports, and going to watch U. Pittsburgh's nationally rated football and basketball teams. Student clubs brings in speakers and/or arrange for student consulting projects with local businesses.

A value-added program for students are the Executive Briefings, noon-hour presentations held several times a month at which chief executives from major corporations come to Katz to speak on career/industry issues. Afterwards, a handful of students join the exec and the dean for lunch.

Equally exciting is the American Assembly Dialogue which brings business leaders to campus to discuss major economic and social issues of the day. Katz is the only school in the nation to hold this event. Past participants include Ivan W. Gorr, Chairman of Cooper Tire and Rubber Co., Ted Turner of Turner Broadcasting System, and Robert Maloney, Chairman, Diebold, Inc.

A final note: the real secret behind Katz's one-year MBA is that many of its students enroll in one of the joint degree programs and earn two degrees, in two years, a solid return on one's time and money.

ADMISSIONS

Katz first considers your college GPA and then in *descending order,* work experience, GMAT score (TOEFL for international students), essays, extracurricular activities, the interview, and letters of recommendation. According to the admissions committee, "Quantitative information such as GPA and GMAT scores are important, but a student's work background, and experiences through their college years can be as important as actual performance numbers on the GMAT or academic record." Minorities, international, and handicapped students are given special consideration. Katz relies on rolling admissions. Each application is individually considered, then evaluated in groups of 100 or more. Students are notified of a decision within four to six weeks of receipt of their completed application. Depending on the circumstances, students may defer admission for up to a year.

STUDENT'S OVERVIEW BOX

FACULTY RATING

HITS AND MISSES

HITS
Accounting
MIS
Finance profs
Student smarts
Visiting execs
Computer/classroom facilities
Pittsburgh

MISSES
Pressure and pace
Faculty
Social life

APPLICANTS ALSO LOOK AT
U Virginia
UC Los Angeles
U Michigan
Duke U.
Penn State U.
Georgetown U.

FOR MORE INFORMATION, CONTACT:
Joseph M. Katz
Graduate School of Business
Mervis Hall
Pittsburgh, PA 15260
(412) 648-1700

PURDUE UNIVERSITY: KRANNERT GRADUATE SCHOOL OF MANAGEMENT

ADMISSIONS FACTS

Type of school   Public

Demographics

No. of men	194
No. of women	76
No. of minorities	34
No. of int'l students	34

EQUAL TREATMENT GRAPH

Women

Minorities

0   2   4 (GPA)

■ Student Opinion   □ National Average

Admissions Statistics

Avg. GMAT	608
Avg. undergraduate GPA	3.26
Avg. age at entry	26
No. of applicants	1,060
No. accepted	306
No. enrolled	153

Deadlines and Notifications

Regular application	rolling
Regular notification	within 6 weeks
Special dates	3/01 (int'l students)

Focus of Curriculum

General Management with specialization in an "option(s)" area

Academic Specialties

Production/Operations Management, Finance, Strategic Management, Technology

Special Programs

Washington Campus Program, Externship Program, Big Ten MBA Job Fair, MS in Human Resources Mgmt,

FINANCIAL FACTS

In-state tuition	$2,520
Out-of-state tuition	$8,190
On-campus housing	$5,500

ACADEMICS

Krannert offers two basic graduate management degrees: one in Industrial Administration (MSIA), and one in Management (MS). MSIA students complete their program in eleven months, including a summer session. This permits them to return to the job market sooner (most already have an area of expertise and solid work experience). Students in both programs share the same core course requirements in the functional areas. MSIAs are limited to three electives. By contrast, MSs take up to nine, although they must declare an "options area." Both programs emphasize a quantitative and analytical approach and also rely heavily on computer modeling.

The school seeks out students "who are comfortable with using technology, understanding their potential for competitive advantage and being able to enhance the adoption of technology in corporations." Not surprisingly, they then attract students with technical and/or quantitative backgrounds. Explained one, "Krannert is quantitatively forward. There are many engineering types here." The quantitative base, says one student, "gives us the tools to be efficient managers, but I question whether we'll be effective managers."

One of the assets that draws students to Krannert is a national reputation in operations management. Raved one, "Krannert deserves to move into the top twenty B-school rankings." But another complained, "The Operations program is overrated, although it's seeking to reposition itself. It should be more closely tied to the engineering school."

Students at Krannert gave the administration good marks. Wrote one, "the school now considers students' concerns and problems. Decision-makers are accessible and they're genuinely concerned." This sense of satisfaction apparently has much to do with the newly restructured curriculum, which now features two eight-week modules instead of the traditional sixteen-week semester. The shorter modules lighten up the core requirement load, provide students greater exposure to a variety of courses, and permit them to take more electives during the first year. One area that remains a problem: the faculty, which students rated below the national average. Of their teaching philosophy, one student wrote: "They're overwhelmingly conservative. They believe in free markets, free people, private investment, and small federal government with limited power. Amen."

PLACEMENT AND RECRUITING

According to the school, in 1992 "Students had an average of twelve interviews on campus and more than two job offers per student." Seventy percent of the student body was placed by graduation. Eighty-five percent within three months. Leading recruiters: Amoco, Ford, General Motors, IBM, Merck, Proctor and Gamble, and Westinghouse. Wrote one would-be tycoon, "I doubled my salary with my MBA." But one student found "opportunities few and far between for students in operations management—unnerving because Purdue is ranked high in this field." Part of the problem is that the school has been hit by the recession. "The Placement Center is striving hard to adjust to changing economic conditions," wrote one job-seeker. Here's a competitive edge: the Externship Program in which students visit a company during their spring break and "shadow" an executive.

PURDUE UNIVERSITY: KRANNERT GRADUATE SCHOOL OF MANAGEMENT

STUDENT LIFE/CAMPUS

Krannert is located in West Lafayette, Indiana, in a semi-urban community two hours from Chicago and an hour from Indianapolis. The B-school computers/classrooms are state-of-the-art. Krannert students work out at the "Co-Rec," an awesome gym featuring amusement park-like facilities—from bowling to golf courses to archery. Although the social scene is below average, it does exist. Planned events include school picnics in the fall and the annual alumni/student banquet. Weekends are spent catching up on sleep, playing in the intramural sports leagues, and attending informal get-togethers. Wrote one student, "Krannert draws primarily from the Midwest—Minnesota down to Texas. But a surprisingly large group of students come from California, New York, and abroad." Writes another, "People are great—must be that Midwest charm! But it ain't life in the big city."

The Krannert School is, by design, a small program with approximately 150 students in the entering class each fall. This fosters a cooperative, team atmosphere. Wrote one, "The small size facilitates a group atmosphere both in and out of the classroom." It makes "class participation more animated, group projects more fun, social life more accessible." First-years go through the core courses together so they have a "cohort experience." Further drawing them together are study groups, which are considered the "nucleus" of case preparation and schoolwork. Students are competitive, "but don't have a killer mentality." This may have something to do with the new emphasis on ethics and touchy-feely skills, as well as the school's unique Personal Leadership Development Plan. Interested students sign up for the program during orientation week and design a personal program of coursework and leadership experiences. Krannert also boasts a "no-nonsense, hard-work atmosphere," although at times this borders on the excessive. Still, recruiters attribute a midwest work ethic to Krannert grads: newly minted MBAs don't expect to start at the top, they expect to work hard to get where they want to go.

ADMISSIONS

The admissions office reports, "Although applicants come from diverse backgrounds in terms of education, experience, and cultures, they tend to have in common a strong analytical and problem-solving background." Krannert first considers an applicant's GPA, then in *descending* order of importance: GMAT scores, work experience, interview, letters of recommendation, essays, extracurriculars. They report that "interviews are encouraged, but not currently required as part of the application process." Applications are handled on a rolling admissions basis; students are notified of a decision three to six weeks after their file is completed. Students can defer admission up to two years, and twenty to twenty-five percent of applicants are accepted with no work experience. Krannert uses a self-managed application (you accumulate documents and submit them all together) so applicants know the application is complete at the time of submission.

STUDENT'S OVERVIEW BOX

FACULTY RATING

HITS AND MISSES

HITS
Innovative curriculum
Quant skills
Student smarts
Student government
Facilities

MISSES
Social life
Students with no work experience
Workload
West Lafayette

APPLICANTS ALSO LOOK AT
UC Berkeley
Indiana U.-Bloom.
Indiana State U.
U Michigan
UNC Chapel Hill
U Illinois-C.U.
Ohio State U.

FOR MORE INFORMATION, CONTACT:
Krannert Graduate School
of Management
1310 Krannert Center, Room 104
West Lafayette, IN 47907-1310
(317) 494-4365

RENSSELAER POLYTECHNIC INSTITUTE SCHOOL OF MANAGEMENT

ADMISSIONS FACTS

Type of school	Private

Demographics

No. of men	142
No. of women	48
No. of minorities	2
No. of int'l students	80

EQUAL TREATMENT GRAPH

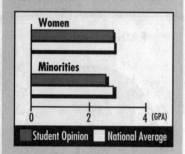

Admissions Statistics

Avg. GMAT	572
Avg. undergraduate GPA	3.07
Avg. age at entry	26
No. of applicants	303
No. accepted	249
No. enrolled	100

Deadlines and Notifications

Regular application	5/01
Regular notification	within 6 weeks
Special dates	N/A

Focus of Curriculum

Specialized

Academic Specialties

Management of Technology, Technological Entrepreneurship, MIS, Health Systems Management

Joint Degrees

JD/MBA, MBA/MS in Engineering and other fields of study.

Special Programs

3-2 Undergraduate MBA, International Exchange in seven countries, Summer "Bridge" Program for Minority Students

FINANCIAL FACTS

In-state tuition	$14,340
Out-of-state tuition	$14,340
On-campus housing	$5,200

ACADEMICS

Rensselaer Polytechnic Institute (RPI) School of Management offers two degrees: a traditional MBA, and its newest complement, the Management & Technology (M&T) MBA. The traditional MBA offers the basic two-year formula with a technical/quantitative slant. The M&T program, which students talk most about, emphasizes the integration of the traditional business areas with each other and with technology. Explained one student, "RPI has moved from a traditionally-based MBA to a more entrepreneurial/general management program utilizing technology." As one might expect, the program also features a heavy technical/quantitative slant and attracts engineering types with strong math and computer backgrounds. To bolster "softer" skills, RPI requires its techie types to take a leadership seminar. Students also report, "Group work is a very important part of the program." According to one M&T MBA, plenty of English majors make it here too: "Not having a technical background has not hindered my status in the program." The single most exciting aspect about the program, writes one MBA, is that "it involves lots of student consulting in technological areas," and is a "hot bed for new ventures." Enthused one student "the strongest contribution to my education has been the year-long, team-based, product development program." Explained one student, "RPI is very much involved with entrepreneurial activities through the Incubator Project and Technology Park, which provides students real-life experience in working with start-up, high-tech companies." But students also said the school offers other less technologically-oriented programs. The Health Systems Management Concentration is reportedly excellent.

Professors received good grades. Explained one student, "The good ones are awesome," although there are some not-so-eloquent teachers. More impressive, given the dedication to cutting-edge research, is that "faculty are very accessible and assist students outside of class." Raved this techie, "One professor is a world authority in the Business Incubator concept. Through my work with him and other faculty, I've obtained a summer position doing consulting in the Ukraine." All in all, students agree, "RPI's new M&T program is one of the most innovative programs around." But students also agree, "The program is still in its infancy and rough around the edges."

PLACEMENT AND RECRUITING

A rare find—a group of B-school students who report they're reasonably satisfied with their placement office and the range of opportunities available. This may be due to the truly *unique* offerings of an RPI MBA. Its hi-tech ingredients provide students a competitive edge. And as more companies become technology driven, the M&T MBA becomes more appealing. Summed up one student about employment potential through RPI, "What this school needs more than anything else is a full-time placement coordinator for the B-school. Otherwise excellent." Seventy-three percent of RPI MBAs had been placed within three months of their 1992 graduation.

RENSSELAER POLYTECHNIC INSTITUTE SCHOOL OF MANAGEMENT

STUDENT LIFE/CAMPUS

With only 200 students in the whole school of management, RPI is defined by high student/faculty interaction and small classes, although core classes tend to be larger. The workload is a killer. The vast majority of students study outside of class a whopping thirty to forty hours a week. Study groups provide some relief. During the second year, the academic workload levels off. But second-years take a practicum in a local industry which requires fifteen to twenty-five hours a week. At least it's not homework. Class participation and presentation count as a high percentage of the grade in many courses.

RPI students are intensely competitive and driven. But students appreciate a helping hand from their peers and frequently reciprocate. The emphasis on teamwork lightens up the industrious mentality of the scientific types. Reports one student, "The program is so group-oriented, it's not difficult to hang around classmates because I spend so much time with them." While the majority agree they like and enjoy each other, the social scene is hindered by all the academic activities both in and outside the classroom. Most events are scheduled through the MBA Association and include happy hours, barbecues, golf events, and guest speaker series. The majority of students live off-campus in Troy and Peekskill. About thirty percent of the students live on campus in graduate housing which is considered extremely attractive.

A final note: Students agree the student body is both professionally and ethnically diverse. There's a large percentage of international students, almost forty percent, and minority students—roughly twenty percent.

ADMISSIONS

The admissions office considers your college GPA most important. After that, in *descending* order, the office considers your GMAT score, work experience, extracurricular activities, interview, letters of recommendation, and essays. A TOEFL of 580 or greater is required of those who speak English as a second language. The school favors applicants with a technically-oriented undergraduate background: "Our focus is the intersection of management and technology. Everything we do begins with the conviction that for all firms in all future markets, sustainable competitive advantage is built upon a technological foundation."

STUDENT'S OVERVIEW BOX

FACULTY RATING

HITS AND MISSES

HITS
Quantitative skills
Ethnic & racial diversity
Entrepreneurship
Student Consulting

MISSES
Marketing
Social life
Troy

APPLICANTS ALSO LOOK AT
U Texas/Austin
Syracuse U.
Cornell U.
Case Western Reserve

FOR MORE INFORMATION, CONTACT:
School of Management
Lally Management Center
Troy, NY 12180-3590
(518) 276-6789

RICE UNIVERSITY: JESSE H. JONES GRAD. SCHOOL OF ADMINISTRATION

ADMISSIONS FACTS

Type of school	Private

Demographics

No. of men	121
No. of women	55
No. of minorities	13
No. of int'l students	18

EQUAL TREATMENT GRAPH

Women

Minorities

0   2   4 (GPA)

■ Student Opinion □ National Average

Admissions Statistics

Avg. GMAT	622
Avg. undergraduate GPA	3.2
Avg. age at entry	27
No. of applicants	631
No. accepted	205
No. enrolled	97

Deadlines and Notifications

Regular application	3/01
Regular notification	rolling
Special dates	N/A

Focus of Curriculum

Specialized

Academic Specialties

Accounting, Finance, Entrepreneurship

FINANCIAL FACTS

In-state tuition	$7,500
Out-of-state tuition	$7,500
On-campus housing	$5,800

ACADEMICS

As one student put it, "Within Houston, Rice is acknowledged as the 'Harvard of the Bayou.'" Indeed, Rice is well-known for its top-flight program and high-quality students. According to the school, "Legal and governmental analysis is stressed, both as a first-year course and as a perspective from which to view business activity." An international perspective and the development of strong communication skills are also pervasive components in the curricula. Wrote one student, "Rice is an innovative school that has done a good job of balancing theory and the real world." Explained another, "The lack of being accredited allows great flexibility in responding to the changing business environment." Perhaps because the MBA program was originally an offshoot of the school's master's in accounting program, the curriculum strongly emphasizes quantitative skills. Observed one, "Over half the class concentrates in finance, it's definitely the strongest major." Added another, "The accounting, finance, and statistics courses are first-rate."

First-year students take thirteen required courses which make use of team projects, case study, and oral presentations. Wrote one MBA, "The school emphasizes the articulation of ideas over book-type learning." Indeed, oral presentations feature heavily in a student's total class grade. During the second year, students devote their electives to one or two concentrations.

A few students complained of a lack of variety in the courses offered. Explained one, "There tends to be an over-concentration on certain areas." However, across the functional areas of business, students rated their skills as very strong. There was only one notable weak spot—operations. Another problem area, though not academic, seemed to be with the administration, whom students feel could do more to run things smoothly.

Professors are highly regarded for their teaching and generous after-class accessibility. This is helped by a low student-faculty ratio of 7:1. But over and over students told us, "The single most important thing about the school is the use of adjunct professors from the local business community. They are extraordinary and bring a sense of reality to the academic world." Put more bluntly, one student wrote, "Many professors get paid big bucks by companies for their advice. We get it for free." One student hit a sour note: "Too many first-time teachers teaching core courses."

PLACEMENT AND RECRUITING

Wrote one student, "If you want to work in the Southwest, Rice is the school to go to." Still, like the students at most of the other B-schools, Rice students feel their career placement office could do a better job in enticing a greater range of companies. A majority of the students told us they contacted alumni in their job search and, overall, were pleased, though not overwhelmed with their help. One request is that the school promote itself more. Explained one student, "The school is seriously under-recognized due to its small graduating class size. Only corporate recruiters seem to know about us."

RICE UNIVERSITY: JESSE H. JONES GRAD. SCHOOL OF ADMINISTRATION

STUDENT LIFE/CAMPUS

Rice boasts a highly demanding academic program. There is a steep learning curve in many of the core courses. Unsurprisingly, students report a heavy workload. "The first year is *very* tough," wrote one, "but the second year is more practical and interesting." Outside of class, students spend an average of thirty-five to forty-five hours doing school work/studying. The majority say it's very important to do most or ALL of the assigned reading. On the plus side, almost everyone works in a study group and benefits from the collective expertise as well as support of the other members.

One student's comments typified the prevalent feeling here: "Rice's small size contributes to much of the successful MBA experience." With only 100 students in the entering class, students report, "Interaction between students is both frequent and substantial. I know everyone in my MBA class at Rice." Adds a first-year, "Our class is tight and genuinely interested in assisting one another through what has proven to be a rigorous first year." Students say they're competitive, but this is kept in check by the culture of cooperation. Still, one student said, "grades are over-emphasized, but this may come more from the students." On the whole, students say classmates are "very bright."

Of Rice's home city, one student wrote, "Being located in Houston is an advantage." The student clubs take advantage of the city's offerings and organize visits to Houston area businesses. Reported another, "Coming from out of state, I found Houston a comfortable and friendly town." For an urban environment, Rice offers a surprisingly tranquil and beautiful campus. A tree-lined, three-mile jogging path encircles the campus. On- or off-campus, students report that housing is affordable and very attractive. Both intramural sports and golf are popular. Favorite watering holes are Valhalla (the campus pub) and Kays. Monthly parties on Herring Hall's patio are also popular.

A final note: students at Rice agree that theirs is not an ethnically and racially diverse community. Wrote one student, "The school should work to recruit more minority students into the program. Blacks make up less than one percent of the class. This is not representative of the real world."

ADMISSIONS

The Jones admissions department considers the following criteria most important: essays, college GPA, letters of recommendation, and work experience. Extracurricular activities are also considered. An interview is not required. According to the school, "each applicant receives a comprehensive evaluation due to the composition of our admissions committee, which includes two graduating MBA students, a recent alumnus or alumna, a tenured faculty member, and the admissions director. We do not select or reject an applicant based solely on his or her academic record or GMAT score; instead we evaluate each applicant in the context of the entire application." Decisions are made on a rolling basis.

STUDENT'S OVERVIEW BOX

FACULTY RATING

HITS AND MISSES

HITS
Finance dept.
Classmates are smart
Library

MISSES
Marketing dept.
Ethnic & racial diversity
Off-campus housing

APPLICANTS ALSO LOOK AT

Arizona State U.
U Texas-Austin
U Houston
U Texas-Arlington
VA Polytech Institute
U Iowa

FOR MORE INFORMATION, CONTACT:

Jesse H. Jones Graduate School of
Administration
P.O. Box 1892
Houston, TX 77251
(713) 527-4918

UNIV. OF ROCHESTER: WILLIAM E. SIMON GRADUATE SCHOOL OF BUSINESS ADMINISTRATION

ADMISSIONS FACTS

Type of school	Private

Demographics

No. of men	312
No. of women	98
No. of minorities	25
No. of int'l students	164

EQUAL TREATMENT GRAPH

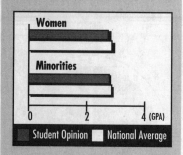

Admissions Statistics

Avg. GMAT	616
Avg. undergraduate GPA	3.27
Avg. age at entry	26
No. of applicants	1148
No. accepted	360
No. enrolled	150

Deadlines and Notifications

Regular application	6/01
Regular notification	within 3 weeks
Special dates	N/A

Focus of Curriculum

Specialized, 11 concentrations, options to pursue a double major

Academic Specialties

Accounting, Finance, Operations, Information Systems

Joint Degrees

MBA/MS in Nursing, MBA/Masters in Public Health, MS in Manufacturing Management, MS in MIS, MS in Mgmt. of Manufacturing Information Systems.

Special Programs

The Executive Seminar Series, International Exchange Programs.

FINANCIAL FACTS

In-state tuition	$16,980
Out-of-state tuition	$16,980
On-campus housing	$5,000

ACADEMICS

Simon is a school with strong potential, renown for its academic research, scholarly faculty, and finance and accounting programs. The curriculum is oriented around the basic concepts of microeconomics. Supply and demand price theory is emphasized and used as a framework for understanding how firms operate in the free market system. First-year courses are theoretical and lecture-oriented. There is an emphasis on basic concepts as well as on analytical tools used to aid managers in making decisions—such as probability and decision analysis. Courses are integrated across disciplines and may be team-taught by faculty. A first-year, third quarter "capstone course" pulls together the previous courses and focuses on Total Quality Management. "Contemporary Issues in Management," a program students rave about, permit's first-years to select topics of interest to their class and invite experts in to discuss them. Topics are then woven into the capstone courses. Although students build general management skills, they must specialize in one of eleven concentration areas. Second-year courses use case studies and experiential learning to integrate principles from the first-year.

Overall, students said the program stresses quantitative methods. Claimed one, "While they're trying to become less of a quant school, there is still too much emphasis on quantitative subjects." But one MBA advised, "Someone with a non-quantitative background can survive." Student's self-assessment of their skills showed erratic strengths. For example, while students rated their finance, accounting, quantitative, and teamwork skills as high, they were less confident about their marketing, general management, and operations skills. Simon students are taught by senior, tenure-track faculty who rank among the nations top five in academic journals. But the heavy focus on research may dilute teaching quality. Professor's are more highly regarded for their after-class accessibility.

PLACEMENT AND RECRUITING

Students may interview in Manhattan through the New York Recruiting Program. In 1992, "twenty-five percent of the class obtained positions with New York City-area businesses." Over 200 companies interviewed on-campus. Seventy-five percent of the graduating class had a job by graduation. Ninety percent within three months. The big recruiters were Proctor and Gamble, Xerox, Bausch and Lomb, Merrill Lynch, and First Empire State Corporation. Although students said they were moderately happy with the placement office itself, they were dissatisfied with the range of companies recruiting. An overwhelming number of students took matters into their own hands, contacted alumni and found them helpful.

UNIV. OF ROCHESTER: WILLIAM E. SIMON GRADUATE SCHOOL OF BUSINESS ADMINISTRATION

STUDENT LIFE/CAMPUS

A hallmark of Simon's program is the cohort and study group experience. Entering students are grouped together in sections, or cohorts, which stick together for the first three-quarters of the program. The school also pre-assigns students to study groups constructed to operate as mini-management teams. Some students complained about this emphasis on group work. Complained one, "Everything is done in groups. I feel it's overemphasized here; I wish there were more individual work." Students say they're competitive: "Students that come here actually want to learn. They're not here just for the three letters, MBA." However, competition is not cutthroat; students say their classmates are cooperative and interested in helping each other.

Students agree that the student body is ethnically and racially diverse. A whopping forty percent of students are international, twenty-five percent are women. One of the more popular events on-campus are the bi-monthly Broaden Your Horizons, lunchtime presentations by foreign students about their country. It's standing room only when Brazilians defend their country's inflation, Canadians discuss their health care system, and the presenters offer classmates a buffet of their native foods.

Simon boasts a brand-spanking new B-school building. Inside it features state-of-the-art facilities and computers, and an elegant, clubby atmosphere. Wrote one student, "Aside from the fact that it's a snow magnet, this campus is perfect." Some of the brutal weather can be avoided by using the indoor tunnels beneath the campus. As for the town of Rochester, it offers the quintessential college-town experience. Students doled out high marks for the affordability and comfort of both on and off-campus housing. On-campus townhouses are especially nice for married students with families. Off-campus, students opt for shared Victorian homes in the trendy Park Avenue section of town.

ADMISSIONS

Two-thirds of Simon's class starts in September; the remaining third start in January and complete the program in an accelerated eighteen-month schedule.

The admissions committee considers the following criteria (not listed in order of importance): essays, college GPA, letters of recommendation, and GMAT. Interviews are required of applicants with fifteen months or fewer of prior full-time work experience. For all others, interviews are strongly encouraged. Decisions are made on a rolling admissions basis. Applicants are notified of a decision within three weeks of applying.

Accepted students may defer admission for up to two years.

STUDENT'S OVERVIEW BOX

Overall Happiness

Academic Satisfaction

50   75   100%

■ Student Opinion   □ National Average

FACULTY RATING

■ Student Opinion   □ National Average

HITS AND MISSES

HITS
Finance
Quantitative skills
Teamwork
Facilities

MISSES
Marketing dept.
Social life

APPLICANTS ALSO LOOK AT

UC Berkeley
U Texas-Austin
U Michigan
New York University
Cornell U.
Ohio State U.
Carnegie Mellon U.
SUNY Buffalo
Columbia

FOR MORE INFORMATION, CONTACT:
William E. Simon Graduate School of
Business Administration
Rochester, NY 14627
(716) 275-3533

UNIV. OF SOUTHERN CALIFORNIA GRADUATE SCHOOL OF BUSINESS ADMINISTRATION

ADMISSIONS FACTS

Type of school	Private

Demographics

No. of men	285
No. of women	140
No. of minorities	34
No. of int'l students	89

EQUAL TREATMENT GRAPH

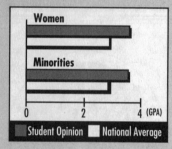

Women

Minorities

0   2   4 (GPA)

■ Student Opinion ■ National Average

Admissions Statistics

Avg. GMAT	622
Avg. undergraduate GPA	3.2
Avg. age at entry	27
No. of applicants	1,289
No. accepted	402
No. enrolled	190

Deadlines and Notifications

Regular application	4/01
Regular notification	within 3 weeks
Special dates	N/A

Focus of Curriculum

Specialized

Academic Specialties

Accounting, Finance, Entrepreneurship, Organizational Behavior

FINANCIAL FACTS

In-state tuition	$15,730
Out-of-state tuition	$15,730
On-campus housing	$7,000

ACADEMICS

USC has a reputation as a top-notch B-school. A revamped curriculum emphasizes the '90s themes seen at many progressive B-schools: globalization, leadership, communication skills, ethics, the use of technologies in problem-solving, and according to the school, "the inter-relatedness of management issues." A primary emphasis is teamwork; almost every course features some kind of partnering. Like many programs, USC organizes the first-year core courses sequentially so that concepts and skills build upon earlier ones. What's unique about USC is that they employ a staggered model; not all courses begin and end at the start or conclusion of a semester. Courses segue from one functional area to another to create an integrated learning experience. Two times a semester, a core faculty member "exports" him- or herself into a colleagues class to team-teach an issue related to more than one functional area, for example, finance and marketing. During the second year, students have up to four electives to specialize and one requirement—the field consulting project. To USC's credit, this hands-on training program has been in place for twenty years. But that doesn't mean the consulting projects aren't up-to-date. In the past few years, students have consulted to small, high growth companies in the inner city as well as to not-for-profit organizations.

USC offers a lot to the would-be business leader. A recent raid on hot professorial talent from other B-schools has beefed up several departments. Stand-outs include Finance, Real Estate, Health Care Advisory Services, and Organization Behavior, the latter of which is nationally renown. Particularly strong is Accounting and Entrepreneurship. As for where students judge their strengths to be, accounting, finance, marketing, and general management seem to be the areas in which USC MBAs feel they're getting their best training. Students feel less confident about their computer skills. The vast majority say the B-school is well-run. An unusual find at a top-flight school, students say getting into the most popular courses is a breeze. They also say they've played a significant role in the development of the curriculum. Reported one MBA, faculty members who design the program are "very responsive—willing to adapt program accordingly." They're also terrific teachers. But students say "incompetent teachers," mostly in the form of adjunct professors who teach second year courses, roam the same halls.

PLACEMENTS AND RECRUITING

The school reports an average of 180 companies hire and/or recruit on campus every year for full-time positions. Approximately seventy-five percent of the class has a job offer by graduation.

Students are moderately satisfied with the services of the career placement office and the range of companies recruiting. They are most enthusiastic about the power and reach of the alumni network. Wrote one student, "Big school. Big alumni base, over 9,000 people." Explained another, "I came here for the West Coast Trojan alumni network."

UNIV. OF SOUTHERN CALIFORNIA GRADUATE SCHOOL OF BUSINESS ADMINISTRATION

STUDENT LIFE/CAMPUS

USC boasts a 150-acre park-like campus sitting right in the middle of L.A. On the plus side, it's a short ride to the bright lights of downtown L.A. On the minus side, it's just a short ride to Watts, one of L.A.'s less appealing neighborhoods. However, for an urban school, USC boasts a lower crime and violence rate than most other large research universities located in or near an urban areas. Despite the relative safety of the campus, most students opt to take advantage of the L.A. lifestyle and live in the beach communities of Manhattan, Hermosa, and Redondo Beach about a thirty-minute drive away. There is rarely a shortage of things to do on campus, or in L.A. As one student put it, "USC is a great school in many ways—academics, extracurricular activities, sports, etc." Social activism is extremely popular. Shortly after the L.A. riots in the spring of 1992, USC entrepreneur students provided mentoring to owners of stricken businesses and helped them apply for disaster loans.

Like most B-schools, USC takes its entering class of 200 students and divides them into smaller sections of fifty students each. Section-mates take all the first-year courses together and according to USC MBAs, do a lot of "first-year bonding." They also do a lot of work. Students spend approximately thirty to forty hours a week studying outside of class. This tapers off by the second year. Apparently the school's emphasis on team work has paid off. Over and over, students praise USC for its "healthy balance on competition and teamwork." There's competition, but this is mostly self-driven. Teamwork, and the desire to help a classmate is the overriding ethic. But all this touchy-feely stuff doesn't come at the expense of smarts. Students say classmates are bright and professionally diverse. Wrote one "People here are of high-caliber and bring a lot of their work background into the classroom."

USC attracts a twenty-one percent international population, but it falls short in attracting minorities—only eight percent make up the student body.

ADMISSIONS

According to the school, USC considers essays, college GPA, letters of recommendation, extracurricular activities, work experience, GMAT scores, leadership, and interviews. USC recommends that applicants be proficient in mathematics, through calculus. USC goes by rolling admissions. Students are notified of a decision approximately three weeks after receipt of completed application, including test scores. The final deadline for applicants is April 1, 1994. Students who are placed on a waitlist decision are notified of a post by June 30th. On a case-by-case basis, students may defer admission for one year.

According to the school, "We are a member of the Consortium for Graduate Study in Management, offering fellowships for talented minorities."

STUDENT'S OVERVIEW BOX

Overall Happiness

Academic Satisfaction

50   75   100%

■ Student Opinion   □ National Average

FACULTY RATING

■ Student Opinion   □ National Average

HITS AND MISSES

HITS
Accounting dept.
Finance dept.
Students professionally diverse
Gym
Los Angeles

MISSES
On-campus housing
Computer skills

APPLICANTS ALSO LOOK AT
UC Berkeley
Northwestern U.
UC Los Angeles
U Michigan
U Texas-Austin
Claremont Graduate School
UC Irvine
Georgetown U.

FOR MORE INFORMATION, CONTACT:
Graduate School of
Business Administration
Bridge Hall 101, University Park
Los Angeles, CA 90089-1421
(213) 740-7846

SOUTHERN METHODIST UNIVERSITY: EDWIN L. COX SCHOOL OF BUSINESS

ADMISSIONS FACTS

Type of school	Private

Demographics

No. of men	180
No. of women	60
No. of minorities	14
No. of int'l students	19

EQUAL TREATMENT GRAPH

Student Opinion ■ National Average

Admissions Statistics

Avg. GMAT	606
Avg. undergraduate GPA	3.1
Avg. age at entry	25
No. of applicants	412
No. accepted	221
No. enrolled	123

Deadlines and Notifications

Regular application	5/15
Regular notification	within 6 weeks
Special dates	3/01 (scholarship)

Focus of Curriculum

General Management

Academic Specialties

Accounting, Finance

FINANCIAL FACTS

In-state tuition	$15,892
Out-of-state tuition	$15,892
On-campus housing	$4,000

ACADEMICS

As one student put it, Southern Methodist University (SMU) has long been known for its "outstanding ties to the Dallas business community." More recently, SMU has become known for its progressive curriculum, a result of the school's transformation from a one-year to a two-year program. The most exciting part of this change has been the addition of the Business Leadership Center (BLC), through which students tailor their learning to their individual needs. According to the school, the BLC builds students' skills in four areas: Preparing for Academic and Career Success; Communication Skills; Team Work and Team Building; and Coaching, Developing, Motivating, and Influencing. Over and over, students told us this program is a huge plus. Explained one, "The BLC offers corporate-like training. I feel confident now that I could give an A-rated presentation."

The first year curriculum consists of ten core courses, and runs concurrently with BLC seminars to allow students opportunities to practice new skills in the classroom. Second-year students take five required courses and have up to five electives. The underlying themes in the curriculum are international business and issues in leadership. Again, BLC seminars are interwoven throughout the program, as are career enhancement workshops. Wrote one student, "The school has a very demanding, yet rewarding curriculum." As for the new program itself, most students told us so far, so good. Said one, "It's great and has a lot of potential."

The majority of students told us SMU doesn't just pay lip service to administrative responsiveness and student involvement. One student wrote, "The administration asks for our opinion and suggestions. We can, and have, improved the program." Overall, students gave themselves high marks for their skills in the functional areas, a strong indicator that the trendy topics have not come at the expense of the basics. Students rated themselves sky-high in areas such as teamwork, interpersonal, and presentation skills. Strong marks also went to their general management, finance, accounting, and computer skills. An area in need of some strengthening was operations.

PLACEMENT AND RECRUITING

The majority of students report they are not satisfied with the efforts of the career services office nor the range of companies recruiting. Complained one student, "Career placement needs to be more supported by administration." Although one explained, "The two-year program is still new, hence the needed improvement in career placement. It's improving though!" According to the school, "Ninety-five percent of those who wanted paid internships obtained them with companies like Northern Telecom, Procter and Gamble Distributing Co., JC Penney Co., and EDS."

Clearly SMU's strong suit, students were most satisfied with the opportunities afforded them through the mentor program. Wrote one MBA, "The school provides excellent access to the business community and alumni through the mentor program."

SOUTHERN METHODIST UNIVERSITY: EDWIN L. COX SCHOOL OF BUSINESS

STUDENT LIFE/CAMPUS

The SMU B-school is housed in a three-building complex. The facilities in these buildings got high marks across the board. Reported one student, "Excellent computer labs." Students are also pleased with the library and the state-of-the-art gym. Both off-campus and on-campus housing is reportedly attractive and readily available.

Students at SMU spend their time outside of class playing intramural tennis and volleyball. A favorite event is the spring golf tournament. Every Thursday night is drink-and-be-happy hour. On weekends, groups of students venture off-campus to enjoy the city delights of Dallas.

Although SMU is located in a major metropolitan area, it lacks the diversity of an urban school. Only ten percent of the student body is international, seven to eight percent are minority. And students we surveyed agreed—the student body is not ethnically and racially diverse.

ADMISSIONS

The SMU admissions office told us that a strong college GPA is most important, and then in *descending* order, GMAT scores, work experience, interview, extracurricular activities, essays, and letters of recommendation. Work experience and the interview are not required, but highly recommended. Non-U.S. applicants must take the TOEFL exam. The school writes, "Admissions staff evaluate all facets of an application and are subjective with their evaluations." They look for students who are "focused and highly motivated." Rolling admissions decisions begin to be made in January for the full-time entering class. The final deadline for filing an application is May 15, 1994. Students are notified of a decision within four to six weeks of receipt of the completed application. On a case-by-case basis, students may be placed on a waitlist.

STUDENT'S OVERVIEW BOX

FACULTY RATING

HITS AND MISSES

HITS
Accounting dept.
Helping other students
On-campus housing

MISSES
Marketing dept.
Ethnic & racial diversity
Placement

APPLICANTS ALSO LOOK AT

U Texas-Arlington
Arizona State U.
U Texas-Austin
Texas Christian U.
Vanderbilt U.
Baylor U.

FOR MORE INFORMATION, CONTACT:
Edwin L. Cox School of Business
282 Crow Building
Dallas, TX 75275
(214) 768-3000

STANFORD UNIVERSITY: STANFORD GRADUATE SCHOOL OF BUSINESS

ADMISSIONS FACTS

Type of school	Private

Demographics

No. of men	502
No. of women	204
No. of minorities	169
No. of int'l students	169

EQUAL TREATMENT GRAPH

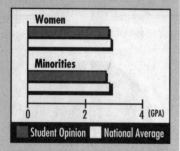

Women

Minorities

0   2   4 (GPA)

Student Opinion   National Average

Admissions Statistics

Avg. GMAT	N/A
Avg. undergraduate GPA	N/A
Avg. age at entry	26.7
No. of applicants	4,109
No. accepted	494
No. enrolled	359

Deadlines and Notifications

Regular application	rolling
Regular notification	within 6 weeks
Special dates	N/A

Focus of Curriculum

General Management

Academic Specialties

Accounting, Finance, General Management, Marketing, Strategic Management, Non-profit Management

Joint Degrees

MBA/PhD-School of Engineering, MBA/MS-Manufacturing Systems Engineering, JD/MBA, MBA, MBA Public Management

Special Programs

Health Services Management option, The Speakers Platform

FINANCIAL FACTS

In-state tuition	$19,236
Out-of-state tuition	$19,239
On-campus housing	$7,000

ACADEMICS

The Stanford Graduate School of Business is indisputably one of America's great B-schools. If you study here, you will study among the nation's best and brightest, learn from Nobel-prize winning faculty, and gain access to power employers. The first year core curriculum is extremely demanding, so much so that students frequently complain that it causes a synaptic melt-down. It's common for first-years to experience panic attacks about whether they'll make it or not. Despite their fears, almost no one flunks out.

The school is broken into three quarters: fall, winter, and spring. First-years are required to take eleven core courses and usually have time for two electives. Core courses focus on four broad areas: organizational behavior; business and the changing environment; economics; functional areas such as accounting, finance, marketing, operations; and computer modeling, decision analysis/statistics. According to Stanford, "Most students take four courses each quarter, although first-year students must take five during at least one quarter." Students can take exemption exams to place out of cores. Second-years choose from over 100 electives. Wrote one student, "Elective classes often work with local businesses; it's great to see real-world applications of knowledge." Some favorite electives are: Management Strategies in the Nonprofit Environment, Personal Creativity in Business, Power and Politics in Organizations, and Topics in Philanthropy. The interest in nonprofit topics is related to the popularity of the school's Public Management Program (PMP) which students describe as excellent. MBAs can earn a PMP certificate by taking three public management electives in addition to their required courses. Of the professors, students report: "Although there are out-liers on the faculty—duds along with the truly out-standing teachers—on average they get the job done." Less-than-exciting teaching tends to occur in core courses. Some of the best learning experiences are found in the visiting speakers program. Wrote one student "this is a great place to meet entrepreneurs such as Scott McNealy, CEO of Sun Microsystems and Steve Jobs."

PLACEMENT AND RECRUITING

In 1992, 211 companies interviewed on-campus. Here are the leading recruiters: consulting heavyweights Bain & Company, Booz Allen, and Boston Consulting Group (to name a few); computer firms Microsoft, Intel, and Dun Microsystems; I-Banks First Boston, Morgan Stanley, and Merrill Lynch; and package-goods companies Clorox, Proctor and Gamble, and Kraft. A large number of graduates go to work for smaller, high-growth ventures in both the Silicon Valley and elsewhere. Fifteen percent of the class took a job overseas. Ninety-seven percent of the class had a job within three months of graduation. Average starting salaries were among the three highest of schools profiled in this book. The median starting salary was $65,000—a solid return on one's investment. The only complaint was about the recruiting grind which students said is "unbelievably pressure-packed, especially when classmates have offers and you don't."

STANFORD UNIVERSITY: STANFORD GRADUATE SCHOOL OF BUSINESS

STUDENT LIFE/CAMPUS

Much of student life revolves around the student clubs, of which there are over fifty including one for spouses and partners. To judge by the responses to our survey, students enjoy each other. Raved one, "The most valuable resource is the student body, 670+ energized folks who love to have fun." Located in suburban Palo Alto, Stanford is what California dreamin' is all about: sunny days, breathtaking views, hot tubs, year-round swimming in the school's outdoor pool and just a few hours' drive away, skiing in Lake Tahoe. A sprawling golf course on campus makes golf clubs de rigeur. Friday afternoons are reserved for Liquidity Preference Functions (LPF)— a veritable beerfest. Real food shows up when the LPF is sponsored by a corporation. Tuesdays nights, the "Friends of Arjay Miller", a.k.a. FOAM, (which includes everyone). As for the campus, it's beautiful. Spanish style buildings feature red-tiled roofs, "a Stanford trademark." On-campus housing is available, but dorm-like. Most students opt to rent shared-houses in the hilly communities nearby. Many of these belong on the cover of Architectural Digest and are expensive (a four bedroom runs $1,800-$2,400 per month). But house/hot tub parties are one of the chief forms of social entertainment.

Students agree that the student body is ethnically and socially diverse, boasting a minority population of twenty-four percent, and women, twenty-nine percent. Claimed one, "Diversity is more than recruiting rhetoric at Stanford. There are plenty of former I-bankers and consultants. But classmates also include a professional soccer player, a labor union leader, an air-force pilot, and professional triathlete." All in all however, students agreed that "Stanford is an absolutely wonderful place to go to school."

ADMISSIONS

The admissions selection process considers the following credentials: college transcript, essays, GMAT score, letters of recommendation, and extra-curricular activities. Notes the school, "The admissions committee is as interested in learning about you as a person as it is in knowing what you have accomplished. Two of the fundamental values of the B-school are that students learn from one another but also engage in thoughtful reflection. The essay questions are designed to lead you to the first step on the path to self-discovery, which is part of the process of becoming a more sensitive and effective manager." The office of admissions considers affirmative action for Native Americans, Mexican Americans, African-Americans, and Puerto Ricans. Applications are batched in one of three rounds: November 10th, January 7th, and March 9th. According to the school, "the earlier you apply, the better." College seniors are admitted with a mandatory two-year deferral.

STUDENT'S OVERVIEW BOX

FACULTY RATING

HITS AND MISSES

HITS
Gen management
Teamwork skills
Classmates are smart
Cozy Student Community
Library
Placement

MISSES
Gym
Getting into popular courses

APPLICANTS ALSO LOOK AT
Cornell U.
UC Los Angeles
U Chicago
U Texas-Austin
U Michigan
UNC Chapel Hill
U Virginia
Dartmouth College
U Penn
Harvard

FOR MORE INFORMATION, CONTACT:
Stanford Graduate School of Business
Stanford, CA 94305-5015
(415) 723-2766

225

Syracuse University School of Management

ACADEMICS

Like many B-schools, Syracuse has responded to the obvious weaknesses of theory-based programs and retooled its curriculum to reflect the times. The new program addresses topics such as globalization, ethics, and managing total quality. Distinct to Syracuse, and worthy of an honorable mention, is the "management and the natural environment" theme, which focuses on the responsibilities of business in environmental issues. Of the new curriculum, one student wrote "Syracuse's MBA program has successfully incorporated the most up-to-date management styles." But one MBA observed, "it still has kinks in it that need to be worked out."

The first-year curriculum is extremely regimented. Wrote one annoyed student, "Class selection is not flexible." Translation: you have to take what they tell you. This consists of the unifying theme courses, personal skills development courses such as "teamwork and groups" and "computer proficiency," and professional core courses. During the second year, students choose from seven elective courses and complete their remaining core courses. Electives can be used to specialize, or pursue a general management program. Areas of study include human resources, innovation management, law and public policy, managerial statistics, and transportation and distribution. Students can also pursue interdisciplinary studies, a huge bonus for MBAs who itch to study at Syracuse's Newhouse Graduate School of Public Communications, a top-rated program.

In the complaint department, students rated their professors below average. Apparently, the emphasis on research is a problem: "Professors should be rated more on their teaching ability and less on publishing and research. Too many don't have a clue as to what it takes to teach." Students also told us the administration is not receptive to student's needs. Observed another, "The school is more concerned with what looks good on paper than whether the program is functional or not." In all likelihood, some of this has to do with calibrating what works and doesn't and adjusting the delivery of the new program accordingly. Stay tuned for next year.

The overwhelming majority of students said they picked Syracuse because it was close to home. Over a dozen students told us they chose Syracuse because it is the designated B-school in their army controller program. Many students mentioned the new curriculum, government program, and university atmosphere as major drawing cards.

PLACEMENT AND RECRUITING

The Career Center offers services such as a résumé book, a mock interview day with area recruiters, a weekly newsletter, and panels featuring visiting alum and corporate recruiters. Students at Syracuse feel the career center could stand improvement. In particular, students would like to see a greater range and number of companies recruiting on campus. Not the type to let that stand in their way, the majority of students in our survey contacted alumni in their job search. Unfortunately, here, too, alumni were not as helpful as students hoped they'd be. Only sixty-seven percent of the class of '92 had been placed by the autumn after their graduation.

SYRACUSE UNIVERSITY SCHOOL OF MANAGEMENT

STUDENT LIFE/CAMPUS

A small program to begin with—only 240 in each class—Syracuse makes the program even smaller by sectioning students into groups of forty each.

Students report they are burdened with a heavy workload. This is the result of the pace and breadth of the new curriculum. They study an average of twenty-five to thirty hours a week and report a moderate, though not killer amount of pressure. Papers and class participation are the preferred instruments of the grading system. A fairly competitive atmosphere prevails, although overriding this is a student body interested in helping others. Nonetheless, students like, but aren't in love with each other.

Students report they're satisfied with the school's facilities, although one student wrote, "The school needs more computer support." The campus itself is beautiful—a 200-acre spread of grassy lawns and historical-landmark buildings. The town of Syracuse has a secluded, rural feel. The weather in winter—misery. A decent, though not robust social scene exists here. Particularly noteworthy is Syracuses's "Friday Shared Experience" program which is a lot less touchy-feely than it sounds. Fridays are class-less, held open for job fairs, debates, or just goofing off.

ADMISSIONS

The admissions office considers (not listed in order of importance) your essays, college GPA, letters of recommendation, extracurricular activities, work experience, and GMAT score. An interview is required. Writes the school, "We use a subjective process to evaluate candidates. Admissions formulas or models are not used. Each candidate is evaluated based upon his or her individual qualifications. Weaknesses in some areas can be offset by strengths in other areas. Personal interviews are very important and can be conducted in Syracuse and major cities throughout the U.S." Decisions are made on a rolling admissions basis. Applicants are notified of a decision four weeks after a completed application has been received. Waitlisted applicants are notified of a spot by July 1st. Upon request, accepted applicants may defer admission for up to two years.

STUDENT'S OVERVIEW BOX

Overall Happiness

Academic Satisfaction

50   75   100%

■ Student Opinion ■ National Average

FACULTY RATING

■ Student Opinion ■ National Average

HITS AND MISSES

HITS
Finance dept.
Ethnic & racial diversity
Library

MISSES
Marketing dept.
Stay in touch
Recruiting

APPLICANTS ALSO LOOK AT

U Pennsylvania
U Michigan
UC Los Angeles
U Arizona
Rensselaer P.I.
SUNY Buffalo
New York University
U Rochester

FOR MORE INFORMATION, CONTACT:

School of Management
Crouse-Hinds School of
Management Building
Syracuse, NY 13244
(315) 443-3850

UNIV. OF TENNESSEE AT KNOXVILLE COLLEGE OF BUSINESS ADMINISTRATION

ADMISSIONS FACTS

Type of school   Public

Demographics

No. of men   123
No. of women   38
No. of minorities   10
No. of int'l students   12

EQUAL TREATMENT GRAPH

■ Student Opinion ■ National Average

Admissions Statistics

Avg. GMAT   580
Avg. undergraduate GPA   3.2
Avg. age at entry   26
No. of applicants   485
No. accepted   124
No. enrolled   80

Deadlines and Notifications

Regular application   4/01
Regular notification   within 3 weeks
Special dates   3/01 (int'l students)

Focus of Curriculum

Technology

Academic Specialties

Technology

Joint Degrees

JD/MBA, BA/MBA in five years

Special Programs

The MBA Symposia, TOMBA, The Oak Ridge National Library (ORNL)

FINANCIAL FACTS

In-state tuition $2,308
Out-of-state tuition $5,908
On-campus housing $3,800

ACADEMICS

The University of Tennessee/Knoxville (UTK) B-school has overhauled its program to introduce a new paradigm for learning: cross-functional courses, team-teaching, team-building, global study, and experiential exercises. This roll-up-your-shirtsleeves, activity-based program offers students more real-world experience than they could hope to find at most other B-schools. Indeed, UTK is the most innovative program in its regional area, and students rave about the new curriculum. Here's what they say: "Our focus is on customer service and quality, rather than learning the individual functions." "UTK's new MBA program is both innovative and comprehensive. We will be well-prepared to serve as cross-functional leaders."

According to the school, "The centerpiece of the core curriculum is a year-long case experience involving students in the running of their own business. Working in teams and focusing on the themes of customer value and organizational systems, students make the management decisions necessary to keep the business in operation. They solve large and complex problems and then give formal presentations to executives who have faced similar problems."

Distinct to UTK is the Oak Ridge National Laboratory (ORNL) which offers students access to pioneering technology. According to the school, "students develop marketing strategies for commercializing technologies developed by ORNL. Selected students from any concentration may serve as consultants and market analysts who work with scientists from ORNL to identify, research and, when possible, market technologies with commercial potential.

As structured as the first year is, the second year is unstructured. Students take eight specialized electives to build an area of concentration. This allows them to tailor a course of study to their career objectives. Up to four electives may be taken in a single area; the remaining electives may be used to form a second concentration or support the major one. Overall, students told us they've struggled with finance and accounting. A dozen or so say their quantitative skills also need bolstering. Complained one, "Those without business backgrounds should have programmed learning modules to catch up in accounting, computers." However, they judge their skills in marketing, general management, operations, interpersonal, teamwork, and presentation skills to be quite strong. Students report the "key learnings here have been how to think—not what to think."

PLACEMENT AND RECRUITING

Particularly noteworthy is the one-semester mandatory business placement course designed to provide students strategies for an independent job search. Its effectiveness is reflected in Tennessee's 1993 placement rate of ninety-four percent. Students report they are satisfied, but hardly happy with the services of the job placement office. In addition, they're disappointed with the number and range of companies recruiting. Still, an overwhelming number of students used the school's resources to contact alumni. Overall, they found them to be helpful, though not critical to the job search.

UNIV. OF TENNESSEE AT KNOXVILLE COLLEGE OF BUSINESS ADMINISTRATION

STUDENT LIFE/CAMPUS

UTK features a very small program. A maximum of 100 students are admitted each year. These are divided into two sections of fifty each. All entering students participate in the same year-long first year program. Students describe a heavy workload, and hit the books an average of thirty to forty hours a week. This results in a fair amount of pressure, though not enough to provoke an anxiety attack. To lighten the load, the majority of students work in study groups.

Observed one student, "The focus here is on learning and not on competition." A unique grading system also encourages cooperation in which "grading is based on team and individual performance and comprehensive written evaluations, NOT exams."

Students report a high quality of life. This is due in part to the terrific social scene and in part to a campus that boasts state-of-the-art facilities. TOMBA, the Tennessee Organization of MBAs is the professional and social association for full and part-time MBA students. The heart and soul of student life, TOMBA not only organizes the social events for students, but organizes the network of UTK MBA alums, runs a professional speaker series, and orchestrates a major community service project. All MBA students are expected to join. As for UTK's hometown, one student wrote, "Knoxville is a great town to go to school in, but you wouldn't want to live here full-time." Known for its great basketball and football teams, one Big Orange supporter wrote, "Sports is huge."

A note on diversity: although students agree that interaction among ethnic groups is easy and relaxed, there are unfortunately few minority students with whom that assertion can be tested.

ADMISSIONS

According to the admissions office, your GMAT scores are considered most important. After that, in *descending* order, your college GPA, work experience, interview, essays, extracurricular activities, and letters of recommendation come into play. "Since the UTK program is relatively small," writes the office of admissions, "we can give a good deal of individual attention to our applicants in order to determine whether ours is the right program for them and whether they are right for our program. As often as possible, we invite students to visit the campus, sit in on classes, and talk with current MBA students. In addition, we involve the faculty and administration in the admissions process."

STUDENT'S OVERVIEW BOX

FACULTY RATING

HITS AND MISSES

HITS
Marketing dept.
Helping other students
Library

MISSES
Accounting dept.
Ethnic & racial diversity
Placement

APPLICANTS ALSO LOOK AT
UNC Chapel Hill
Penn State U.
U Georgia
U Virginia
U Alabama-Tuscaloosa
Georgia Tech

FOR MORE INFORMATION, CONTACT:
College of Business Administration
527 Stokely Management Center
Knoxville, TN 37996-0550
(615) 974-5033

UNIVERSITY OF TEXAS AT ARLINGTON COLLEGE OF BUSINESS ADMINISTRATION

ADMISSIONS FACTS

Type of school	Public

Demographics

No. of men	440
No. of women	212
No. of minorities	47
No. of int'l students	89

EQUAL TREATMENT GRAPH

Admissions Statistics

Avg. GMAT	550
Avg. undergraduate GPA	3.2
Avg. age at entry	30
No. of applicants	670
No. accepted	298
No. enrolled	190

Deadlines and Notifications

Regular application	6/30
Regular notification	N/A
Special dates	6/01 (int'l students)

Focus of Curriculum

Specialized

Academic Specialties

Finance, Accounting, Information Systems

FINANCIAL FACTS

In-state tuition	$840
Out-of-state tuition	$3,290
On-campus housing	N/A

ACADEMICS

Most students would agree with the one who wrote, "The University of Texas–Arlington (UTA) offers the 'most bang for the buck' of any MBA program in North Texas. It's just as good as, if not better than Southern Methodist University or Texas Christian University." Wrote another, "I chose UTA because of its affordability *and* flexibility." Indeed, if you're a working student, UTA is a natural first choice. Students may begin the program in either the fall, spring, or summer semester—part-time or full-time. The majority of classes are offered at night. In addition, a student's course of study depends on his or her prior academic background. For example, students with little business background start with a series of "foundation courses." Students with prior academic work in business may waive out of equivalent foundation courses or simply go on to the "advanced" courses. Expect loads of math; the curriculum has a strong quantitative slant. Concentrations are available in one of the following areas: accounting, economics, finance, information systems, management, international management, management science, marketing, and real estate. Raved one MBA, "I have been very pleased with the quality of the classes." The majority of students report they feel well-trained by their studies in accounting and finance—UTA power subjects—and report above average quantitative skills. Students were less confident of their skills in marketing, operations, and presentations/communications. "The program is very good at the basic tools," wrote one student, "but is weak in application via simulations and experiential activities."

As for the faculty, one student commented, "Most of the professors make learning relevant to the 'real world'; not just theory. They're also willing to help you one-on-one outside of class." But as pleased as students are with their profs, students are displeased with the school's administration. One student complained, "This University nickels and dimes its students to death with fees, essentially a hidden cost, since fees are not publicized." Griped another, "I have been frustrated by the bureaucratic 'policies and procedures' that the school operates under." A frequent complaint was about the facilities—the library, computers, and campus—which are considered inadequate. Still one MBA countered, "UTA is striving to improve and has improved things since I began." Summed up another, "this is a good, solid, well-balanced program."

PLACEMENT AND RECRUITING

According to the school, "Seventy-six of the one 131 students who graduated in 1988-89 responded to the College's annual salary survey. Almost ninety-five percent of the respondents were employed. The average salary was $38,824. The salary range was $22,000 to $90,000." Explained one student, "Starting salaries are lower than some of the other MBA schools in the state since recruiting is not a strength." Added another, "This school is not well thought of across the country. However, in the Dallas/Fort Worth metro area, the school is very respected and carries a lot of weight with local companies."

UNIVERSITY OF TEXAS AT ARLINGTON COLLEGE OF BUSINESS ADMINISTRATION

STUDENT LIFE/CAMPUS

UTA is geared towards the commuter/part-timer. Wrote one typical student "UTA is close to home and work. I wouldn't give up working full-time to attend school." The majority of students are married. All of this translates into a commuter school atmosphere: the student body is less than cohesive, the on-campus social life dead. Wrote one student, "Being a commuter school, I sorely miss the camaraderie that my undergrad university provided. It also hurts networking opportunities." Explained another, "This is a large school, with a large student body. And there isn't much interaction outside of the classroom." Still many MBAs weren't bothered by the lack of esprit de corps. Huffed one, "This is a commuter school. I'm not interested in the social activities it has to offer."

On a happier note, UTA MBAs agree, the student body is both professionally and ethnically diverse. Roughly eighteen percent of the student body is foreign. Reported one, "Nice mix of working, non-working, foreign and domestic students." Although one student noted, "There are more geeks here than at any other school in America" and another wrote, "this school is proudly homophobic!" As for their smarts, one MBA noted, "UTA students have appreciable academic skills." According to our survey, students are moderately competitive. As one student put it, "constructive competition is encouraged." This means that students aren't the note-stealing type. On the other hand, they're not the most helpful either. A large number of students say their teamwork skills aren't the kind to win anyone Mr. or Ms. Congeniality. Still, the majority work in study groups. The workload is considered reasonable given student's nine to five workday schedule.

A final note: for the rare student who want to attends full-time and live on-campus, one student told us, "School housing is almost unavailable. You have to wait for a very long time, and the opportunity to get something is zero."

ADMISSIONS

While it accepts more applicants than it rejects, Arlington does expect its entering class to have a great deal of work experience to draw from. GMAT scores rank next in importance, followed by undergraduate GPA and letters of recommendation.

STUDENT'S OVERVIEW BOX

Overall Happiness

Academic Satisfaction

50   75   100%

■ Student Opinion ■ National Average

FACULTY RATING

■ Student Opinion ■ National Average

HITS AND MISSES

HITS
Accounting dept.
Diverse work experience
On-campus housing

MISSES
Marketing dept.
Social life
Placement

APPLICANTS ALSO LOOK AT
Brigham Young U.
Rice U.
Georgia State U.
Baylor U.
Memphis State
Texas Christian U
U Dallas
Southern Meth. U.

FOR MORE INFORMATION, CONTACT:
College of Business Administration
P.O. Box 19376, UTA Station
Arlington, TX 76019
(817) 273-3004

UNIVERSITY OF TEXAS AT AUSTIN GRADUATE SCHOOL OF BUSINESS

ADMISSIONS FACTS

Type of school	Public

Demographics

No. of men	727
No. of women	256
No. of minorities	157
No. of int'l students	147

EQUAL TREATMENT GRAPH

Women

Minorities

0 2 4 (GPA)

■ Student Opinion ■ National Average

Admissions Statistics

Avg. GMAT	634
Avg. undergraduate GPA	3.3
Avg. age at entry	26
No. of applicants	3,839
No. accepted	919
No. enrolled	468

Deadlines and Notifications

Regular application	rolling
Regular notification	within 8 weeks
Special dates	2/01 (int'l students)

Focus of Curriculum

Specialized;

Academic Specialties

Accounting, Management Information Systems, Marketing, Human Resources

Special Programs

Foreign Study, The Master in Professional Accounting Program.

FINANCIAL FACTS

In-state tuition	N/A
Out-of-state tuition	N/A
On-campus housing	$4,500

ACADEMICS

The University of Texas/Austin (UT) is one of the nation's finest public B-schools. In addition, it has a reputation for offering one of the best values. Students agreed, the "bang for the buck" is unbeatable. Among the academic strengths of the school are accounting, human resources, and information systems management (ISM), the last of which is supported by a major grant from IBM and utilizes CLASSROOM 2000, a special facility designed for advanced ISM study. Particularly noteworthy is the marketing department, which focuses on brand management and consumer and trade promotions. Unique opportunities are found in the Systemic Business Relationships Program, which is co-sponsored with Proctor and Gamble and 3M, and provides marketing students customer-focused internships in the summer between the first and second year.

The first year is extremely structured. The second year is flexible—students tailor their programs by choosing from over 170 electives. Up to five may be chosen for concentration in an area. Distinct to UT is the Quality Management Consortia which is made up of fourteen small companies who make a two-year commitment (via funding and sponsoring internships) to classroom education and on-site implementation of Total Quality Management (TQM). Roughly twenty students work as consultants to bring TQM principles to the companies' workplaces. Equally exciting is MOOT CORP a venture competition program offered as part of the technology management and entrepreneurship concentration. Students develop detailed, business plans and then match them against those of their peers at schools such as Harvard, Purdue, and Wharton. Entries are judged by a panel of who's who-like corporate leaders.

The most common complaints were about lightweight academics, assignment of busy work, and placement. But according to students, the administration has begun a campaign to correct this. Thus far, UT plans on developing a "market-driven curriculum." The administration has supported research at corporations across the country to determine what skills are needed in the marketplace—both short- and long-term. If a course doesn't provide students knowledge they can use, it's dropped.

PLACEMENT AND RECRUITING:

Students were less than satisfied with the career center. Complained one, "The placement office does little (except make my life miserable) because they are disorganized." Over 300 companies interviewed on-campus. Roughly eighty percent of the graduating class had a job within three months of graduation. The hot recruiters: Apple, Lotus, IBM , Xerox, 3M, Proctor and Gamble, Ford Motor Company, the Big Six accounting firms, major I-banks, Wells Fargo, and McKinsey. An overwhelming number of students contacted alumni in their job search and found them helpful.

UNIVERSITY OF TEXAS AT AUSTIN GRADUATE SCHOOL OF BUSINESS

STUDENT LIFE/CAMPUS

UT is housed in the George Kozmetsky Center for Business Education, a 350,000 square-foot complex of four interlinked buildings containing classrooms, research centers, and computer laboratories. As for Austin itself, students ranked UT's hometown as one of the nation's best. Close to the midway point between Dallas, Houston, and San Antonio, Austin boasts a mixture of high culture, tropical weather, and outdoorsy vacation activities such as boating, rock-climbing, fishing, and horseback riding. And just in case you were concerned, one Texan we surveyed assured us "Austin does not have cows walking down the street." Indeed, Austin is home to dozens of entrepreneurial, high-tech companies. Much of student life revolves around the Graduate Business Council which sponsors activities such as sports events and informal get-togethers. Students also plan their orientation week, graduation week events, and host the Friday night Distinguished Lecturer Program.

From class assignments to consulting projects, group work dominates UT. Not surprisingly, students rated themselves as outstanding team-players. Students here are competitive, but "supportive and willing to help others." High ranking also went to classmates' "smarts."

Minority enrollment is particularly high because UT participates in a twelve-school consortium which recruits and funds gifted minority candidates. In 1992, Ford Motor Co. asked the school to put together a team of Hispanic students to develop a plan to recapture market share in the Hispanic automobile purchasing category. Ford was so impressed with the proposal, they flew the students to Dearborn headquarters for a two-day series of presentations to top brass.

ADMISSIONS

The admissions office uses the following criteria to evaluate applicants (not listed in order of importance): GMAT scores, essays, academic record and college GPA, work experience, and letters of recommendation. Work experience and an interview are not required, but strongly encouraged. Writes the school: "Although grades and GPA are important, other areas receive substantial consideration. Personal and professional goals, achievements, extracurriculars, community involvement, and evidence of leadership and management abilities are considered in the admissions decision. While work experience is not mandatory, less than ten percent of admitted students enter our program without some type of professional employment experience." UT-Austin makes decisions on a rolling admissions basis. Advises the school, "Appy as early as possible." Applicants are notified of a decision within six to eight weeks. Waitlisted students are notified of a decision between June 1st and August 16th. On a case by case basis, the admissions committee allows students to defer admission for up to two years.

STUDENT'S OVERVIEW BOX

FACULTY RATING

HITS AND MISSES

HITS
Accounting
Marketing
Teamwork
Ethnic & racial diversity
Austin

MISSES
Placement

APPLICANTS ALSO LOOK AT

Northwestern U.
Dartmouth College
Cornell U.
Rice U.
Columbia U.
Tulane U.
U Rochester
New York University

FOR MORE INFORMATION, CONTACT:

Graduate School of Business
21st and Speedway
Austin, TX 78712
(512) 471-7612

TEXAS A&M UNIVERSITY COLLEGE OF BUSINESS ADMINISTRATION

ADMISSIONS FACTS

Type of school	Public

Demographics

No. of men	349
No. of women	155
No. of minorities	25
No. of int'l students	24

EQUAL TREATMENT GRAPH

Women	
Minorities	
0 2 4 (GPA)	
■ Student Opinion ■ National Average	

Admissions Statistics

Avg. GMAT	597
Avg. undergraduate GPA	3.2
Avg. age at entry	25
No. of applicants	840
No. accepted	425
No. enrolled	258

Deadlines and Notifications

Regular application	2/01
Regular notification	within 4 weeks
Special dates	N/A

Focus of Curriculum

General Management

Academic Specialties

General Management, International Business

Joint Degrees

MBA/MA in International Management with Johannes Kepler University, MBA with Ecole Superieur de Commerce, Master of Science in five business fields

Special Programs

Study Abroad in five countries.

FINANCIAL FACTS

In-state tuition	$1,202
Out-of-state tuition	$4,058
On-campus housing	$3,000

ACADEMICS

Plenty of Texas A&M B-school students agreed with the Aggie (as they like to call themselves) who wrote "a bargain!" Even for out-of-state residents, this school offers one of the lowest tuition rates in the country. But Texas A&M has more than price going for it. It also boasts a national reputation, and according to students, "a great location." The school's new updated curriculum starts off with an outward bound-style orientation, followed by an integrative three-week course called Markets and Corporate Strategy, which describes how businesses operate with diverse stockholders such as customers, the public, and investors. Students also take a two-semester long executive leadership and development program, the kind that focuses on '90s issues like ethics and cultural diversity. To get a head start on the job search, students also take an equally long career development seminar. Unique to Texas A&M is a required summer term in which students focus on international business as well as work in an internship. During the second year, students take a variety of "directed" and "free" electives. Here's the good news: elective hours can be earned through internships, study abroad, or foreign language classes. Everything here features a global slant.

Not everyone appreciates Texas A&M's new program. Wrote one student, "There's more coursework. But it should be more challenging in quality, not *quantity*." Griped another, "The new schedule cuts out people like myself who can no longer work part-time to pay for school." It may be too soon to judge this program. But the marks students gave themselves for academic preparedness in all the major disciplines were only slightly above average. The highest scores were in the areas of accounting, general management and teamwork. The lowest were in operations and computers. The majority of students say this school is meeting their academic needs. As for the faculty, professors receive good grades for their teaching. Students award them even higher grades for their after-class accessibility. But there were a few gripes. Wrote one Aggie, "Teachers sometimes take a conservative viewpoint without reference to more liberal viewpoints." Griped another, "There needs to be better communication among professors with regard to scheduling exams."

PLACEMENT AND RECRUITING

Aggie MBAs share their placement center with the undergraduate school which makes them unhappy. Unsurprisingly, students gave this department below-average grades and complained about their less-than-aggressive efforts to bring in a greater number and range of companies on-campus. Last year, over 110 recruiters visited the school to interview Texas A&M MBAs. But students say it's not enough. Blasted one student, "The recruitment of MBAs here is terrible. I could count the number of internships available on my hands. Until they rectify the situation I can't recommend this school." A positive note: students rave about the "Aggie network" and say alumni are responsive. This last may explain A&M's ninety-three percent placement rate for 1993.

TEXAS A&M UNIVERSITY COLLEGE OF BUSINESS ADMINISTRATION

STUDENT LIFE/CAMPUS

As one student put it, "There's a lot of work, mostly cases, which becomes routine." By all accounts, the workload is heavier under the new program and in the first year, but it's not overwhelming. The majority of students study an average of twenty to twenty-five hours a week. A sizeable number report reading rather than deeply analyzing cases is the way to go. In most classes, exams count heavily towards the grade.

Students here are competitive, but also cooperative. This doesn't mean they're great buddies. Half of students surveyed don't particularly enjoy or hang out with classmates. Among those who feel the complete opposite, one raved, "I love the people here," and another wrote, "Hospitality and friendliness are pervasive characteristics of peers and the community." The problem then may stem from the fact that Aggies feel their classmates lack professional experience, a complaint we heard over and over. Griped one, "Too many students here have no work experience. That really dilutes classroom learning, which is what B-school is supposed to be about." One student told the admissions office, "Focus less on GMAT scores and more on work experience." Another area of complaint: diversity and tolerance. Students agree that Aggies are not racially diverse. Wrote one, "Like everywhere, there is a need for more minority representation (Hispanics, blacks, and females). There's only one African-American male among almost 450 students." Bummed another, "Too much prejudice among students." On the upside, a new B-school building offers excellent facilities and computer labs, although students want longer computer center hours and their own business library. As for the town of College Station, students say it's okay. Wrote one, "Being from a metropolitan area, I enjoy the small-town atmosphere. But it gets old occasionally." The majority of students live off-campus in housing that is affordable though not especially beautiful. Extracurriculars are sponsored by the MBA/MS Association which holds a case competition, executive lecture series and recruiter/faculty/student golf tournament.

ADMISSIONS

While Texas A&M has no cut and dried formula for selecting MBA applicants, they do hold them to fairly rigorous standards. Above all, your GPA and GMAT score ought to be well above average. Beyond those, your work experience (they like to see a résumé), personal essay, recommendations, and the quality and rigor of your undergraduate program are all taken into consideration. Leadership in any pursuit also plays well with the admissions committee. There are no set math requirements, but A&M appreciates a strong quantitative background in its applicants.

STUDENT'S OVERVIEW BOX

FACULTY RATING

HITS AND MISSES

HITS
Accounting dept.
Classmates are smart

MISSES
Marketing dept.
Lack diverse work experience
Placement

APPLICANTS ALSO LOOK AT
U Iowa
U Texas-Austin
U Texas-Arlington
Texas Christian U.
U Houston
Baylor U.

FOR MORE INFORMATION, CONTACT:
College of Business Administration and
Graduate School of Business
Masters Programs Office
331 Blocker Building
College Station, TX 77843-4113
(409) 845-4714

Texas Christian University: M.J. Neeley School of Business

ADMISSIONS FACTS

Type of school	Private

Demographics

No. of men	92
No. of women	39
No. of minorities	12
No. of int'l students	24

EQUAL TREATMENT GRAPH

Admissions Statistics

Avg. GMAT	560
Avg. undergraduate GPA	3.0
Avg. age at entry	27
No. of applicants	290
No. accepted	201
No. enrolled	107

Deadlines and Notifications

Regular application	4/30
Regular notification	within 5 weeks
Special dates	5/30 (int'l students)

Focus of Curriculum

General Management

Academic Specialties

Finance, Marketing, Management

Teaching Methodology

Case Study, Lecture

FINANCIAL FACTS

In-state tuition	$2,988
Out-of-state tuition	$2,988
On-campus housing	N/A

ACADEMICS

As one student put it, Texas Christian University (TCU) is a "good business school that probably doesn't promote itself enough to get rated in most publications." Perhaps, but we heard students' kudos about the program loud and clear. What did they say about TCU? Plenty. Many students agreed with the ones who wrote "Best school for the money" and "the curriculum is challenging." Praised another, "It's like a big family here. Professors won't hold your hand and baby you through the material, but they're certainly concerned that you grasp the concept before moving on." In particular, students were most enthusiastic about the high level of personal attention they receive. Reported one, "Administration and staff are totally devoted to students." Summed up another, "TCU avoids the assembly line approach to MBA programs."

TCU offers students a basic, two-year generalist MBA. During the second year of the program, students can concentrate their studies in one of six areas: decision sciences, finance, management, management information systems, or marketing. Explained one MBA, "I came here to get basic business skills—computer, managerial and specifically, marketing strategy know-how from Dr. David Cravens, one of the gurus of the U.S." Across the board, students report they feel well-prepared by their training in areas such as marketing, finance, accounting, general management and teamwork. Perhaps because TCU is one of a select few schools that boasts a Center for Productive Communication, students gave themselves sky-high marks for their presentation and interpersonal skills. Confirmed one student, "There is a great emphasis placed on communication and presentation skills. The Center for Productive Communications is a major asset." Another major asset, literally, is the Educational Investment Fund with cash and securities totalling $1.2 million—one of the largest student-run portfolios in the nation. Here students are offered incomparable hands-on experiences in investment management. For more hands-on experience, students can participate in the Student Enterprises Program whereby teams of students act as paid consultants to various profit and not-for-profit organizations. The only complaint in this otherwise MBA utopia was "TCU places too much emphasis on standardized test scores. They're hardly willing to give someone a chance that doesn't meet their criteria."

PLACEMENT AND RECRUITING

According to students, TCU is the best school to go to for "GREAT connections to businesses in the Dallas/Fort Worth area." Claimed one student, "Of all the schools in the area, TCU has by far, the strongest ties to the business community." Of course, this makes getting a job all that much easier. Confirmed one student, "Excellent placement rate and many local job contacts."

TEXAS CHRISTIAN UNIVERSITY: M.J. NEELEY SCHOOL OF BUSINESS

STUDENT LIFE/CAMPUS

TCU is a small school. Total enrollment is kept to 300 students—half the size of the national average. Classes are small too—core classes average thirty-five students, electives twenty. The workload can be substantial, though it is hardly ever overwhelming. Wrote one student, "If you want unbelievable academic pressure, you won't find it here." Indeed, the majority of students study only fifteen to twenty-five hours a week.

Enthused one MBA, "The best part of TCU is the friendliness and accessibility of the people (students, faculty, administration, and community." Raved another, "It's easy to get to know people and get help with problems." As one might expect, students here are competitive, but not into backstabbing. The school's emphasis on team work creates a supportive and friendly atmosphere.

Most students would agree with the one who wrote, "I enjoy the company of my fellow classmates." As for the make-up of the student body, TCU MBAs said fellow classmates are smart and professionally diverse, but unfortunately, not racially diverse.

Much of the social whirl is handled through the MBA Association which organizes parties and a designated eatery/bar of the week for Thursday night no-class-Friday get-togethers. As for TCU's hometown of Fort Worth, students think it's terrific. Most MBAs live off-campus in apartment complexes in the Hulen area of Fort Worth, a ten minute commute by car from campus. Only one apartment complex is within walking distance of school.

ADMISSIONS

According to the school, your GMAT scores are considered most important. After that, in descending order, your college GPA, work experience, essays, extracurricular activities, letters or recommendation, and interview. Work experience and interview are not required for admission. All applicants are required to have completed a three hour undergraduate course in Financial Accounting. Students must demonstrate sound quantitative skills. Writes the school, "Because of TCU's small size, applicants receive a high level of personal attention in the application process. The Director of Admissions personally reviews every file and is available to prospective students throughout the application process. While a student's GMAT and undergraduate GPA are important, TCU is committed to producing leaders in business. To that end, the Admissions office examines the entirety of a student's application and does not base decisions on GMAT and grades alone." Decisions are made on a rolling admissions basis. Students are notified of a decisions within three to five weeks of receipt of the completed application. The final deadline is April 30th, although applications may be accepted thereafter if space is available. Accepted applicants are not permitted to defer admission.

STUDENT'S OVERVIEW BOX

Overall Happiness

Academic Satisfaction

50   75   100%

Student Opinion   National Average

FACULTY RATING

Student Opinion   National Average

HITS AND MISSES

HITS
Finance dept.
Classmates are smart
Safety

MISSES
Ethnic diversity
Gym
Library

APPLICANTS ALSO LOOK AT

Arizona State U.
U Texas-Austin
U Texas-Arlington
Baylor U.
Southern Meth. U.
Texas A&M

FOR MORE INFORMATION, CONTACT:

M.J. Neeley School of Management
P.O. Box 32868
Fort Worth, TX 76129
(817) 921-7490

TULANE UNIVERSITY: A.B. FREEMAN SCHOOL OF BUSINESS

ADMISSIONS FACTS

Type of school	Private

Demographics

No. of men	193
No. of women	63
No. of minorities	24
No. of int'l students	73

EQUAL TREATMENT GRAPH

Women

Minorities

0   2   4 (GPA)

■ Student Opinion   □ National Average

Admissions Statistics

Avg. GMAT	603
Avg. undergraduate GPA	3.1
Avg. age at entry	26
No. of applicants	535
No. accepted	286
No. enrolled	99

Deadlines and Notifications

Regular application	5/01
Regular notification	within 4 weeks
Special dates	4/01 (int'l students)

Focus of Curriculum

General Management, students have option of specializing.

Academic Specialties

International Business, Marketing, Finance

Joint Degrees

MBA/JD, MBA/Master of Public Health, MBA/MA in Latin American Studies, Part-time MBA program available

Special Programs

Study Abroad, International Internships

FINANCIAL FACTS

In-state tuition	$17,225
Out-of-state tuition	$17,225
On-campus housing	$5,575

ACADEMICS

Touted as an "up-and comer," Tulane has retooled its curriculum to focus more on global business, the managerial role, and the social and political environment in business. The result is a unique course of study. First-years now take two "focus modules" which encourage collegial bonding among students. The first module is called the "Job of the Executive" and is delivered during the first week of school. Students learn why they need to study all the disciplines, and how that multi-functional knowledge is used in the workplace. The module also exposes students to the social and ethical contexts in which businesses operate. The second module is called "Career Development" and focuses on networking, résumé writing, and career strategies to get students into the job search process early in their MBA schooling. Along with the modules, first-years take the more traditional core courses which are theoretical and lecture-oriented. Second-years go on to modules three and four, which focus on Total Quality Management and Leadership. The case method is heavily used. Two of the nine required electives for second-years may be taken outside the Freeman school in other university programs. Popular B-school electives include Cases in Finance and Negotiations, International Business, and Strategic Marketing which features a business simulation game. Students told us the finance and entrepreneurship departments are particularly strong. Several students described the first year as a "killer" and "high pressure."

To judge by the responses to our survey, Tulane manages to create a strong international environment not just with course work and foreign study, but with the very makeup of its student body. Again and again students told us this makes for a complete learning experience. Wrote one, "The high percentage (thirty-four percent) of international students in the first-year class offers a fantastic perspective in the global business environment." Agreed another, "International students facilitate continuous cultural interaction." To assist international students in their transition to American studies, the school offers a special International Student Orientation Program. But there were complaints. Some problem areas are class scheduling, too few uses of case study, and career placement. Overall, students describe the academic program at Tulane as providing a "very high quality education with a value-added approach to teaching." Raved another "Tulane is an excellent B-school—small, friendly, and in New Orleans!"

PLACEMENT AND RECRUITING

Approximately eighty organizations interviewed on campus in 1991-1992. Despite all this, students say they are disappointed with the services. Wrote one, "The placement office is of little assistance in finding a job." Help is on the way, however; a new placement director was appointed in June 1993. Despite complaints, Tulane enjoys solid placement rates. In 1992, eighty percent of the class had a job by graduation. Leading recruiters were Andersen Consulting, Ford Motor Company, KPMG Peat Marwick, Ernst & Young, Hibernia National Bank, Wachovia Corporation, and Freeport-McMoran.

TULANE UNIVERSITY: A.B. FREEMAN SCHOOL OF BUSINESS

STUDENT LIFE/CAMPUS

According to the school, Tulane's location in New Orleans plays a critical role in the success of the program. Students strongly agree. Wrote one, "New Orleans is a town that's in a class of its own." Said another, "New Orleans is an extremely broadening experience." Ready yourself for a diet of crawfish, Po' boys, and a night life that undergrads regularly travel thousands of miles to partake in.

Like most B-schools, Tulane is housed in just one building. But in this case, it's spectacular. Goldring/Woldenberg Hall is a newly built (1986) seven-story complex featuring an auditorium, group study rooms, classrooms, and a three-story atrium. Hang-out time is enhanced by a second-floor outdoor patio which surrounds the entire building. The building also houses a state-of-the art technology/computer center, a library, an audio/visual studio complete with television studio and editing and viewing room, a computer classroom with forty-four networked laptops, and a computer integrated manufacturing laboratory used for simulating manufacturing processes. Wrote one student, "The physical facilities—building, classrooms, services—are advanced."

One student's remarks typified the prevalent attitude here: "The best students here are on par with the smartest you'll find anywhere, and a great deal cheaper to hire than those from some of the top schools." In 1992, eighty percent of the class had a job by graduation. Students also said, "The group spirit is outstanding," and students are friendly and cooperative. Reported another, "We help each other with homework, projects, and studying for tests." The overwhelming majority of students rated classmates as highly competitive. Yet one student countered, "Even though Tulane has a very competitive environment, students help each other." One student added, "The school makes an effort to take care of you; they know your name."

ADMISSIONS

The admissions considers GMAT scores and college GPA most important, and then in *descending* order of importance, work experience and interview (required for all domestic applicants), essays, letters of recommendation, and extracurricular activities. Tulane uses a rolling admissions process; students are notified of a decision three to four weeks after the application file is complete. The final deadline for domestic applicants is May 1, 1993; for international students, April 1, 1993. All applicants are automatically considered for merit-based fellowships at the time of admission. College seniors are admitted with a mandatory deferral of two years.

Tulane features an unusual five-year MBA sub-matriculation program. Wrote one student, "The five-year program is excellent and extremely competitive. Students in this program were among Tulane's best undergraduates."

STUDENT'S OVERVIEW BOX

FACULTY RATING

HITS AND MISSES

HITS
Quant
Ethnic & racial diversity
Internationalization
Innovative curriculum
Gym
New Orleans

MISSES
Placement

APPLICANTS ALSO LOOK AT
Duke U.
U Texas-Austin
UNC Chapel Hill
U South Carolina
Emory
Vanderbilt U.
Rice U.

FOR MORE INFORMATION, CONTACT:
A.B. Freeman School of Business
Goldring/Woldenberg Hall, Suite 200
New Orleans, LA 70118-5669
(800) 865-5410
(504) 865-5402

VANDERBILT UNIVERSITY: OWEN GRADUATE SCHOOL OF MANAGEMENT

ADMISSIONS FACTS

Type of school	Private

Demographics

No. of men	297
No. of women	94
No. of minorities	42
No. of int'l students	59

EQUAL TREATMENT GRAPH

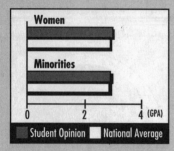

Women

Minorities

0 2 4 (GPA)

■ Student Opinion □ National Average

ADMISSIONS STATISTICS

Avg. GMAT	607
Avg. undergraduate GPA	3.14
Avg. age at entry	25
No. of applicants	912
No. accepted	446
No. enrolled	191

Deadlines and Notifications

Regular application	3/15
Regular notification	within 6 weeks
Special dates	N/A

Focus of Curriculum

General Management

Academic Specialties

General Management, Human Resources, Services Marketing

FINANCIAL FACTS

In-state tuition	$17,500
Out-of-state tuition	$17,500
On-campus housing	$5,400

ACADEMICS

Although for years this school has been known as a southern powerhouse, the Owen Graduate School of Management has recently burst onto the national B-school scene. Indeed, several students said they chose Owen because of its "up-and-coming attitude." From the get-go, Owen delivers a solid education. A first year, non-credit course called Mathematics for Managers bolsters rusty skills with a rapid review of algebra, calculus, and linear equations. Professors teach the major disciplines from a cross-functional point of view. A year-long course, Managerial Problem Solving and Communication, serves up the kind of fare that allows managers to translate ideas into actionable programs. But the topping on the cake is the chance to take electives from two of the school's research centers—the Operations Roundtable and the Center for Service Marketing—which students say provide cutting-edge insights. During the second year, students can opt to add an "international emphasis" by taking three international electives. One of the international electives, International Management and Issues, features a visit to a foreign country with the Dean and several faculty. Each year students in this course decide where they want to go, and whom they want to meet with. The most recent class traveled to Korea and Taiwan. Owen MBAs may also earn degree credit for advanced language study. Much praise was also heaped on the school's human resources management program, which students say is "tops."

Distinct to Owen is an elective track of Services Marketing Courses, which address issues of customer satisfaction and service quality management. Students in these tracks work as apprentices with companies such as AT&T, American Airlines, and The National Symphony on their services marketing and customer relationships.

Owen MBAs are happy with the high level of interaction between faculty and students, a factor bolstered by small classes (an average of twenty-five to thirty-five students in each). Owen MBAs feel very well-prepared by their studies in marketing, finance, human resources, quantitative methods, computers, and presentation skills. The administration garners positive reviews, and, overall, students say this program is meeting, and exceeding, their expectations.

PLACEMENT AND RECRUITING

In 1992, over 160 companies interviewed Owen students. Ninety-five percent of the class had a permanent job offer within three months of graduation. The major recruiters were: AT&T, American Airlines, Andersen Consulting, MCI, G.E., Pepsico, Northern Telecom, Deloitte & Touche, Ford, UPS, Sara Lee, Proctor and Gamble, and M&M Mars. According to students, the school was affected by the recession in terms of there being a limited range of companies recruiting on-campus. One student added, "Average starting salaries starting to rise, but could be better. Remember though, a large number of students stay in the South with low cost of living." Reported another, "Owen has just hired a full-time staff member to tackle international placement and recruiting."

VANDERBILT UNIVERSITY: OWEN GRADUATE SCHOOL OF MANAGEMENT

STUDENT LIFE/CAMPUS

Like many small schools, Owen provides its students with an intimate learning environment. With only 180 students in each class, students tend to know each other. Wrote one student, "One key aspect of Owen is its personal culture. Everyone is a person here, not a number." Adds another, "Tight group of students. Everyone helps each other." Students are competitive, but not cutthroat. While the workload is not up-all-night impossible, it can be tough. Students hit the books roughly thirty hours a week. The overwhelming majority utilize study groups to get the benefit of many heads applied to a single problem. Students are intelligent and professionally diverse. Observed one MBA, "Everyone brings something to the table."

Owen offers one-stop schooling. Everything is located in one building, which students describe as "outstanding." Equally awesome is the athletic center, which, in addition to every piece of exercise equipment you can imagine, also features an indoor climbing wall. As for Owen's hometown, students say Nashville is great. Ninety percent of the students live off-campus and find the cost of living reasonable. On-campus, the student-run clubs sponsor many activities: a lecture series, community service work, student-consulting projects, baseball games, a golf tournament, and the Fall Ball.

ADMISSIONS

The admissions office considers your work experience most important, then in descending order, your college GPA, interview, GMAT scores, essays, letters of recommendation, and extracurricular activities. Although the school adds, this order "differs according to the background of various candidates."

The interview is an "integral part of the admissions process," advises the school. "It allows a candidate to present key aspects of their background, character, and aspirations that are not easily conveyed in writing. The primary objectives in the interview are to assess career aspirations and explore motivation and clarity of purpose." Although not required, it is recommended that students take a calculus course to demonstrate strong quantitative skills. The school goes by rolling admissions. But there is no final deadline. Writes the school, "Serious candidates will apply by May 1st."

Applicants with two or more years' work experience getting their application in by the first Friday in December will have a decision by the end of January. Applicants who would benefit from additional work experience may defer admission for up to two years. Keep in mind that applications are up by twenty percent at this school.

STUDENT'S OVERVIEW BOX

FACULTY RATING

HITS AND MISSES

HITS
Quantitative skills
Helping other students
Gym

MISSES
Accounting dept.
Ethnic & racial diversity
Off-campus housing

APPLICANTS ALSO LOOK AT
U Tennessee-Knox
U Texas-Austin
U Alabama-Tuscaloosa
Northwestern U.
Emory U.
Boston College
Notre Dame U.
U Virginia

FOR MORE INFORMATION, CONTACT:
Owen Graduate School of Management
401 21st Avenue
Nashville, TN 37203
(615) 322-6469

UNIV. OF VIRGINIA: COLGATE DARDEN GRADUATE SCHOOL OF BUSINESS ADMINSTRATION

ADMISSIONS FACTS

Type of school	Public

Demographics

No. of men	311
No. of women	156
No. of minorities	69
No. of int'l students	70

EQUAL TREATMENT GRAPH

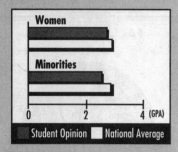

Women

Minorities

0   2   4 (GPA)

■ Student Opinion □ National Average

ADMISSIONS STATISTICS

Avg. GMAT	610
Avg. undergraduate GPA	3.0
Avg. age at entry	27
No. of applicants	1,890
No. accepted	488
No. enrolled	232

Deadlines and Notifications

Regular application	3/15
Regular notification	within 8 weeks
Special dates	12/01 (early action)

Focus of Curriculum

General Management

Academic Specialties

General Management

FINANCIAL FACTS

In-state tuition	$6,855
Out-of-state tuition	$14,227
On-campus housing	N/A

ACADEMICS

Darden is part of a state-affiliated university with a well-deserved reputation as one of the best B-schools in the nation. The program provides a general management education for individuals who expect to be "excellent general managers later and strong functional managers early in their career." The foundation for this is the case study method. According to the school, "In analyzing each case, students develop a variety of practical skills: how to define important issues, when and how to apply analytical techniques, and how to make decisions after evaluating alternatives." Translation: the case method at Darden teaches students to think on their feet, to quickly develop practical solutions to real problems and to consider functional issues in a "big picture" context. Advised one Dardenite, "Case study is THE best approach to training/education." As for the quality of education, students describe Darden's program as "a top-notch learning experience." Wrote one, "We are extremely well prepared to become general managers in many different types of companies." The curriculum features a heavy emphasis on quantitative applications.

First-year MBAs take nine required courses which introduce students to the functional areas. But this feels more like one nine-month multifunctional course. Alas, no electives allowed. One student wrote, "Very regimented first year." Second-years take three core electives and thirteen "free" electives. A major component of the second year is the Directed Study which involves working with a faculty member on a managerial issue involving field research. Students craft their own course of study and projects; many involve outside consulting with companies such as Pepsico.

Students noted several reasons for choosing Darden: low cost combined with prestige, cozy student community, and the case study method. A surprising number of students said they selected Darden because of its tough-as-nails reputation. Many mentioned the school's long-standing emphasis on values and ethics as a drawing card. Reported one, "Business ethics are a fixture at Darden—a truly humanizing aspect that is integrated throughout the curriculum." As for the faculty, Darden's top the charts. Gushed one student, "The enthusiasm, intelligence, and devotion of the faculty sets Dardens academic experience far above that of any other top-tier program."

PLACEMENT AND RECRUITING

Students at Darden are very happy with the placement center. Raved one student, "Half of each year's graduates obtain jobs through Career Placement; the remainder through alumni and faculty referrals and personal contacts." More than 150 companies recruit on-campus. The major recruiters: Booz Allen, Carrier Corp, Citibank, Coca-Cola, Eli Lilly, IBM, MBA Enterprise Corps, McKinsey, Merrill Lynch, Signet Bank. By graduation in 1992, seventy-five to eighty percent of students were placed. Three months after graduation, eighty-five to ninety percent had jobs. Raved one successful student, "I have an offer from my number one job choice—all thanks to Darden."

UNIV. OF VIRGINIA: COLGATE DARDEN GRADUATE SCHOOL OF BUSINESS ADMINSTRATION

STUDENT LIFE/CAMPUS

Students told us Darden offers "a happy environment." Located in the college town of Charlottesville, the UVA campus is beautiful. But the B-school buildings are not. The good news is a state-of-the-art facility is scheduled to be completed in 1995. Nearly fifty percent of the first-year class lives in a nearby apartment complex, christened Darden Gardens. Several other apartment complexes are within walking distance, which alleviates some of Darden's parking problems. Two-bedrooms go for $400-$500 per month. Many students rent shared farmhouses in the Blue Ridge Mountains (a ten-minute commute) for roughly $1,000 per month.

Students here claim there is "excellent diversity ethnically." Backing up that assertion is a "high percentage of women, which makes Darden unusual among B-schools." But as for racial/gender harmony, Darden has a ways to go. Accusations about minority student discrimination, and a "hostile climate" for female and junior faculty surfaced at Darden in the spring of 1992. The brouhaha came to such a head, the school has since undertaken many initiatives—from student forums on minority and gender issues to a faculty task force—to tackle the problems.

Students perform eighty to one hundred hours of schoolwork every week. A typical complaint was that a three-night caseload leaves little time for student clubs and activities. Wrote one, "Married with children, time management can be a problem." Still, one reported, "Darden is not as difficult as people say. You have to be disciplined and keep up with the work so as not to be killed by cold calls. Second year is a lot less stressful." But Darden gets bonus points for providing an environment as supportive as it is demanding. Students are pre-assigned study groups intentionally structured to create a mix of skills and expertise.

Students are competitive, but not cutthroat. Darden's small size fosters a close-knit, homey atmosphere. Wrote one MBA "Classmates are bright and supportive. They're not out to get each other." Observed another, "Everyone shares in each other's triumphs and troubles."

ADMISSIONS

According to the admissions office, each of the following components count one-third in the admissions decision: "Academics (GPA, GMAT); work/professional experience; and personal attributes (essays, interview, extracurriculars.)" The interview is strongly encouraged but not required. The committee explains, "Darden is committed to evaluating many facets of an individual's background. The committee looks for evidence of competitive academic performance, intellectual ability, significant work and life experiences, as well as other qualities of character that cannot be quantitatively measured. Factors such as breadth of perspective, international exposure and diversity are also taken into consideration."

Applications are processed in one of three rounds. Early Action applicants are notified of a decision by January 15th. Students are rarely granted a deferral; possible reasons for one are military obligation or visa restrictions.

STUDENT'S OVERVIEW BOX

FACULTY RATING

HITS AND MISSES

HITS
Finance
Student smarts
Students professionally diverse
Cozy student community
Tuition
Campus

MISSES
Workload
On-campus housing

APPLICANTS ALSO LOOK AT
Stanford U.
Harvard
Columbia U.
William & Mary (A)
Cornell U.
Dartmouth
UNC-Chapel Hill
Duke
U Penn

FOR MORE INFORMATION, CONTACT:
Colgate Darden Graduate School
of Business Administration
P.O. Box 6550, North Grounds, UVA,
Massie Road Extended
Charlottesville, VA 22906
(800) UVA-MBA-1 (804) 924-7281

WAKE FOREST UNIVERSITY: BABCOCK GRADUATE SCHOOL OF MANAGEMENT

ADMISSIONS FACTS

Type of school	Private

Demographics

No. of men	175
No. of women	43
No. of minorities	6
No. of int'l students	31

EQUAL TREATMENT GRAPH

Admissions Statistics

Avg. GMAT	603
Avg. undergraduate GPA	3.0
Avg. age at entry	25
No. of applicants	432
No. accepted	237
No. enrolled	112

Deadlines and Notifications

Regular application	rolling
Regular notification	within 4 weeks
Special dates	4/01 (int'l students)

Focus of Curriculum

General Management

Academic Specialties

General Management, International Business

Joint Degrees

MBA/JD; MBA/MD

Special Programs

Babcock Leadership Discussions Series; Partners in Education; Babcock World Business Games.

FINANCIAL FACTS

In-state tuition	$13,500
Out-of-state tuition	$13,500
On-campus housing	$4,000

ACADEMICS

Wake Forest (WF) stresses a general management perspective in a program that is as grounded in the traditional basics as it is in the experiential aspects of business education. Extensive use is made of case study analysis and presentation. But the program is also peppered with role plays, field projects, teamwork exercises, and business simulation games. In particular, oral and written skills are emphasized; students typically make two or more presentations. The first-year curriculum immerses students in the major disciplines and is extremely structured. Courses are organized in such a way as to present the field of management as a unit rather than as a series of stand-alone subjects. Writes the school, "For example, an organizational behavior exam may be based on cases taught in accounting, marketing, and analytical methods." But academic analysis only goes so far; a course on interpersonal behavior brings in the soft skills. Of primary importance is the study of international business. Many students participate in the East Asia Management Program, which includes a trip to Pacific Rim countries, or join the large number of MBAs who opt for a summer job abroad. During the second year, students specialize, or develop an "elective, yet coherent" course of study. Either way, the overriding framework here is of a general-ist, macro perspective. One valuable stepping stone at WF is the Mentor Program, which matches students with executives who have similar career interests. WF MBAs rave about this program, which allows them to make important contacts in the business community.

Professors are widely praised for their exceptional teaching skills and extraordinary accessibility. Compared to other schools in this survey, students at WF are among those reporting the highest rate of academic expectations being met or exceeded. Across the board, students say they feel well-prepared by their courses. This includes the functional areas of business as well as soft and quantitative skills. The single area where self-rated competency was not unanimous was operations; one fourth of the students felt their skills needed bolstering. The administration garners mixed reviews. While students report it's easy to get into popular electives, a not insignificant number feel the school isn't run as smoothly as it could be.

PLACEMENT AND RECRUITING

Like most B-schools, WF's Career Planning and Placement Office serves up a full plate of career services—from mock interviews to job strategy workshops. The office distributes a résumé book of second-year students to hundreds of corporations. They also participate in the MBA Consortiums in Atlanta and New York to present students to organizations not recruiting on campus.

Still, while students say the career office is not horrible, they certainly don't think it's operating at peak efficiency. In particular, students are dis-appointed with the range of companies recruiting. The smart move at WF is to utilize alumni and mentor relationships. The overwhelming majority of students said they did just that and found individuals they contacted helpful.

WAKE FOREST UNIVERSITY: BABCOCK GRADUATE SCHOOL OF MANAGEMENT

STUDENT LIFE/CAMPUS

Depending on the next day's case load, students spend anywhere from four to six hours a night preparing their insights for in-class discussion. During the first year, class participation typically counts for forty to fifty percent of the grade. To emphasize teamwork and provide WF MBAs with an academic support system for the case method, WF pre-assigns students to study groups. This reduces much of the anxiety. The overriding culture is supportive. As one might expect, WF MBAs like each other. Indeed, classmates intend to stay friends long after that last case is cracked. Students say the intelligent student body is also professionally diverse and enriches their learning experience.

According to our survey, the library and gym are great. Indeed, all the facilities are. The B-school just moved into the Professional Center for Law and Management—a spanking new building shared with the law school—although the verdict's not in on how these two will fare as roommates. Expect powerful alliances. Students say the local area and campus is beautiful. The majority opt for off-campus living in nearby apartments. International students are provided housing on-premises in the Wake Forest MBA International House. The social scene teems with activity. Surprisingly, students here, unlike at other B-schools, date a lot. Those law school collaborations may already have begun. Group activities include picnics, intramural sports, and anything involving the great outdoors.

ADMISSIONS

Work experience tops the list of admissions criteria at Babcock, followed by quality of undergraduate curriculum and GPA, GMAT scores, reputation of undergraduate school, personal statement, interview and recommendations. Think about two years of full-time labor before applying to the program.

STUDENT'S OVERVIEW BOX

FACULTY RATING

HITS AND MISSES

HITS
Finance dept.
Helping other students
On-campus housing
Social life

MISSES
Accounting dept.
Ethnic & racial diversity
Placement

APPLICANTS ALSO LOOK AT

U Virginia
Notre Dame U.
VA Polytech Inst
UNC Chapel Hill
Ohio State U.
Emory U.
U South Carolina
Vanderbilt U.

FOR MORE INFORMATION, CONTACT:

Babcock Graduate School of
Management
Box 7659 Reynolds Station
Winston-Salem, NC 27109
(919) 759-5422
(800) 722-1622

UNIV. OF WASHINGTON GRADUATE SCHOOL OF BUSINESS ADMINISTRATION

ADMISSIONS FACTS

Type of school	Public

Demographics

No. of men	315
No. of women	162
No. of minorities	71
No. of int'l students	57

EQUAL TREATMENT GRAPH

Admissions Statistics

Avg. GMAT	622
Avg. undergraduate GPA	3.24
Avg. age at entry	28
No. of applicants	1,064
No. accepted	338
No. enrolled	200

Deadlines and Notifications

Regular application	3/01
Regular notification	rolling
Special dates	N/A

Focus of Curriculum

General Management

Academic Specialties

Marketing, Finance, Entrepreneurship, International Business, Environmental Management

Joint Degrees

MPAccounting, JD/MBA, MBA/MAIS, MBA/MHA Health Administration.

Special Programs

Overseas Study, Engineering and Manufacturing Management, Environmental Management Program, International Management Fellows Program.

FINANCIAL FACTS

In-state tuition	$3,537
Out-of-state tuition	$8,850
On-campus housing	$4,650

ACADEMICS

The University of Washington (UW) is ideal for students who have no prior academic coursework in business. The first year consists of introductory level courses in the major disciplines. A new curriculum emphasizes the interrelationships of these disciplines in a single, year-long course which also stresses ethics and international business. Students also take modules on leadership, diversity, and communications. These modules are taught by both B-school faculty and Seattle area business executives. During the second year, students work on satisfying the international business requirement. Wrote students, "UW is very Asian Rim and Computer-Industry oriented," the latter is due to the influence of high-tech Seattle companies such as Microsoft, and Physio Control. Expect a lot of math; the curriculum is numbers-oriented. There's also a heavy-duty research requirement.

Enthused one student about this school, "Best plus—every class incorporates total quality management (TQM) issues. Everyone had to do a twenty-minute video on TQM." Many students raved about another plus, the Business Diagnostic Center, which matches student volunteers with local companies in need of management expertise. Distinct to UW is the new environmental management (EM) program, the first of its kind in any MBA program in the nation. Here students earn an EM certificate by taking a series of team-taught environmental courses. As part of the program, students are placed in internships with companies such as Amoco and Pepsico. There's also a new program in entrepreneurship and innovation which provides students an opportunity to interact with some of Seattle's home-grown entrepreneurs. One student asserted, "This is a great experience; eighty percent of the first-year students were involved this year." MBAs have completed projects for Starbucks Coffee, Boise Cascade, and the Seattle Theater Group. As for the faculty, students report a high degree of variability in their teaching skills. Wrote one MBA, "Many profs are great." Others said, "Many are out of touch with the times," and "The quality of the faculty lags behind that of the students." Partly offsetting this, professors are said to be widely accessible and committed.

According to our survey, students feel especially well-prepared by their courses in finance, accounting, and teamwork. They also report a high level of confidence in their general management, quantitative, and computer skills. MBAs feel less certain about their operations and presentation skills. But overall, students say this program is worth the investment of time and money. Exclaimed one, "A fantastic value in MBA education!"

PLACEMENT AND RECRUITING

In 1992, roughly fifty companies recruited on-campus. To interview with a greater number of companies, students participated in several job fairs. By graduation, sixty percent of the class had been placed in a full-time position. According to our survey, students are disappointed with the career center as well as with the range of companies recruiting. But according to one student, "The career center appears to be building a strong base for future years."

UNIV. OF WASHINGTON GRADUATE SCHOOL OF BUSINESS ADMINISTRATION

STUDENT LIFE/CAMPUS

Students report a moderate to heavy workload and study an average of twenty to thirty hours a week. The vast majority of MBAs say they don't take shortcuts; it's important to do all or most of the reading. But students don't feel like they're in a pressure cooker. Study groups, which were recently introduced in the program, allow students to leverage off member's expertise and collaborate on schoolwork. The entering class of 180 is divided into cohorts of forty-five students each who take all the first-year courses together with the same faculty. According to students, this provides an intimate learning environment and encourages cooperation. Indeed, the best part of life here is the sense of community and camaraderie among students. UW MBAs are good friends. They intend to stay friends long after graduation. As one might expect, students here are noncompetitive. A new grading system of High Pass, Pass, Low Pass, and Fail helps this along. In the upcoming year, students will receive individual performance evaluations from the faculty. Of the extremely bright student body, students report they are also professionally very diverse.

One student's comments capture the prevalent feeling here: "New facilities are badly needed, especially a larger student lounge, although the computer lab is pretty good." A new business building is currently in the works. Complains another, "The library specializes in pre-war literature."

As for Seattle, students note, "UW is located in a great city," and they enjoy "the scenery and lifestyle of Western Washington." Indeed UW is paradise for outdoorsy-types. Just an hour away are the Cascade Mountains. The university itself sits on Lake Washington and is surrounded by Puget Sound. As one might expect, biking, hiking, and skiing, are favorite activities. So it's no surprise that the school attracts recreation-oriented folk. It's not unusual for there to be an Olympic medalist in the entering class. A current student is the female world champion in water-skiing. An outgoing student is a nationally recognized alpine climber who regularly practiced on the indoor climbing wall located in UW's awesome gym. For the less athletically inclined, there are plenty of student club activities. Two favorites: international theme parties, and comfort food night (this year's entree: Rice Krispie Treats).

ADMISSIONS

The admissions office considers the following criteria (in no particular order): essays, college GPA, extracurricular activities, work experience, the interview and GMAT scores. Letters of recommendation are not considered. Decisions are made on a rolling basis. "We strongly encourage early application," writes the office of admissions.

STUDENT'S OVERVIEW BOX

Student Opinion   National Average

FACULTY RATING

Student Opinion   National Average

HITS AND MISSES

HITS
Accounting
Total quality management
Diverse work experience
Seattle

MISSES
Facilities
Library
Presentation skills

APPLICANTS ALSO LOOK AT
UNC Chapel Hill
Stanford U.
U Colorado at Boulder
Duke U.
U Texas-Austin
U Tennessee-Knox
U Michigan

FOR MORE INFORMATION, CONTACT:
Graduate School of Business
Administration
110 MacKenzie Hall DJ-10
Seattle, WA 98195
(206) 543-4660

WASHINGTON UNIVERSITY: JOHN M. OLIN SCHOOL OF BUSINESS

ADMISSIONS FACTS

Type of school	Private

Demographics

No. of men	215
No. of women	83
No. of minorities	35
No. of int'l students	60

EQUAL TREATMENT GRAPH

Admissions Statistics

Avg. GMAT	602
Avg. undergraduate GPA	3.17
Avg. age at entry	26
No. of applicants	810
No. accepted	369
No. enrolled	146

Deadlines and Notifications

Regular application	4/30
Regular notification	within 5 weeks
Special dates	N/A

Focus of Curriculum
General Management

Academic Specialties
General Management

Joint Degrees
MBA/JD; MBA/MS in Social Work; MBA/MA in Architecture.

Special Programs
The MBA Enterprise Corps; Foreign Study.

FINANCIAL FACTS

In-state tuition	$16,750
Out-of-state tuition	$16,750
On-campus housing	$8,000

ACADEMICS

While Olin has recently added innovative components to its program, the school's traditional, generalist formula remains intact. First-year students get a thorough grounding in the functional areas. Courses are sequenced to incorporate learning from prior courses. Still, non-quant types find it rough going here; there is a heavy emphasis on applied mathematics and microeconomics. Second-years craft their own study with electives in the Olin school and other University departments. So far, standard fare. But the program that everyone talks about is Olin's Management Center. Here companies pay for teams of MBAs to come on-site and consult on matters ranging from marketing to strategy. Both Apple Computer and Monsanto have asked Olin students to advise them on select issues. Social responsibility is also promoted—student teams perform pro bono consulting to organizations in the nonprofit sector such as the St. Louis Food Bank. The school is so committed to this program they suspend classes for a week so students can focus exclusively on their consulting. Another experiential learning program that has received a lot of press is TYCOON, a twelve-day computerized business simulation game which is taught in conjunction with a strategy course. A new exciting program is the dual degree MBA/MA in East Asian studies in which students study Japanese or Mandarin Chinese and complete a semester or internship in their target country (China, Taiwan or Japan.)

Olin may be considered a go-getter school, but according to the students in our survey, it hasn't earned its stripes yet. Although the majority of Olin MBAs said this program is meeting their academic expectations, a third said they're less than satisfied. Still, one MBA asserted, "I think the educational and developmental experience at Olin is *very* underrated." The administration gets equally mixed reviews. Griped one student, "If Olin operated more like the successful businesses we study, we would all benefit more from the experience. There is an adversarial relationship between students and the administration." Professors get decent grades for their teaching, but better grades for their accessibility. Again, this depends on who you ask. Raved one student, "Intelligent faculty stimulate creative thinking and express a genuine concern for students." But another student griped, "The use of non PhD professors without business backgrounds seriously undermines the quality of education here."

PLACEMENT AND RECRUITING

Early in the program Olin groups students by their potential professional path. They then work as a team to research a particular industry. According to the school, "We maintain yearly contacts with about 600 companies that want information about Olin MBAs, and nearly 120 of them send recruiters to conduct on-site interviews." Olin also has close ties with St. Louis area businesses. In 1992, eighty percent of the graduating class was placed within three months of commencement. The median starting salary was $45,000. Major recruiters were Andersen Consulting, Monsanto, MBA Enterprise Corp, Edison Brothers, NBD Bank, Towers Perrin, Ralston Purina, Procter & Gamble, American National Bank, and Wells Fargo Bank.

WASHINGTON UNIVERSITY: JOHN M. OLIN SCHOOL OF BUSINESS

STUDENT LIFE/CAMPUS

There's a steady and heavy dose of work, especially during the first year. Students prepare for class roughly twenty-five hours a week. Almost fifty percent say it's not necessary to do all of the reading. Everyone works in a study group, which is considered an integral part of the learning experience. The small size of the school (150 students in each full-time class) offers many advantages: small classes, personal attention, and a supportive environment. Students are primarily noncompetitive. Surprisingly, only slightly more than fifty percent of those we surveyed said classmates go out of their way to help each other.

From classrooms to computing facilities, Olin MBAs enjoy top-notch, well-appointed facilities. As for the campus itself, it's amazingly beautiful. Students also say housing is plentiful and attractive. Most live off-campus in nearby apartments. The heavy social scene at WU ranges from weekly Friday afternoon keg parties, to student-fundraisers such as the charity run for Florida Hurricane victims. For an unusual dining experience, students attend one of the many International Pot-Luck Dinners, sponsored by the International Business Council. Last year, a student from Cazakhstan served a horse dish and freaked everyone out. Other major clubs (not sponsoring horse dinners) are: Entreprenuers Club, Business Minority Council, International Business Council, Joint Ventures, Marketing Club, Operations and Manufacturing Club, Voluntary Action Committee, Women in Management, and Masters Consulting Group.

A final note: students agree WU is ethnically and racially diverse. As for equal treatment, WU practices what it teaches. The associate dean is one the few women in her position in the nation.

ADMISSIONS

According to the admissions office your work experience is considered most important. After that, the school considers in descending order, your college GPA, GMAT scores, essays, letters of recommendation, extracurricular activities, and interview. Writes the school, "the interview is not required, but strongly recommended and can be a determining factor in whether a student is admitted." The school also requires students to submit a very detailed work history. Admissions are handled on a rolling basis; students are notified of a decision three to five weeks after their application is received. The final deadline is April 30th, 1994. Students who are waitlisted are notified of a position by June 1st. Students may defer admission for up to one year for work or cost related situations. Students who defer must pay a deposit to hold a spot in the class.

STUDENT'S OVERVIEW BOX

Overall Happiness

Academic Satisfaction

50   75   100%

■ Student Opinion □ National Average

FACULTY RATING

■ Student Opinion □ National Average

HITS AND MISSES

HITS
Accounting
Operations
Students professionally diverse
Cozy student community
Library

MISSES
Marketing
Recruiting

APPLICANTS ALSO LOOK AT
UNC Chapel Hill
Indiana U.-Bloom.
U Michigan
Vanderbilt U.
Emory U.
U Texas-Austin

FOR MORE INFORMATION, CONTACT:
John M. Olin School of Business
Campus Box 1133
One Brookings Drive
St. Louis, MO 63130-4899
(314) 935-7301
(800) 622-3622

COLLEGE OF WILLIAM AND MARY GRADUATE SCHOOL OF BUSINESS

ADMISSIONS FACTS

Type of school	Public

Demographics

No. of men	127
No. of women	74
No. of minorities	24
No. of int'l students	11

EQUAL TREATMENT GRAPH

Women	
Minorities	

0   2   4 (GPA)

Student Opinion ■ National Average

Admissions Statistics

Avg. GMAT	580
Avg. undergraduate GPA	3.0
Avg. age at entry	27
No. of applicants	413
No. accepted	165
No. enrolled	101

Deadlines and Notifications

Regular application	5/01
Regular notification	within 4 weeks
Special dates	6/15 (P/T students)

Focus of Curriculum

General Management

Academic Specialties

General Management

FINANCIAL FACTS

In-state tuition	$3,750
Out-of-state tuition	$9,570
On-campus housing	$7,500

ACADEMICS

William and Mary (W&M) starts its program off with an Outward Bound-type three-day orientation. Approximately 100 entering students dangle and swim their way through a high-ropes course and raft-building exercise on the James River. Students are also divided into six-person study groups in which they will work for the first year. To get these would-be MBAs ready for school, a battalion of eighteen professors introduce them to the case study method.

During the first year, students take thirteen core courses. The first year also includes a topics program on issues such as business versus environmental concerns, cultural diversity, and the changing world of finance. The year ends with a week-long computerized simulation game through which student teams compete against one another in the international recreational shoe market. During the second year, W&M MBAs specialize or continue their generalist studies. Some diverse electives are: Manufacturing Planning and Control Systems, Negotiations, Doing Business in Japan, and International Marketing. But this may be close to all there is. Wrote one student, "Because we're small, we don't have a great selection of classes." But working directly with a professor in an independent study does afford practical and unusual opportunities for study. In the past, students have studied decision-making, human bias, and sports negotiation.

As one student put it, "Faculty make this place great." Another student's comments typified the prevalent feeling here: "Emphasis is on teaching! Nobody is an out-of-touch research hound." Over and over, professors were described as "friendly" and "extra-accessible." Of course, we heard about some exceptions. One student said, "Some are an embarrassment to higher education." Several students complained to us about the administration—"This place is run like a typical government agency." Still, the vast majority of students praise W&M for its solid general management education and extremely low cost.

PLACEMENT AND RECRUITING

The Office of MBA Placement offers students a wide range of counseling, workshops, and other career strategy programs. To promote students for summer jobs, they distribute an Internships Résumé Book to over 100 employers. In one impressive program, students are matched with volunteer "MBA Career Coaches" from the nearby business community. In addition, the alumni association sponsors many career and regional events. Wrote one student, "Great alumni contacts."

Students at W&M tend to agree with students at other B-schools—economic times are tough and the career placement often doesn't deliver. In particular, W&M's 1993 placement rate of eighty percent is about average for schools in our survey. W&M MBAs wish the school would increase the range of companies recruiting on campus.

COLLEGE OF WILLIAM AND MARY GRADUATE SCHOOL OF BUSINESS

STUDENT LIFE/CAMPUS

The most attractive aspect of life at W&M is the sense of community fostered by the school's small size. Students report "lots of individual attention," "small classes," and "a supportive environment." Close working relationships are fostered by the study group concept. As you might expect, students here are only moderately competitive. The emphasis is on helping one another. They like and enjoy each other. What they don't like is the heavy workload. Wrote one student, "It seems like all we're being taught is how to react to huge amount of work in a limited time frame; i.e., 'head games,' just to see if we can stay sane." But they can handle it. Of the professionally diverse student body, students told us they're "among the brightest around."

Students describe W&M's hometown of Williamsburg as "a great place to go to school—quiet and quaint." With easy access to Virginia Beach, Richmond, and D.C., students say they can get away when they need to. They also describe the campus as beautiful. Spanking new graduate housing right on the premises offers great accommodations for both single and married students. Note: don't expect a very active spouse/significant other program. A popular activity is MBA athletes for charity and community service.

ADMISSIONS

According to the admissions office, the following criteria are weighed equally: GMAT scores, work experience, college GPA, letters of recommendation, and essays. Applicants can use a computer diskette to apply; it works on a DOS base system. William and Mary features a five rounds admissions process and notes it is advisable to apply in the first three. Round deadlines are: December 4th, January 15th, February 26th, March 31st, and May 4th, the final deadline. Early Action applicants are notified of a decision by December 18th. General applicants are notified of a decision three weeks after the application has been received. On a case-by-case basis, students can defer admission for up to one year. There is an admissions deferment program for college seniors.

STUDENT'S OVERVIEW BOX

Overall Happiness

Academic Satisfaction

50 75 100%

■ Student Opinion □ National Average

FACULTY RATING

■ Student Opinion □ National Average

HITS AND MISSES

HITS
Quantitative skills
Helping other students
On-campus housing

MISSES
Finance dept.
Ethnic & racial diversity
Recruiting

APPLICANTS ALSO LOOK AT
UNC Chapel Hill
U Virginia
U Georgia
Emory U.
Georgetown U.
George Mason U.
VA Commonwealth
VA Polytech Institute

FOR MORE INFORMATION, CONTACT:
Graduate School of Business
Blow Memorial Hall, P.O. Box 8795
Williamsburg, VA 23187-8795
(804) 221-2900

UNIVERSITY OF WYOMING COLLEGE OF BUSINESS

ADMISSIONS FACTS

Type of school	Public

Demographics

No. of men	34
No. of women	11
No. of minorities	1
No. of int'l students	N/A

EQUAL TREATMENT GRAPH

Admissions Statistics

Avg. GMAT	551
Avg. undergraduate GPA	3.3
Avg. age at entry	26
No. of applicants	71
No. accepted	58
No. enrolled	28

Deadlines and Notifications

Regular application	3/30
Regular notification	immediate
Special dates	N/A

Focus of Curriculum

General Management

Academic Specialties

General Management

FINANCIAL FACTS

In-state tuition	$1,250
Out-of-state tuition	$3,750
On-campus housing	$3,166

ACADEMICS

Beautiful, rugged, pristine: when University of Wyoming students describe the natural setting in which they're located, these are the words they use. But a room with a view won't cost you much. This state-run B-school is among one of the least expensive programs included in this book. As one student told us, it "offers the best bargain for academic education." That education includes small classes and a high level of student/faculty interaction. Said one student, "The most outstanding asset of this school is the student-teacher ratio. You really get to know your professors." Reported another, "Faculty members provide excellent examples of what it means to be a professor. They're good teachers. There's a fair balance between their research and commitment to students."

An unusual twist among B-schools: students with non-business degrees must take Common Body of Knowledge (CBK) courses as prerequisites for the core MBA program. While this does get everyone on solid footing, one student gripes, "CBK classes are geared too heavily to quantitative aspects of business. More qualitative courses should be available to balance the two." Another twist: students have to maintain a 3.00 GPA (on a 4.00 scale). More than two "C's" and it's probation time. After completing CBK requirements, students take core MBA courses and electives in an extremely unstructured program. For example, a student can take a psychology course in another graduate department and have it count towards the MBA degree. But several students told us this program is not as diverse in offerings as it appears to be. Wrote one, "Electives are scarce. There should be more grad level international courses." Added another, "There should be required communications courses." There is one unusual requirement for graduation: students must write a thesis to demonstrate their writing and research capabilities. As for how they feel about their skills, students report they feel well-prepared by their studies in general management, quantitative methods, and computers. They're less confident of their marketing and accounting skills. Still, as one might expect, students are unanimous: Wyoming is well worth the investment of time and money.

UNIVERSITY OF WYOMING COLLEGE OF BUSINESS

STUDENT LIFE/CAMPUS

As one MBA put it, "The program is not real high-pressure which makes it more enjoyable." Agrees another, "The workload is manageable." Two-thirds of the students report it's important to do all or most of the reading, the rest say shortcuts are fine. The majority work in study groups, although one MBA griped, "Should be more mandatory group work." What students seem to appreciate most at Wyoming is the small, homey atmosphere. Wrote one: "Students are warm and supportive. Everyone knows each other." This does, of course have its down side. There isn't a lot privacy in a graduate program of only sixty students. But there's also isn't backstabbing competition.

Wyoming is an outdoorsy type of person's paradise. You are easily within an hour of rock climbing, hiking, skiing—any outdoor activity conceivable.

Steamboat is a frequent roadtrip destination. But bring more than ski pants—Wyoming winters are l-o-o-o-ng. As for the school's hometown of Laramie, students say it's safe and civilized, if not a bit boring. Most students live on-campus in affordable, accessible housing. There are few social outlets on-campus or in the town of Laramie. The primary student club is the Graduate Business Council which sponsors career-related events as well as Friday afternoon get-togethers at the campus beer garden. Wrote one MBA, "We certainly party," but much of this occurs in informal gatherings over a pot-luck dinner.

ADMISSIONS

Wyoming accepts about two-thirds of its MBA applicants (about half of whom wind up enrolling) on the basis of GPA, GMAT score, personal interviews, work experience, quality of undergraduate curriculum and essays.

STUDENT'S OVERVIEW BOX

Overall Happiness

Academic Satisfaction

50   75   100%

■ Student Opinion □ National Average

FACULTY RATING

■ Student Opinion ■ National Average

HITS AND MISSES

HITS
Quantitative skills
Classmates are smart
On-campus housing

MISSES
Marketing dept.
Diverse work experience
Placement

APPLICANTS ALSO LOOK AT
(not available)

FOR MORE INFORMATION, CONTACT:
College of Business
P.O. Box 3275 University Station
Laramie, WY 82071-3275
(307) 766-6858

YALE UNIVERSITY SCHOOL OF ORGANIZATION & MANAGEMENT

ADMISSIONS FACTS

Type of school	Private

Demographics

No. of men	279
No. of women	117
No. of minorities	45
No. of int'l students	105

EQUAL TREATMENT GRAPH

Women

Minorities

0   2   4 (GPA)

■ Student Opinion ■ National Average

Admissions Statistics

Avg. GMAT	651
Avg. undergraduate GPA	3.31
Avg. age at entry	27.5
No. of applicants	1,216
No. accepted	457
No. enrolled	201

Deadlines and Notifications

Regular application	3/30
Regular notification	within 8 weeks
Special dates	N/A

Focus of Curriculum

Specialized

Academic Specialties

Finance, Management in the Public and Non-profit sectors

Special Programs

The Outreach Management Consulting Group; Externship Program; Internship Fund.

FINANCIAL FACTS

In-state tuition	$19,275
Out-of-state tuition	$19,275
On-campus housing	$7,500

ACADEMICS

The Yale School of Organization and Management (SOM) doesn't offer an MBA. It offers a master's in public and private management (MPPM), which one student describes as "the true master's of management degree, an MBA-plus." Another student describes it as "a hybrid of an MBA and MPA program." Whatever the description, SOM's primary mission is to "educate managers for business *and* government *and* nonprofit organizations." But students feel the "and" tends to get lost in the translation of what this program is about. Wrote one emphatic student, "This school is misunderstood. Its goal is to prepare quality general managers for ALL sectors—public, private, and non-profit—not just one." There is an emphasis on the interrelatedness of these areas. Given the historical interface between business and government, Yale considers its integrated, multi-sector approach to management simply more pragmatic than a strict MBA curriculum.

According to one student, "SOM does a very good job of bridging the similarities of management in the three sectors and highlighting the differences." In addition to their sector studies, first-year students take an intensive group of core classes in the typical, functional areas of business; hence the description, "MBA-plus." There is a strong emphasis on quantitative as well as soft skills. Second-year students focus on a specialization and have up to seven electives. An outstanding department is finance. Wrote one student, "Our reputation as non-profit public sector school detracts unfairly from the quantitative rigor and excellence of the finance faculty and curriculum." Overall, students describe a rigorous and intellectual program. They say the program is meeting their academic expectations. They rave about the quality of their education. Professors also garner rave reviews. Students describe them as "great teachers" and "very accessible." Adds one student, "Regular review sessions and personal tutors are available if needed (free of charge)." Despite all this, there are academic weak spots, especially by an MBA's standards. A large number of students report they feel only adequately prepared in operations management and computer skills. Still most students would agree with this student "SOM is one-of-a-kind."

PLACEMENT AND RECRUITING

The career development office offers students the standard fare—mock interviews, résumé preparation, etc. On top of this, Yale offers an on-line contacts database and an aggressive alumni network program. The latter includes participation in a student/alumni mentoring program and referrals and job postings from within alumni's companies.

Overall, Yale students are dissatisfied with the range of companies recruiting on campus. But one student explained, "Our placement office has the daunting task of finding jobs for 400 people who have 400 different career goals. We are hurt by the fact that companies aren't going to come here and find a lot of people who fit their molds." Still, according to one student, "Yale has had tremendous success in placing banking and finance people due to the reputation of its finance department and faculty." The school's niche positioning in other areas hasn't hurt either. In 1992, approximately eighty-five percent of the class had a job by graduation.

YALE UNIVERSITY SCHOOL OF ORGANIZATION & MANAGEMENT

STUDENT LIFE/CAMPUS

According to our survey, students are the heart and soul of this program. As one Yalie put it, "The student body is one of the school's great strengths—tremendous geographic, academic, and professional diversity—both in terms of background and objectives. This range of perspectives makes classroom discussion especially interesting." Agreed another, "Since group work is emphasized, the high quality/diversity of students adds to the learning experience."

Students report a demanding workload and spend an average of thirty-five to forty hours a week preparing for class. Wrote one student, "There is a heavy infusion of weekly problem sets during the first year requiring in-depth analysis and complete write-ups." No doubt this requires hard work, but students aren't competing for grades. SOM's non-competitive scale of grading (proficient, pass, and fail) de-emphasizes student-against-student competition. Still, like many MBAs, students report a fair amount of academic pressure, although one student says this "varies because it's self-imposed." Students rave about the support and helping hands of classmates. One student gushes, "The small size (200 per class) allows for a true sense of community. We *really* enjoy and work well with each other." Exclaims another, "Our student body is warm, friendly, cohesive—I love it here!" Apparently these warm feelings will continue after graduation. Shared one student, "Classmates will be friends and assets for life."

As for Yale's hometown of New Haven, students say, "It's a crime-ridden city with nothing going for it." Still, the majority of students opt to live off-campus in apartments in the city's residential neighborhoods, inland or along the Long Island Sound. Students say off-campus housing is both attractive and reasonably priced. Wrote one student, "We don't rely on public transportation but on Yale University shuttles which are very convenient, efficient, and free." One student boasted that SOM has the "best golf course of any B-school in the country." Beyond golf, students report an active and varied social life, though this doesn't include dating. Students tend to socialize and travel in packs.

A note on the student body: thirty-six percent of the students are international, representing twenty-six different countries. Wrote one student, "This makes Yale culturally stimulating. Also impressive is the integration of the international students into all school activities." Reported another, "Above average number of married students, and those with children."

ADMISSIONS

Applicants to Yale better have excellent GPAs and GMAT scores if they hope to attract the attention of the admissions committee, which accepts less than a quarter of those apply to the MBA program. Work experience, letters of recommendation, and a strong background in mathematics complete the list of admissions criteria.

STUDENT'S OVERVIEW BOX

Overall Happiness

Academic Satisfaction

50   75   100%

■ Student Opinion ■ National Average

FACULTY RATING

■ Student Opinion ■ National Average

HITS AND MISSES

HITS
Finance
Diverse work experience
Classmates are smart
Faculty

MISSES
Marketing
On-campus housing
New Haven

APPLICANTS ALSO LOOK AT

U Pennsylvania
U Virginia
Cornell U.
MIT
New York University
Columbia U.
U Cincinnati
U Texas-Austin

FOR MORE INFORMATION, CONTACT:
School of Organization and
Management
Box 1A, Yale Station
New Haven, CT 06520-7368
(203) 432-5932

Index

257

Index

I

J

K

L

W

Y

About the Author

Nedda Gilbert is a graduate of the University of Pennsylvania and holds a masters degree from Columbia University. She has worked for The Princeton Review since 1985. In 1987, she created The Princeton Review corporate test preparation service, which provides Wall Street firms and premier companies tailored educational programs for their employees. She currently resides in Chicago.